Constitutional Politics and the Judiciary

Recent confrontations between constitutional courts and parliamentary majorities, for example in Poland and Hungary, have attracted international interest in the relationship between the judiciary and the legislature in Central and Eastern European countries. Several political actors have argued that courts have assumed too much power after the democratic transformation process in 1989/1990. These claims are explicitly or implicitly connected to the charge that courts have constrained the room for manoeuvre of the legislatures too heavily and that they have entered the field of politics. Nevertheless, the question to what extent this aggregation of power has constrained the dominant political actors has never been examined accurately and systematically in the literature. The present volume fills this gap by applying an innovative research methodology to quantify the impact and effect of courts' decisions on legislation and legislators, and to measure the strength of judicial decisions in six CEE countries.

Kálmán Pócza is a senior research fellow at the Institute for Political Science of the Hungarian Academy of Sciences and associate professor at the Pázmány Péter Catholic University Budapest. He is the Principal Investigator of the JUDICON research project (www.judicon.tk.mta.hu).

Routledge Research in Constitutional Law

This series features thought-provoking and original scholarship on constitutional law and theory. Books explore key topics, themes and questions in the field with a particular emphasis on comparative studies. Where relevant, titles will engage with political and social theory, philosophy and history in order to offer a rounded analysis of constitutions and constitutional law. Series Editor: David Marrani
Available titles in this series include:

Democracy and the Human Rights Act
Republican Analysis of Citizen Power
Dennis Dixon

Constitutional Acceleration within the European Union and Beyond
Edited by Paul Blokker

Philosophy, Obligation and Law
Bentham's Ontology of Normativity
Piero Tarantino

Constitution-making and Human Rights in the Sudans
Edited by Mohamed Abdelsalam and Lutz Oette

Constitutional Politics and the Judiciary
Decision-making in Central and Eastern Europe
Edited by Kálmán Pócza

EU Law, Fundamental Rights and National Democracy
Eduardo Gill-Pedro

For more information about this series, please visit:
www.routledge.com/Routledge-Research-in-Constitutional-Law/book-series/CONSTLAW

Constitutional Politics and the Judiciary

Decision-making in Central and Eastern Europe

Edited by
Kálmán Pócza

Routledge
Taylor & Francis Group
LONDON AND NEW YORK

First published 2019 by Routledge

2 Park Square, Milton Park, Abingdon, Oxfordshire OX14 4RN
52 Vanderbilt Avenue, New York, NY 10017

Routledge is an imprint of the Taylor & Francis Group, an informa business

First issued in paperback 2020

British Library Cataloguing-in-Publication Data
A catalogue record for this book is available from the British Library

Library of Congress Cataloging-in-Publication Data
Names: Pâocza, Kâalmâan, 1976- editor.
Title: Constitutional politics and the judiciary: decision-making in Central and Eastern Europe / edited by Kâalmâan Pâocza.
Description: Abingdon, Oxon; New York, NY: Routledge, 2019. | Includes bibliographical references and index.
Identifiers: LCCN 2018033001 | ISBN 9781138607644 (hardback)
Subjects: LCSH: Constitutional courts–Europe, Eastern. | Constitutional courts–Europe, Central.
Classification: LCC KJC5456 .C668 2019 | DDC 347.43/035–dc23
LC record available at https://lccn.loc.gov/2018033001

ISBN: 978-1-138-60764-4 (hbk)
ISBN: 978-0-367-52355-8 (pbk)

Typeset in ITC Galliard
by Deanta Global Publishing Services, Chennai, India

Contents

List of Figures *ix*
List of Tables *xii*
List of abbreviations *xiii*
List of judicial cases *xiv*
List of contributors *xix*

1 Introduction 1
KÁLMÁN PÓCZA

Outline of the volume 3
Notes 6

2 Research methodology 8
KÁLMÁN PÓCZA AND GÁBOR DOBOS

2.1 Introduction 8
2.2 Literature overview 8
2.3 Units of observation: judicial rulings 11
2.4 Components and elements of judicial rulings 12
2.5 Mapping the diversity of judicial rulings 18
2.6 Measuring the strength of judicial rulings 21
2.7 Network analysis of dissenting opinions 24
2.8 Further research projects 25
Notes 27
References 30

3 The Czech Constitutional Court: Far away from political influence 32
KATARÍNA ŠIPULOVÁ

3.1 Introduction 32
3.2 Constitutional setting 33

3.3 Research design and methodological particularities 36
3.4 General observations: the Czech Constitutional Court as an inconspicuous constrainer? 38
3.5 Trends in majority rulings 44
3.6 Trends in dissenting opinions 49
3.7 Qualitative evaluation 54
3.8 Conclusions 56
Notes 57
References 59

4 The German Federal Constitutional Court: Authority transformed into power? 61
OLIVER W. LEMBCKE

4.1 Introduction 61
4.2 A powerful Court 61
4.3 General impressions 66
4.4 Trends in majority rulings 72
4.5 Trends in dissenting opinions 78
4.6 Qualitative evaluation 81
4.7 Politically important cases 85
4.8 Conclusions 87
Appendix 88
Notes 89
References 91

5 The Hungarian Constitutional Court: A constructive partner in constitutional dialogue 96
KÁLMÁN PÓCZA, GÁBOR DOBOS AND ATTILA GYULAI

5.1 Introduction 96
5.2 Origins and structure of the Hungarian Constitutional Court 96
5.3 General characteristics: a Court of outstanding performance? 100
5.4 Trends in majority rulings 104
5.5 Trends in dissenting opinions 113
5.6 Conclusions 121
Appendix 122
Notes 122
References 124

6 The Polish Constitutional Tribunal: Deference beyond the veil of activism 126
ARTUR WOŁEK AND IGA KENDER-JEZIORSKA

6.1 Introduction 126
6.2 Origins of the court and institutional setup 127
6.3 General observations: a barrier for politics or a part of it? 132
6.4 Trends in majority rulings 134
6.5 Trends in dissenting opinions 146
6.6 Conclusions 150
Notes 151
References 152

7 The Romanian Constitutional Court: Muddling through democratic transition 155
CSONGOR KUTI

7.1 Introduction 155
7.2 Historical background and institutional arrangements 156
7.3 Methodological peculiarities and caseload 161
7.4 Trends in the strength of majority rulings 164
7.5 Trends in the strength of unconstitutionality rulings 171
7.6 Analysis of the presidents' performance 172
7.7 Analysis of dissenting opinions 174
7.8 Conclusions 177
Appendix 179
Notes 179
References 183

8 The Slovak Constitutional Court: The third legislator? 184
ERIK LÁŠTIC AND MAX STEUER

8.1 Introduction 184
8.2 Origins and institutional design 184
8.3 Three Courts 186
8.4 Methodological specifics of the Slovak case 187
8.5 Assessing the trends 190
8.6 Landmark cases 198
8.7 Conclusions 205
Appendix 206
Notes 206
References 209

9 Courts compared: The practice of constitutional adjudication in Central and Eastern Europe 213
KÁLMÁN PÓCZA, GÁBOR DOBOS AND ATTILA GYULAI

9.1 Introduction 213
9.2 Rulings and decisions 214
9.3 Ruling types compared 216
9.4 Frequency of strength values compared 223
9.5 Average strength of judicial rulings in comparison 228
9.6 Dissenting opinions compared 240
9.7 Conclusions 243
Notes 245

Index 247

Figures

3.1 Number of decisions and rulings (CCC) 36
3.2 Number and average strength of rulings (CCC) 39
3.3 Frequency of ruling types I (CCC) 44
3.4 Frequency of ruling types II (CCC) 46
3.5 Average strength of rulings (by presidents) (CCC) 48
3.6 Average strength of rulings (by presidents and majorities) (CCC) 49
3.7 Number of rulings and dissenting opinions (CCC) 50
3.8 Average strength of rulings (by judges) (CCC) 51
3.9 Dissenting coalitions at the CCC 52
4.1 Caseload of the FCC (1951–2016) 63
4.2 Trust in the FCC (1984–2012) 65
4.3 Annual average input and output of the FCC (1990–2016) 66
4.4 Number of decisions and rulings (FCC) 68
4.5 Frequency of ruling types I (FCC) 69
4.6 Configurations of rulings (percentages and numbers) (FCC) 70
4.7 "Corridors" of the strength of rulings (FCC) 71
4.8 Average strength of rulings (FCC) 72
4.9 Average strength of rulings (by Senates) (FCC) 73
4.10 Judicial activism vs. judicial self-restraint (FCC) 74
4.11 Average strength of rulings (by year of complaint) (FCC) 75
4.12 Average strength of rulings (by presidents and vice-presidents) (FCC) 77
4.13 Average strength of rulings (by "top five" judges) (FCC) 78
4.14 Number and average strength of rulings (by judges) (FCC) 79
4.15 Annual peaks and lows in aggregated average strength of rulings (FCC) 84
5.1 Number and average strength of rulings (HCC) 103
5.2 Frequency of ruling types I (HCC) 104
5.3 Frequency of ruling types II (HCC) 105
5.4 Average strength of rulings (by presidents) (HCC) 111
5.5 Average strength of rulings (by presidents and majorities) (HCC) 112
5.6 Number of rulings and dissenting opinions (HCC) 113
5.7 Average strength of rulings (by judges) (HCC) 115

5.8 Proportion and strength of dissenting opinions (HCC) 116
5.9 Average difference to majority rulings and frequency of dissenting opinions (HCC) 117
5.10 Dissenting coalitions 1990–2015 (HCC) 118
5.11 Dissenting coalitions 1990–2010 (HCC) 120
6.1 Number of decisions and rulings (PCT) 131
6.2 Frequency of ruling types I (PCT) 135
6.3 Frequency of ruling types II (PCT) 139
6.4 Number and average strength of rulings (PCT) 145
6.5 Number of rulings and dissenting opinions (PCT) 148
6.6 Dissenting coalitions 1993–2015 (PCT) 149
7.1 Number of decisions and rulings (RCC) 164
7.2 Number and average strength of rulings (RCC) 165
7.3 Frequency of ruling types I (RCC) 169
7.4 Frequency of ruling types II (RCC) 172
7.5 Average strength of rulings (by presidents and majorities) (RCC) 173
7.6 Average strength of rulings (by judges) (RCC) 174
7.7 Number of rulings and dissenting opinions (RCC) 175
7.8 Dissenting coalitions 1992–2015 (RCC) 177
8.1 Number of decisions and rulings (SCC) 188
8.2 Number and average strength of rulings (SCC) 191
8.3 Frequency of ruling types I (SCC) 193
8.4 Frequency of ruling types II (SCC) 194
8.5 Average strength of rulings (by presidents and majorities) (SCC) 194
8.6 Number of rulings and dissenting opinions (SCC) 196
8.7 Number of rulings and dissenting opinions (by judges) (SCC) 196
8.8 Dissenting coalitions (SCC) 197
8.9 Average strength of rulings (by judges) (SCC) 197
9.1 Number of decisions and rulings in comparison 215
9.2 Ruling/decision rate of six courts 215
9.3 Ruling/decision rate of six courts (by years) 216
9.4 Distribution of ruling types (by courts) 220
9.5 Distribution of strength values (by courts) 223
9.6 Distribution of 'non-zero' strength values (full dataset) 224
9.7 Distribution of 'non-zero' strength values (FCC, HCC, RCC compared) 224
9.8 Distribution of 'non-zero' strength values (CCC, PCT, SCC compared) 226
9.9 Standard deviation of average 'non-zero' strength values in comparison 227
9.10 Standard deviations of average 'non-zero' strength values (FCC, HCC, RCC compared by years) 227
9.11 Standard deviations of average 'non-zero' strength values (CCC, PCT, SCC compared by years) 228

9.12 Average strength values compared 229
9.13 Average 'non-zero' strength values compared 230
9.14 Average strength of rulings (HCC, PCT compared by years) 231
9.15 Average strength of rulings (FCC, SCC compared by years) 232
9.16 Average strength of rulings (CCC, RCC compared by years) 233
9.17 Average strength of 'non-zero' rulings in comparison 234
9.18 Differences of average strengths of rulings with and without 'non-zero' rulings 235
9.19 Average strength of rulings with and without 'non-zero' rulings (HCC by years) 236
9.20 Average strength of rulings with and without 'non-zero' rulings (PCT by years) 236
9.21 Average strength of rulings with and without 'non-zero' rulings (FCC by years) 237
9.22 Average strength of rulings with and without 'non-zero' rulings (SCC by years) 237
9.23 Average strength of rulings with and without 'non-zero' rulings (CCC by years) 238
9.24 Average strength of rulings with and without 'non-zero' rulings (RCC by years) 238
9.25 Proportion of rulings with at least one dissenting opinion in comparison 241
9.26 Rulings with at least one dissenting opinion (CCC, HCC, SCC compared by years) 242
9.27 Rulings with at least one dissenting opinion (FCC, PCT, RCC compared by years) 243

Tables

2.1 Components and elements of rulings 13
2.2 Possible combination of the elements of judicial rulings 19
2.3 Ruling types (weak, average and strong forms of rulings) 20
2.4 Weighting of the elements of rulings 22
3.1 Caseload of the Czech Constitutional Court 40
4.1 Short timeline of institutional changes and reforms (FCC) 63
4.2 Motion types, numbers and success rates (FCC) 67
4.3 Average strength of rulings (by Senates) (FCC) 73
4.4 Rulings and dissenting opinions (1990–2015) (FCC) 79
4.5 Dissenters (more than once) and dissenting coalitions (FCC) 80
4.6 Votes (FCC) 80
4.7 Selected types of rulings (FCC) 81
A.1 Frequency of ruling types II (in %) (FCC) 88
A.2 Ranking of "politically important" cases (FCC) 88
A.1 Frequency of ruling types III (in %) (HCC) 122
6.1 Number of rulings decided by the full bench 2007–2015 (PCT) 143
A.1 Frequency of ruling types III (RCC) 179
8.1 Workload of the SCC 190
A.1 Frequency of ruling types III (SCC) 206
9.1 Distribution of ruling types (full dataset with and without RCC) 217
9.2 Distribution of ruling types II (full dataset with and without RCC) 217
9.3 Distribution of ruling types (by courts) 218
9.4 Frequency of prescriptions (FCC) 219
9.5 Frequency of Temporal Effects (FCC) 219
9.6 Frequency of completeness (PCT) 220
9.7 Frequency of Temporal Effects (PCT) 220
9.8 Number of rulings with and without rejections (by courts) 221
9.9 Ruling types without rejections I (full dataset) 221
9.11 Ruling types without rejections (by courts) 222
9.10 Ruling types without rejections II (full dataset) 222
9.12 Distribution of prescriptions (FCC) 225

List of abbreviations

CC	constitutional court
CCC	Czech Constitutional Court
CEE	Central and Eastern Europe
CIIA	constitutional interpretation in abstracto
CR	constitutional requirement
DO	dissenting opinion
FCC	German Federal Constitutional Court
HCC	Hungarian Constitutional Court
OM	unconstitutionality by legislative omission
PCT	Polish Constitutional Tribunal
PROC	procedural unconstitutionality
RCC	Romanian Constitutional Court
REF	refusal
REJ	rejection
SCC	Slovak Constitutional Court
SoC	strength of cases
SoR	strength of rulings
SUBST	substantive unconstitutionality

List of judicial cases

Czech Constitutional Court

Pl. ÚS 1/92
Pl. ÚS 5/92
Pl. ÚS 16/93
Pl. ÚS 31/96
Pl. ÚS 33/97
Pl. ÚS 36/01
Pl. ÚS 5/03
Pl. ÚS 16/04
Pl. ÚS 6/05
Pl. ÚS 13/05
Pl. ÚS 20/05
Pl. ÚS 77/06
Pl. ÚS 9/07
IV. ÚS 1777/07
Pl. ÚS 3/09
Pl. ÚS 24/09
Pl. ÚS 27/09
Pl. ÚS-st. 31/10
Pl. ÚS 49/10
IV. ÚS 276/11
Pl. ÚS 10/13
Pl. ÚS 28/13

German Federal Constitutional Court

BVerfGE 1, 1
BVerfGE 1, 281
BVerfGE 6, 309
BVerfGE 8, 51
BVerfGE 12, 205
BVerfGE 35, 79

BVerfGE 36, 1
BVerfGE 82, 60
BVerfGE 82, 322
BVerfGE 83, 37
BVerfGE 83, 238
BVerfGE 84, 9
BVerfGE 84, 304
BVerfGE 85, 264
BVerfGE 87, 1
BVerfGE 87, 234
BVerfGE 88, 87
BVerfGE 88, 203
BVerfGE 91, 1
BVerfGE 92, 26
BVerfGE 93, 37
BVerfGE 92, 365
BVerfGE 95, 335
BVerfGE 99, 165
BVerfGE 99, 300
BVerfGE 100, 1
BVerfGE 101, 158
BVerfGE 103, 111
BVerfGE 105, 197
BVerfGE 105, 313
BVerfGE 106, 62
BVerfGE 106, 166
BVerfGE 106, 310
BVerfGE 108, 169
BVerfGE 110, 33
BVerfGE 111, 160
BVerfGE 111, 226
BVerfGE 111, 382
BVerfGE 112, 118
BVerfGE 112, 226
BVerfGE 115, 1
BVerfGE 115, 259
BVerfGE 116, 96
BVerfGE 121, 30
BVerfGE 122, 210
BVerfGE 123, 267
BVerfGE 125, 175
BVerfGE 127, 31
BVerfGE 127, 293
BVerfGE 132, 134

BVerfGE 132, 195
BVerfGE 133, 59
BVerfGE 133, 241
BVerfGE 134, 1
BVerfGE 135, 1
BVerfGE 135, 259
BVerfGE 136, 9
BVerfGE 137, 185
BVerfGE 138, 1
BVerfGE 138, 136
2BvL 17/09
BVerfGE 139, 285
BVerfGE 140, 65
BVerfGE 140, 160

Polish Constitutional Tribunal

W 6/93
K 16/93
K 17/93
P 1/94
K 2/94
K 6/94
K 11/94
K 12/94
W 1/95
K 4/95
K 13/95
K 18/95
K 27/95
K 19/96
K 26/96
K 39/97
K 4/99
K 2/07
K 44/07
K 54/07
K 55/07
K 3/09
K 6/09
K 10/09
K 11/10
P 8/11
K 14/11

K 35/11
K 40/12
SK 61/12
K 16/13

Romanian Constitutional Court

71/05.03.2002
279/22.03.2006
657/09.10.2006
321/29.03.2007
1258/08.10.2009
1414/04.11.2009
1415/04.11.2009
1237/06.10.2010
1431/03.11.2010
1609/09.12.2010
2/04.01.2011
53/25.01.2011
1039/2012
334/26.06.2013
449/06.11.2013
471/14.11.2013
511/12.12.2013
417/03.07.2014
662/11.11.2014

Slovak Constitutional Court

I. ÚS 39/93
I. ÚS 5/94
PL. ÚS 8/94
PL. ÚS 16/95
I. ÚS 7/96
PL. ÚS 17/96
I. ÚS 61/96
II. ÚS 31/97
II. ÚS 65/97
I. ÚS 30/99
PL. ÚS 17/00
PL. ÚS 3/01
PL. ÚS 12/01
PL. ÚS 3/02
PL. ÚS 6/04

PL. ÚS 10/05
PL. ÚS 29/05
PL. ÚS 23/06
PL. ÚS 3/08
PL. ÚS 17/08
PL. ÚS 13/09
PL. ÚS 19/09
PL. ÚS 102/2011
PL. ÚS 105/2011
PL. ÚS 4/2012
PL. ÚS 11/2012
PL. ÚS 8/2013
PL. ÚS 40/2014
PL. ÚS 36/2015
PL. ÚS 44/2015
PL. ÚS 45/2015
PL. ÚS 53/2015
PL. ÚS 7/2017

List of contributors

Gábor Dobos is a junior research fellow at the Hungarian Academy of Sciences (Institute for Political Science, Centre for Social Sciences) and PhD candidate at the Corvinus University of Budapest. He is primarily interested in the local politics of Hungary, election pledges and constitutional adjudication. His recent publications include "Hungary – Are Neglected Regional Elections Second-Order Elections?", in: Arjan H. Schakel (ed.): *Regional and National Elections in Eastern Europe: Territoriality of the Vote in Ten Countries.* London: Palgrave Macmillan, 2017 (with Réka Várnagy); "How to Measure the Strength of Judicial Decisions – A Methodological Framework", *German Law Journal* 18(2017):6 (with Kálmán Pócza and Attila Gyulai). Contact: dobos.gabor@tk.mta.hu

Attila Gyulai is a research fellow at the Institute for Political Science, Centre for Social Sciences of the Hungarian Academy of Sciences. His fields of research are the political theory of Carl Schmitt, political realism, democratic theory and the Hungarian political system. His recent English-language publications include "The Lesson of Carl Schmitt's Realism. The Autonomy and the Primacy of the Political", *Theoria* 155 (forthcoming 2018); "How to Measure the Strength of Judicial Decisions: A Methodological Framework", *German Law Journal* 18(2017):6 (with Kálmán Pócza and Gábor Dobos); "Taming the Extreme: Hungarian Black Metal in the Mainstream Publicity", in: Emilia Barna, Tamás Tófalvy (eds.) *Made in Hungary: Studies in Popular Music.* London, Routledge, 2017. Contact: gyulai.attila@tk.mta.hu

Iga Kender-Jeziorska is a PhD student at the Political Sciences Doctoral School of the Corvinus University of Budapest. She has presented her research at national and international conferences (Urban Drug Policies, Warsaw 2016; Stadt Nach Acht, Berlin 2017; Local Public Policies and their Environment, Cracow 2018; 26th Annual NISPAcee Conference, Iasi 2018). She co-coordinates X. Working Group on Non-Governmental Organizations within Network of Institutes and Schools of Public Administration in Central and Eastern Europe. Her research focus is drug policy in the context of human rights and public health, with focus on young people. She is also active in the non-governmental sector in the field and is involved in the work of the Civil Society Forum on Drugs by the European Commission. Contact: iga.jeziorska@sin.org.pl

Csongor Kuti is an assistant professor at University of Arts Tîrgu Mures. He earned his PhD from Central European University. His publications include *Post-Communist Restitution and the Rule of Law*. Budapest, Central European University Press, 2009; "Miners' Canary", *Journal of Constitutional Law in Eastern and Central Europe*, 16 (2009):1; "In Courts We Trust?", *Acta Juridica Hungarica*, 54 (2013):4; "Justice and Restitution", in: Sabine Fischer, et al. (eds): *Movements, Migrants, Marginalisation. Challenges of Societal and Political Participation in Eastern Europe and the Enlarged EU*, Ibidem Publishers, Stuttgart, 2007. Contact: csongi@excite.com

Erik Láštic is an associate professor at the Department of Political Science, Faculty of Arts at the Comenius University in Bratislava, Slovakia. His research focuses on various aspects of politics and policy making in Central and Eastern Europe, including legislative politics and referendum. He has published dozens of articles and chapters domestically and internationally (e.g. Routledge, Springer, Sage). Recent publications: "Into the Labyrinth: The Rewards for High Public Office in Slovakia" (with Katarína Staroňová), in: B. Guy Peters, Marleen Brans (eds.): *Rewards for High Public Office in Europe and North America*. London, Routledge, 2012; "If It Works, Fine, If Not, So What? Initiatives in Slovakia", in: Maija Setälä and Theo Schiller: *Citizens' Initiatives in Europe: Procedures and Consequences of Agenda-Setting by Citizens*. London, Palgrave Macmillan, 2012. Contact: erik.lastic@uniba.sk

Oliver W. Lembcke is an associate professor of political science at Erfurt University (Germany). He studied political science, history and law in Kiel and Cambridge (Mass.) and he received his PhD (s.c.l.) from Jena University. He is a member of the chairman committee of the section on Politics and Law of the German Political Science Association. His research interests are in the field of comparative politics and political theory with a focus on the principles and practice of modern constitutionalism, e.g. on human rights and human dignity, on forms of constitutional authority and on the judicial governance in different institutional settings. Recent publications include, among others: *Politics and Law* (2017), *Authority and Symbolic Legislation* (2016), *Democratic Theory* (2 vols., 2016/2018 forthcoming), *Personhood* (2015) and *Human Dignity* (2013). Contact: mail@oliver-lembcke.de

Kálmán Pócza is a senior research fellow at the Institute for Political Science of the Hungarian Academy of Sciences and an associate professor at the Pázmány Péter Catholic University Budapest. He is the principal investigator of the JUDICON project. He was a visiting research fellow at the University of Notre Dame, University of Tübingen and University of Fribourg. His recent publications include "Distrust in Government: A Comparative Historical Analysis", in: László Kontler, Mark Somos (eds.): *Trust and Happiness in the History of European Political Thought*. Leiden: Brill, 2017; "How to Measure the Strength of Judicial Decisions: A Methodological Framework", *German Law Journal* 18(2017):6 (together with Gábor Dobos and Attila Gyulai); "Democratic Theory and Constitutional Adjudication", *Acta Juridica Hungarica* 56(2015):2–3. Contact: pocza.kalman@tk.mta.hu

Katarína Šipulová is a senior researcher at Judicial Studies Institute (Masaryk University Brno). She earned her PhD at the Masaryk University Brno and the MSt title in Socio-Legal Research at the University of Oxford. Her main area of interest is transitional justice and democratization of the Central and Eastern European countries. Katarína Šipulová worked as head of the International Department of the Czech Supreme Court. She has been an active member of several research projects dealing with human rights as well as international law and its impact on domestic jurisprudence (e.g. international human rights treaties in national legal systems, implementation of ECtHR case law against the Czech Republic). Katarína was co-leader of a project on the application of EU law by the Czech civil courts conducted by the Supreme Court in 2012. Her publications include "Ideology and International Human Rights Commitments in Post-communist Regimes: Cases of the Czech Republic and Slovakia", in: Marlene Wind (ed.): *International Courts and Domestic Politics*. Cambridge University Press, 2018; "DH v Czech Republic Six Years Later: On the Power of an International Human Rights Court to Push through Systemic Change", *Netherlands Quarterly of Human Rights*, 32(2014):3. Contact: katarina.sipulova@law.muni.cz

Max Steuer is a PhD candidate at the Department of Political Science at the Comenius University in Bratislava. His research interests include political institutions, particularly constitutional courts in Central Europe, freedom of speech and democracy and legitimacy in the EU. Max has been involved in several research projects and in academic service, for example, as editor-in-chief of *Politikon: The IAPSS Journal of Political Science*. He has published, among others, "Constitutional Pluralism and the Slovak Constitutional Court: The Challenge of European Union Law", *The Lawyer Quarterly* 8(2018):2; "Kto a ako vyberá strážcov? Legitimita výberu sudcov Ústavného súdu SR v komparatívnej perspective" ["Who Selects the Guardians and How? The Legitimacy of the Selection of Judges of the Slovak Constitutional Court in a Comparative Perspective"], *Právník* 156(2017):4; "A Subordinate Issue? An Analysis of Parliamentary Discourse on Freedom of Speech in Slovakia", *Czech Journal of Political Science* 15(2015):1. Contact: max.steuer@uniba.sk

Artur Wołek is a public policy and administration professor at the Jesuit University of Krakow Ignatianum. Previously he was an associate professor at the Warsaw School of Economics and WSB-National-Louis University. In the 1990s, he also worked as an advisor with the Prime Minister's Office for Constitutional Reform and as the director at the Windsor Group, a think tank. Books authored include: *Słabe państwo* [*A Weak State*] (2012) and *Demokracja nieformalna. Konstytucjonalizm i rzeczywiste reguły polityki w Europie Środkowej po 1989 r.* [*Informal Politics. Constitutionalism and Effective Rules of Politics in Central Europe*] (2002). Books edited include: *Nieodrobiona lekcja. Polityki publiczne w Czechach i Polsce* [*The Lesson Not Done. Public Policies in Poland and the Czech Republic*] with Ondřej Krutílek (2013) and *Udana transformacja na peryferiach?* [*Successful Transformation on the Peripheries?*] with Justinas Dementavičius (2013). Contact: wolekak@kr.onet.pl

1 Introduction

Kálmán Pócza

Recently, political backlash against constitutional courts seems to have become a more or less general phenomenon in several Central European countries. In the last years, several political actors in the region have expressed their discontent with the juridification of politics and practice of judicial supremacy. They have argued that courts assumed too much power after the democratic transformation process in 1989/1990, and that they have used this power in an illegitimate way. These claims are explicitly or implicitly connected to the charge that courts have constrained the room for manoeuvre of the legislatures (and the executive) too heavily and that they have entered the field of politics. Thus, backlash against them should be interpreted rather as an act of balancing the power relationships between courts and legislatures (or other branches of political power).

Nevertheless, the question to what extent this aggregation of power and authority has constrained the dominant political actors *in fact* has never been examined accurately and systematically in the literature. Of course, there are several pieces and volumes focusing on the clashes between courts and legislatures (or courts and executives), but these are rather illustrative investigations with no coherent methodological background. The JUDICON research project[1] elaborated a systematic method to (1) map the diversity and (2) measure the strength of judicial decisions. This new methodology facilitates assessing systematically the multi-faceted reality of constitutional adjudication and measuring the strength of judicial decisions. In order to fit research to reality, a scale has been elaborated to answer the question to what extent courts have constrained the legislatures in general. A major impulse for presenting a new methodology came from a survey of the scholarly literature and its comparison with the reality of constitutional adjudication.

Our starting hypothesis was that the practice of constitutional adjudication in Central Europe (CE) has been more diverse than has been supposed by legal research. Our findings partly confirm this hypothesis. In fact, some courts have employed more tools available to them; thus, diversity of judicial rulings in these countries has been more characteristic than in other Central and Eastern European (CEE) countries. Hence, the diversity of judicial decisions in CEE presents a mixed picture. However, most courts were very careful in their practice and were inclined to select tools which were in no sense radical and which constrained only slightly their parliaments. In this sense, with the exception of some courts, constitutional adjudication in Central Europe has been very careful and the courts' practice proved to be highly self-restrained. We expected that the German Federal Constitutional Court (FCC) and the Hungarian Constitutional Court (HCC) had performed outstandingly and constrained their legislatures more heavily than any other court in the region, since these two courts have always been considered the strongest courts in the legal scholarship. In some respects, this hypothesis has been confirmed. In other aspects, however, we were compelled to contest it. While constitutional adjudication in Hungary proved to be the most diverse, the HCC constrained the room for manoeuvre of the legislature to a lesser degree than its counterparts in Germany or Slovakia. While the most powerful court was clearly the first Slovak court (1993–2000), the constitutional adjudication of the Romanian Constitutional Court (RCC) and the Polish Constitutional Tribunal (PCT) could be best characterized as highly moderate and restrained. These findings are all the more interesting since, beyond the Hungarian one, these two courts had to bear the most direct and impulsive attacks from political actors. Consequently, the general argument of the political actors of these countries, which states that courts intruded into the field of politics and illegitimately constrained the democratically elected legislatures, seems to be inadequate and should be considered rather as a fictitious narrative which aims to underpin the political intentions of the dominant actors. Not surprisingly, it was the German Federal Constitutional Court (FCC) which became more frequently a "positive legislator" and prescribed the *Bundestag* most frequently how to remedy unconstitutionality. Since the FCC built up its authority slowly and is by far the oldest court as compared to other courts of the region, it was not astonishing that the FCC included positive prescriptions either in the operative part, the headnote (*Leitsatz*) or in the justification of its decisions. Recently established courts of the CEE region have dared only very rarely to become positive legislators, and this is true for the three courts of the region which found themselves under heavy strain from the second half of the 2000s, i.e. the Romanian Constitutional Court, the Hungarian Constitutional Court and the Polish Constitutional Tribunal. This does not mean, however, that the Czech Constitutional Court (CCC) was able to completely escape the politicization of its operation. While the CCC was clearly the most isolated court and the behaviour of the CCC judges could not be explained by political circumstances or the influence of political parties, the CCC had the highest number of rulings with at least one dissenting opinion during the 1990s. This polarization is all the more interesting, since in the last decade of the 20th century judges of the other courts in the region only rarely published dissenting opinions. Trends in and network analysis of dissenting opinions indicate that political polarization of the courts commenced in the early 2000s in almost all CEE countries. Thus, challenging the non-partisan position of the courts is not unprecedented or a new phenomenon, even if the international media first realized this polarization process only after the attacks against the courts in the second decade of the 2000s.

As a general assessment, we will argue in this edited volume that the narrative of politicians referring to the ever-growing extension and misuse of judicial power seems to be somewhat incorrect, while political polarization of the courts became a more widespread phenomena as early as from the first years of the 2000s, which has been, in turn, generally neglected in the legal scholarship to date.

Outline of the volume

This volume is about the practice of constitutional adjudication in Central Europe with a special focus on the puzzling relationship between constitutional courts and legislatures. It does not concentrate on either the theory of judicial or legislative supremacy or the institutional design which, of course, might influence both constitutional adjudication and the relationship between these institutions. Furthermore, it will deliberately avoid any philosophical questions concerning the legitimacy of judicial review, and its main approach is certainly not in line with classical works of (European) legal scholarship. It does not aim to find an answer to the question of supremacy, nor does it approach the question of the relationship between the judiciary and the legislature from a merely legalistic point of view. Instead of philosophical, theoretical and purely legal questions, we have decided to explore empirically and systematically the practice of constitutional adjudication in Central Europe with a special focus on the diversity of judicial decisions and the strength of the constraint they exercise on the legislatures. Consequently, this work fits rather in the field of empirical legal research, which has a rich tradition in the American legal research community but is relatively unknown in the European context.[2]

This book is a product of the JUDICON research project,[3] in which we have focused on six Central European countries (Czech Republic, Germany, Hungary, Poland, Romania and Slovakia) between 1990 and 2015 and formulated two aims: first, we have elaborated a new methodology to map the diversity and measure the strength of judicial decisions (methodological part). Second, based on this coherent methodology and the database created by the project, we have explored the diversity and measured the strength of judicial decisions in six Central European countries (descriptive part). Having these aims in mind, we formulated two research questions:

How differentiated are the decisions of the Central European constitutional courts? (diversity of judicial decisions)

To what extent have these differentiated decisions of Central European constitutional courts constrained the room for manoeuvre of the legislature? (strength of judicial decisions)

A major impulse for formulating our research questions came from a survey of the scholarly literature and its comparison with the reality of constitutional adjudication. Obviously, there is an almost inexplicable discrepancy between the theory and practice of constitutional adjudication. The main deficiency of research on constitutional adjudication consists of an unsophisticated dichotomous approach that merely categorizes decisions of constitutional courts as positive or negative, i.e. as decisions that concluded in declaring the constitutionality or unconstitutionality of a given legal regulation. This approach is deeply inconsistent with the worldwide practice of constitutional adjudication, since the latter has shown widespread differentiation of judicial decisions over the last thirty years. Interestingly, constitutional adjudication in Central Europe shows striking diversification and is, consequently, decades ahead of empirical research on judicial behaviour. Refined practices of constitutional adjudication clearly exceed the upholding/strike down dichotomy, applied in the research on constitutional adjudication, by declaring a variety of provisions like legislative omission, procedural unconstitutionality, determining constitutional requirements, declaring complete or partial, *ex tunc* or *pro futuro* annulment or giving some prescription as to how to remedy unconstitutionality. Mapping this diversity of judicial decisions is one of the main aims of this book.

Furthermore, diversity of judicial decisions implies that we might be able to arrange judicial decisions into a ratio scale and evaluate them according to their strength. Although in legal terminology, the strength of a judicial decision seems to be a concept rather difficult to interpret, "strength" as used in this research project shows the extent to which constitutional courts restrict the room for manoeuvre of another constitutional organ (in this research project, the legislatures). While all decisions of a constitutional court have the same legal binding force, they may reduce the scope of legislative activities to varying degrees. For example, in cases the methodological chapter of the volume describes as formal unconstitutionality, legislatures made "only" a procedural mistake in the adaptation of the bill. After having corrected this procedural flaw of the legislative process, they might adopt the same law, often even with the same content. On the other hand, in cases of substantive unconstitutionality, the regulation should be changed substantively, i.e. its content should be transformed to meet the constitutionality criteria. In the second case, constitutional courts significantly narrow down the scope of legislative activities, since the court has found the content, rather than the way the bill was adopted, unconstitutional. Consequently, a decision based on substantive unconstitutionality is stronger than one based on formal unconstitutionality because it might limit the legislature's room for manoeuvre more heavily. It is important to note that by measuring the strength of judicial decisions, on no account do we want to measure the impact of judicial decisions. The term "strength" as used in our research might be best described with a boxing metaphor: measuring strength is measuring the power of a punch, and by no means the kind of impact this punch had on the other boxer. It is not considered whether this opponent could have side-stepped or is only slightly shaken, in spite of the fact that it was a very strong punch. To put it briefly, strength is not measured by the intensity of the impact of a decision.

To explore the diversity and measure the strength of judicial decisions, we have elaborated a new methodology which is apt to give a more nuanced picture of the practice of constitutional adjudication in Central Europe. We present the details of this methodology in Chapter 2. After assessing the literature on the empirical analysis of judicial decisions, we define the unit of observation of the research, which is also quite different from common approaches to judicial decisions. Since decisions of the constitutional courts might contain several rulings, we disaggregate all judicial decisions into rulings (units of observation). Neglecting the fact that court decisions are usually complex entities distorts all empirical analysis, a practice that should definitely be avoided. By disaggregating the decisions into rulings, we will certainly avoid this common mistake of empirical legal research. Beyond this fundamental novelty considering the unit of observation, we also present the main components and elements, i.e. the building blocks, of all judicial rulings. Naturally, in practice all courts do not employ all of the elements as presented in the chapter. Nevertheless, our fundamental aim is to present the tool-box judges might use in configuring their rulings. The elements presented should be considered as a repository of possible instruments judges can select from to make their decisions. In the next step, we present ruling of types which are aggregations of different elements of judicial decisions into the categories of weak, average and strong forms of rulings. By contracting the elements into ruling types, we are able to shed light on the diversity of rulings of courts in Central Europe: some combinations, i.e. ruling types, are completely absent from certain courts' practice, while others are clearly preferred. Declaration of substantive unconstitutionality with *pro futuro* temporal effect without any positive prescription has certainly been a preferred ruling type of the Polish Constitutional Tribunal, while the same court has never interpreted the constitution *in abstracto.* Concerning the second research question about the extent courts have constrained legislature's room for manoeuvre, we will introduce a scale based on certain fundamental principles that will serve as the starting point of the empirical analysis dealing with the strength of judicial decisions. The next section of the chapter deals with the explanation of weighting the elements of judicial decisions. Certainly, this part of the project might implicate some debate, but we hope to clarify the most important questions and dispel all concerns regarding the measurement of the strength of judicial rulings. Next we clarify the methodology of analyzing dissenting opinions and dissenting coalitions, and in the last section of the chapter we deal with future research based on the JUDICON dataset the authors of the project are to conduct.

Chapters 3 to 8 include country studies presenting the results of the coding process and the analysis of the relevant countries' datasets. The country studies follow the same coherent structure as the research methodology. We have structured each chapter in line with our predefined questions. Each country study will introduce the respective constitutional court by outlining its historical origins, the court's position within the constitutional system, its main competencies and institutional peculiarities or special processes unknown elsewhere in the region. Naturally, the courts' formal powers might have explanatory power concerning the diversity and strength of judicial rulings, but we have applied a different perspective. We intended to map and measure Central European courts' judicial decisions. Consequently, although the authors of the country studies refer to the (missing) formal powers of the relevant court, our main focus will be on the next parts of the studies. First, we asked the authors to present their general impressions of the court's activity based on the evaluation of the JUDICON dataset of their respective countries. We wanted to know whether there were any kinds of country-specific phenomena concerning case selection, coding processes, dissenting opinions, decision procedures or other elements deviating from our consistent coding rules. After these general impressions, we asked the authors to assess the trends in majority rulings. Questions pointed to whether there were preferred or missing ruling types, whether any changes or trends are observable in the court's ruling types, and we also asked the authors to try to find explanations for these trends and changes in ruling types. Similarly, we asked them to assess the trends and changes in the strength of majority rulings, and to determine whether these changes are linked to changes in political conditions or changes in the court's composition. On the other hand, in some countries, there were no clear trends discernible. In these cases, we asked the authors to find an answer to the absence of trends. Since in most countries the court's president has a special influence on its activity, every study (except for the German one) has a section on the comparison of the president's performance with that of the majority rulings. Subsequently, there will be an analysis of dissenting opinions. Here, once again, there are some countries (foremost Germany) where the number of dissenting opinions is so low that they cannot be analyzed. In other countries, however, trends in publishing or not publishing dissenting opinions are clearly recognizable, as are judges who have been more willing to give dissenting opinions. Also, the authors were able to assess individual judges' performance concerning the frequency and strength of dissenting opinions, as well as their relative difference from the rulings' strength of the majority position. Since we have also prepared a network analysis of dissenting opinions within the JUDICON project, the country studies touch upon the question of dissenting coalitions, i.e. identifying the judges who were willing to join each other for a dissent. As a concluding part, a qualitative evaluation closes the country studies where the country experts deal with specific cases and court decisions.

In the last chapter of the book (Chapter 9), we undertake a general assessment of the performance of Central European courts. In this chapter, we compare the courts' performance from the perspectives of dominant or missing ruling types, the uniformity or diversity of ruling types, the frequency of the strength values of majority rulings, the average strength of majority rulings both in general and their longitudinal changes and the trends in dissenting opinions. While there are several earlier assessments of Central European courts, this chapter will provide a comprehensive quantitative look at the practice of constitutional adjudication based on a comparable dataset. In this sense, this chapter contains several new insights not accessible before the creation of the JUDICON dataset.

Notes

1 See: www.judicon.tk.mta.hu
2 It should be stressed, however, that recently several initiatives have been launched which indicate that the field of empirical legal studies is becoming more and more popular, even in Europe. The first and the second Conference on Empirical Legal

Studies in Europe held in Amsterdam (2016) and in Leuven (2018), as well as the activity of Law and Court Standing Group of the European Consortium of Political Research (ECPR) and several research projects at various European universities like JUSTIN (Masaryk University Brno), iCOURTS (University of Copenhagen) or PluriCourts (University of Oslo) are excellent examples which demonstrate that various methods of empirical legal studies are nowadays more widespread in the European research community than a few years ago.

3 The JUDICON research project (www.judicon.tk.mta.hu/en) has been supported by the Hungarian Academy of Sciences (Centre for Social Sciences) and the Pázmány Péter Catholic University Budapest (Faculty of Humanities and Social Sciences KAP16-1.1-1.6 Grant). We are indebted to all interns of the project and especially to Adrienn Vajda who helped us in editing all figures and tables of the volume.

2 Research methodology

Kálmán Pócza and Gábor Dobos

2.1 Introduction

Over the last 30 years, the global spread of judicial review has been undoubtedly one of the most notable political developments not only in Western countries but all around the world (Stone Sweet 2000; Hirschl 2004; Ginsburg 2008). After the 1989/1990 transition process, constitutional courts (CCs) have also been established in Central and Eastern Europe; however, their performance is widely varied. Some of them have played no more than a marginal role in the processes of democratization and democratic consolidation, while others have been among the most important (political) actors in the new democracies of Central Europe. Although the evolution and practice of constitutional adjudication in Central Europe have been discussed by several path-breaking and excellent books (Schwartz 2000; Procházka 2002; Sadurski 2014; Bricker 2016) and edited volumes (Sadurski 2002; Luchterhandt et al. 2007) mapping the theory and practice of constitutional adjudication in Central Europe, they fail to present a coherent and systematic empirical analysis of constitutional adjudication in Central Europe. Most of these fundamental works have been edited volumes without a well-defined and coherent methodological approach, or they otherwise exhibit some weaknesses in referring to various illustrative examples as evidence of the proposed thesis. Incoherent methodological approaches and mere illustrative examples, however, are not sufficient for proving the hypotheses derived from theories of constitutional adjudication and theory.

2.2 Literature overview

Systematic empirical research on Central European constitutional adjudication is practically absent in this field.[1] Although the literature of legal studies has extensively analyzed the position of Central European constitutional courts in the system of separation of powers, to date few systematic empirical researches have been conducted on the operation or functioning of these institutions. Projects which consider, for example, the practice of constitutional adjudication in Hungary have a mainly philosophical character (Kis 2000; Győrfi 2001; Tóth 2009) as they tend to use a normative approach and, with a few exceptions (Boulanger 2013;

Halmai 2014; Szente 2016), do not focus on contextual analysis of the judicial practice. Thus, the systematic empirical research our project attempts to conduct has scant precedents in the Central European region.

Although over the last 20 years an increasing number of scientific articles and books with multi-faceted approaches have been published on the operation/functioning of constitutional courts and constitutional adjudication in Western Europe, several methodological problems and questions of the research on courts are still unanswered. Since a general overview of the state of the art of the political science research on constitutional courts has been provided by Dyevre (2010) and Hönnige (2010), it is more expedient to briefly refer to the literature regarded as the sources and inspiration for our methodological approach.

In elaborating a new approach, more sophisticated in evaluating the strength of judicial decisions taken *vis-à-vis* the legislature, we were inspired first by Brewer-Carías' international research project (2013), which aimed to describe the practices of various constitutional courts considered as positive legislators, i.e. as institutions which to a certain degree penetrate the jurisdiction or the field of competence of the legislative branch. By means of an inductive approach, Brewer-Carías compiled a typology of the decisions of CCs, considering their encroachment upon the competence of the legislature. Since Brewer-Carías' classification has a mere descriptive character, it is informative but not appropriate for a political science analysis of the interaction between legislature and judiciary.

In spite of the fact that the American scholarship on judicial behaviour is the most advanced, there have been no aspirations to analyze judicial decisions in a more differentiated way. Until recently, American scholars also used the "constitutional/unconstitutional" dichotomy in their analyzis of judicial decisions. Only Cass Sunstein's *One Case at a Time: Judicial Minimalism on the Supreme Court* (1999) turned the scholarly interest towards various possibilities judges could (or should) face in judicial decision-making processes. We were greatly inspired by this book.

Since CCs are actors in the political field, theoretical approaches of the political science literature have also produced some reflections on the exact role and strength of CCs within the political system. Interestingly enough, the most powerful theoretical framework of the last decade, the veto player theory, which also informed our research project, ignores the CCs as relevant political actors. According to the original form of this theory (Tsebelis 2002), constitutional courts are "most of the time" not veto players in the political system since they are absorbed by other veto players. Despite this original reluctance, the veto player theory has been applied to analyzing the functioning of European CCs. Volcansek (2000) and Hönnige (2007) challenged Tsebelis' rejection of considering CCs as veto players and demonstrated that, in contrast to Tsebelis' view, CCs are indeed "most of the time" veto players. Although these studies accept that legislatures are able to and sometimes do absorb the veto power of CCs, their empirical analysis has concluded that this is an exceptional rather than a normal situation. Our research project is in accordance with the latter scholars in arguing that the CEE CCs might be considered as veto players depending above all on the political environment. Whether they are "most of the time" absorbed or are real veto players can be demonstrated only in light of the results of the empirical data from the later phases of our research. The question of the diversity and magnitude of various veto powers (thus varieties of judicial decisions) emerged also in the criticism of the veto player theory (Ganghof 2003). Although Ganghof's remarks are revealing, they do not provide a systematic framework for the classification of the strength of a veto power; consequently, a scale of the strength of judicial decisions *vis-à-vis* the legislature cannot build on them. Since they are fragmentary and unsatisfactory, we have to elaborate a scale which can differentiate among veto acts of constitutional courts in terms of their intensity.

De Visser's (2014, 309) recently published, highly valuable comprehensive work has considered the process of the differentiation of judicial decisions. Though this work seems to be the most reflective, one which reckons with the multi-faceted practice of constitutional adjudication in Europe, and we embrace most of its insights, our research project fills some gaps still prevalent after de Visser's descriptive–illustrative empirical work. Our research project set off on the way de Visser marks out, but we turn this into systematic empirical research based on a new methodology. Consequently, we have elaborated a generally applicable scale to measure the strength of judicial decisions and scrutinize not only illustratively but also systematically how courts of the CEE region have used their power.

Bricker has examined empirically and systematically four different courts' adjudication practices in the CEE region. His study (Bricker 2016, 62), however, adopts a methodological approach that does not seem to be able to answer our descriptive research question about the extent to which constitutional courts have constrained legislature. Since Bricker simply differentiates between decisions which uphold a legislative act (constitutionality) and which abrogate it (unconstitutionality), the methodological approach his book applies seems to avoid the most pressing question of our research project.

While research on the temporal effect of judicial decisions (Popelier et al. 2014) and on constitutional dialogues between courts and legislatures (Meuwese and Snel 2013), as well as debates on the remedial power of the courts (Leckey 2016; 2015, 93–191), took into account several factors of the approach presented in this volume, these contributions tend to focus separately on certain elements of judicial decisions and are clearly less comprehensive in comparison to our approach.

Nevertheless, recently a new stream of research has emerged dealing with the formal powers of courts. These projects are very closely related to the present research since they put the question of the strength of constitutional courts in the light of their formal powers (Brinks and Blass 2017). Measuring the formal power of the courts or taking into account the legal and judicial practice or the immediate political context will certainly help in mapping the institutional design, the legal culture and the context in which judges make their decisions. These contributions focus on questions highly related to the present research since they look for determinants of the strength of constitutional courts – or, to put it differently, they try to find an answer to the question "what makes some constitutional courts powerful institutional actors relative to the other branches within their system of government, and others weaker, with far less impact on constitutionally relevant policy outcomes?" (Gardbaum 2017). Measuring the strength or weakness of the courts will give us the chance to explore and check the most plausible explanatory variables for strengths or weaknesses of judicial decisions. Measuring the strength of the court and measuring the strength of judicial decisions are complementary but, at the same time, completely different approaches to the courts: while the former looks for the capabilities of and constraints on the courts, i.e. the circumstances in which the judges make their decisions, the latter considers the relevant activity of the judges and measures the strength of the judicial decisions. Certainly, the capabilities and strength of the institution influence the capabilities of the judges and judicial decision-making, but judges always have alternatives from which they can choose, even if their room to manoeuvre might vary according to the institutional design. Taking these considerations into account, we assert that the approach we present in this volume is a highly innovative one with no precedent in the literature but is, at the same time, closely related to new trends which try to explore the strength of constitutional courts in their own context.

2.3 Units of observation: judicial rulings

In contrast to research of the judicial branch which generally considers one decision as the unit of observation, we take one ruling as our unit of observation. Judicial decisions might contain several different rulings. For example, a decision of the court might contain a ruling that declares an *ex nunc* procedural unconstitutionality annulling a whole law, while another ruling of the same decision declares *ex tunc* substantial unconstitutionality of a paragraph of a different legislative act. To date, researchers have not considered decisions as a complex set of different rulings, which seems, nevertheless, to be a necessary step if we want to have real in-depth analysis of the practice of constitutional adjudication. Sometimes judicial decisions contain only one ruling, but our empirical research has proven that in some countries it is rather uncommon and that judicial decisions generally include more than one ruling.[2] Neglecting the fact that one judicial decision frequently consists of several rulings might seriously distort any kind of empirical legal research since this leads to an unjustified and unacceptable aggregation of units of observations.[3] Thus, we have determined the ruling as the unit of observation. This is justified since two rulings of the same decision might have completely different values: i.e. one ruling might reject a motion dealing with certain legal regulations while another ruling in the same decision might declare unconstitutional some other parts of the same (or another) legal regulation. All this implies that various rulings, as defined by the court, cannot be aggregated into one unit (of observation).

Consequently, our point of departure was that a judicial decision might contain several rulings concerning various parts of different legal regulations.

We disaggregated all judicial decisions into several rulings (if a decision consisted of various rulings). For example, in Decision 47/2009 (IV.21.) the Hungarian Constitutional Court first held that "in the application of Section 12 para. (3) of the Act XXIII of 1992 on the Legal Status of Public Servants, it is a constitutional requirement based on Article 59 and 60 of the Constitution that the deed of oath should not contain any data referring to the public servant's conviction of conscience or religion". This Ruling 1 is a constitutional requirement. As a second ruling of the same decision, the HCC rejected "the petitions aimed at establishing the unconstitutionality and the annulment of Section 12 and Section 13 para. (2) of Act XXIII of 1992 on the Legal Status of Public Servants". Consequently, Ruling 2 of this decision was a rejection. As a third ruling of that very same decision, the HCC terminated "the procedure aimed at the posterior review of the unconstitutionality of Sections 31/A–31/F of Act XXIII of 1992 on the Legal Status of Public Servants", which means that Ruling 3 of this decision was a suspension. As a fourth ruling, it refused in the same decision "the petition aimed at establishing the unconstitutionality and the annulment of Section 13 para. (1), Section 65 para. (2) item d) and Section 102 para. (8) of Act XXIII of 1992 on the Legal Status of Public Servants, and it refused other petitions as well". This means that Ruling 4 of this specific decision of the HCC was a rejection.

Certainly, constitutional courts do not always make unanimous decisions, and sometimes judges express their disagreement by formulating dissenting opinions. Consequently, we have coded not only majority decisions but also dissenting opinions.[4] We have, however, neglected all concurring opinions since they do not concern the tenor, i.e. the operative part of the judicial decisions, which is the focus of our research project. Disaggregating majority decisions and dissenting opinions into rulings implies that the judges' dissenting opinions can be directly linked[5] to rulings of the majority decisions. This allows for avoiding the pitfalls of a simplified analysis that would link whole judicial decisions to dissenting opinions without taking into consideration that various rulings in dissenting opinions might refer to different parts of a majority decision. This means that dissenting opinions are analyzed according to the same components and elements as the majority decisions themselves, and it becomes possible to investigate even individual judicial behaviour.

2.4 Components and elements of judicial rulings

Considering the complexity of judicial decisions, we aimed to elaborate a methodological framework that offers a sophisticated tool for mapping the diversity of the rulings and measuring their strength. To be able to do this, one has to identify the elements in the ruling which affect the diversity and the extent of constraint (see Table 2.1). Obviously, the most important element of the ruling is the provision, which declares a law[6] constitutional or unconstitutional. However, it is also important whether the CC annuls only a part of the law or the whole act (or only a certain interpretation of it). This will be referred to as the completeness

Table 2.1 Components and elements of rulings

I Provision	(Ia) rejection or refusal (REJ/REF)	(Ib) uncons-titutionality by legislative omission (OM)	(Ic) procedural unconsti-tutionality (PROC)	(Id) constitutional requirement (CR)	(Ie) substantive unconstitutionality (SUBST)	(If) constitutional interpretation *in abstracto* (CIIA)
II Completeness	(IIa) qualitative partial annulment		(IIb) quantitative partial annulment		(IIc) complete annulment	
III Temporal effect	(IIIa) *pro futuro*		(IIIb) *ex nunc*		(IIIc) *ex tunc*	
IV Prescription	(IVa) no prescription	(IVb) non-binding prescription		(IVc) directive	(IVd) binding prescription	

Note: Unless otherwise indicated, all tables and figures of the volume are produced by JUDICON project and based on its dataset.

of a ruling. Furthermore, the temporal effect of the annulment can vary, which also influences the diversity and strength of the ruling. These three components (provision, completeness and temporal effect) are always located in the operative part of a judicial decision. Finally, rulings may contain a prescription, which declares how unconstitutionality might or should be corrected – it formulates guidelines or directives which legislatures should transform into a law. A prescription might be found either in the operative part or in the justification of the decision. Although the present research primarily focuses on the operative part (since this contains the directly binding elements), justifications are also considered when they contain prescriptions.

(I) Provision

Rulings of the constitutional court always contain a provision which might differ on the grounds on which the law has been found (un)constitutional: it might declare a refusal or rejection, unconstitutionality by legislative omission, procedural unconstitutionality, interpretation in harmony with the constitution (or constitutional requirements), substantive unconstitutionality or constitutional interpretation *in abstracto.*

- (Ia) Refusal/Rejection (REF/REJ)
  Motions might be rejected on the grounds that the legal regulation under review is completely in accordance with the constitution. They might be refused, however, also without substantive court investigation, due to inadmissibility or by referring to the political question doctrine. The process of the CC might be suspended, which, for the sake of our research project, might be considered as equal to a refusal except when the CC determines some constitutional requirements to be respected by the legislature.[7]
- (Ib) Unconstitutionality by legislative omission (OM)
  Unconstitutionality might emerge not only by the proactive operation of the legislature but also by legislative omissions. Legislative omissions might be caused not only by total inactivity of legislature but also by imperfect or insufficient legislation. Declaring unconstitutionality on these grounds is, however, a mild form of provision, since the constitutional court does not annul any acts of parliament but only calls upon the legislature to regulate something which is not regulated at all, or is regulated in an imperfect or insufficient manner.[8]
- (Ic) Procedural unconstitutionality (PROC)
  By procedural unconstitutionality, we mean all court provisions which abrogate a law due to the failures of the legislative process. Procedural unconstitutionality refers only to the legislative process and not to the substance of legislation. In this case, it is possible for the legislature to pass the bill a second time with the same or highly similar substance. Unconstitutionality means in this sense the violation of procedural rules but not the violation of the formal principles of rule of law.[9] This category includes cases of inaccurate

processes of legislation (like violation of the procedural rules of legislation; violation of the principle of the hierarchy of legal sources; omission of the prescribed consultation in the legislative process; omission of a substantive debate in the legislative process).

- (Id) CONSTITUTIONAL REQUIREMENTS (CR)

  While formally upholding a law, judges might have considerable room to manoeuvre in constraining the legislature by two means: first by judicial interpretation in harmony with the constitution, and second by determining constitutional requirements for either the courts or the legislature. To some extent, constitutional requirements in the operative part of a decision substantially broaden the regulation under constitutional review without the annulment of any of its parts. By giving guidance or directives for the legislature, the court is expanding the text of the law under review; consequently, it turns into a positive legislator. Constitutional requirement or interpretation in harmony with the constitution is suitable, however, for declaring both a particularly weak or a particularly strong provision which constrains the legislative branch seriously or just barely. This means that the court might be a mild or a very rigorous positive legislator.[10]

- (Ie) SUBSTANTIVE UNCONSTITUTIONALITY (SUBST)

  Substantive unconstitutionality constrains legislature more significantly than any previous forms of provisions, since it imposes some substantive barrier on the legislature. Declaring a law unconstitutional based on its content and disharmony with some paragraphs of the constitution is a very strong provision which implies high levels of constraints on the legislature. Consequently, the legislature's room to manoeuvre will be considerably narrowed.

- (If) CONSTITUTIONAL INTERPRETATION *in abstracto* (CIIA)

  An even stronger way to constrain the legislative branch (and the constituent power) is constitutional interpretation *in abstracto*.[11] Constitutional interpretation *in abstracto* means that the CC has been asked to explain and, consequently, to expand the text of the constitution in the operative part of its decision. Since the operative part of a decision usually contains only provisions like rejecting, refusing, suspending or annulling, all other forms of provisions which do not rule but explain and thereby extend the text of the constitution are equal to a constitution writing process. Constitutional interpretation *in abstracto* means the expanding of the text of the constitution; therefore, the constitutional court becomes not merely a positive legislator but a constituent power (*pouvoir constituant*). The court undertakes constitution-making even if it is an implicit rather than an explicit process. Since legislative majorities are usually not equal to supermajorities, and in this case the constitutional court fulfils the role of the constituent assembly or the *pouvoir constituant*, these decisions might be regarded as meaning the strongest constraints of the legislative.[12] Constitution-making means that the legislature's room to manoeuvre is heavily limited, since amending the constitution usually requires a supermajority that only rarely coincides with the legislative majority.

(II) Completeness

Judicial decisions pertain to legal regulations or legal norms. Although it might be uncertain whether a legal norm is contained in one sentence, in an article or in several interconnected articles of a statute (or even of several statutes), we embrace the position of the legislator and assume that the legislator either included all relevant norms concerning a policy issue in a statute or that it referred to other statutes which are interconnected. By assuming this position, we argue that complete annulment means that all paragraphs of a statute have been quashed. Nevertheless, a judicial decision very rarely annuls all sections of a statute; it is more common that only certain parts of it will be quashed. Furthermore, we distinguish between qualitative and quantitative partial annulment. Qualitative partial annulment of the norm might be best grasped perhaps as a negative constitutional requirement.[13] Determining a negative constitutional requirement, in practice, means that the CC found the law (or a paragraph/section/some words of a law) unconstitutional as far as the norm (or legislative act) might have an interpretation which is unconstitutional. However, there might be some other interpretation of the same norm (or legislative act) that is in harmony with the constitution. Consequently, though the CC annulled the norm (law or any part of the law), the legislature might find a solution by adopting the same law (part of the law) by explicitly excluding its unconstitutional interpretation. This is why this kind of ruling is only partial: the ruling of the CC intends to exclude only some kinds of interpretation of the law (or part of the law), some part of the possible meanings of the law but not other kinds of interpretation of the law. In contrast to qualitative partial annulment, quantitative partial annulment means that not only a certain interpretation of some parts of the law but also all possible interpretations and meanings of that part of the law are unconstitutional, while the constitutional court annuls only one or some part(s) (paragraph, section, some words) of the law. In this sense, quantitative partial annulment is "more complete" than qualitative partial annulment since the law might remain in effect, given the possibility that its unconstitutional interpretation is excluded from the text of the law. Quantitative partial annulment thus means that the constitutional court annulled a part of the law – but only a part of it. Complete annulment, in turn, means that all paragraphs of the law have been annulled.[14]

(III) Temporal effect

The temporal effect of the annulment is a further element of all judicial decisions, which affects the strength of rulings and consequently the room for manoeuvre of the legislature. Since *pro futuro* rulings may grant a transitional period, in which the goals of the legislative body might have temporarily been effectuated, this type of ruling seems to be a compromise and has a less dramatic effect on the legislature. This is not the case with *ex nunc* rulings, and even less in the most radical form of rulings (*ex tunc*). While an *ex nunc* ruling comes into effect immediately, leaving no room for the legislator, an *ex tunc* ruling annuls a law retroactively, which creates an especially strong encroachment on the legislative.

(IV) Prescription

As for the prescription determined by the courts, judges have quite a wide range of options: they can formulate recommendations, directives or constitutional requirements, or they can even anticipate what kind of legislative acts might prove to be unconstitutional in the future. They can also prescribe detailed regulation as to how unconstitutionality might be remedied. Since prescriptions vary according to their legal force (or binding effect), it is reasonable to discern four categories reflecting the variegation of prescriptions. Prescriptions which are placed in the operative part of a judicial decision have a clear-cut, legally binding effect (binding prescription) and are functionally equivalent to a constitutional requirement in the operative part of the decision.[15] Both prescriptions (or directives) in the operative part and constitutional requirements expand the text of the law under review; consequently, the court becomes a positive legislator by giving a prescription or a constitutional requirement. By contrast, prescriptions in the justification (or reasoning) have a less clear-cut status concerning their legal effect (non-binding). Prescriptions in the headnotes (*Leitsatz*)[16] of the decision have an ambiguous legal effect: they are more constraining than prescriptions in the justification but less so than prescriptions in the operative part of the decision (directive). Furthermore, several decisions contain no prescription at all (no prescription).

The four elements, namely provision, completeness, temporal effect and prescription, on which our research project focuses might be considered as options from which a judge or the constitutional court makes up a ruling. A ruling results from a mixture of the elements chosen. We checked the presence/absence of all four elements rigorously in each relevant ruling, since even the absence of an element is an indicator of the strength or weakness of a ruling.

We are aware, however, of the fact that certain combinations of these elements are not applicable at all: in the case of unconstitutionality by legislative omission (Ib), completeness (II) and temporal effect (III) are not applicable since no legal norm has been annulled, which is a precondition for referring to the completeness or temporal effect of the annulment. Also, declaring a constitutional requirement in the operative part of the decision (Id) or declaring a constitutional interpretation *in abstracto* (If) both imply that completeness (II) and temporal effect (III) are not applicable, since no sections of the law have been annulled. Annulment is required in order to be able to check for the completeness and temporal effect of the annulment.

Constitutional requirement in the operative part of the decision (Id) and constitutional interpretation *in abstracto* (If) imply that we cannot consider prescription (IV) at all. This is because constitutional requirements are functionally equivalent to prescriptions that expand the text of the law under review – as explained above. Constitutional interpretation *in abstracto* (If), by contrast, expands the text of the constitution; thus, we cannot consider it as a prescription. Beyond these specific cases, in the coding process all four elements of a ruling listed above was checked one by one in four steps.

2.5 Mapping the diversity of judicial rulings

As noted above, our research starts from the assumption that the decisions of the constitutional courts should be considered more diverse than merely declaring constitutionality or unconstitutionality. The components we identified earlier allow judges to select from a wide range of measures to constrain the legislature. Therefore, to answer the first research question of how differentiated the decisions of the Central European Constitutional Courts are, we need to examine the frequency of various combinations of the elements of judicial rulings used by the judges.

2.5.1 Combinations of the elements of judicial rulings

Based on the methodological framework, there are 79 possible combinations of the elements (different types of provision, completeness, temporal effect and prescription). As can be seen in Table 2.2, not all elements can be combined with each other in practice (see NA: not applicable). For example, the court cannot declare omission with *ex tunc* temporal effect and partial annulment, since in this case, there is no existing law to be annulled. Diversity understood as the simple enumeration of the possible elements is, however, only the most basic way to account for the complexity of a court's rulings. As a nominal level of measurement, this merely differentiates between possible combinations of the elements that add up a given ruling; however, the value of the elements remains unconsidered. Still, it offers a step beyond the simple binary differentiation of constitutionality or unconstitutionality.

Obviously, the most important part of any ruling is the provision that reflects the core of the court's standpoint. Examining diversity thus can be approached as the nominal measurement of provisions, since the main direction of a ruling is fundamentally defined by this first element of the ruling.

2.5.2 Ruling types

Since a ruling might be made up of different elements that constrain the legislature in various ways, it is important to explain diversity as the frequency of stronger and weaker combinations. Certain elements combined into one ruling indicate that the constitutional court attempted to significantly reduce the legislature's room to manoeuvre. For example, declaring substantive unconstitutionality of a complete law with *ex tunc* temporal effect and giving a binding prescription is one of the strongest possible constraints. Conversely, declaring *pro futuro* procedural unconstitutionality without any prescription allows the legislature to overcome unconstitutionality without closely following the court's lead. This approach helps us understand the variance and diversity of rulings and their intuitively defined relative strength, while the exact value differences of the various combinations remains undisclosed at this point.

Table 2.2 Possible combination of the elements of judicial rulings

Provision	*Completeness*	*Temporal effect*	*Prescription*
Rejection or refusal (REJ or REF)	NA	NA	NA
Omission (OM)	NA	NA	no prescription non-binding prescription directive binding prescription
Procedural unconstitutionality (PROC)	qualitative partial annulment	*pro futuro*	no prescription
	quantitative partial annulment	*ex nunc*	non-binding prescription
	complete annulment	*ex tunc*	directive
			binding prescription
Constitutional requirement (CR)	NA	NA	Constitutional requirement
Substantive unconstitutionality (SUBST)	qualitative partial annulment	*pro futuro*	no prescription
	quantitative partial annulment	*ex nunc*	non-binding prescription
	complete annulment	*ex tunc*	directive
			binding prescription
Constitutional interpretation *in abstracto* (CIIA)	NA	NA	Constitutional requirement

NA: no combination is possible.

By highlighting the provision and combining it with completeness, temporal effect and prescription, weak, average or strong rulings can be discerned. Since provisions give the tenor of a ruling, it is justifiable to check whether the court (or the dissenting judge) tries to sharpen or, conversely, alleviate the provision by selecting weak, average or strong elements of completeness, temporal effect and prescription.[17] Weak types of rulings (weak omission, weak procedural or substantive unconstitutionality) indicate that the court has tried to soften its provision by determining only a qualitative partial annulment and/or declaring a transitional period by delaying the coming into force of its ruling (*pro futuro*). Weak rulings exclude any implicit or explicit meddling with the competencies of the legislative, which means that no prescriptions will be included in the weak ruling types (marked by white in Table 2.3).[18] In turn, a complete and/or *ex tunc*

Table 2.3 Ruling types (weak, average and strong forms of rulings)

I Provision	(Ia) rejection or refusal (REJ/REF)	(Ib) unconstitutionality by legislative omission (OM)	(Ic) procedural unconstitutionality (PROC)	(Id) constitutional requirement (CR)	(Ie) substantive unconstitutionality (SUBST)	(If) constitutional interpretation *in abstracto* (CIIA)
II Completeness	(IIa) qualitative partial annulment		(IIb) quantitative partial annulment		(IIc) complete annulment	
III Temporal effect	(IIIa) *pro futuro*		(IIIb) *ex nunc*		(IIIc) *ex tunc*	
IV Prescription	(IVa) no prescription	(IVb) non-binding prescription		(IVc) directive	(IVd) binding prescription	

annulment and/or any kind of prescription are obvious signs of the court's resoluteness. Annulling a complete law or making a decision with retroactive effect puts heavy burdens on the legislature, not to mention any interference with its competence by determining positive (binding or non-binding) prescriptions or directives for the legislature. Therefore, these ruling types might be called strong omissions, strong procedural or substantive unconstitutionality (marked by dark grey in Table 2.3). Complete annulments, *ex tunc* annulments or any kind of prescription always indicate a strong ruling type even if other elements are weak or average.[19] In between the two poles of weak and strong ruling types there is, of course, an average type. In this case, the court annuls only a certain part of the law (quantitative partial annulment), its decision will come into force on its announcement (*ex nunc*) and it does not contain any prescription. This is the standard ruling type and, according to the JUDICON dataset, is also the most frequent one (marked by light grey in Table 2.3).[20] To put it simply: if a ruling diverges from this average type and declares a qualitative partial or a *pro futuro* annulment, it is a weak ruling type, but it becomes a strong one if it declares a complete or *ex tunc* annulment, or if it includes any prescriptions.[21]

This classification allows for differentiation of the ruling types more or less intuitively, which, however, can be specified by weighting the elements that make up a ruling. It is thus needed to move from the level of diversity to the exact strength of the constitutional courts' rulings.

2.6 Measuring the strength of judicial rulings

Measuring the strength requires weighting the elements of rulings. Determining or predefining the relationship of the elements to each other is not unconceivable by formulating clear and plausible principles of weighting the elements (see Table 2.4).

(I) Provision

It is obvious that the most important part of a judicial decision is its provision. The range of the scale extends from decisions that reject the motion (without deciding on the merit of the case) or simply find the law constitutional, on the one end of the scale, and decisions in which the constitutional court becomes constituent power (constitutional interpretation *in abstracto*), on the other. There are different types of decisions between these two extremes. The relative weight might be determined according to the following relations.

(Ia) Rejection does not constrain the legislature at all. [0.00]
(Ib) Unconstitutionality by legislative omission merely declares that the legislature must adopt a new regulation but does not constrain the legislature regarding the substance of regulation. [+0.50]

Table 2.4 Weighting of the elements of rulings

I Provision	(Ia) rejection or refusal **[0]**	(Ib) unconstitutionality by legislative omission **[0.5]**	(Ic) procedural unconstitutionality **[1]**	(Id) constitutional requirement **[2]**	(Ie) substantive unconstitutionality **[6]**	(If) constitutional interpretation *in abstracto* **[10]**
II Completeness	(IIa) qualitative partial annulment **[0]**		(IIb) quantitative partial annulment **[0.5]**		(IIc) complete annulment **[1]**	
III Temporal effect	(IIIa) *pro future* **[0]**		(IIIb) *ex nunc* **[0.5]**		(IIIc) *ex tunc* **[1]**	
IV Prescription	(IVa) no prescription **[0]**	(IVb) non-binding prescription **[1]**		(IVc) directive **[1.5]**		(IVd) binding prescription **[2]**

(Ic) Declaring the procedural unconstitutionality of a legal regulation implies that the regulation will be annulled but only due to some procedural mistakes in the legislative process. [+1.00]

(Id) Constitutional requirements constrain the legislature more than the declaration of procedural unconstitutionality since the CC becomes a positive legislator and the substance of the regulation will be altered while upholding the law under review. [+2.00]

(Ie) Declaring substantive unconstitutionality implies that the substance of the legal regulation has been flawed to a degree that the CC could not rectify unconstitutionality by stretching the text of the law under review (i.e. determining a constitutional requirement) but has to abrogate the legal regulation. The guiding principle is that any form of substantive unconstitutionality should be regarded as a stronger decision than any other decision based on procedural unconstitutionality or constitutional requirement. Therefore, the weakest combination of substantive unconstitutionality should always be regarded as stronger than the strongest form of procedural unconstitutionality.[22] [+6.00]

(If) Constitutional interpretation *in abstracto* is regarded as the strongest constraint on the legislator. This is why CIIA must be at least as strong as the strongest decision declaring substantive unconstitutionality [+10.00].[23] It is, however, of utmost importance to remark that CIIA does not always constrain the legislature. CIIA might sometimes rather extend the room of the national legislator to manoeuvre *vis-à-vis* other political actors. In this case, the constitution will be expanded in a way highly favourable for the legislature. This is why we have to make a clear difference between highly constraining CIIA, on the one hand, and highly permissive CIIA on the other. Consequently, CIIAs should also be evaluated case by case. [either +10.00 or 0.00][24]

(II) Completeness

The question of whether the CC annulled the legal regulation totally (complete annulment), partially (quantitative partial annulment) or merely excluded some meanings of a legal term (qualitative partial annulment) is certainly not as important as the provision or a prescription. Thus, we had to add less weight for the strongest form of completeness than for the strongest form of prescription and the provision. This is how qualitative partial annulment is weighted as the weakest form [0.00], quantitative partial annulment as a middle-range [0.50] and complete annulment as the strongest form [+1.00].

(III) Temporal effect

Temporal effect should be considered as important as completeness if we compare the four elements of rulings. Temporal effect is certainly less important than the prescription and even less than the provision. Hence the weight of the three categories are as follows: *pro futuro* [0], *ex nunc* [0.50] and *ex tunc* [+1.00].

(IV) Prescription

Since courts might to some extent replace legislature by determining binding prescriptions, this fourth element (along with its functional equivalent constitutional requirement) must be the second most important and weightiest element of a ruling after declaring the substantive unconstitutionality of a legal regulation. Weights of prescriptions vary according to their placement in the decision: non-binding is placed in the justification, which has a rather uncertain legal effect [+1.00]; directive is placed in the headnote (if there is such a thing in the decision), the legal status of which is still uncertain but might clearly be regarded as a stronger element [+1.50] than prescriptions in the justification. The strongest prescription is placed in the operative part, which has a legal binding effect [+2.00].[25]

2.7 Network analysis of dissenting opinions

Beyond analyzing majority rulings, we will focus also on dissenting opinions (but not on concurring opinions). Dissenting opinions are sometimes formulated by one judge without any other judges aligning with the dissent. Sometimes, however, judges make a coalition in publishing dissenting opinions. A coalition of dissenting judges means that a dissenting opinion written by a judge might also be supported and signed by further judges. A coalition might mean a single case of agreement, but in the practice of the courts some coalitions of two or more judges last, extending to several cases. Dissenter coalitions are considered here in a very restrictive sense: judges form a dissenter coalition only if their dissent has the same strength and is an outcome of the same composition of the elements of judicial decisions. This means that they selected the same components in all four aspects (ruling, completeness, temporal effect and prescription) of the ruling. The same strength of two or more dissenting opinions is not a sufficient condition of a dissenting coalition, since it could be an outcome of a different composition of their dissenting opinions. Two dissenting opinions with the same value [7.00] will not be considered as a basis of judicial coalition if they differ, for example, in their temporal effect and completeness. To put it simply: a dissenting opinion declaring a substantive unconstitutionality [6.00], with qualitative partial annulment [0.00] *ex tunc* [1.00] and without any prescription [0.00] is not considered as a basis of judicial coalition if another judge declared in his/her dissenting opinion a substantive unconstitutionality [6.00] with complete annulment [1.00] but *pro futuro* [0.00] and without any prescription [0.00], since they differ in temporal effect and completeness.

Dissenting opinions have been conjugated, and each interaction of judge "A" with any other judge has been counted in a matrix. Of course, there have been decisions where dissenting opinions were formulated by only one judge, without any other judges aligning with it. These cases have been neglected, since we were interested in dissenting coalitions. The number of interactions between judge "A" and judge "B" shows the strength of the coalition: if the uniformity of their dissenting opinions occurred several times (even if the components of their dissenting opinion differed from time to time), it is considered a strong coalition. This framework of analysis will be applied consequently in all country studies (except Germany, where dissenting opinions were very rare).

2.8 Further research projects

For the JUDICON research project, we have built up a database by coding all relevant decisions of six Central European constitutional courts. As noted above, relevant decisions included only those which affected legislative acts, more precisely the bills and laws of selected Central European countries. Consequently, one of the most obvious ways the research could be continued is to widen and deepen its scope. Including further (Western and Eastern European) countries is certainly an activity which demands more human resources, as well as a heavy workload if we continue coding and analyzing court decisions concerning secondary legislation. Less demanding and, consequently, more feasible activities for the authors of the present volume include selecting and analyzing politically relevant court decisions, applying the attitudinal model or the external strategist model of judicial behaviour or combining the JUDICON dataset with the one of the Comparative Agendas Project (CAP).[26]

2.8.1 Selecting politically salient decisions

Case selection is certainly one of the most important decisions researchers of constitutional adjudication face. In the following analyzes, we have included all relevant decisions of the courts and additionally analyzed selected cases in each country study by applying qualitative methods. Nevertheless, the comprehensive dataset we have built up in the JUDICON project opens up different quantitative strategies in evaluating the results of the coding process. First, one might evaluate all relevant decisions without selecting politically important ones. Therefore, the research project cannot be accused of subjective bias in case selection. In this regard, one does not have to rely on the assumed (political) importance or impact of the courts' decisions. However, this comprehensive strategy also has some shortcomings. Analyzes based on quantitative methods might be blind to some important (political) circumstances. While we might argue that including all decisions of the CCs might increase the objectivity of the analysis, it is of utmost importance to stress that analyzing selected cases by quantitative methods might also be necessary in order to evaluate the activity of the CCs from the perspective of the political significance of certain decisions. Weighting among legal regulations under constitutional review according to their significance to a given country's political life might be a valid research design and should certainly be conducted. Such quantitative research projects might, for example, uncover judges' possible strategies in taking strong rulings against (politically) less important legal regulations adopted by their respective nominating party and against (politically) more important regulations of the opposing side, while being more permissive against (politically) more important legislative regulations adopted by their nominating party and against (politically) less important regulations adopted by the other side.

2.8.2 *The attitudinal and the strategist models*

In some countries, the nomination and election of the judges of constitutional courts are highly politicized processes, i.e. political parties play a key role in selecting, nominating and electing judges. In these countries, the authors of the present volume will be able to determine the nominating party of individual judges with high reliability. By building up a separate dataset which includes the parliamentary voting behaviour of nominating parties, researchers will be able to answer the question posed by the attitudinal model of judicial behaviour. Since the JUDICON project transcends the binary approach of analyzing constitutional/unconstitutional decisions, we will be able to find out how far judges followed the policy and value preferences of their nominating parties. We do not simply respond to the question of the attitudinal model with a simple yes or no, but can also determine judges' relative proximity to their respective nominating parties. This sophisticated approach promises exciting results; thus, this research will certainly be done in the near future.

Another interesting model of judicial behaviour is the external strategist model, which tries to find out whether external circumstances like public opinion (trust in constitutional courts), constitutional courts' *de facto* independence, the margin of parliamentary majority, political fragmentation or polarization have any impact on the judges' behaviour. Since coherent data on trust in constitutional courts in Europe is missing, we have to confine ourselves to the analysis of the data of other relevant factors listed above. Nevertheless, we are keen to check for these independent variables and see whether theoretical assumptions – e.g. that political fragmentation and/or public trust in constitutional courts enhances the leeway of the courts, while the opposite reduces the chances to make tough decisions – are proved or disapproved.

2.8.3 *Comparative Agendas Project*

Last but not least, a huge potential might also be attributed to research which connects the JUDICON dataset with that of the Comparative Agendas Project. Currently only Germany and Hungary have been included into the CAP project, but we hope that further Central European countries will join this exciting project and that further members of the JUDICON project will be also able to analyze which policy issues implicate stronger or weaker decisions of constitutional courts. By doing this, we will be able to map the courts' impact on certain policy areas or see whether there were policy issues courts deliberately avoided. Naturally, the courts' formal competences might heavily influence their chances to influence policy makers or policy issues; however, connecting the two datasets, and analyzing the judicial behaviour according to policy areas, is nevertheless a highly promising research project. Having all this potential research projects in mind, let us start our journey by systematically exploring the practice of constitutional adjudication in six Central European countries.

Notes

1 As an exception, see Bricker (2016). However, as Bricker's work focuses on the constitutionality and unconstitutionality of legislative acts, it cannot answer the question in the focus our own research: to what extent is the legislative constrained by the constitutional court? For an earlier version of the present chapter, see Pócza et al. (2017). Here we would like to thank the *German Law Journal* for their generosity in permitting us to reprint some parts of that paper.

2 We postulated as a general principle that rulings (i.e. units of observations) will be defined by the court, i.e. if the court embraces various legal regulations in one ruling and decides this bunch of legal regulations by declaring them unconstitutional in one ruling, we do not disaggregate this ruling. We assume that the court had good reasons to deal with those legal regulations in a bunch.

3 Obviously, one could argue that we might discern those rulings which are the tenor of the decision, i.e. the politically relevant or important rulings. This argument, however, presupposes that decisions have been disaggregated into rulings, and, on the basis of reasonable criteria, one could select the politically relevant rulings. This approach is certainly not unjustified, but once again it presupposes that decisions have been separated into rulings and we have justified criteria for the selection process.

4 For the codebook, see: http://judicon.tk.mta.hu/en/methodology

5 Occasionally, dissenting judges formulate their general disagreement or criticism in their opinions rather than their specific concerns with a particular ruling. In these cases, it is impossible to link rulings with a related part in the dissenting opinion. Therefore, while these dissenting opinions have also been collected and coded, they have not been analyzed.

6 After detailed consideration, within our framework, we only consider laws, while lower level regulations (e.g. decrees) and court decisions are excluded as they would exceed the scope of the research.

7 Refusals was coded only if there was a dissenting opinion (e.g. the judge claims that the constitutional court should have decided the case on its merits) since refusals are mainly based on technical arguments, i.e. the court could not deal with the case due to some formal deficiencies. In controversial cases, there will certainly be a dissenting opinion that argues that the court should have dealt with the case on its merit.

8 One might argue that finding an omission is much more severe interference with the competencies of legislation; therefore, some clarification is needed as to why we conceive unconstitutionality by legislative omission as a mild form of provision. First of all, we have to stress that a ruling based on legislative omission does not concern the legal system in force, i.e. it does not annul any of the existing legal norms. Furthermore, even if the court assessed an omission but did not propose any solution for how unconstitutionality might be corrected, the legislature is not under direct pressure to act in any form. If the court's decision does not contain any threat or possible sanction (which most of the time is the case in CEE countries), the legislation might simply neglect or disregard the ruling of the court, and *status quo* might be preserved. In this case, the court simply suggested that the legislature act, but if it doesn't want to change the *status quo*, nothing will change. This is why we argue that a ruling which found a statute unconstitutional by referring to legislative omission does not really

compel the legislation to act. By contrast, constitutional requirement and, certainly even more, substantive unconstitutionality mean that *status quo* will be automatically changed by the decision of the court.

9 We are aware of the fact that sometimes it is quite difficult to make an unambiguous distinction between procedural/formal unconstitutionality and substantive unconstitutionality. The term "rule of law" might serve as a transition point between procedural unconstitutionality and substantive unconstitutionality. We have considered that we should include any principle and connotations derived from the rule of law that do not exclude a repeated adoption of the legislative regulation with the same substance as a procedural unconstitutionality. Eventually, however, we decided to code all references to the principle of rule of law or any derivation of it (like accessibility, clarity, calculability, necessary time provided for preparation to comply with the new law, legal certainty and taboo of retroactivity) as substantive unconstitutionality. At the end of the coding process, we will return to these special cases and re-evaluate them one by one in order to clarify whether the decision based on the principle of rule of law excluded a repeated adoption of the legal regulation with the same substance. A further problem emerges concerning the taboo of retroactive legislation in the context of democratic transitions. Since sensible questions of transitional justice definitely collide with this fundamental principle of rule of law, procedural/formal unconstitutionality based on the taboo of retrospective legislation might have a highly restrictive effect on legislation in times of democratic transition. This is why decisions implying conflicts between the principles of the transitional justice and the rule of law should be very carefully analyzed.

10 Since our research aims to analyze judicial decisions quantitatively, we have simply focused on the presence or absence of constitutional requirements and have not evaluated the strength of these requirements one by one. Further qualitative investigation will be needed in order to refine the picture regarding the strength of these constitutional requirements. At this phase of the project, we are focusing on the formal presence of constitutional requirements.

11 Beyond the German Federal Constitutional Court, no court in Western Europe has the competence to declare an abstract and binding interpretation of constitution without reviewing a law filed to the court. By contrast, this kind of constitutional adjudication is not unknown in Central Europe, although even courts in CEE have rarely been asked to exercise it (for this see Hönnige 2007, 132 and Sadurski 2014, 23). Binding constitutional interpretations are not only advisory notes in the justifications of a decision but are included in the operative part of judicial decisions; they should not be confounded with preliminary reference procedure of the ECJ. For an example, see Decision 21/1996 of the HCC (http://hunconcourt.hu/letoltesek/en_0021_1996.pdf).

12 At first glance, it might be not obvious why we are arguing that constitutional interpretation *in abstracto* corresponds to constitution-making or writing. The idea (and problem) that constitutional courts might be not only positive legislators but actors of constitution writing processes has been developed in the legal scholarship in connection to the heavily discussed problem of unconstitutional constitutional amendments. Constraining the constituent power by judicial decisions means, certainly, that the court vindicates the right to be an integrative part of a composite body assumed as *pouvoir constituant*. Also, the concept of post-sovereign constitution-making, as presented by Andrew Arato, hints that the constitutional courts emerged as powerful actors to fill in the gaps and deficiencies of a transitory constitution. In several countries (and especially in Hungary and South Africa), prominent actors of these post-sovereign constitution-making processes were constitutional courts. Both of

these directions of constitutional theories, however, consider either all forms of the activity of constitutional courts in general, or they narrow down the problem to the concept of unconstitutional constitutional amendment. In contrast to these trends, we argue that including lengthy and detailed interpretation of constitutional norms and concepts into the operative part of a judicial decision is clearly an expansion of the text of the constitution. Since the operative part of a decision is undoubtedly legally binding, while the status of justifications is contested in this regard, we argue that binding interpretation of the constitution included into the operative part is equivalent to constitution-making. For this question, see Arato (2016), Stone Sweet (2012, 826) and Vorländer (2006, 20).

13 For the term qualitative/quantitative partial annulment, see Visser (2014, 314).

14 The initial results of the research point out that in Hungary, as opposed for example to Germany, qualitative partial annulment is not a regular decision in the Constitutional Court's practice, which usually considers whether the law should be completely or only partially annulled irrespective of possible interpretations. The comparative aims of the project, however, required the introduction of the category of qualitative partial annulment.

15 Binding prescription (IVd) and constitutional requirement in the operative part of the decision (Id) are essentially the same. The only difference is that while the constitutional requirement does not formally annul the law, a binding prescription is a decision that annuls the law.

16 The comparative aims of the research required the introduction of the category of headnote (or, in the case of the German Constitutional Court, *Leitsatz*), although in some cases (e.g. in Hungary) decisions of the constitutional court do not include such summaries.

17 Obviously, there are no weak, average or strong forms of rejection, constitutional requirements and constitutional interpretation *in abstracto,* since completeness, timing and prescription are not applicable in these cases as described above. Omission might be only strong or weak, since completeness and timing are irrelevant in this case.

18 Weak ruling types include the following combinations of the elements: Ic + (IIa and/or IIIa and/or IVa); Ie + (IIa and/or IIIa and IVa); Id + (IIa and/or IIIa and IVa); Ie + (IIa and/or IIIa and IVa).

19 Strong ruling types include the following combinations: Ib + IVb/IVc/IVd; Ic + (IIc and/or IIIc and/or IVb/IVc/IVd); Ie + (IIc and/or IIIc and/or IVb/IVc/IVd).

20 Average ruling types include the following combinations: Ib + IVa; Ic + (IIb and IIIb and IVa); Ie + (IIb and IIIb and IVa).

21 Strong elements override weak and average forms, which means that if a strong element is included, the ruling will be defined as strong.

22 The strongest form of procedural unconstitutionality consists of procedural unconstitutionality (Ic) + complete annulment (IIc) + *ex tunc* timing (IIIc) + binding prescription (IVd), which gives 5 points in sum (1+1+1+2). The weakest form of substantial unconstitutionality consists of substantive unconstitutionality (Ie) + qualitative partial annulment (IIa) + *pro futuro* timing (IIIa) + no prescription (IVa), which means 6 points in sum (6+0+0+0)

23 The strongest form of substantive unconstitutionality consists of substantive unconstitutionality (Ie) + complete annulment (IIc) + *ex tunc* timing (IIIc) + binding prescription (IVd), which means 10 points in sum (6+1+1+2).

24 In cases of utmost permissibility, the constitutional court might explicitly broaden the legislative's room to manoeuvre. However, as our research focuses on the extent the constitutional court constrains the legislator, we decided not to use negative values and a dedicated scale to evaluate decisions that broaden the legislative's room to

manoeuvre. Since constitutional interpretation *in abstracto* is a weapon only rarely used by constitutional courts, qualitative analyzes might help to determine what broadening in these cases actually means.

25 As noted earlier, we regard binding prescription (IVd) and constitutional requirement in the operative part of the decision to have the same weight.

26 For the CAP project, see: http://www.comparativeagendas.net/

References

Arato, Andrew. 2016. *Post Sovereign Constitution Making: Learning and Legitimacy.* Oxford: Oxford University Press.

Boulanger, Christian. 2013. *Hüten, richten, gründen. Rollen der Verfassungsgerichte in der Demokratisierung Deutschlands und Ungarns.* Berlin: Epubli.

Brewer-Carías, Allan. 2013. *Constitutional Courts as Positive Legislators. A Comparative Law Study.* Cambridge: Cambridge University Press.

Bricker, Benjamin. 2016. *Visions of Judicial Review. A Comparative Examination of Courts and Policy in Democracies.* Colchester: ECPR Press.

Brinks, Daniel M., and Abby Blass. 2017. "Rethinking judicial empowerment: The new foundations of constitutional justice". *International Journal of Constitutional Law* 15 (2): 296–311.

Dyevre, Arthur. 2010. "Unifying the field of comparative judicial politics: towards a general theory of judicial behavior". *European Political Science Review* 2 (2): 297–327.

Ganghof, Steffen. 2003. "Promises and pitfalls of veto player analysis". *Swiss Political Science Review* 9 (2): 1–25.

Ginsburg, Tom. 2008. "The global spread of constitutional review". In *The Oxford Handbook of Politics and Law*, edited by Keith E. Whittington, 81–99. Oxford: Oxford University Press.

Gardbaum, Stephen. "What Makes for More or Less Powerful Constitutional Courts?" UCLA Public Law & Legal Theory Research Paper Series No. 17–37, 2017, 7.

Győrfi, Tamás. 2001. *Az alkotmánybíráskodás politikai karaktere* [*The Political Character of Constitutional Adjudication*]. Budapest: INDOK.

Halmai, Gábor. 2014. "In memoriam magyar alkotmánybíráskodás" ["In memoriam Hungarian constitutional adjudication"]. *Fundamentum* 18 (1–2): 36–64.

Hirschl, Ran. 2004. *Towards Juristocracy, the Origins and Consequences of the New Constitutionalism.* Cambridge: Harvard University Press.

Hönnige, Christoph. 2007. *Verfassungsgericht, Regierung und Opposition. Die vergleichende Analyse eines Spannungsdreiecks.* Wiesbaden: VS Verlag.

Hönnige, Christoph. 2010. "Beyond judicialization: why we need more comparative research about constitutional courts". *European Political Science* 10 (3): 346–358.

Kis, János. 2000. *Alkotmányos demokrácia* [*Constitutional Democracy*]. Budapest: INDOK.

Leckey, Robert. 2015. *Bills of Rights in the Common Law.* Cambridge: Cambridge University Press.

Leckey, Robert. 2016. "The harms of remedial discretion". *International Journal of Constitutional Law* 14(3): 584–607.

Luchterhandt, Otto, Christian Starck and Albrecht Weber. eds. 2007. *Verfassungsgerichtsbarkeit in Mittel- und Osteuropa.* Baden-Baden: Nomos Verlag.

Meuwese, Anne, and Marxin Snel. 2013. "Constitutional dialogues: an overview". *Utrecht Law Review* 9 (2): 123–140.

Pócza, Kálmán, Gábor Dobos and Attila Gyulai. 2017. "How to measure the strength of judicial decisions? A methodological framework". *German Law Journal* 18(6): 1557–1586.

Popelier, Patricia, Sarah Verstraelen, Dirk Vanheule and Beatrix Vanlerberghe. eds. 2014. *The Effects of Judicial Decisions in Time*. Cambridge: Intersentia.

Procházka, Radoslav. 2002. *Mission Accomplished. On Founding Constitutional Adjudication in Central Europe*. New York/Budapest: CEU Press.

Sadurski, Wojciech, ed. 2002. *Constitutional Justice East and West*. The Hague/London: Kluwer Law International.

Sadurski, Wojciech, ed. 2014. *Rights Before Courts. A Study of Constitutional Courts in Postcommunist States of Central and Eastern Europe*. Dordrecht/New York: Springer.

Schwartz, Herman. 2000. *The Struggle for Constitutional Justice in Post-Communist Europe*. Chicago: University of Chicago Press.

Sunstein, Cass. 1999. *One Case at a Time: Judicial Minimalism on the Supreme Court*. Cambridge (Mass.): Harvard University Press

Stone Sweet, Alec. 2000. *Governing with Judges. Constitutional Politics in Europe*. Oxford: Oxford University Press.

Stone Sweet, Alec. 2012. "Constitutional Courts". In *The Oxford Handbook of Comparative Constitutional Law*, edited by Michael Rosenfeld and András Sajó, 816–830. Oxford: Oxford University Press, 2012.

Szente, Zoltán. 2016. "The political orientation of the members of the Hungarian Constitutional Court between 2010 and 2014". *Constitutional Studies* 1 (1): 123–149.

Tóth, Gábor Attila. 2009. *A szövegen túl. Értekezés a magyar alkotmányról*. [*Beyond the text. Essay on the Hungarian constitution*]. Budapest: Osiris.

Tsebelis, George. 2002. *Veto Players. How Political Institutions Work*. Princeton: Princeton University Press.

de Visser, Maartje. 2014. *Constitutional Review in Europe. A Comparative Analysis*. Oxford: Hart Publishing.

Volcansek, Mary. 2000. *Constitutional Politics in Italy*. London: MacMillan Press.

Vorländer, Hans. 2006. "Deutungsmacht. Die Macht der Verfassungsgerichtsbarkeit". In *Die Deutungsmacht der Verfassungsgerichtsbarkeit*, edited by Hans Vorländer, 9–36. Wiesbaden: VS Verlag.

3 The Czech Constitutional Court

Far away from political influence

Katarína Šipulová

3.1 Introduction

Constitutional courts undoubtedly belong among the core players in the governance of Central and Eastern Europe (CEE). This specific position reaches back to their role in democratic transitions (Hirschl 2004; Ferreres 2004; Ginsburg 2003). Not only did constitutional courts represent a symbolic break with the past (Teitel 2000; Grudzinska-Gros 1994; Uitz 2007, 51), but they were also generally considered better equipped to address the missing societal understanding and consensus on the nature of rights (Schwartz 2004). In the political turmoil and rush of (often chaotic) institutional reconstructions, it was often the constitutional courts that were left to fill in the gaps in imperfect transitional constitutions and to articulate values underlying the new democratic regimes (Sadurski 2014).

The idea of a constitutional court as an institution protecting the constitutional core and challenging the absolute supremacy of legislator reaches back to the end of the 19th century. However, it became fully implemented only after the Second World War. While it is true that Central and East European constitutional reconstructions started from *tabula rasa* after 1989 (Hesse and Johnson 1995), the search for viable models of constitutional review was deeply embedded in external incentives. Post-war proliferation of the Kelsenian model of constitutional review within Western Europe and a facilitation of the rule of law processes were conditioned by the integration into the Council of Europe and the European Union (Sadurski 2014).

In a way, constitutional courts were among the institutions set to guarantee the smooth transition and protection of the democratic transitions, setting the limit to competences of other political actors and constraining the legislative and executive power in activities violating the rule of law principles embedded in democratic regimes.

Yet recent developments remind us how fragile and prone to political pressure constitutional courts are. Several CEE countries faced strong political interference and a backlash against the judiciary, reflected in forced court packing, cut of courts' competences and undue pressure on decision-making (Kosař 2016). Even autocratic leaders need the judiciary to legitimize their own regime, and thus constitutional courts, with their competence to overturn legal acts, are a logical target. The case of the Czech Constitutional Court (CCC), in this sense, is a peculiar story. It started as a sort of low-key actor (especially compared to Hungary or Poland) and steadily increased its powers in the domestic political arena due to engagement in several high-profile cases related to constitutional reforms of the party and electoral system and the position of EU law. At least, that is the typical narrative of qualitative studies.

Building on the starting hypothesis that the practice of constitutional adjudication in the CEE region is far more diverse than originally suggested by existing legal research, the aim of this chapter is to confront this narrative with empirical data and analyze how much the Czech Constitutional Court really constrained the legislator in constitutional review cases decided from 1993 until 2015. The second section introduces constitutional settings and constitutional debates, which led to the creation of the Czech and Slovak Federal Constitutional Court (CSFCC) and subsequently the independent CCC. It analyzes the competences of the Czech Constitutional Court, political actors engaged in the process of selection of its judges. The third section addresses methodological issues related to the Czech case, and the fourth section briefly summarizes general trends present in the case law of the CCC and its changes over time. The fifth section offers a longitudinal analysis of the majority decision-making, while the subsequent sixth section uncovers not so often discussed dissents and coalitions of judges voting in minorities against the final ruling. Finally, the chapter closes with a network analysis of the behaviour of individual judges and discusses the most relevant, crucial cases influencing the jurisprudence and position of the CCC within the political system. The chapter shows that the CCC built its renomé despite leaving the legislator considerable room to manoeuvre, which, in return, might have helped prevent more serious political interference and undue pressure.

3.2 Constitutional setting

Before diving directly into the discussion of the CCC's competences, it is vital to better understand the overall structure of the Czech political system and the interactions of the CCC with other actors of the legislative process. The section therefore first explains the character of the Czech political system and then discusses the constitutional legacy.

The political system of the Czech Republic is typically described as a parliamentary system (Kopeček and Strmiska 2005). A 2012 constitutional amendment introducing a direct election of the President of the Republic spurred a discussion on the shift in the character of the political system (Brunclík 2014, 57–77). Nevertheless, the bicameral parliament still represents the core institution of the Czech political system. It consists of the Chamber of Deputies with 200 members (the lower chamber) and a Senate (an upper chamber with 81 senators). The lower chamber is typically considered the domain of the political combat between the governing and opposition parties (Kopeček and Petrov 2016). The upper chamber has had a historically weaker and less prestigious position.[1]

The importance of the Chamber of Deputies increases with a look at the character of the Czech governments, which usually consist of coalitions formed between two to three political parties. Over the last 25 years, however, the coalitions proved not to be particularly strong, with several governments disintegrating before the end of their electoral term (Kopeček and Strmiska 2005). This was apparent especially in the periods 1996–1998 and 2010–2012, when we witnessed several abrupt changes in the governmental coalition, along with falls and formations of caretaker governments.[2]

Nevertheless, although their character has changed over time, the parliamentary institutions are strongly ingrained in Czech political culture. The constitutional review of legislation, on the other hand, was re-introduced into the system only after the fall of the communist regime. The very first Czech experience with a constitutional judiciary reaches back to the First Czechoslovak Republic following the First World War. The first Czechoslovak Constitutional Court, established in 1921, drew inspiration from the Kelsenian model of constitutional judiciary. The Court was composed of seven judges appointed by the President of the Republic (three judges), the Supreme Court and the Supreme Administrative Court (two judges each) for ten years. The actual impact of the interwar constitutional court was, however, very limited, due to its extremely restricted set of competences. The constitutional review was evoked in practice only twice.

The 1968 Constitutional Act presumed an establishment of the Czechoslovak Federal Constitutional Court; however, the constitutional provision never saw implementation during the communist era.[3] The establishment of the Czech and Slovak Federal Constitutional Court (CSFCC) was therefore perceived as one of the core assignments of the November 1989 revolution. The Act on the CSFCC was formally enacted on 27 February 1991 as one of the key constitutional acts after the transition. The CSFCC consisted of 12 judges appointed for seven years by the federal President from three lists of eight nominees, submitted by the Federal Assembly, Czech National Council and Slovak National Council. There was a strict condition of parity between Czech and Slovak judges.[4] No career judges serving under the communist regime were nominated: new judges were chosen from academics (five judges) and former dissidents/deputies representing new democratic parties and civil movements (seven judges).

The political atmosphere of the early post-transitional months influenced the CSFCC's powers and was reflected in the design of its competences.[5] Moreover, President Havel saw the CSFCC as a crucial actor and mediator of disputes between both federal republics. Therefore, the constitution pre-set its competences in a way which opened the door for the CSFCC to become a very strong political actor in terms of Hirschl mega-politics, i.e. issues of utmost political significance that define and divide whole policies, ranging from electoral matters, to regime change, identity and nation-building processes (Hirschl 2004, 31). However, due to the very short durability of the Czech and Slovak Federal Republic (1990–1992), this particular competence was never implemented in practice. The CSFCC started its decision-making activity in March 1992, and within the short ten months of its existence, it issued a little over 1,000 decisions and managed to establish itself with a few politically salient judgements, developing core principles adopted by the Czech Constitutional Court later on.[6]

The Czech Constitutional Court (CCC), established in 1993, has retained most of the institutional and competence structure of its federal predecessor. As previously mentioned, the CCC exists in a parliamentary system with a relatively strong position of the President of the Republic and a bicameral parliament composed of the Chamber of Deputies (ChD), the lower chamber, and the Senate, the upper chamber. Contrary to the Slovak Constitution, the CCC is regulated in the fourth chapter of the Czech Constitution, standing outside the general judiciary. It is characterized as a judicial body protecting the constitutionality and safeguarding its institutional framework and functional linkages (Rychetský et al. 2015). The constitution characterizes the main role of the CCC as an institution settling disputes emerging from the system of checks and balances, as one of the most important safeguards of the judiciary against the legislative and executive power and as an institution protecting individuals and minorities against the will of the majority (Klokočka 1996, 365–370; Wagnerová 1996, 25). The CCC represents a specialized and concentrated constitutional judiciary. Its jurisdiction is rather broad, including the abstract and concrete constitutional review, individual complaints, review of constitutional complaints on presidential elections, review of elections and competence disputes between other constitutional institutions.[7] In practice, however, its main task is the review of constitutionality, dominantly exercised via individual constitutional complaint proceedings, which amounts to ca. 98 percent of its caseload (Kosař-Vyhnánek 2018, 29). The CCC also decides on the compatibility of international treaties with the Czech Constitution and can pre-emptively review the possibility of the Czech Republic taking on new international commitments.

The Court is composed of 15 judges nominated and appointed by the President of the Republic following the Senate's approval.[8] This means that the President of the Republic has a particularly strong say in the CCC's composition and more or less nominates the whole Court every ten years. Thus, the CCC is often named in relation to that: the first CCC (1993–2002) as Havel's Court, the second CCC (2003–2012) as Klaus' Court and the third (2013–) as Zeman's Court. The first independent CCC appointed by President Havel (1993–2002) comprised mostly judges of the CSFCC, academics and members of the Czech opposition movement, typically deputies of Civic Forum (*Občanské fórum*, OF) during the 1989–1992 era.[9] Apart from the very first CCC, every other nomination by Klaus and Zeman faced some controversies and disputes in the Senate (Šimíček 2016, 230).

The CCC decides either in chambers with three judges (there are four such chambers) or in a plenary session. The plenary session decides in constitutional control cases. It also adopts the work schedule which creates an algorithm for the case assignment.[10] Interestingly, the President of the CCC and the two Vice-Presidents are not permanent members of any chamber but rather rotate among them. Otherwise, the composition of chambers was fixed up to 2016, when the

CCC approved a new scheme of rotation, according to which the chambers were to be reshuffled every two years.[11]

The position of the President of the CCC is relatively a strong one, regarding both competences and informal practice. The President of the CCC is appointed by the President of the Republic. Although formally, the President of the CCC is considered to be a *primus inter pares* (Kosař-Vyhnánek 2018, 34), he also has a certain informal influence on the nomination of constitutional judges,[12] the composition of chambers, court administration and budget, which is of particular importance as the CCC has its own independent budget section. The President of the CCC also formally represents the CCC and acts on its behalf vis-à-vis other constitutional actors: for example, she/he formally represents the CCC in the legislative process where the CCC has a competence to comment on new legal acts.[13] The position of the CCC's President is further strengthened by the missing judicial council or other body of judicial self-governance which would represent the judiciary. Instead, the triangle of apex court presidents typically serves as an informal platform representing the whole judiciary vis-à-vis other branches of power (Kosař 2016).

3.3 Research design and methodological particularities

The following section highlights the most important elements of the research design and distinguishes the elements in which the Czech Republic differed from the general methodological scheme. The research addresses the constitutional review proceedings of the CCC from 1993 to 2015, analyzing altogether 285 decisions containing a total of 367 individual rulings (Figure 3.1).

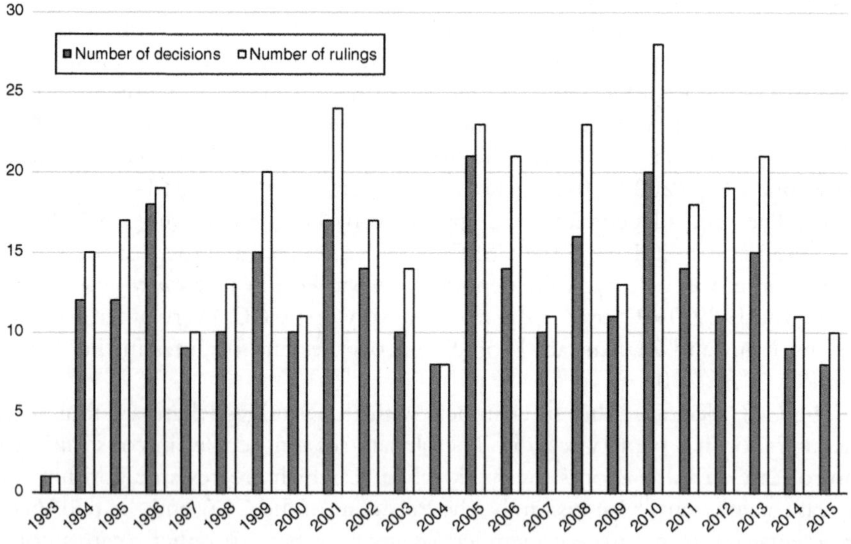

Figure 3.1 Number of decisions and rulings (CCC)

Some aspects should be highlighted regarding the methodology and the categorization of these rulings. First, as the project deals with constitutional review of legislation, the material scope of the Court's jurisprudence was framed by Article 87 para. 1 letters a) and b) of the constitution.[14] Contrary to the Slovak Constitutional Court and other courts in the region, the CCC does not have the competence of constitutional interpretation *in abstracto*.[15] Moreover, although the project addresses exclusively the constitutional review proceedings, several other competences of the CCC directly or indirectly constrain the legislator: similarly to *a posteriori* abstract and concrete constitutional review cases individual complaints, separation of powers disputes or the review of the constitutionality of a political party's dissolution, a referendum or international treaty ratification can impact the competences and exercise of legislative power. Yet the majority of cases concerning legislative acts came from the constitutional review cases. Only privileged dignitaries may initiate an *a posteriori* abstract review: the President of the Republic, a group of MPs or senators, the government. In practice, the vast majority of petitions were initiated by MPs (Kosař-Vyhnánek 2018), which means that the parliament, and the Chamber of Deputies in particular, was the main arena and actor both initiating and targeted by the constitutional review.[16]

Second, according to Article 89 of the Czech Constitution, the decisions of the CCC are enforceable immediately after their announcement. An enforceable decision is binding on all authorities and persons. This means that decisions on the unconstitutionality of legal norms are enforceable immediately following their publication in the Collection of Laws (Rychetský et al. 2015, 931). When it comes to the temporal effect of the derogatory competence of the CCC, in most cases the contested legal provision or an act found unconstitutional is annulled with an *ex nunc* effect, i.e. after the publication of the decision of the CCC in the Collection.[17] Occasionally, the CCC can authorize the effect of the annulment *pro futuro*.[18] A slightly more problematic debate surrounded the question of whether the CCC can annul the legal norm retroactively (*ex tunc*), as the Czech constitutional order and its understanding of the principles of democracy expressively refuses retroactivity (Filip et al. 2007). The CCC itself is very restrictive in the interpretation of the temporal effect of its derogatory competence, especially in the abstract control of constitutionality.[19] Therefore, the *ex tunc* effect is not relevant for the present analysis.

Third, the JUDICON project introduces the categorization of ruling types into refusal/rejection, unconstitutionality by legislative omission, procedural unconstitutionality, constitutional requirements, substantive unconstitutionality and constitutional interpretation *in abstracto* (see Chapter 2, Section 2.4). Not all of these types, however, can be found within the competences of the CCC or identified from the rulings of the CCC's decisions. For example, the declaration of unconstitutionality by legislative omission is particularly rare with the CCC. There were very few cases where the Court found the parliament violating the constitution because of its legislative inactivity. The core problem with this category is that the prevailing interpretation of the Czech Constitution and the separation of powers principle suggests that the directly elected legislator cannot be penalized for non-activity or otherwise ordered to act and pass a legal norm by other political authorities, by an authority which does not have a direct legitimacy (Vojtek 2007; Malíř 2008).[20] In this respect, the CCC has so far respected this principle and acted as a self-constrained actor. The only exceptions were situations of a particular historical importance, or cases of a conflict with the Constitution or international human rights treaties' provisions.[21]

Similarly, a few remarks need to be made about the categories of constitutional requirements and prescriptions. Typically, a ruling by the CCC states only whether the contested provision of the legal norm, or the whole legal act, violates the constitution or any other binding international human rights treaty. Yet, sometimes the CCC includes constitutional requirements or any kind of prescriptions in the decision's reasoning. Still, these situations are quite rare, suggesting consequently that the CCC is acting mostly as a self-constrained court and leaves quite a wide margin for manoeuvre by the legislator.

3.4 General observations: the Czech Constitutional Court as an inconspicuous constrainer?

Before analyzing the strength of the CCC's rulings, it is worth looking at the overall chronological trends in the development of its case law. This section will first examine the inspirational sources for the CCC, then compare them with the general patterns of the CCC performance, offering several explanations for the CCC behaving as an inconspicuous constrainer.

It was previously suggested that the CCC started with a rather high level of legitimacy, building on the legacy of its federal predecessor (CSFCC). Although the CSFCC issued only eight relevant judgements during its ten months of existence, some of those had significant repercussions for the political system.[22] In 1992, 99 members of the Federal Assembly, former Communist Party of Czechoslovakia deputies petitioned the CSFCC, claiming that vetting of public officials introduced in the Big Lustration Act contradicted democratic principles and the international human rights commitments of the Czech Republic. In the judgement Pl. US 1/92, the CSFCC responded with transferring the *materieller Rechtsstaat* principle into Czech law and creating a solid basis for a value-embedded interpretation of the transition. A democratic regime, according to the CSFCC, has an obligation to protect its principles. Not only did this become a cornerstone for almost all future transitional jurisprudence, heavily referenced and quoted in almost a hundred Czech Constitutional Court's decisions, but the judicial adjustment of lustration processes also shaped the party competition in the Czech parliament and political arena in the early 1990s (David 2011, 2006; Nedelsky 2004).[23]

Taken together with competences and activism of constitutional courts emerging in neighbouring countries, Poland and Hungary in particular, the CCC could draw rich inspiration and strong incentives to become an active opponent and strong constrainer of the legislator. In fact, it started as a very low-key actor.

Figure 3.2 portrays the development of the analyzed constitutional adjudication of the CCC from 1993 to 2015. Overall, the performance of the Court was relatively even, with more dramatic changes happening only in the period around 2004–2007 and 2007–2009. The low-key start in the 1990s, with the rulings' strength typically moving around 3 points, and especially dropping to 2.21–2.30 points in the second half of the 1990s, is somehow surprising, given the existing legal literature identifying the first CCC as a particularly strong actor in policy issues related to the democratic transition and subsequent transition processes. Yet the systematic empirical data shows little evidence of such influences.[24]

It is necessary, however, to remind the reader that this research project does not arbitrarily select politically salient judgements but rather analyzes all relevant rulings of the constitutional courts and thus looks at a more general performance of the courts, which should be expected to differ from the most controversial and typically discussed and publicized cases.

It is also worth mentioning here that the general case load of the CCC gradually rose over time, with 523 petitions in 1993 (47 to be decided by the plenum of all judges) to 4,946 petitions in 2012. The number of petitions to be decided by the plenum, which includes both individual petitions and constitutional review cases, is much more constant (Table 3.1). Yet, we can see that the steep rise to 4.5 points in strength value of the rulings relevant for our research project in 2004 clearly correlates with a comparatively lower number of relevant rulings delivered in constitutional review cases (see Figure 3.2). Similarly, the dramatic drop in 2007 may coincide to a certain degree with an overall lower number of delivered rulings.

Figure 3.2 therefore suggests certain trends in the strength of the rulings, which might correlate with (a) a changing agenda of the CCC (i.e. changing character of contested legal acts and changing practice of other actors to make use of the judicial review procedure) and (b) the political and economic background.

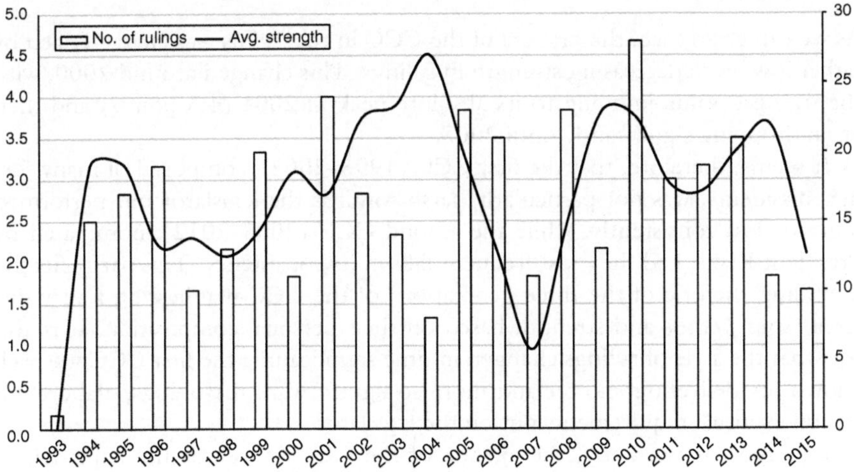

Figure 3.2 Number and average strength of rulings (CCC)

Table 3.1 Caseload of the Czech Constitutional Court

Year	*Number of petitions to be decided in panels*	*Number of petitions to be decided in a plenum*	*All (various) petitions*
1993	476	47	523
1994	829	33	862
1995	1224	47	1271
1996	1462	41	1503
1997	1975	46	2021
1998	2170	30	2200
1999	2543	24	2567
2000	3077	59	3136
2001	3006	39	3045
2002	3140	44	3184
2003	2496	52	2548
2004	2713	75	2788
2005	2982	58	3040
2006	3455	94	3549
2007	3302	29	3331
2008	3208	42	3250
2009	3394	38	3432
2010	3726	60	3786
2011	3967	38	4005
2012	4915	31	4946
2013	4022	56	4078
2014	4057	27	4084
2015	3858	34	3892

Note: The petitions decided by the whole plenum of constitutional judges are not only constitutional review cases; some individual petitions can be decided by the plenum as well. Nevertheless, the constitutional review of legislation represents a significant majority of these cases.

Source: www.concourt.cz

As we can clearly see, the first era of the CCC in the 1990s was characterized by rather low, even decreasing strength in rulings. This changed around 2000, with the strength value jumping to its absolute peak in 2004 (4.5 points) and then again dropping significantly until 2007.

It seems, therefore, that the first CCC (1993–2002), composed of many former dissidents, was not particularly harsh towards the legislator but performed more or less consistently, while the second CCC (2003–2012), nominated by President Klaus, had the most frequent falls in its consistency. This partly fits the prevailing rhetoric of the three generations of the CCC manifesting a very different spirit, ethos and strength based on their personal composition. It is also true that the style of rulings changed in time significantly; the first CCC was well known for delivering shorter and more straightforward reasonings, elaborating less on eventual requirements put on the legislator.

But, most importantly, the agenda of the CCC as well as the approach of political actors towards the judicial review changed significantly. While Kessler's Constitutional Court (1993–2002) mostly addressed issues of what Hirschl identifies as mega-politics (Hirschl 2004, 31), the petitions reaching the second CCC (2003–2012) broadened the scope of the judicial review to other areas such as social policy or the quality of the legislative process (Kopeček and Petrov 2016). The first CCC, therefore, especially during the first electoral period, decided mostly on topics which had a fundamental impact on the design of the Czech democratic regime, such as transitional justice and coming to terms with the communist past. In the second and third electoral term, many petitions contesting the constitutionality of the electoral system itself reached the CCC. Other important topics addressed fundamental rights and the independence of the judiciary (Šipulová 2017). It is also worth noting that, typically, the initiators of the constitutional review of legislation in the 1993–1996 era were mostly opposition MPs (Kopeček and Petrov 2016). The power distribution in the Chamber of Deputies between the centre-right Klaus governments (1993–1997) and leftist opposition therefore played a huge role. It is also expected that it was mostly the leftist parties who contested the constitutionality of the legislation coming to terms with the previous regime.

When it comes to the second possible correlating variable, the political turmoil serves as a good explanatory factor in the CCC's activity. As Kopeček and Petrov (2016) previously showed, individual actors relied on judicial review as a political tool overturning a majority vote with varying frequency based on the atmosphere in the parliament, and mostly coalition stability in the Chamber of Deputies. A mild reduction in the strength of rulings after 1996 coincides with the minority government led by Klaus (1996–1997), when internal political crises and party conflicts led to a certain decrease in the number of petitions for judicial review reaching the plenum of the CCC. With the Klaus government losing its clear majority (June 1996), the opposition fought the fiercest legislative battles directly on the floor of the Chamber of Deputies instead of turning to the CCC. As will be demonstrated later, a significant decrease in the number of petitions (and hence issued rulings) might distort the statistical results of the average strength of rulings for the respective years.

The continuous rise in the strength of rulings at the very end of the 1990s correlates with the overall higher rate of petitions for the constitutional review submitted to the CCC and, more importantly, petitions related again to Hirschl's mega-politics. A significant portion of these petitions addressed (a) restorative transitional justice issues influencing the state's budget and fiscal policies and (b) the electoral reform of 2000. The latter reform was spurred by the extraordinary situation in Czech politics: the 1998 elections led to the creation of the so-called Opposition Agreement, under which the two biggest parties, the leftist Czech Social Democratic Party (*Česká strana sociálně demokratická*, ČSSD) and rightist Civic Democratic Party (*Občanská demokratická strana*, ODS) formed a special contract: the agreement allowed the Social Democratic Party to assume power as a single-party minority government with the support of the Civic Democratic Party in opposition, which was promised far-reaching reform of the electoral system (Nikolenyi 2003, 325–344).

The situation led to a huge debate across the party system, with small political parties seeing the Opposition Agreement and prepared electoral reform as a direct threat to political plurality (Lebeda 2000; Birch et al. 2002, 81). The divisive reform which passed successfully in 2000 was one of the most closely followed petitions contested before the CCC. Although not completely successful, the overturn of the most controversial elements, i.e. the new recalculation of votes to seats, was one of the most important checks the CCC implemented on the legislator in its history. The decision Pl. US 42/2000 prevented an important change of the political system and protected the pluralistic character of the party system. Moreover, the CCC firmly stated that there are limits to the legislator's arbitrariness and prevented any similar institutional changes in future.

From the legislative point of view, the period 2002–2006 was characterized by preparatory works and EU law approximation, which was also reflected in the CCC's jurisprudence. Compared to Slovak constitutional reform and preparations, which were led in a very pro-active and euro-optimistic atmosphere also related to the fall of Mečiar's government and the recommencement of the democratization process, the Czech constitutional development was rather sceptical, opting to follow the German example and preparing a substantive review of the impact of EU law on the Czech legal and constitutional order. Nevertheless, the CCC also issued several strong rulings finding legislative acts unconstitutional in the light of the EU integration (e.g. Pl. ÚS 39/01). In relation to the so-called euro-amendment of the Czech Constitution, one particularly influential and highly debated decision should be taken into account. On 25 June 2002, the CCC, in case Pl. ÚS 36/01, suggested that international human rights treaties are part of the Czech constitutional order; therefore, should the general court have doubts about the compatibility of any legal provision with a binding international human rights treaty, it cannot independently decide to not apply the conflicting national provision but has to request a constitutional review and an annulment of the problematic domestic provision before the CCC. This decision was important from several points of view: first, it contested the constitutional amendment in which the legislator aimed to change the position of international human rights commitments in relation to national constitutional order. The CCC did not agree and overruled such a conception, assigning to the concerned treaties a primacy and direct effect. It needs to be said that this was one of the very few and very first instances of the CCC reviewing a constitutional amendment substantively. Second, the judgement aimed at strengthening the position of the CCC within the concentrated system of constitutional control and entrusting the role of sole watchdog of the legislative system to the CCC.[25]

Apart from the changes in constitutional order caused by the euro-amendment, we should also mention the political turmoil surrounding the judicial nominations of the second CCC. While President Havel was more or less unified in constitutional judges' nominations with the legislator,[26] the same definitely cannot be said for President Klaus. Václav Klaus became the President of the Republic in 2003, after having served several electoral terms as prime minister. His idea of the Czech Constitutional Court differed from Havel, having in mind a more docile institution, since, although the CCC still kept a rather low profile, it started showing its teeth in several politically salient decisions, eventually becoming an increasingly influential player (Kosař and Vyhnánek 2018). Moreover, Klaus had to face the Senate, which has been established in 1996 and soon got into serious tensions with the new President. Shortly after his appointment, the Senate refused four candidates nominated by President Klaus; one of them, Aleš Pejchal, who later became the Czech judge at the European Court of Human Rights after a controversial election, was even refused twice. The situation escalated around 2004 when four constitutional judges were missing and the CCC could not decide in plenum on constitutional review cases.[27] Although the CCC delivered some comparatively strong rulings in 2004, the overall number of rulings was very low, which might have influenced the statistical average performance of the CCC. It took two years before the Court sat again with a full composition.

From 2008, the strength of the CCC's rulings rose again. Although the annual average did not differ all that much from the first CCC, the media portrayal of the Court changed profoundly and the CCC, thanks to several politically salient cases, cemented its role as an influential political actor. A case best demonstrating the renewed vigour of the CCC was the decision Pl. ÚS 27/09. The Court annulled the Constitutional Act, shortening the electoral term of the Chamber of Deputies, and as a result postponing the parliamentary elections for seven months. The case was, obviously, politically highly salient: the ad hoc shortening of the electoral period was contested by one MP, who claimed his fundamental political rights were being violated. It was the second time the CCC directly changed the composition of power of the political arena in the Czech Republic. The decision spurred a heated discussion and raised many critical voices against the CCC, partly strengthening and partly damaging its reputation, legitimacy and relations with the legislator (Roznai 2014). Moreover, the decision had far-reaching consequences from a procedural point of view, as the CCC confirmed its own competence to review the constitutionality of constitutional acts. Overall, however, it seems that the average strength of rulings was slowly falling, which might suggest the presence of a certain learning curve within the Czech parliament. The legislative process in both the Chamber of Deputies and the Senate does contain the revision of constitutionality and works with existing CCC decisions, so a certain autolimitation of parliament is definitely taking place inside of the legislative process.

In conclusion, however, although the CCC did not generally act as a court heavily constraining the legislator, it proved to be a strong actor in certain periods of political instability (e.g. 2001–2002) or in periods when its own position was endangered by other actors of the political system (2009). Interestingly, already in the late 2010s the CCC has been perceived as one of the strongest constitutional courts in the region (Kosař-Vyhnánek 2018). Although it has made decisions in several widely discussed and controversial cases, it seems to have built its reputation without explicitly constraining the parliament.[28] Nevertheless, it seems that the Czech case does not support the often presented assumption that the success of democratic transition correlates with the constitutional courts constraining the legislator and removing the rule of law violations from legal documents (Smith 2017).

3.5 Trends in majority rulings

A different type of perspective describing the activity of the CCC towards the legislator relates to the analysis of the types of rulings typically issued by the CCC in constitutional review cases. The following section therefore looks more closely at the composition of the types of rulings in different time periods, examining the existence of various trends and particularities in the CCC's decision-making, which might better explain the average development of the strength of its rulings.

3.5.1 Trends in ruling types

Figure 3.3 captures the development of trends in the use of different ruling types in constitutional review cases and illustrates in more detail the method of the CCC's work and its changing approach towards both legislative review and requirements laid on the legislator.

Looking at the very beginning of the 1990s, when the CCC came into existence, it seems that the variability of the ruling types slowly evolved. While in 1993–1994, the CCC exclusively issued rulings rejecting petitions or finding a substantive violation, in the second decade, the representation of other types of rulings became far more diverse. As previously mentioned, unconstitutionality by omission remained one of the extremely rare types of rulings, as review of the missing activity of the legislator has been considered by Czech constitutional scholars and practitioners as a tool which borders on interference of the Court with legislative activity and the sphere of influence of parliament. The CCC typically constrained itself *vis-à-vis* the review of constitutionality and did not presume

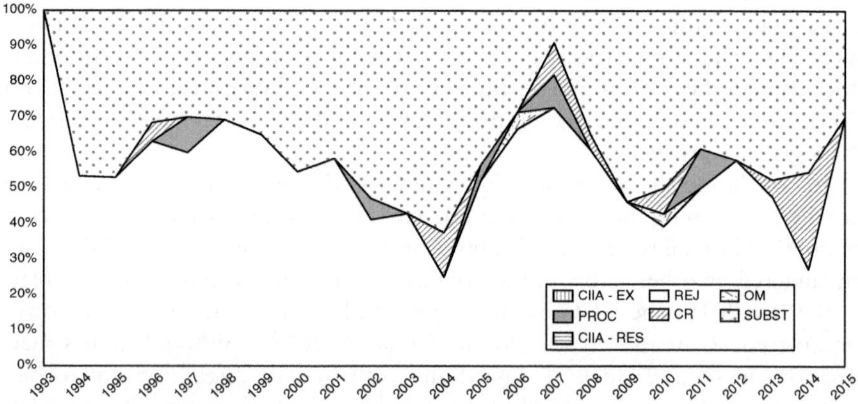

Figure 3.3 Frequency of ruling types I (CCC)

how the legislator should act when implementing its decision. We only have two examples of such activity by the CCC: Pl. ÚS 20/05 of 28 February 2006 and Pl. ÚS 9/07 of 1 July 2010. Incidentally, both cases relate to transitional justice policies and therefore represent part of Hirschl's mega-politics. The first case, Pl. ÚS 20/05, touches upon the problem of regulated rents in apartments, a legacy of the communist era and planned economy. The CCC stated here that the long-existing non-activity of parliament, which failed to adopt a specialized legal norm regulating the conditions under which the landlord is allowed to raise the rent and change the conditions of the contract for his or her tenants, violates the constitution, the Charter of Fundamental Rights and Protocol No. 1 to the European Convention on Human Rights. While it limited the prescription towards the parliament to a statement that specialized norm should be adopted, it also prescribed how the general courts should decide in individual cases in order to correct the unconstitutionality until the legislator could act. As previously mentioned, the second case addressed the non-activity of parliament in relation to the return of property to churches, which was nationalized by the Communist Party. Although most of the transitional justice issues, restitutions of individual property included, were legislatively addressed in the early 1990s, church property remained a hot potato dividing the political sphere and the public until the 2010s. The pressing societal interest in solving the issue, therefore, pushed the CCC to state that even non-activity of the parliament may lead to unconstitutionality. However, even here the CCC did not prescribe how parliament should act and limited its reasoning to a statement that inactivity established unconstitutionality.

The most varied combination of ruling types fell into the period between 2004 and 2014. While it is true that this period closely correlated with the new composition of the Constitutional Court (the second CCC being active between 2003 and 2012), review of the legislative process became a significant part of the constitutional review proceedings, with the CCC stepping more and more often into the internal rules and requirements of the legislative process. The politically most important decision in this area (Pl. ÚS 77/06), from 2007, involved the Court stopping the widespread practice of some MPs attaching seemingly small and insignificant proposals in amendments, often of procedural character, to unrelated legislative acts which were in the final stage of their approval in parliament. The CCC found these "legislative riders" unconstitutional because they circumvented the whole legislative process and debate necessary in a democratic state. The declaration of procedural unconstitutionality constrained the legislator in its future drafting process and had broad repercussions for the system of parliamentary legislative negotiations.

It is apparent that the ruling type of constitutional requirement became more frequently used over time, again especially in the third decade of the CCC. Two explanations might be valid here: first, with the growing autolimitation of parliament (and higher stress being put on the pre-emptive control of constitutionality in the legislative process), the CCC can find the conforming interpretation more easily, which leaves the legislator and authorities implementing legislative provisions more room to manoeuvre. Second, the more frequent use might also relate to the more frequent implementation and application of the European Convention on Human Rights and other human rights treaties. In some cases, the missing provision or provision with a lower standard of individual fundamental rights protection might be supplemented with the direct use of the Convention articles. This would correspond with the growing practice of judicial compliance and application of Convention principles by Czech courts (covering an even broader range of issues due to the expanding jurisprudence of the European Court of Human Rights). The explanation is also supported by an overall increasing focus put on the Convention in the legislative process (Smekal and Vynánek 2018).

Figure 3.4 provides us with an even more refined look at the constitutional adjudication of the CCC. While most of the rulings finding procedural unconstitutionality were concentrated in the second half of the examined period, the majority of these rulings were of strong character. Interestingly, the highest proportion of the strong type of procedural unconstitutionality can be found in 1997 (10 percent), followed by a radical decline in occurrence until 2003. In the last three years (2012–2015), no procedural unconstitutionality was found by the CCC in the review of legislation. We also previously mentioned that constitutional requirements and more room to manoeuvre left for the legislator are concentrated in the later era of the CCC. While Kessler's Court had only a single occurrence of this practice in 1996, this type of ruling became more frequent in 2004, after access to the European Union and the publication of the "insolvency judgement" Pl. ÚS 36/01. Although the CCC issued this judgement in June 2002, the new approach towards the interpretation of international human rights law and binding ratified treaties might still have influenced the overall development. In 2014, the percentage of this type of ruling reached as high as 27.3 percent.

We should devote the very last remarks regarding the type of rulings to substantive unconstitutionality. While, apart from the period 2005–2007, Figure 3.3 shows a rather balanced share of rulings rejecting the petitions and finding a

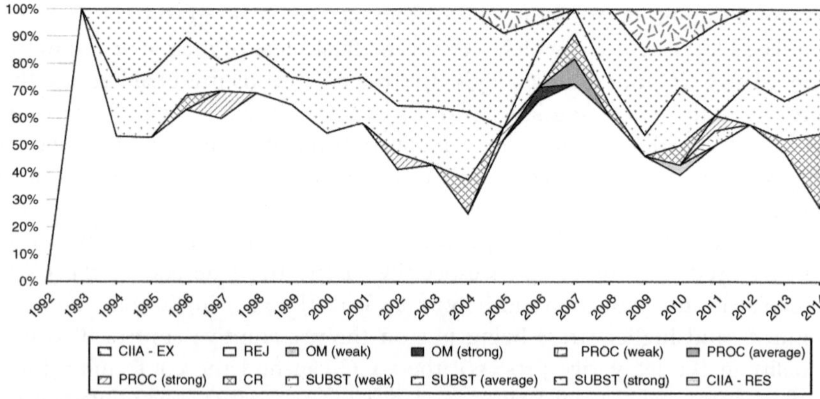

Figure 3.4 Frequency of ruling types II (CCC)

substantive violation, Figure 3.4 illustrates more closely other characteristics found in these substantively unconstitutional rulings. While Kessler's CCC used mostly rulings of weak or average character (oscillating around 15–20 percent) – 20 percent for the weak type and 26.7 percent for the average in 1994, for example – strong rulings of the substantive unconstitutionality type only emerged much later, in 2005 (8.7 percent of all rulings from that year). Although the share of strong substantive rulings also remained modest later on (15.4 percent in 2009), it definitely became more frequent up to 2011. Between 2011 and 2015, the CCC did not issue any type of strong substantive unconstitutionality ruling. The variance might correspond with the previous narrative of the raising strength and activism of the second and third CCC, as well as more diverse actors petitioning for a constitutional review and bringing a wider range of policy issues to the CCC.

3.5.2 The role of the presidents

The previous overview of the average strength of majority rulings and types of rulings did not suggest a clear relation to the three "generations" of the CCC. The presence and use of different types of rulings, apart from the constitutional requirements, seems highly fragmented and mostly incidental, perhaps related to a policy area of the contested legislation. Yet it is still worth looking more closely at individual compositions of the CCC and their performance under different presidents. Typically, the presidents shape judicial institutions, and strong court presidents with many competences are especially notable in the CEE region (Kosař 2016; Kosař 2017). As explained above, the position of the CCC's President is a relatively strong one, regarding both competences and informal practice.

The history of the CCC involves three different presidents: Zdeněk Kessler, former MP of the Federal Assembly between 1990 and 1992 and a member of new democratic political parties (Civic Forum and Civic Democratic Party subsequently) created shortly after the 1989 revolution. Kessler's Court (1993–2002) consisted mostly of dissidents and lawyers with personal experience of the previous communist regime. A few very strong personalities joined the Court, Vladimír Čermák and Vladimír Klokočka being among the most significant and influential scholars, lawyers and political scientists discussing the shape and principles of democracy. Strong backgrounds in sociology and political sciences (complementing their legal education) also undoubtedly influenced their position in constitutional review cases.

The second President, Miloš Holeček, remained in power for a very short time period (March to July 2003): he took over the ending mandate from Kessler, who stepped down from the position due to serious health problems. Holeček, previously the Vice-President of the Court, acted as a President of the CCC for only four months. After the end of his mandate in July 2003, he left the Court and returned to the Regional Court in Brno. The data in Figure 3.5 is slightly misleading, due to the extremely short period of time under Holeček's presidency. Moreover, it is widely known that although Holeček served as one of the judges of

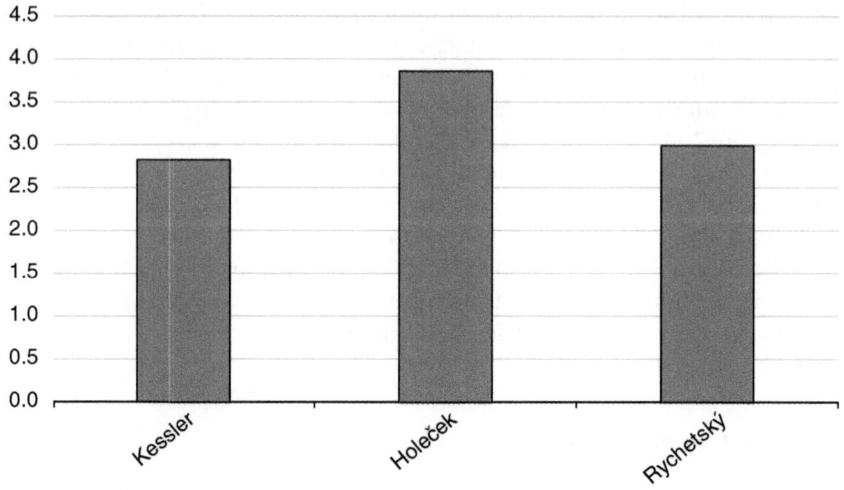

Figure 3.5 Average strength of rulings (by presidents) (CCC)

the first CCC, the era of his chairmanship was marked by a disruptive conflict with other judges regarding the possibility of sitting on a panel deciding the case which a particular judge had publicly commented on before joining the CCC. This conflict significantly worsened relationships inside the Court and created an opposition between the President of the CCC and the majority of the other judges.

As shown above, the average strength of rulings issued under the presidency of the third President of the CCC, Pavel Rychetský (2003 through the present), was almost the same as Kessler's Court performance. It is necessary to point out, however, that Pavel Rychetský is now serving his second term as President of the CCC, and the project analyzes altogether 13 years of his presidency. Although the narrative of the legal literature and historical works on the CCC typically identifies the first CCC as the most influential and the strongest one, the statistics actually show that when it comes to general relationship towards the legislator, Rychetský's Court proves to hold an even stronger stance.

Figure 3.6 captures the aforementioned problem of Holeček's Court and the existing disruption between the President and the rest of the judges in 2003 quite precisely. The difference in strength between the two lines demonstrates the deviation existing between the strength of rulings of CCC Presidents and the Court's average. Overall, it can be said that both Kessler and Rychetský were for the most part well in sync with the rest of the judges. The huge fall of the President's strength to 0.0 points in 2003 correlates with the deteriorating health and strength of Zdeněk Kessler, who eventually left the Court. While Miloš Holeček was in no position to renew the constraining force of the President towards the majority of judges, Rychetský quickly regained his power and influence. Furthermore, the peak in 2013 shows how much the strength of CCC

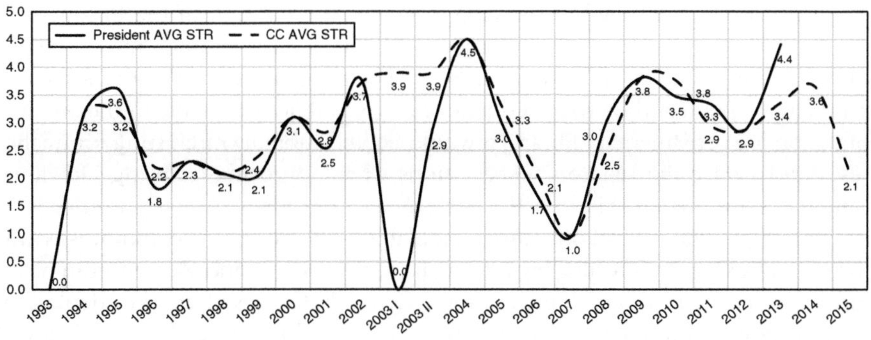

Figure 3.6 Average strength of rulings (by presidents and majorities) (CCC)

rulings here depended on the President himself: 2013 correlates with the year of Rychetský's reappointment after Zeman was elected in a historically first direct presidential election. The strength of the President of the CCC, who started with particularly good relationships with Zeman, also strengthened due to a change in the position of other judges appointed by new President Zeman. This change in the personal composition of the Court and the temporary solution of the second crises surrounding the appointment of new judges and previous conflicts between Klaus and the Senate, helped Rychetský to strengthen his position (with his rulings' strength reaching 4.5 points in 2013). The minor divergence between the majority of the Court and the President of the CCC might have resulted from the peculiar situation when the re-appointed President of the CCC chaired a partly changed, newly nominated Court.

Apart from the two occasions described above, the presidents were more or less in line with the other CCC judges. Whether this also allowed them to establish a strong leadership will be further examined in a discussion on dissenting opinions and coalitions formed inside the CCC.

3.6 Trends in dissenting opinions

Compared to the trends in majority rulings, the practice of attaching dissenting opinions to the Court's decisions tells us more about the internal structure and voting coalitions between individual judges.

In contrast to the Hungarian case, it is not possible to clearly identify political subjects or parties standing behind the nomination of individual candidates for the position of constitutional judge. The judges are nominated by the President of the Czech Republic, whose motivation in choosing individual names is not always clear. Depending on the relationship of the President of the Republic with the President of the CCC, or his own membership in a political party, he might have listened to recommendations from the CCC President, legal experts or his own party members seeking to strengthen or weaken the Court. No clear-cut relation between dissenting opinions of individual judges and the profile of political parties can therefore be identified in the Czech case, as the position of the President of the Republic or the Senate on the right–left political axis is much more complicated than in Hungary, for example. Nevertheless, as the Senate's questioning of candidates nominated by the President of the Republic is available in the archives of the online parliamentary library, it would be undoubtedly interesting for further research to trace the senators' expectations when approving/refusing individual candidates and match this with the performance of judges. A first, intuitive look suggests that, while Havel opted for candidates with strong anti-communist sentiments, opposing the socialist legal formalism, both Klaus and Zeman nominated more conservative judges. Furthermore, Zeman's CCC shifted the ideological composition of the CCC more towards the left, while the earlier nominees of Havel and Klaus were ideologically more diverse (Kosař and Vyhnánek, 2018, 16).

It is also widely known that President Klaus was very critical of Havel's Court, opposed the Court's activism in constitutional review proceedings and pointed out on several occasions that an unconstrained constitutional court violates the principles of a democratic system (Kühn and Kysela, 2006). Klaus aimed for a weaker, more docile Court. Sometimes, it is suggested that he achieved the historically highest gender balance because he believed that female nominees were weaker.

Figure 3.7 demonstrates the overall presence of rulings with at least one dissenting opinion over time. Interestingly, apart from 1993, the very first year of the CCC's existence, there was no year when the judges did not publish at least one dissenting opinion. The practice of publishing dissenting opinions is therefore widespread and well established with the CCC. At first sight, the proportion of dissents seems to be more or less stable. The number of dissents in individual years rises and falls with the overall number of rulings. Yet it is possible to see a more significant drop in the number of dissents in 2009 and, in contrast, a

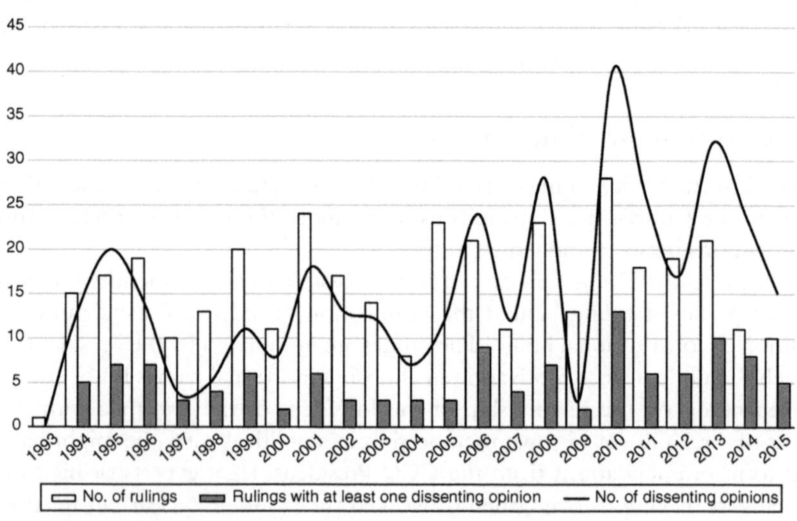

Figure 3.7 Number of rulings and dissenting opinions (CCC)

distinctive rise in the following year, 2010, when the number of dissents reached almost half the rulings in issued decisions.

The trends in the number of dissenting opinions are not easy to identify, as the overall numbers seem to be quite fragmented. Yet a certain trend of a more frequent use of dissents can be traced, especially in the second half of the second CCC and the third CCC. As previously mentioned, only three dissents were issued in 2009, while the following year, their number jumped as high as 40. In the last years (2013–2015), the number of rulings with at least one dissenting opinion seems to have been slightly decreasing, yet the overall proportion of rulings with at least one dissenting opinion increased significantly. This extreme rise could be a partial result of the coming end of the term and growing discrepancies and differences between the judges. Some of the judges of the second Court, finishing their second mandate in a row, are well known for attempting to make a grandiose exit. On the other hand, 2013 saw the CCC getting used to a new composition and mix of judges, renewed offices and new incoming nominees.

3.6.1 Judges clustered

If we were to dissect the behaviour of individual judges and compare the strength of their rulings when they join the majority with their dissents, the collected data shows that David, Fenyk, Cepl and Zarembová have the highest score. Figure 3.8, however, informs us to a greater degree about the factual influence and strength of these judges inside the Court. While there are no significant differences in the values of majority rulings, the individual judges differ profoundly in the values of their dissents. Cepl, Fenyk, David and Zarembová acted as the most significant constrainers in their dissents, although we need to point out that at the time of the research, Fenyk and David were fairly new judges with a very low overall number of decided cases. Similarly, Filip, Suchánek and Šimíček, judges with the lowest score of constraining dissent, all belong to the third CCC and had only

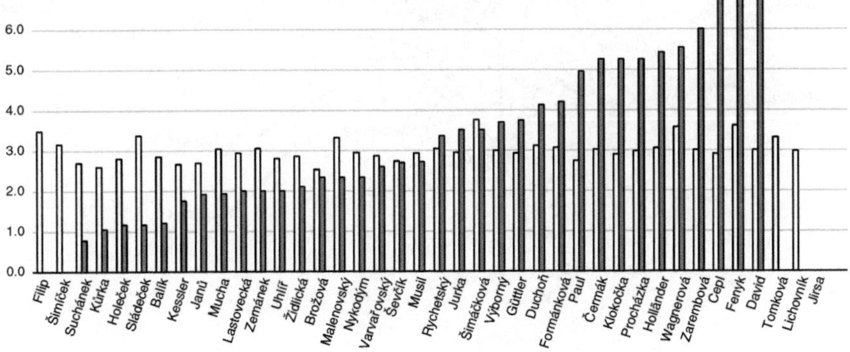

Figure 3.8 Average strength of rulings (by judges) (CCC)

been sitting for two years at the time the project was completed. Frequently, dissenting judges were mostly those with an academic background: Klokočka, Cepl, Fenyk or judges coming from other apex courts (David).

3.6.2 Network analysis

Dissenting opinions are not always raised individually. On the contrary, judges quite often form coalitions based on their shared opinion about an issue.

Figure 3.9 shows the complete network of dissenting interactions between all judges serving on the CCC between 1993 and 2015.[29] As previously mentioned, the Czech system of constitutional judge selection does not allow for a clear-cut analysis of political interests and parties supporting the judges' nomination. As all constitutional judges are appointed by the President upon their approval by the Senate, all judges in the network are portrayed as nominated in a complete consensus of left- and right-wing parties.

Interestingly, there are no absolutely isolated judges; however, two judges, David Uhlíř and Jiří Zemánek, have so far formed only one coalition between themselves. It is worth noting that both are among the newest judges, appointed only in 2014, although at the time the data collection of the JUDICON project was finished, Zemánek had already served on the CCC for almost two years.

Similarly, new judges joining the CCC since 2013 are based in the left part of the network analysis and, as might be expected, coalitions of these judges with judges who have served on the Court for a longer time are still somewhat rare. Furthermore, the connections between these judges reflect some previous ties: Vojtěch Šimíček, Kateřina Šimáčková and Jan Filip are all members of the Department of Constitutional Law and Political Sciences at the Masaryk University Law Faculty. Moreover, Šimáčková and Šimíček both arrived at the CCC from the Supreme Administrative

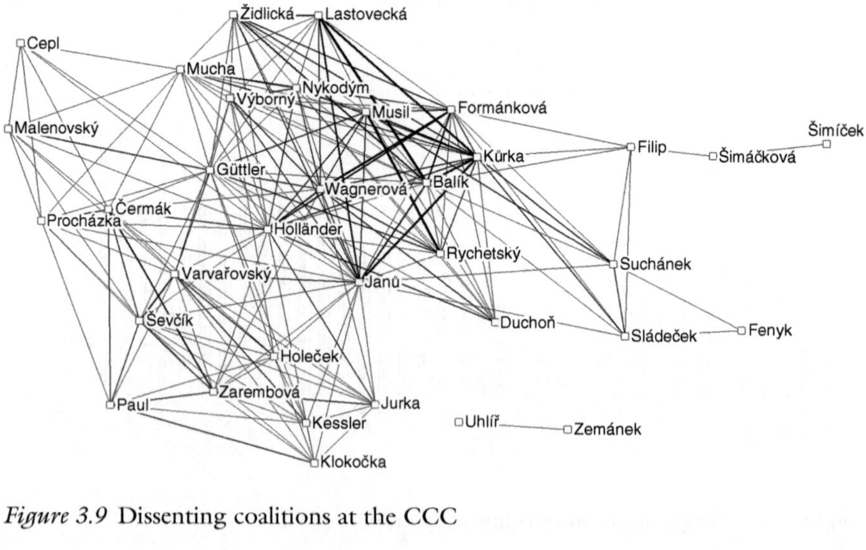

Figure 3.9 Dissenting coalitions at the CCC

Court. Jaroslav Fenyk is also a new judge who previously both practised and taught criminal law at the Masaryk University Law Faculty. However, he (interestingly enough) does not have any connection with his Law Faculty colleagues.

The right part of the network analysis captures the first (Kessler) Court. The most frequent strong coalitions with many other judges belong to Vlastimil Ševčík. But overall, although most of the proceedings included in the analysis are rulings of the plenum of judges, some of the coalitions of the Kessler CCC copy interactions between judges sitting on the same panel. Nevertheless, although the first CCC generally had many connections between judges, the coalitions were clearly not stable, and judges frequently interacted across all plenum.

The middle of the network illustrates the Rychetský Court and judges serving (for the most part) between 2003 and 2013. Several points follow from the network. First, the number of coalitions clearly increased during the second CCC, and the use of dissenting opinions stabilized as a more frequent practice. While the first Court acted as a somehow unified authority, with Zdeněk Kessler guarding and protecting the legitimacy and unity of the voice of the Court towards other actors of the political system, the CCC under Rychetský's first presidency seems to have been much more polarized. Dissenting opinions and deep cleavages between judges became a common practice, and some commentators have even suggested that differences and disputes between individual judges ran so deep that judges sitting on the same panel did not communicate with each other (Kmec 2010). The inclusion of a dissenting opinion of judges being in a minority was fairly common in this period with judges from academic backgrounds or other political aspirations. The strongest coalitions present within the triangle Balík–Kůrka–Lastovecká, or Wagnerová–Holländer–Formánková–Kůrka, copied both the composition of the small chambers and the ideological closeness of judges. While the left–right division is easily identifiable only with some judges (such as Eliška Wagnerová or Vlasta Formánková), the network suggests other possible cleavages, such as the ideological position towards the activism of the CCC. Both Holländer and Wagnerová, like Rychetský, were proponents of a strong model of constitutional adjudication nearing the German model of the *Bundesverfassungsgerichtshof.* Another possible cleavage might be the professional past of constitutional judges (academic career, private sphere, courts, etc.).

In summary, it can be concluded that while the Czech example of the interactions between constitutional judges does not easily uncover political orientation and loyalty towards a certain leftist or rightist ideology based on a subject who appointed the judges, certain other cleavages dividing the judges are suggested. Clearly, previous relationships and background shared between judges before joining the CCC play a huge role. To some degree, a similar past professional orientation might also be at play. What would perhaps be most interesting to research in the future is the ideological stance of judges towards judicialization (or self-constrained court), their position *vis-à-vis* international human rights law and its effects or, possibly, even the connection between judges re-appointed (or actively voicing their interest in being repeatedly appointed) and their activity in issuing dissenting opinions.

Unfortunately, although the President of the Republic clearly nominates judges with certain expectations – whether Klaus who, although not very successfully thanks to the Senate's vetoes, tried for a more mellow, constrained Constitutional Court, or Zeman, who initially propagated diversity among the constitutional judges (looking especially at their previous background and differentiation between judges coming from practice and from academia) – the behaviour of judges based on the President's preferences are only barely traceable. First, approval by the Senate calls for a certain consensus across the political scene, as was clearly shown during the crises created by President Klaus. Second, the Czech system allows for a change of all judges (currently most of the judges due to some judges ending their mandate pre-emptively) at the same time. With a ten-year period, this also means that judges are most likely not prone to be reappointed by the same President, or the same composition of the Senate.

3.7 Qualitative evaluation

Finally, we will briefly look at the qualitative evaluation of some of the judgements identified by the quantitative model as either little or very constraining towards the legislator. A group of judgements identified by the qualitative scaling as very constraining includes ten decisions and 16 rulings. Ten rulings were issued by the first Court, four rulings by the second Court and two rulings by the third Court. All these decisions were issued in *a posteriori* review. Altogether, eight dissenting opinions were joined to two decisions, both from the period of the first CCC. When it comes to the individual characteristics of these decisions, all rulings pointed at the violation of various parts of the rule of law principle, but what is even more surprising, all target the principle of the rule of law and the prohibition of retroactivity. In all cases, the CCC annulled all contested legal acts with *ex nunc* effect. As expected, typically for its practice, the CCC did not include any remedy directly into the wording of the rulings. Nevertheless, the reasoning of individual decisions included some rather important general indicators and interpretative points showing the legislator how to proceed in order to safeguard the principle of the prohibition of retroactivity in future legislative norms. When it comes to the material scope and content of individual decisions, Pl. ÚS 16/93 from 24 May 1994 targets one of the formative issues of the era, restitutions and nationalization of individual property. Here, while reviewing the Land Act (Act No. 229/1991 Coll.), the CCC, although admitting a special character of the enacted legal norm disturbing some of the relationships existing during the Communist era, found that the retroactive effect of contested legal norms overarches the aim of the act and cannot be justified by the public interest in coming to terms with the past. The principle of the legal certainty and the prohibition of retroactivity was also pointed out by the CCC in the other cases; only one of those targeted transitional justice issues: Pl. ÚS 10/13 of 29 May 2013, a decision reviewing (*a posteriori*) the constitutionality of Act No. 429/2012 Coll. on the restitution of the church property. The rest of the cases were undoubtedly important for the formation of certain formal criteria and ground principles of the legislative process. In this sense, the decisions without doubt constrained the legislator, because the wording of the rulings not only pointed out the deficits of current contested legal norms, but in its reasoning set a certain set of rules (core principles) for future legislative activity. Nevertheless, most of these decisions are not typically considered by (legal) scholarship as formative jurisprudence of the CCC.

When it comes to decisions and rulings constraining the legislator in a more subtle way (the category of constitutional requirement or procedural unconstitutionality), leaving parliament a wider margin of appreciation and room for the implementation of the new legal provisions, the CCC issued altogether 31 significant rulings (in 23 decisions). Only three of those fit the period of the first Court, which sits well with our previous interpretation that the very first CCC oscillated almost exclusively between either rejections or substantive findings of unconstitutionality. Approximately half of these rulings were joined by dissenting opinions, which demonstrates a lower interest of judges in issuing a dissent in less salient cases. When it comes to the calibration of individual categories and the characteristics of these decisions, their rulings requested either interpretation of provisions in harmony with the constitution, or they stated procedural unconstitutionality of the legislative process which had led to the enactment of the contested legal norm. Therefore, typically, the CCC annulled the entire acts, not only individual provisions, but with a *pro futuro* effect, i.e. softening the effect of the constraint put on the legislator, following from the annulment.

An in-depth evaluation of individual decisions confirms the initial expectation raised in the overview of majority decisions' trends: rulings requiring an interpretation in harmony with the constitution (constitutional requirements) are far more frequently used after the 'Insolvency judgement' (Pl. ÚS 36/01), and most of them refer not only to the constitution but also to the European Convention on Human Rights, suggesting a possible conforming interpretation or direct application of the Convention. Regarding the subject matter, the decisions do not cover a common policy area.[30] In two cases, however, the CCC explicitly stated the need to be a self-constrained actor (Pl. ÚS 3/09) and not to supplement the positive legislator (Pl. ÚS 49/10).

The finding of procedural unconstitutionality and failures in the legislative process have been mostly common since about 2007. The cases regarded various issues from regional elections (Pl. ÚS 13/05) to competence disputes and limitations of powers of individual constitutional actors (Pl. ÚS 33/97). Interestingly, one of the cases included in this section is the "legislative riders" case (Pl. ÚS 77/06), which had a particularly significant effect on the legislative process, with the CCC attempting to set clear rules limiting potential obstructions. Therefore, while it might be concluded that these cases did not constrain the legislator substantively, the CCC tied the hands of those legislative authorities which tried to acquire more competences or circumvent core legislative (and democratic) rules.

3.8 Conclusions

The chapter analyzed the patterns existing in the constitutional review cases of the Czech Constitutional Court. We started with pointing out the surprising lack of knowledge on the decision-making of CEE constitutional courts and their position in the political system – all the more surprising considering the widespread literature suggesting how important actors constitutional courts were in forming narratives of transitional justice and embedding new political systems in rule of law and democratic values.

The combination of both qualitative and quantitative analysis of the CCC constitutional review proceedings showed several interesting observations. First, although typically considered a strong and influential constitutional court, this hypothesis has not been proven by the empirical data of the JUDICON project. The CCC has not constrained the Czech parliament extensively; on the contrary, it has often acted very self-restrictively. That being said, the Court has indeed reviewed a fair share of acts and legislative provision and has even quashed plenty of cases under the review, yet has nevertheless stuck to self-constraining and moderate tactics, often leaving the parliament a large space to manoeuvre when reacting to CCC's rulings. Yet, the CCC stepped up the game in instances when most politically salient cases were at play (confirming Hirschl's hypothesis about the judicialization of mega-politics), especially those related to the core of the democratic system (election and electoral rights) and transitional justice policies. Yet, the CCC stuck to the practice of softening the constraining effect of rulings, finding substantive violations of the constitution with temporal effects or no/minor suggested remedies.

Second, there is only a very scant relationship between the trends in ruling types and political situation. This might be a result of three phenomena: (a) institutional fragmentation: the system of constitutional judge nomination, which is less politically conditioned than in other countries of the region; (b) political fragmentation: the high political fragmentation due to the proportionate electoral system; and (c) policy fragmentation: the gradual widening of both actors and policy scope of constitutional review.

The specific character of the first post-revolution Court guided its decision-making activity in a rather different direction than later composition under Rychetský's chairmanship. This is reflected in both the agenda considered by the CCC and the strength of issued rulings. The very first era was marked by particular transition-oriented topics, different understanding of the rule of law principle (which Teitel [1997] describes as transitional rule of law) and peculiar composition when most of the judges came from intellectual 1989 elites. The second and third CCC became more polarized, although, interestingly, it was the third CCC nominated by Zeman which had the most coherent ideological consistency, with most judges leaning towards the left. Yet, as there was no clear party logic present during the CCC judges' nominations, the CCC managed to keep a clear distance from political influence and was able to decide more according to the internal value-based considerations of individual judges.

Nevertheless, the combination of the three types of fragmentation seems to have helped the CCC to become the constitutional court most isolated from various external political factors within the region. This is all the more supported by the CCC's own approach and tactic of moderating the constraining effect of its rulings and leaving the legislator with room for rather wide discretion. It will only be seen in future developments whether this tactic and distinctive characteristic of the Czech political context will help the CCC become a less fragile institution in the face of upcoming political turbulence.

Notes

1 Actually, the weak position of the upper chamber reaches back to the beginning of the 1990s. Although the independent Czech Constitution of 1992 did presume the establishment of the Senate, the very first election to the chamber was only held in 1996. The importance and usefulness of the upper chamber is still debated in the political arena today, with some political parties suggesting its removal.

2 Czech parliamentarianism is quite often characterized as a type of Startori's "assembly government" with typically volatile coalitions facing difficulties when pushing through their political agenda.

3 Similar to other federal institutions. Although the Constitution of 1968 characterized Czechoslovakia as a federation, respective federal institutions were never reformed into a federal form.

4 Constitutional Act No. 23/1991, Art. 10–15.

5 See Article 3 of the Constitutional Act No. 91/1991 Coll.

6 One of the most important cases decided by the CSFCC was the Lustration judgement, no. Pl. ÚS 1/92, in which the CSFCC established the principle of *materieller Rechtsstaat*.

7 The Constitution identifies initiators as a group of 41 deputies or 17 senators (i.e. more than one-fifth for both chambers), a general court, General Prosecutor, an individual if petitioning violation of her rights, the CCC's own panel and the President of the Republic.

8 It is worth noting that while the Constitution requires unconditionally an approval by the Senate (Article 84 para. 2), the Act on the Czech Constitutional Court stipulates that a President's nominee becomes a judge if the Senate does not vote within 60 days. See also Wagnerová (2007) on Article 6.

9 Contrary to the Slovak Constitutional Court, the CCC retained most of the Czech judges of its federal predecessor. Moreover, as there was not yet a Senate, the judges were approved by the Chamber of Deputies.

10 Article 40 of The Act 91-1991 Coll.

11 CCC, Plenary Resolution No. Org. 60/15, December 2015.

12 Although the constitutional judges are appointed by the President of the Republic after approval by the Senate, the President of the Republic sometimes consults the CCC's President beforehand on the nomination. This was the case of the first and the beginning of the third CCC under the chairmanship of Pavel Rychetský.

13 Although in practice, this competence is delegated to the General Secretary of the CCC.

14 The annulment of statutes or individual provisions thereof (a) and the annulment of other legal enactments or individual provisions thereof (b).

15 See Article 128 of the Slovak Constitution.

16 Yet, the concrete review is much more common, typically initiated by ordinary courts challenging the legislation. Article 95 para. 2 of the Czech Constitution.
17 See Article 70 of the Act on the CCC.
18 See, for example, judgement Pl. ÚS 28/13. The CCC can postpone the effect in a situation if the immediate annulment of the norm would lead to even graver abuse of constitutional rules.
19 See, for example, Pl. ÚS 31/96, Pl. ÚS 5/03, IV. ÚS 1777/07, Pl. ÚS 24/09, Pl. ÚS 13/05, Pl. ÚS 6/05, Pl. ÚS 27/09.
20 See also judgements of the CCC Pl. ÚS 36/08 of 8 July 2010, Pl. ÚS 2/03 of 19 March 2003, or Pl. ÚS 20/05 of 28 February 2006.
21 The first one concerned the restitution of church property, which was presumed by a constitutional federal law but unimplemented 20 years after the revolution (Pl. ÚS 9/07), while the second one (Pl. ÚS 20/05) regarded the regulated rents and the lack of legislation establishing the situations upon which the owners of the flats with regulated rents might raise the rent.
22 Pl.US 1/92, 26 November 1992, on a review of Act No. 451/1991 Coll. Big Lustration Act (Velky lustracni zakon), and Pl. US 5/92, 4 September 1992.
23 The CSFCC annulled a few provisions of the Lustration Act regarding the vetting of repercussions for collaborators (people listed in secret police files as persons co-operating with the regime) due to the high unreliability of archived documentation. It was a widespread practice that some people were included in the lists of collaborators without them knowing about it, either because the StB planned to approach them in the future or tried to tarnish their reputation (David 2011).
24 One of the very few examples is an article by Kopeček and Petrov on the judicial review of legislation from the point of view of the relation between the CCC and parliament (Kopeček and Petrov 2016).
25 Several empirical studies, however, suggest that this decision was not rigorously followed, especially not by the apex courts – the Supreme and Supreme Administrative Court. For more elaboration see Petrov and Šipulová (2016).
26 Havel opted for a CCC composed of former dissidents. Consequently, the past and the relation of nominees to the former regime was a key determinant. What also helped the conformity with the legislator was the fact that Havel consulted many influential bodies before making his list of nominees and included most of the Czech judges of the CSFCC. For more on the nomination, see Kosař and Vyhnánek (2016).
27 The situation repeated at the very end of 2011 and 2012, when the number of judges dropped again to 13, as the Senate originally refused two Klaus nominees, Jan Sváček and Zdeněk Koudelka (the latter eventually became a constitutional judge after his re-nomination by President Zeman).
28 Some of the most discussed cases internationally did not come from a constitutional review but other types of procedures, mostly individual complaints. See, for example, the CCC crossing swords with the Court of Justice of the European Union in the Holubec case (Pl. ÚS 5/12), or the review of the Lisbon Treaty (Pl. ÚS 29/09).
29 The Czech Constitution allows a repeated mandate (for ten years) of a constitutional judge. There is no proportional system for the exchange of judges. The new constitutional judges are therefore appointed either after the mandate of a serving judges runs out (which endangers the continuousness of the Court, as most of the serving judges finish their mandate in the same year) or with retirement age. So far, there have been two big changes in the CCC's composition: in 2003 and 2013.
30 Policy areas cover just satisfaction and immaterial damage (Pl. ÚS 16/04), judicial rehabilitation, (II. ÚS 173/95) protection of state ownership (Pl. ÚS 12/06), deprivation of legal capacity (IV. ÚS 3102/08).

References

Birch, Sarah, and Millard, Frances, and Popescu, Marina, and Williams, Kieran. 2002. *Embodying Democracy. Electoral System Design in Post-Communist Europe*. New York: Palgrave Macmillan.

Brunclík, Miloš. 2014. "'Mezi Berlínem a Paříži' Kam kráčí politický režim České republiky" ["Between Berlin and Paris: Where Does the Political Regime of Czechia Go?"]. In *O komparativní politologii a současné české politice* [*On Comparative Political Science and Current Czech Politics*], edited by Michal Kubát and Tomáš Lebeda, 57–77. Prague: Karolinum.

David, Roman. 2006. "From Prague to Baghdad: Lustration Systems and Their Political Effects". *Government and Opposition* 41 (3): 347–72.

David, Roman. 2011. *Lustrations and Transitional Justice: Personnel Systems in the Czech Republic, Hungary, and Poland*. Philadelphia: Pennsylvania Studies in Human Rights.

Ferreres, Victor. "The Consequences of Centralizing Constitutional Review in a Special Court. Some Thoughts on Judicial Activism". SELA (Seminario on Lationoamérica de Teoría Constitutcional y Política) Papers 39, 2004. http://digitalcommons.law.yale.edu/yls_sela/39.

Filip, Jan, Holländer, Pavel, and Šimíček, Vojtěch. 2007. *Zákon o Ústavním soudu. Komentář* [*Commentary on the Constitutional Court Act*]. 2nd edition. Prague: C. H. Beck.

Ginsburg, Tom. 2003. *Judicial Review in New Democracies: Constitutional Courts in Asian Constitutionalism*. Cambridge: Cambridge University Press.

Grudzińska-Gross, Irena. 1994. *Constitutionalism in East Central Europe: Discussions in Warsaw, Budapest, Prague, Bratislava*. Bratislava: Czecho-Slovak Committee of the European Cultural Foundation.

Hesse, Joachim Jens, and Johnson, Nevil, eds. 1995. *Constitutional Policy and Change in Europe*. Oxford: Nuffield European Studies.

Hirschl, Ran. 2004. *Towards Juristocracy*. Harvard: Harvard University Press.

Klokočka, Vladimír. 1996. *Ústavní zřízení evropských států* [*Constitutional Setting of European States*]. Prague: Linde.

Kmec, Jiří. 2010. "Ústavní soudci, mluvíte spolu?" ["Constitutional Judges, Do You Speak to Each Other?"] *Jiné právo*, May 2. http://jinepravo.blogspot.cz/2010/05/ustavni-soudci-mluvite-spolu.html.

Kopeček, Luboš, and Petrov, Jan. 2016. "From Parliament to Courtroom: Judicial Review of Legislation as a Political Tool in the Czech Republic". *East European Politics and Societies and Cultures* 30 (1): 120–46.

Kopeček, Luboš, and Strmiska, Max. 2005. *Politické strany a stranicke systémy ve srovnávací perspective [Political Parties and Party Systems in Comparative Perspective]*. Prague: Portál.

Kosař, David. 2016. *Perils of Judicial Self-Government in Transitional Societies*. New York: Cambridge University Press.

Kosař, David. 2017. "Politics of Judicial Independence and Judicial Accountability in Czechia: Bargaining in the Shadow of the Law between Court Presidents and the Ministry of Justice". *European Constitutional Law Review* 13 (1): 96–123.

Kosař, David, and Vyhnánek, Ladislav. 2016. "Senát a výběr soudců Ústavního soudu" ["Senate and Selection of Constitutional Court Judges"]. In *Dvacet let Senátu Parlamentu České republiky v souvislostech* [*20 Years of the Senate of the Parliament of the Czech Republic*], edited by Jan Kysela. 2–16. Prague: Leges.

Kosař, David, and Vyhnánek, Ladislav. Forthcoming. "The Constitutional Court of Czechia". In *The Max Planck Handbooks in European Public Law Volume III: Constitutional Adjudication (I)*. Oxford: Oxford University Press.

Kühn, Zdeněk, and Kysela, Jan. 2006. "Nomination of Constitutional Justices in Post-Communist Countries: Trial, Error, Conflict in the Czech Republic". *European Constitutional Law Review* 2: EuConst 183–208.
Lebeda, Tomáš. 2000. "Přiblížení vybraných aspektů reform volebního systému" ["Some Aspects of the Electoral System Reforms"]. *Politologický časopis* 7: 245–47.
Malíř, Jan. 2008. *Odpovědnost členských států za škodu v právu Evropské unie: Studie ze soudcovské tvorby práva* [*State Liability for the Violation of EU Law: Studies of Judicial Decision Making*]. Prague: Charles University, Law Faculty.
Nedelsky, Nadja. 2004. "Divergent Responses to a Common Past: Transitional Justice in the Czech Republic and Slovakia". *Theory and Society* 33 (1): 65–115.
Nikolenyi, Csaba. 2003. "Coordination Problem and Grand Coalition: The Puzzle of the Government Formative Game in the Czech Republic, 1998". *Communist and Post-Communist Studies* 36: 235–344.
Petrov, Jan, and Šipulová, Katarína. 2016. "International Human Rights Treaties in the Case Law of Domestic Courts: Supreme Court and Supreme Administrative Court". In *Making Sense of Human Rights Commitments: A Study of Two Emerging European Democracies*, edited by Hubert Smekal, Katarína Šipulová, Ivo Pospíšil, Jozef Janovský and Petr Kilian, 183–212. Brno: MUNI Press.
Roznai, Yaniv. 2014. "Legisprudence Limitations on Constitutional Amendments? Reflections on the Czech Constitutional Court's Declaration of Unconstitutional Constitutional Act". 8 ICL 29.
Rychetský, Pavel, Langášek, Tomáeš, Herc, Tomáš, and Mlsna, Jan. 2015. *Ústava České republiky. Ústavní zákon o bezpečnosti ČR. Komentář* [*Commentary on the Constitution of the Czech Republic*]. Prague: Wolters Kluwer.
Sadurski, Wojciech. 2014. *A Study of Constitutional Courts in Postcommunist States of Central and Eastern Europe*. 2nd edition. Dordrecht: Springer 2014.
Schwartz, Herman. 2004. *The Struggle for Constitutional Justice in Post-Communist Europe*. Chicago and London: University of Chicago Press.
Senate of the Czech Republic, transcript of 23 June 2000. Available at http://www.senat.cz.
Šimíček, Vojtěch. 2016. "Výběr kandidátů na soudce Ústavního soudu a jejich schvalování Senátem" ["The Selection of Nominees for Constitutional Court Judges and Their Approval by the Senate"]. In *Dvacet let Senátu Parlamentu České republiky v souvislostech* [*20 Years of the Senate of Parliament of the Czech Republic*], edited by Jan Kysela, 225–240. Prague: Leges.
Šipulová, Katarína. 2017. *The Role of Constitutional Courts in De-Communization Processes in the Czech Republic and Slovakia*. MSt thesis. Oxford: Oxford University. Unpublished manuscript.
Smekal, Hubert, and Vyhnánek, Ladislav. 2018 (forthcoming). *Beyond Compliance*. Prague: Wolters Kluwer.
Smith, Brian Clive. 2017. *Judges and Democratization. Judicial Independence in New Democracies*. Oxford: Routledge.
Teitel, Ruti. 1997. "Transitional Jurisprudence: The Role of Law in Political Transformation". *Yale Law Journal* 116: 2016–80.
Teitel, Ruti. 2000. *Transitional Justice*. Oxford: Oxford University Press.
Uitz, Renata. 2007. "Constitutional Courts in Central and Eastern Europe: What Makes a Question Too Political?" *Juridica International* 13: 47–59.
Vojtek, Petr. 2007. *Odpovědnost za škodu při výkonu veřejné moci: komentář* [*State Liability for the Execution of Public Power*]. 2nd edition. Prague: C. H. Beck.
Wagnerová, Eliška. 1996. *Ústavní soudnictví* [*Constitutional Judiciary*]. Prague: Linde.

4 The German Federal Constitutional Court

Authority transformed into power?

Oliver W. Lembcke

4.1 Introduction

The preliminary Constitution of the Federal Republic of Germany (*Grundgesetz*) entered into force 24 May 1949. More than two years later, the Federal Constitutional Court (FCC) of Germany was created in 1951 (Table 4.1). It was on 28 September that the Court officially went into session, but the judges had already started to take up their work and had published their first decision after the first week of September 1951.[1] Following the defeat of the Nazi regime and its reign of terror in Germany and all over Europe, the main political purpose of the new constitution was to restore the rule of law and to ensure basic rights in a way that ensured every individual would be effectively protected against harm and abuses of power, especially by state officials. The key idea was to establish a form of "sovereignty under law", and the FCC was thought to be a centrepiece in this constitutionalist framework (Beyme 2017, 44; Lembcke 2007, 85). The wide range of competences that was attributed to the FCC reflects this intention of the framers. The FCC, however, succeeded in stretching its bases of power and legitimacy in ways that helped to promote its own status even beyond the framers' idea of a Court specialized in matters of constitutional law. This accomplishment affects the distribution of power between the key actors of the political system. But in what ways? Does the FCC use its power, status and legitimacy to restrain the legislator, or even to become a superior form of legislator? These are empirical questions. They have been usually treated by case studies of the FCC analyzing specific fields of jurisdiction or policies by means of qualitative methods. This chapter intends to present a quantitative analysis focusing on the restraining effects of the FCC's jurisdiction on the government as the main policymaker in the German parliamentary system. It specifically aims to answer a two-fold question. To what extent does the FCC translate its power of competences and status into strong judicial rulings? And are these rulings restraining or replacing the legislator as the prime policymaker?

4.2 A powerful Court

4.2.1 Competences and organization

The Court has been vested with a rich arsenal of competences. They range from the power of (*a posteriori*) judicial review on law-making and administrative regulation, including any kind political action with substantial effects on the public sphere, ranging from the scrutiny of elections or banning political parties to the power of concrete review of individual complaints against both Court and administrative decisions, even in rare cases of individual complaints made directly against legislative acts. Moreover, the FCC also exerts review power in matters of competence conflicts related to the federalist organization of the state or related to any other conflict between main political actors. Against this background, it is obvious that the FCC belongs to the category of powerful constitutional courts (Alizivatos 1995). It comes as no surprise, therefore, that the FCC has been held as a role model of institutional designing, at least in terms of its competence structure.[2]

The organization of the FCC is determined by a three-fold structure with the two separate Senates as its core units, in which constitutional case matters are resolved (Schlaich and Korioth 2015, 26). The two Senates can be described as an almost fully autonomous entity; they have equal powers and work, in principle, independently from each other. Each bench of the Senates contains eight judges, of which the *Bundestag* elects four judges per Senate and the *Bundesrat* elects the other four judges, in both cases with a two-thirds majority.[3] All of the FCC judges are trained lawyers, qualified by two state examinations in law, and every judge serves as a (full-time) public office holder for one term of twelve years at maximum (with an age limit of 68 years).[4] Among them, at least three members of each bench must be career judges coming from other German high Courts.

Whereas the "hard cases" are decided in the two Senates, the bulk of work, at least on a daily level, is done by the Chambers (Zuck 2015, 444; Schlaich and Korioth 2015, 190, 338; Farahat 2016, 110). These Chambers were established exclusively to tackle the vast number of individual complaints, which are typically decided by three judges per chamber, unless the complaint presents a matter that is of general importance for the jurisdiction of the FCC. In these cases, the individual complaint is lifted to the Senate level and deliberated and decided by the full bench of eight judges.

Unlike, for instance, the US Supreme Court, the FCC does not have the competence of a free case selection. The Chambers are, therefore, a necessary institutional response to the caseload, which is, for example, lacking in Romania (see Kuti in this volume), and to the individual constitutional complaints, which account for the largest share of the caseload by far, with almost 97 percent at present.

On rare occasions, the judges of the FCC assemble in a plenary session (Schlaich and Korioth 2015, 26). The decision-making of the FCC in such a plenum has been called for, so far, mainly in situations when the unity of the Court's jurisdiction was at stake, with one of the two Senates signalling to deviate from the other's earlier jurisdiction. This overall organizational structure has been in place since 1951. However, since then several reforms, mostly up to the 1970s, have tried to adapt the FCC to its manifold purposes (Schlaich and Korioth 2015, 56, 187; Wöhrmann 1987), mainly induced by challenges of a fast and steadily growing increase of caseloads that called for changes and readjustments (Figure 4.1).

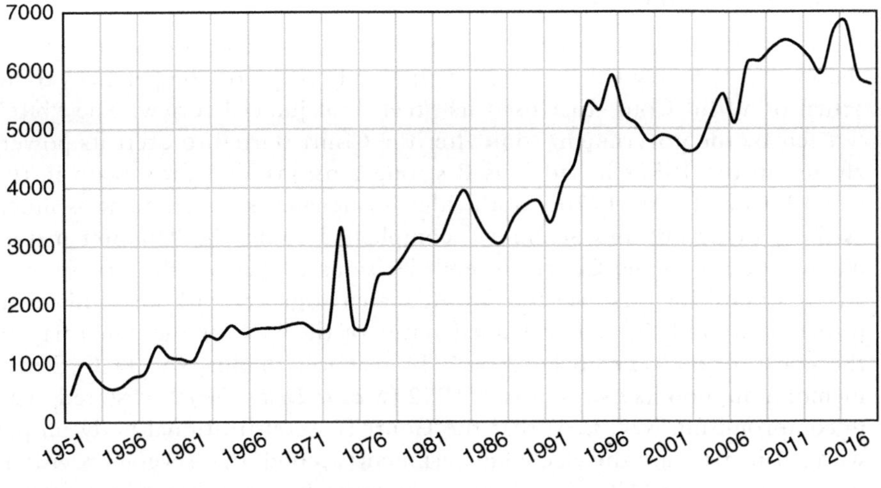

Figure 4.1 Caseload of the FCC (1951–2016)

Table 4.1 Short timeline of institutional changes and reforms (FCC)

1951	• The legislation regulating the organization and structure of the FCC (BVerfGG) was first announced in March 1951 (BGBl. I S. 243) and entered into force on 17 April 1951.
1952	• The FCC filed a memorandum on its own status as a constitutional body (27 June 1951).
1956	• Readjustment of the competences between the two Senates. • The option of (non-binding) judicial expertise by the FCC (used on three occasions before this reform) was scrapped.
1963	• Reduction of the number of judges per Senate: eight judges at each bench.
1971	• With the beginning of the year the reform entered force, unifying term limits (twelve years max.) and age limits (retirement age at 68). • In addition, the option of dissenting opinion was introduced, and the first (official) dissenting opinion was published on 4 January 1971.
1993	• In the wake of institutional changes due to the German reunification, the BVerfGG was renewed on 11 August 1993 (BGBl. I S. 1473) with the latest amendment in July 2017 (BGBl. I S. 2730).
1996	• Establishment of a press bureau.
2008	• The FCC no longer performs the additional role as the constitutional court of Schleswig–Holstein, which established its own constitutional tribunal.
2015	• Reform of the election procedure on 24 June 2015 (BGBl. I S. 973). Instead of delegating its electoral power to a special committee, the judges of the FCC are now selected by parliament in a full plenary session.

4.2.2 Critical junctures

With the benefit of hindsight, it was less the external reforms that paved the way from a new Court vested with a wide range of competences to an actual powerful Court that used its "teeth" of judicial review. The "bite" was felt by the government soon after the Court started to exert its power; already in the 1950s it had caused strong tensions, and then again in the late 1960s and early 1970s. Both sides – Adenauer's government as much as those of Brandt and Schmidt – complained about the "counter-majoritarian" power of the Court. Several decisions evoked harsh criticism and strong opposition.[5] However, only Adenauer together with his minister of justice contested the self-acclaimed status of the FCC as the "guardian of the constitution" (Lembcke 2015). In reaction to this, the FCC filed a memorandum on its own status in 1952 (*Status-Denkschrift*). It stated in an uncompromising way, first, that the Court is a constitutional body on par with parliament and the elected government; second, that several provisions of the law on the FCC (*Bundesverfassungsgerichtsgesetz*, BVerfGG) are not in line with this interpretation (for example the supervision of the ministry of justice over the FCC). It declared, therefore, thirdly, the present state of affairs as unconstitutional until the legislator had acceded to the demands of the Court. It was an unprecedented act, an act of "self-empowerment" (Lembcke 2007) or even a "judicial coup d'état" (Stone Sweet 2007) that ultimately turned this institution into an authority within the political system of Germany. It was successful mainly because the public believed widely in the constitution and trusted the FCC in its role as a reliable "guardian". Ever since then, there have been many cases of criticism, sometimes disrespectful and bordering contempt.[6] Yet even these have been mainly directed toward the jurisdiction and much less intensively towards the institution itself. Under these circumstances, so far the FCC has successfully managed to recover even after long periods of criticism, for instance in the first half of the 1990s, when the Court, especially the First Senate, was criticized for its liberal-progressive attitude toward, among others, drugs, the military and religion (Lembcke 2006).

4.2.3 Judicial reputation

A key factor that helped the FCC to maintain its powerful position in the German political system is the trust of citizens in "their" Court. The level of trust in the Court is considerably high compared to other main political institutions (Figure 4.2). It was about 20 percentage points higher in the mid-1980s, and the gap widened to a 30 percentage point difference during the first decade of the 2000s. However, the situation is less clear in the wake of crisis management after 2007, which seems in general to be favourable for the government with a peak in 2012, compared to levels of trust in the 2000s years before. The reunification of Germany after 1989 – with relatively low (but rising) levels of trust

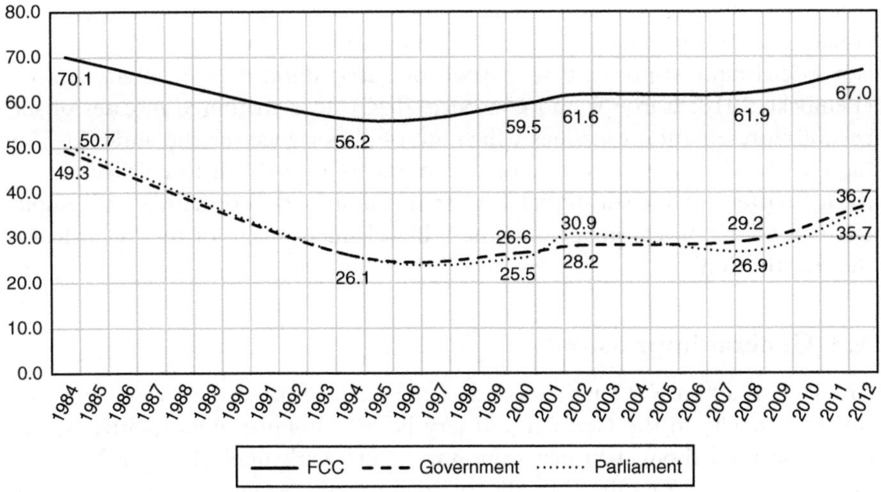

Figure 4.2 Trust in the FCC (1984–2012)

by the former citizens of East Germany (German Democratic Republic, GDR) (Lembcke 2006) – together with a longer period of intensive criticism during the first half of the 1990s reduced the amount of trust in the FCC substantially. It saw a drop of about 15 percentage points, succeeded by a slow but steady recovery during the years of the 2000s, regaining around 10 percentage points of trust within the following ten years. Since then, around two-thirds of German citizens view the FCC as trustworthy.[7]

"Trustworthy" in this respect means that German citizens, by a wide margin, believe in the Court's role of protecting the constitution – a role that the FCC has endowed with the self-acclaimed image as the "guardian of the constitution". In other words, the judges of the FCC have successfully defined the institution as the representative and, by the same token, as the authority of the constitution by means of their interpretations. This success has significantly changed the power structure of the political system in favour of the FCC, at least in the sense that the Court itself determines to a large degree the limits of its own power (Lembcke 2007; Jestaedt et al. 2011). This in itself is a form of power, based on the widely accepted status that the Court not only has the competence ("the right") to interpret the constitutional principles and provisions, but has also become the "mouth" of the constitution, to use a famous phrase of Montesquieu, or, at least, the constitution's "verified" translator.[8] This "power of Hermes", the power of the translator, is solidified by the high approval rating of the constitution.[9] These approval ratings result from strong feelings most Germans have about their constitution, in many ways similar to the US, where the constitution has an almost sacral status as the common ground for society and politics alike (Vorländer 1989).

The two sources of the FCC's legitimacy, the constitution (normative legitimacy) and the trust of the citizens (empirical legitimacy), relate to each other (Majone 2001), mediated by the Court's reputation. Reputation – like authority – is a special kind of power that is based on recognition by the public audience (Lembcke 2013; Garoupa and Ginsburg 2015). It is attributed in cases of successful representation of values which are of importance for the audience. The high levels of trust indicate a reputation of the FCC as the distinguished authority in matters of constitutional law, transcending the normative and empirical dimensions of legitimacy into the self-acclaimed image of the "guardian of the constitution".

4.3 General impressions

The FCC is a "busy" Court. Soon after the judges started their work, the institutional novelty in the German judiciary became popular among citizens, who quickly learned about their new option to "go to Karlsruhe" (Lamprecht 2011). Since the German reunification, the caseload has on average increased even more compared to the period prior to 1989. Yet so far, the institutional operability has not been affected by this increase. Instead, the FCC has established a relatively stable equilibrium between the cases brought before the Court (input) and the cases decided by the Court (output), measured by the annual average (Figure 4.3).

The present chapter focuses on the period from 1990 to 2015. Within these twenty-five years, only a small volume of cases is the subject of the research question (Table 4.2). The sample includes all judicial reviews (abstract and concrete review) during this time span, the procedures of competence collisions – as far as the parliament is concerned, and restricted to the national level

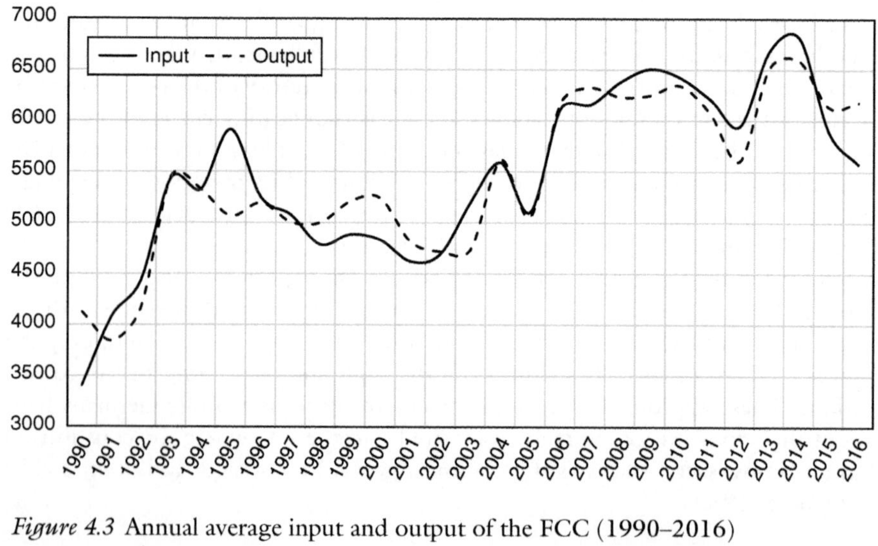

Figure 4.3 Annual average input and output of the FCC (1990–2016)

Table 4.2 Motion types, numbers and success rates (FCC)

Type of motions(selected)	*Motions per year (Ø)*	*Motions until 2016 (N)*	*Quota of motions (%)*	*Decisions 1990–2015 (N)*	*Rulings 1990–2015 (N)*	*Success rate (%)*
Concrete review (BvL)	54.8	3.563	1.6	148	172	38.4
Abstract review (BvF)	2.7	173	0.1	48	76	46.0
Competence collision (BvE)	3.3	214	0.1	21	32	56.3
Constitutional complaint (BvR)	3313.2	215.360	96.6	5	7	42.9*
Other	55.6	3.612	1.6	—	—	—
Motions in total	3429.6	222.922	100	222	287	—

Source: Official statistics of the FCC (cumulated). *Success Rate of individual complaints overall: 2.3%.

(excluding competence conflicts between the national government and the *Bundesländer*) – and, finally, a handful of selected individual complaints that, first, were directed against a piece of legislation (and not directed against an administrative or a court decision) and, second, had been bundled together with concrete review motions by the FCC.

The core unit of the data set, to be sure, is not the case brought before Court, but the ruling of the FCC. One case can, and usually does, include more than one ruling. As for the FCC, however, the ratio 1:1.3 between decisions and rulings is close, at least compared to other constitutional courts, e.g. the Polish Constitutional Tribunal (see Chapter 6 in this volume) or the Hungarian Constitutional Court (see Chapter 5 in this volume). In addition, the overall number of the FCC rulings is considerably low, like the Slovak Constitutional Court (see Chapter 8 in this volume), with some years having a particularly small annual average of rulings (Figure 4.4).

A closer look at the rulings reveals some of their characteristics. First of all, Figure 4.5 mirrors the difficulty of discerning a clear-cut tendency, and, moreover, that the low strength of the rulings (SoR) relates to the low number of rulings; this is especially true for two of the outliers, the aggregated scores of the years 2000 and 2011. Yet, the figure also displays a relationship between the number of rulings declaring substantial unconstitutionality and the SoR in general, indicated by similar curves (cyclical) and a relationship between rejections and the SoR (anti-cyclical). After the exclusion of refusals (rejection due to formal considerations), more than 50 percent of motions brought before the Court are at least partly successful. In other words, once the FCC decides on the merit the odds are quite high that the complainants "have a case", and more often than not the ruling will be in their favour. Among the various types of non-rejections,

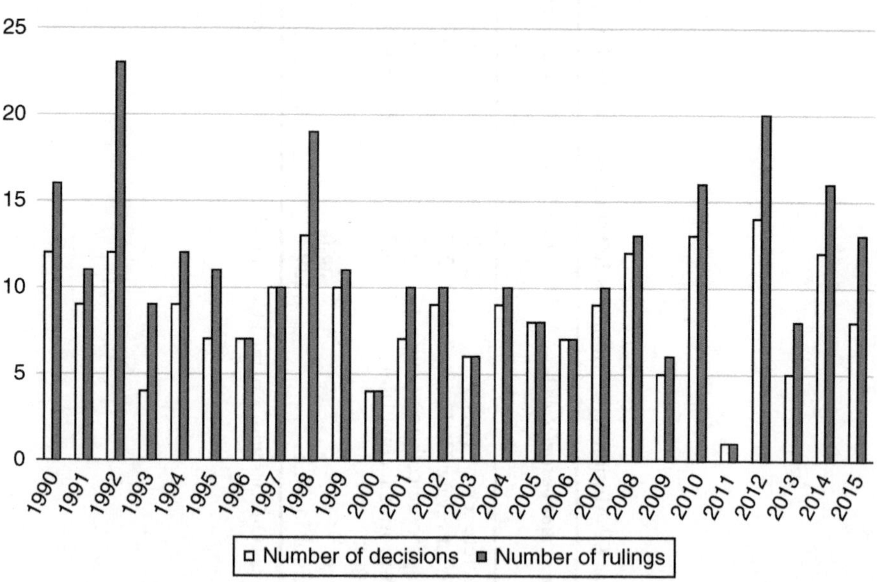

Figure 4.4 Number of decisions and rulings (FCC)

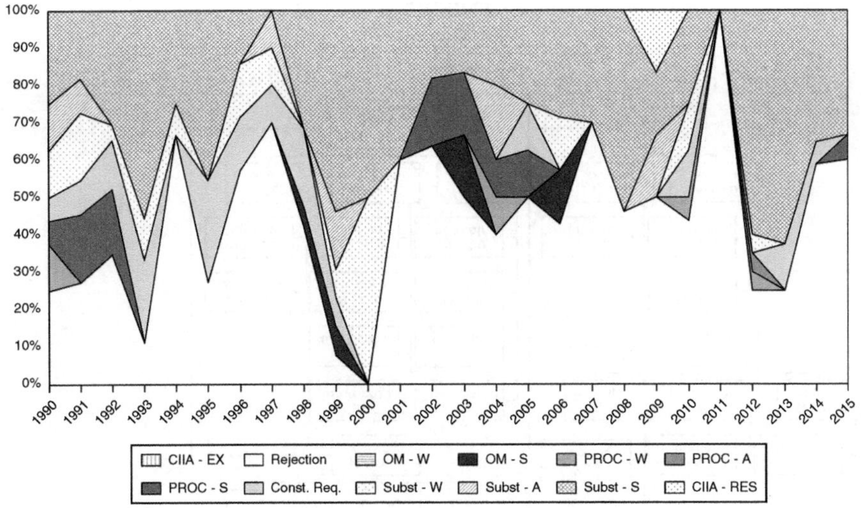

Figure 4.5 Frequency of ruling types I (FCC)

the rulings declaring substantial unconstitutionality outnumber by far (43 percent) the rest of the ruling types. Some of them are, practically speaking, of no relevance at all. The legislative omission is a case in point (n = 1).

If the FCC encounters circumstances in which the judges find the legislator should live up to its constitutional obligations, they do not ask for it by declaring legislative omission without binding consequences but *demand* it by declaring the legislative act as unconstitutional, typically combined with other elements. What are these elements that add up to rather *strong* substantive unconstitutionality (85 percent, compared to roughly 15 percent *weak* substantive unconstitutionality)?[10] To answer this question, the configurations of the rulings need to be taken into account (Figure 4.6).

The configurational analysis of the *strong* substantive unconstitutionality shows that they are typically connected with *pro futuro* in combination with a broad remedy.[11] The operating idea behind this configuration is the following. Once the FCC prescribes a change of the legal or political *status quo*, it allows for some time. But it cuts both ways. In cases in which the FCC does not allow any time (*ex tunc* rulings), the judges usually refrain from prescribing broader forms of remedy. Again, this holds true for partial (*ex tunc* 33 percent, no remedy 81 percent) as much as complete annulments (*ex tunc* 48 percent, no remedy 65 percent). Of course, there are other than these two configurations. But they can serve as a framework of analysis that shows some of the instruments and the way they are used by the constitutional judges to refine their rulings and gradate the restraints on the legislator.

Like the type of the legislative omission, the types of procedural unconstitutionality, or constitutional interpretation *in abstracto* (CIIA), do not play an important role. The CIIA presupposes a situation in which the constitution does

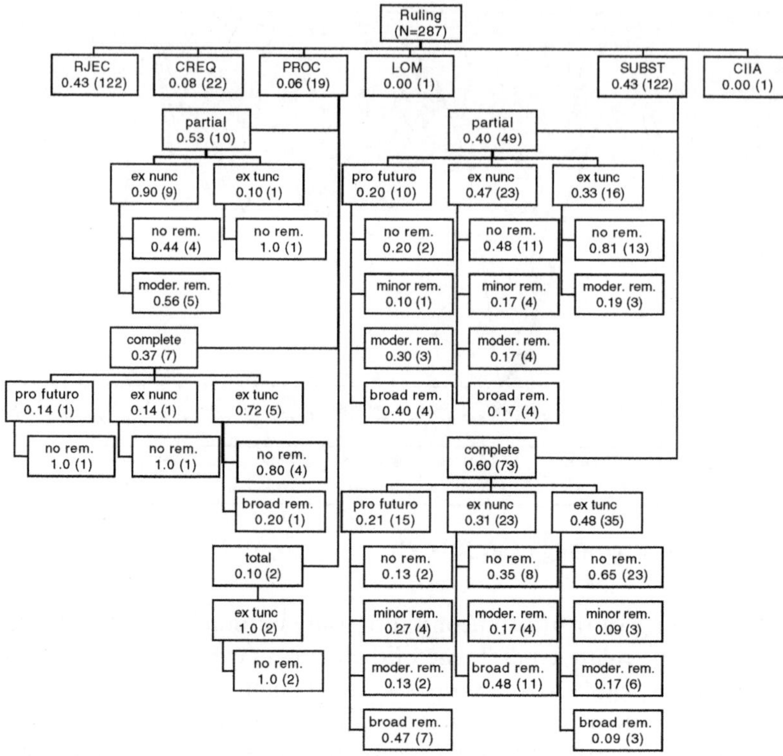

Figure 4.6 Configurations of rulings (percentages and numbers) (FCC)

not provide any substantial guidance. Considering the "rich" and rigid German constitution (Beyme 2017, 44; Lijphart 2012, 204), this is obviously not the default position of the FCC. On the contrary, the FCC has framed the German Basic Law (*Grundgesetz*) as an expression of normative principles – and in the beginning even as an expression of "objective values"[12] – mainly due to basic and human rights, and in particular because of the principle of human dignity. In this perspective, the concept of the CIIA is marginal at best.

As for procedural unconstitutionality, this type is almost a *quantité négligeable* with only 6 percent of all ruling types. One explanation is that since 1945 Germany has become a solidified constitutional democracy under the rule of law, in which procedural rules of law-making are generally acknowledged and respected by the political actors. The fact that the judges applied 50 percent of this ruling type in the first three years after reunification indicates that the context of regime transition might be, at least in the German case, a factor explaining the relevance (and the lack of it) of this type (Table A.1 in the Appendix).[13]

It may come as a surprise that the FCC does not rely on a variety of ruling types, with an almost fifty–fifty split between rejections on the one side and rulings of substantial unconstitutionality on the other. Together these two types account for more than 80 percent of all rulings. However, this does not mean that the judges in Karlsruhe see their ruling as a matter of "black and white". Instead, they use the techniques of gradating the impact of their decisions by refining the configuration of the ruling, especially with respect to the type of substantial unconstitutionality. With these instruments, the FCC has created room for strategic considerations in their relationship with the government and its majority in parliament.

The scatterplot in Figure 4.7 illustrates this room for leeway. It displays the strength of rulings (SoR, with values from 0 to 10) by time frame (year) and with that visualizes two corridors of strategic refinement, defined by two lines of the rulings' average strength (average value with and without rejections). The first corridor starts above the line of rejection at the bottom of the scatterplot and stops shortly before the line of average strength (3.6) of all rulings, including the rejections. The second corridor covers the range from the second line of average without rejections: 6.4 to the maximum of strong rulings (10). What preliminary conclusion can be drawn from this visualization?

- The FCC makes use of the full range of instruments: the Court does not shy away from "strong" rulings (up to the maximum value), nor do the judges try to maximize their constraining impact on the legislator over the years.
- In general, the judges seem to make use of the leeway that the constitutional interpretation of the different cases provides for. Seen in this light, they take up the role of a maker and moulder of refined and adjusted rulings, displaying a sense of proportion in their judgements. However, these rulings are typically either rather strong or weak.
- With only very few exceptions, the corridor between the two lines of average (average value with and without rejections) is strikingly empty. The main factor explaining these findings lies in the specific configuration of the different elements that determine the relative SoR. Moderating aspects of the judgements do not bridge the gap between the two corridors. Put simply, moderate decisions exist only inside the two corridors, not outside of them.

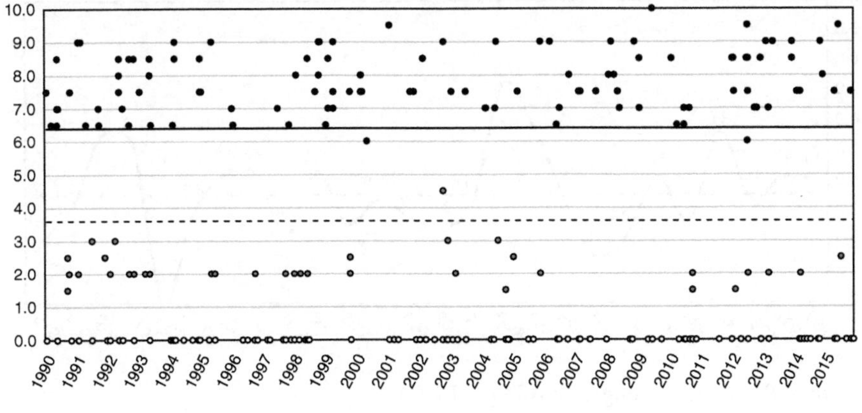

Figure 4.7 "Corridors" of the strength of rulings (FCC)

4.4 Trends in majority rulings

The two corridors of the SoR display a full picture of the FCC's rulings, but this picture is too fine-grained for discerning major trends. What are the periods in time of a strong jurisdiction? And what are those of a weak jurisdiction? Is it likely that these periods are induced exogenously or are driven by forces within the Court?

4.4.1 The FCC and its two Senates

As a starting point for such a kind of structural-quantitative analysis, it is necessary to switch the perspective from the SoR at a case-per-case level to the average SoR over a longer period. The chart in Figure 4.8 provides an overview on an annual basis. *Prima facie*, the only trend that is discernible is that there is no trend at all. The line plot oscillates up and down in a rather short period of time.[14] It is basically a "zig-zag" line of the FCC's ruling. However, it should be noted that this finding is consistent with earlier insights into the "either–or" character of the FCC's ruling according to the analyzes of the "corridors" and the configuration of the SoR.

To go one step further, it is also worth pointing out again that the term German Federal Constitutional Court is, of course, only a "signifier" for the average of the SoR by the two Senates. This reminder begs the question to what (if at all) these two entities differ from each other in terms of the SoR? Table 4.3 gives a quick insight. Based on the average per year, the rulings of both Senates display a wide value range – with the Second Senate being more "moderate" than the First Senate. Moreover, both Senates seem to oscillate between periods of strong and weak rulings, yet the First Senate appears to be more "volatile".

These impressions are confirmed by the plot displaying the SoR for each Senate of the last twenty-five years (Figure 4.9). Instead of a robust trend over

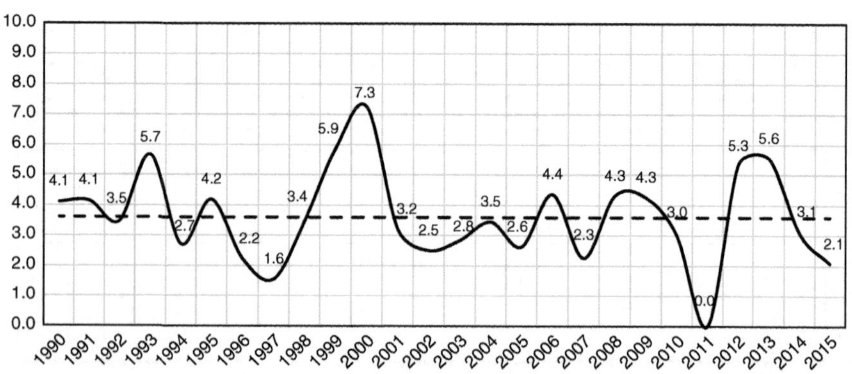

Figure 4.8 Average strength of rulings (FCC)

Table 4.3 Average strength of rulings (by Senates) (FCC)

	Average	*Min. and max.*	*Strong periods*	*Weak periods*	*Dynamics*
First Senate	4.15	0–9	1990–1991, 1993, 1999–2001, 2004–2006, 2009, 2012–2013, 2015	1992, 1994, 1996, 2002, 2007–2008, 2010–2011	"Heart rate"
Second Senate	3.25	0–7.5	1994, 2000, 2008	1991, 1997, 2001, 2011, 2014– 2015	"Waves"

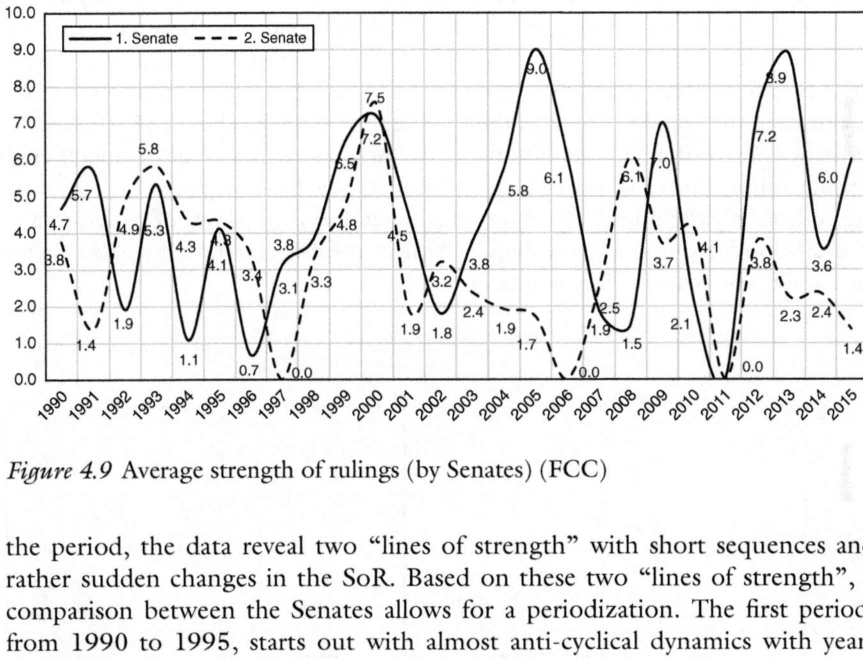

Figure 4.9 Average strength of rulings (by Senates) (FCC)

the period, the data reveal two "lines of strength" with short sequences and rather sudden changes in the SoR. Based on these two "lines of strength", a comparison between the Senates allows for a periodization. The first period, from 1990 to 1995, starts out with almost anti-cyclical dynamics with years where the difference in strength is rather huge (e.g. 1991, 1994) and years in which the rulings of both Senates on average are close to each other (e.g. 1993, 1995). The second period lasts from 1996 to 2002, in which the annual SoR in each of these years is "mirrored" with a small delay. This period of adaptation is succeeded by a third period of rather short anti-cyclical dynamics (2003–2006), but with a strong discrepancy in the years 2005–2006. This pattern repeats itself twice with sequences of adaption (2007–2011, 2014) and deviation (2012–2013, 2015).

What kind of conclusion can be drawn from these observations? First, both Senates exert their power by means of strong rulings, but they do not do it all the time. Each Senate has also shown periods of self-restraint. Second, the fact that the data do not indicate trends over a longer period suggests that the FCC in general is not driven by an activist agenda. This conclusion does not dispute interpretations claiming that the Court has made use of its power to become a policymaker, but neither the First Senate nor the Second Senate has pursued such a role for a long period.

To provide a more nuanced assessment, without delving too much into this long-standing discussion on the concept of judicial activism (Green 2009), the following "minimal requirements" can be used as a hypothesis for a quantitative analysis. If the FCC is an activist Court, the quantity of rulings and their strength are expected to be high. Using a scatterplot for testing this hypothesis on an annual basis (Figure 4.10), the data in the first quadrant should display a high number of cases indicating the years of judicial activism of the FCC. However, the relatively small sample of cases in this quadrant does not support this hypothesis. Actually, the cases are more or less equally divided over all the four quadrants, providing some evidence for the thesis that the judges make use of the power to deliver strong rulings and, at the same time, use their power to restrain themselves.

In sum, the empowerment of the FCC, combined with the act of self-empowerment shortly after its establishment, did not result in a trend of increasingly strong rulings. Instead, since the 1990s the judges have been exerting time and again not only the power of strong rulings but also the "power of self-restraint", thereby moderating or even scaling back their influence on the key political actors and their base majority in parliament.

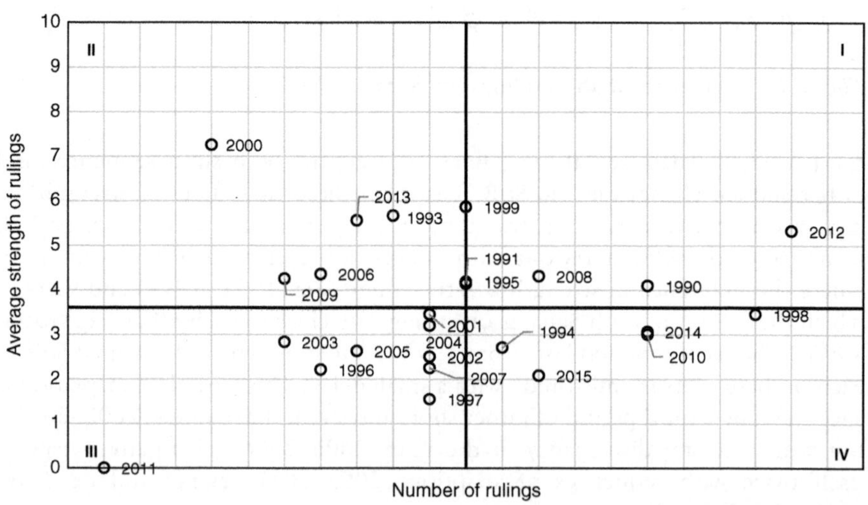

Figure 4.10 Judicial activism vs. judicial self-restraint (FCC)

4.4.2 Political contexts

What are the factors contributing to this moderation of the FCC's power? Are these factors endogenous or exogenous in their nature? To throw some light onto this matter, the SoR is linked to political contexts, especially to changes in government. The underlying hypothesis for this analysis is that changes in government influence the SoR. And there is ***prima facie*** evidence supporting this hypothesis. The rampant rise of strong decisions in 1998 suggests a reaction of the judges to the policies of the centre-left/green coalition that endured from 1998 to 2005. Yet this operationalization is misleading, because it is based on coincidence in time but does not control for the impact and its direction. Most likely, at least within the first years of a newly elected government, the rulings do not impose restraints on its novel legislation but affect the legacy of its predecessors. In this light, it seems a different way of analyzing the data is called for. The key idea of this alternative presented in the line plot in Figure 4.11 is to "mirror back" the data on strength values to the time the complaint was brought before the Court. This method acknowledges the (sometimes huge) difference between the two dates of, first, bringing the complaint before Court by the claimant and, second, delivering the decision by the Court. The guiding assumption is that the data of the complaint might clarify which government's action will be challenged by the claimant. For example, if the complaint has been filed during the time of a left-wing government, it is reasonable to assume that a left-wing legislative act has been challenged. This is why "mirroring back" is needed, which means that this method requires checking for the date when the complaints have been filed. Based on these data, we can discern at least three major periods.

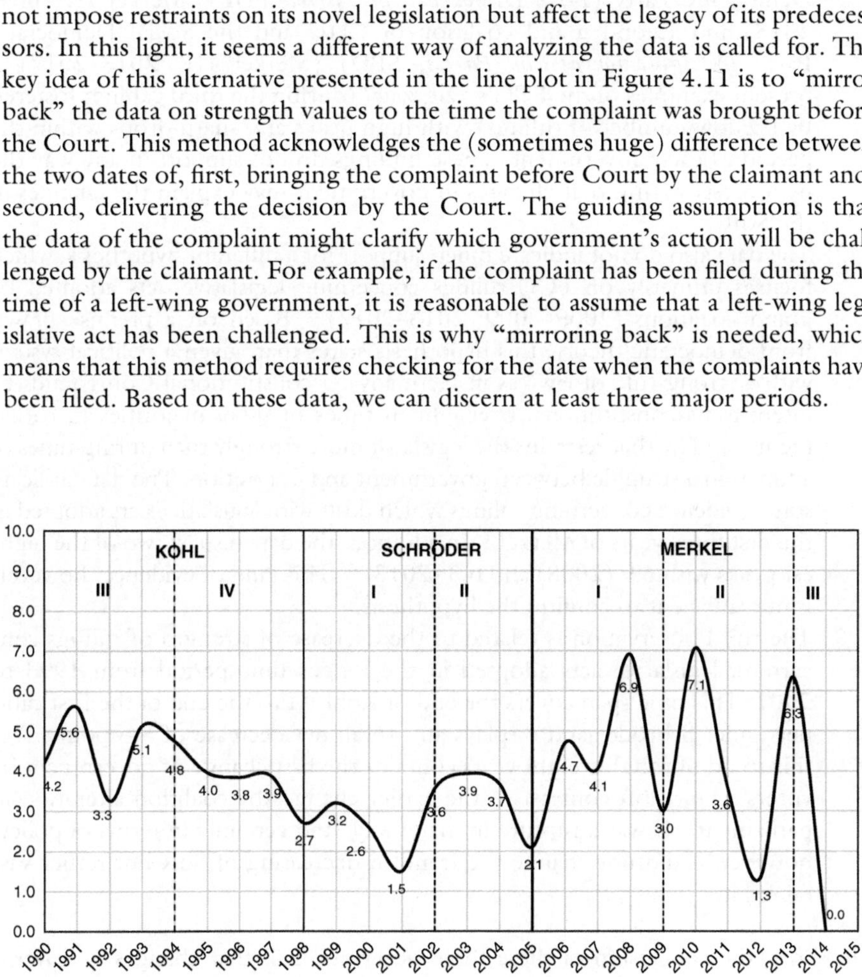

Figure 4.11 Average strength of rulings (by year of complaint) (FCC)

1 Picking up the example of the centre-left/green coalition (Schröder I and Schröder II), the line plot shows a decrease of strength in the rulings of the FCC, which means that the FCC declared weaker rulings on the legislative acts of the Schröder governments compared to the previous Kohl government and the following grand coalition (Merkel I). Moreover, the data display an increase of SoR concerning legislative acts passed by the parliament at the beginning of the first grand coalition under Merkel (2005–2009), followed by a sharp drop of roughly 3 points at the end of Merkel's first chancellorship. The two following cabinets under Merkel – the centre-right coalition of Christian Democratic Union (*Christlich Demokratische Union*, CDU), Christian Social Union (*Christlich-Soziale Union*, CSU) and Free Democratic Party (*Freie Demokratische Partei*, FDP) (Merkel II, 2009-2013) and second grand coalition of CDU and the Social Democratic Party (*Sozialdemokratische Partei*, SPD) (Merkel III, 2013–2017) – present examples of the FCC's "zig-zag" (during the third cabinet fostered by the low number of rulings) with high peaks and sharp drops within the period of each government. These findings do not support in any way the hypothesis stating that changes in government may explain the changes in the SoR.

2 The data also do not indicate much support for a different hypothesis, which focuses primarily on FCC rulings concerning legislative acts adopted by grand coalitions (2005–2009; 2013–2017).[15] Based on a premise drawn from democratic theory, this hypothesis states that, given a political system with a strong rule of law (as in Germany), a constitutional Court tends to intensify its constitutional oversight in times of super-majorities in parliament – and by that restrains the legislator more strongly than during times of a functional struggle between government and opposition. The data indicate some evidence concerning rulings which dealt with legislative acts adopted in the first three years of Merkel I. In addition, the data display two of the highest peaks with 6.9 (2008) and 6.3 (2013).[16] This kind of evidence, however, is not sufficient to confirm the hypothesis.

3 The third observation is related to the decrease of strength of rulings concerning legislative acts adopted in the longer time period from 1993 to 2001. This time span covers the end of Kohl III to the end of the first cabinet under Schröder and displays an overall net decrease of 3.6 points. Yet this trend of roughly eight years contains the first change of government by voters' choice (in contrast to the earlier changes by coalition alteration in parliament). It was a rupture in many ways and certainly in terms of policy; however, it did not change the trend in decreasing of SoR but rather sustained it.

In short, the conclusion of these three observations is that changes in government do not seem to affect (much) the FCC's rulings in terms of their strength. It may be one of the most important exogenous factors that could affect Courts in general, but according to the data it does not do so in the German case.

4.4.3 Inside the Court

But what if we change the perspective and focus on internal changes instead of external ones? If the Court is characterized to a large degree by being independent not only in a normative sense but also empirically, then the factors explaining the SoR may be found within the Court. Are there factors that cause the outcome of the rulings determining whether they are weak or strong? Is, for instance, the "zig-zag" as the dominant pattern an expression of internal incoherence? Or is it due to an asymmetrical distribution of power among the judges?

In some countries, court presidents can play a leading role, particularly if they have the status of ***primus inter pares***, connected, for instance, with the power of determining the reporting judge. As for the FCC, the additional competences of the President are very limited and mainly linked to the representative function that comes with the office. One of the reasons for this very limited extra power is that the FCC is composed of two more or less separate and autonomous Senates, each with its own chairman. It should therefore not come as a surprise that the individual record of strength is within the range of the other judges' scores (Figure 4.12).[17]

The bar chart displays the average performance of the several presidents and vice-presidents during their term. Taken together, the individual results of the SoR scores of the nine judges show that their performances are relatively similar. Most of this group have individual scores ranging from 4.0 to 5.0 with small exceptions (but no statistical outliers). Correspondingly, the standard deviation of this group is rather small (0.614), particularly in comparison with the general standard deviation (0.897). Among the group of presidents and vice presidents, only Ferdinand Kirchhof (at present, vice president of the First Senate) belongs to the group of judges with strong rulings, based on the average score of his rulings (Figure 4.13).

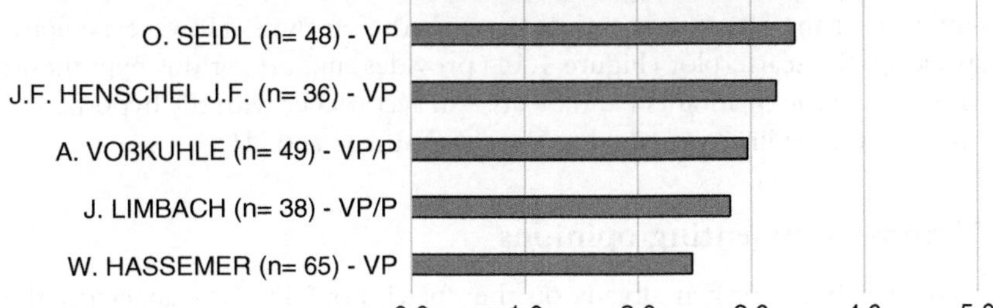

Figure 4.12 Average strength of rulings (by presidents and vice-presidents) (FCC)

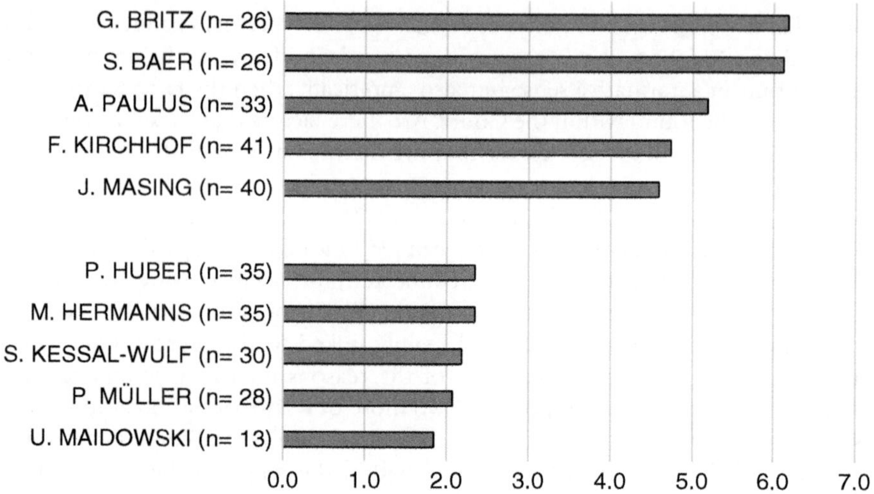

Figure 4.13 Average strength of rulings (by "top five" judges) (FCC)

Within this group of judges with a score of strong rulings on average, the maximum SoR is slightly above 6.0 and the minimum SoR close to 5.0. In contrast, the scores of judges with a very "moderate" record are relatively close to each other, with an SoR around 2.0. It is noticeable in both sub-groups that judges with a higher number of rulings are leaning more towards the average FCC SoR.

These findings inspire the following hypothesis, which states that the longer the judges are in office (measured here by their number of rulings) the more they adjust in terms of their individual scores of SoR. Theoretically, this assumption can be linked to a neo-institutional approach that frames "the bench" as an institution made of formal and informal rules, in which experience dealing with these different rules matters. Under these circumstances, the emergence of a "logic of appropriateness" (March and Olsen 2006) is likely to prevail, guiding the behaviour and interactions of judges and promoting in some ways a common understanding of "appropriate" rulings. This, of course, is more a theoretical ad hoc augmentation of the hypothesis and deserves further analysis. However, empirically speaking, the scatterplot (Figure 4.14) provides support for this hypothesis: the SoR scores in the quadrants I and IV are – in accordance with the hypothesis – closer to the average line compared to the quadrants II and III.

4.5 Trends in dissenting opinions

Some light has been thrown already on the "black box" FCC by analyzing the individual SoR scores of the judges. Several questions remain, of course. Among them, the question of factions inside the Court is of importance. In the case of the FCC, the database for such an analysis is rather thin, due to the lack of

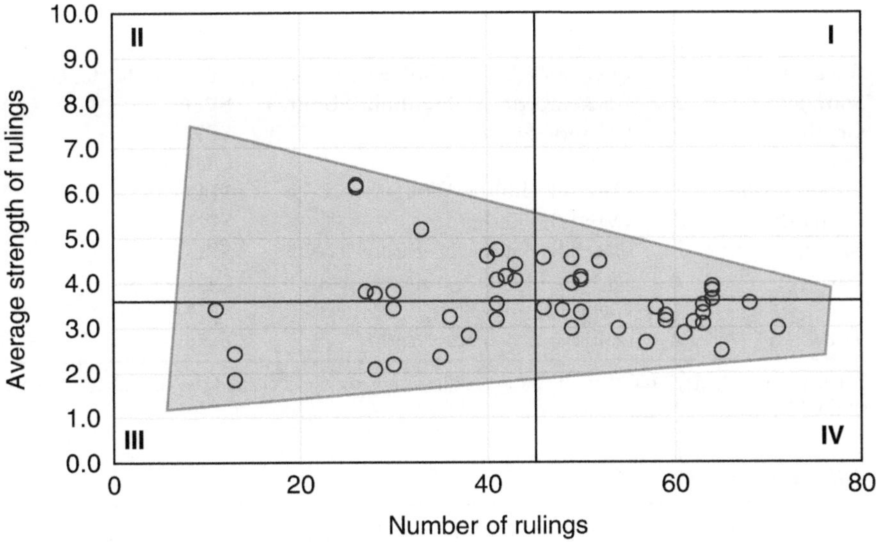

Figure 4.14 Number and average strength of rulings (by judges) (FCC)

Table 4.4 Rulings and dissenting opinions (1990–2015) (FCC)

	N	%
Rulings	287	89.1
Concurring opinion	8	2.5
Dissenting opinion	27	8.4
Total	322	100.0

individual data. The majority decisions may include a vote, sometimes even several votes on different passages of the decision, but they usually do not provide any reliable information of the individual voting behaviour of the judges.[18] In the German case, the primary source for such an analysis has always been the dissenting opinions,[19] but these data are also rather scarce, at least for the time span under scrutiny (Table 4.4).

From 1990 to 2015, the judges of the FCC did not deliver dissenting opinions very often. Their share is less than 10 percent of the data set, and the picture does not change much if concurring opinions are included in the sample. Moreover, the dissenting opinions are rather evenly spread: roughly one-third of the judges delivered a dissenting opinion no more than once, only three judges three times (Table 4.5).

To be sure, dissenting opinions can be a sign of polarization (a high number of dissenting votes by many judges) or disintegration (a high number of the same judge or group of judges).[20] In this light, the FCC appears to be an integrated Court with a functional and inclusive decision-making process, in which typically the different positions and arguments are heard, discussed and, after some time

Table 4.5 Dissenters (more than once) and dissenting coalitions (FCC)

Name	*N*	*Coalition*	*Party**	*N*
Böckenförde	2	Böckenförde–Graßhof–Kirchhof	SPD–CDU/CSU	1
Sommer	2	Böckenförde–Mahrenholz–Sommer	SPD	1
Graßhof-	3	Graßhof–Sommer	SPD	1
Osterloh	3	Haas–Papier	CDU/CSU	1
Lübbe-Wolff	2	Osterloh–Lübbe-Wolff	SPD	1
Gerhardt	3	Osterloh–Gerhardt	SPD	2
Masing	2	Osterloh–Gerhardt–Lübbe-Wolff	SPD	1
Gaier	2	Di Fabio–Mellinghoff–Landau	CDU/CSU	1
		Gaier–Masing–Baer	SPD–Green	1
Total	19	centre-left vs. centre-right	7:3	10

* The variable "party" refers to the party that has suggested and elected the candidate as a judge of the FCC.

Table 4.6 Votes (FCC)

b	*8:0*	*7:0*	*6:0*	*7:1*	*6:1*	*6:2*	*5:2*	*5:3*	*4:3*	*4:4*	*NA*
N (303)	40	3	3	15	3	12	3	11	1	3	205

of refinement, decided. An indicator of this assumption is the documented voting record of the judges (Table 4.6).[21] In 49 percent of the publicly documented votes (n = 94), the judges decided the case unanimously.[22] In addition, 35 percent of the decisions are at least carried by a clear majority.

These findings, which show an FCC striving for an integrated decision-making process, are in line with the research of qualitative studies. Mainly based on interviews, these studies stress the consensus orientation within the Court as the informal "logic of appropriateness" (Lembcke 2007, 259).[23] However, this logic does not always prevail. In cases in which a consensus cannot be reached, the dissenting opinions may fulfil different functions (see Kelemen 2018):

- Pluralist authority. The dissenting opinion demonstrates a different option for deciding the case, which might be more acceptable for groups that have suffered defeat before the FCC.
- Critical communication. If the critique comes from inside, it might be taken as a signal to the majority of the judges to check carefully whether this line of jurisdiction should actually be pursued further.
- Open source for discourse. Finally, the dissenting opinions might also serve as an open source for everyone who wants to be equipped with (usually well-reasoned) arguments that can be re-introduced into the discourse to keep it going.

To what extent these functions are of importance is an empirical question. It should be noted, though, that the data indicate a rather partisan outlook with respect to the coalitions of dissenters: none of the coalitions was "bi-partisan";

the judges exclusively joined ranks with others of the same ideological camp. The sample is too small to draw far-reaching conclusions from it. Yet it at least provides grounds for a clear-cut hypothesis and for further research.

4.6 Qualitative evaluation

The data set contains 287 rulings. 43 percent of which are rejections, while 57 percent belong to another type of ruling. The large majority of non-zero rulings, i.e. other than rejections, are rulings of substantial unconstitutionality (roughly three-quarters); the rest – roughly a quarter – are spread over four different types of ruling (Table 4.7). In addition, Table 4.7 also contains a special sub-group, the type of substantive unconstitutionality based on formal legal principals of the rule of law (FORM). This kind of substantive unconstitutionality, as contrasted to procedural unconstitutionality, is a tricky phenomenon, as explained in the methodological chapter of the present volume.[24] The FCC has made use of this type with reference to (i) the legal principle that measures should not have retroactive effects and to (ii) the principle of legal clarity.

For an evaluation of the validity of the index, we now take a closer look at the SoR. Does the score, as predetermined by the JUDICON project, match the real impact of these decisions?

To start with the ***constitutional interpretation in abstracto*** (CIIA): it concerns a ruling related to the Treaty of Lisbon, delivered in June 2009 (BVerfGE 123, 267). In line with previous decisions in the context of the EU, most notably the Maastricht decision of the year 1993 (BVerfGE 89, 115), the FCC takes a grand view on the state of affairs in terms of EU integration and the importance of democratic accountability, the role of the national political actors and the normative guidelines of the *Grundgesetz* in this respect. The FCC repeats its key notion that the delegation of national competences to the EU is not simply a one-way road. It is high politics of great normative importance – signalled by the concept of "constitutional identity" (Rode 2012). For this reason, the delegation process must be embedded in an institutional framework of democratic context, and in such a context it is necessary, according to the Second Senate, to strengthen the German parliament. The maximum SoR score of 10 already indicates that this ruling must be understood as a very strong decision. The reason for this is two-fold.

Table 4.7 Selected types of rulings (FCC)

	CR	*PROC*	*OM*	*FORM*	*CIIA*
Number	22	19	1	8	1
Senate (1st–2nd)	14–8	1–18	0–1	6–2	0–1
Motion Types	4	3	1	2	1
Competence conflicts	2	10	—	—	1
Abstract review	8	8	1	6	—
Concrete review	10	1	—	2	—
Individual complaints	2	—	—	—	—
Average SoR Score	2.00	2.5	2.5	7.6	10.0

First, the FCC creates and lays out its own vision of the new dynamic role the German *Bundestag* should assume in this process of heightened institutional integration of the EU (BVerfGE 123, 267 [434]). Second, it leaves the government together with its parliamentary majority without any room to manoeuvre at all. Instead, it links the necessary institutional changes in the German national arena favouring the parliament to the ratification of the Lisbon treaty (BVerfGE 123, 267 [270]).[25] On a more general note, however, it seems necessary to highlight the somewhat paradoxical direction of the SoR score in this case. In general, the score measures the restraint of the FCC toward the legislator; the Lisbon ruling, however, deviates from this kind of logic. Here, the judges deliver their decision with the consequence of strengthening the parliament. It is an example of a "forced empowerment" of the legislator by the FCC.[26]

Like the CIIA, the *legislative omission* (OM) is a rare type of ruling employed by the FCC.[27] The data set contains only one case, but a politically important one concerning the Financial Equalization Scheme between the German *Länder* (*Länderfinanzausgleich*, LFA) from the year 1999 (BVerfGE 101, 158 [227]). The LFA has been a contested topic ever since then. The ruling of the judges reflects this history of political power struggle with an attempt to make the voice of reason heard. By introducing the notion of legal principles on which the bargaining process should be based, the judges identify such a constitutional duty in Art. 106 III 4 GG and oblige the legislator to deliberate on such a framework – true to the maxim "first arguing, then bargaining". It characterizes this ruling that large parts of it read as helpful suggestions for a more principled financial equalization scheme by emphasizing, at the same time, the parliamentary leeway for discourse and solutions (BVerfGE 101, 158). Nevertheless, the very fact that the FCC declares a deadline is a clear indication that the Court means business. After a (rather long) period of three years, the parliament must come forward with a framework for the financial equalization scheme, or the LFA becomes unconstitutional (BVerfGE 101, 158 [237]). Because of these legal consequences, which are in effect close to a moderate ruling type of a procedural unconstitutionality, the SoR score of 2.5 seems appropriate.

In contrast to the ruling types of OM and CIIA, *constitutional requirements* (CR) have been quite often employed by the judges, although with ups and downs during the last twenty-five years (Table A.1 in the Appendix). As a ruling type, CRs are technically part of a rejection; however, the FCC uses them as an explicit and binding condition for validating the norm under scrutiny (Schlaich and Korioth 2015, 319–24, Moench 1977, 19–30). This is a judicial technique that usually saves the government time and resources, and it has been used by the FCC mostly in the fields of jurisdiction dealing with social welfare and labour law (41 percent). CRs are generally viewed as status quo "friendly", because they keep laws or legal provisions intact. Nevertheless, they can be used by judges to impose their own reading of the constitution in a way that is practically "patronizing" the legislator. At least potentially, there are a variety of different kinds of CRs; and in fact, the analysis of the FCC reveals some of these differences. It seems that most of the times CRs are used for clarifying a legally important concept and its consequences (e.g. BVerfGE 87, 234). But CRs can also cut deeper and appear then to be more intervening (e.g. BVerfGE 136, 9) and correcting (e.g. BVerfGE 133, 241). All in all, these are nuances which should matter in a qualitative approach but less so in this kind of quantitative-structural approach. Seen in this light, the rather low SoR score (at 2.0) without any refinements or adjustments seems to be appropriate.

On the surface, the ruling type of substantial unconstitutionality due to formal legal principles of the rule of law (FORM) resembles the procedural unconstitutionality (PROC) type.[28] In both cases the FCC operates most of the time like a Court of cassation (Häußler 1994, 102) which restraints itself with respect to the remedy, but unmakes the invalid legal provision *ex tunc*. In addition, neither ruling type dominates the FCC's action. The share of PROCs is only 6 percent of all ruling types, and the amount of FORM cases is even less than that (Table 4.7). However, there are differences between these two ruling types.

- *Motion type*. PROC cases have a focus on election and party conflicts with 53 percent of all PROC (Meyer 2015; Sachs 2016, 86, 128). These matters are typically brought before the Court via politically contested competence conflicts (*Organstreit*), whereas FORM cases reach the FCC via abstract or concrete review procedures with a clear focus on social welfare and finance (tax) matters (Pilz 2015; Schreiber 2014).
- *Legal issues.* Typical complaints of the FORM cases claim a lack of protection of legitimate expectations and are based on the legal principle regulating retroactive effects of legal provisions (e.g. BVerfGE 116, 96; BVerfGE 127, 31). To a lesser extent, these rulings also refer to the principle of legal clarity (e.g. BVerfGE 108, 169; BVerfGE 110, 33). PROC cases are not only more politically contested but are also less homogenous in terms of the legal issues involved. These issues cover the competence conflicts related to federalism (e.g. BVerfGE 111, 226; BVerfGE 112, 226) as much as inter- and intra-institutional conflicts (e.g. BVerfGE 106, 310), procedures of the decision-making process (e.g. BVerfGE 127, 293) and many topics concerning resources of the political actors (e.g. BVerfGE 85, 264; BVerfGE 111, 382).
- *SoR scores.* The different levels of the SoR scores (PROC: 2.47; FORM: 7.56) reflect the different reasons for the unconstitutionality. In the case of FORM, it is the content that is ruled unconstitutional by the FCC and not "only" the process, which is usually the main issue in PROC cases. In addition, the "underperformance" of the PROC rulings is quite striking. Only one of the nineteen rulings (BVerfGE 106, 62) comes close to the theoretical maximum SoR score of 5.0. This is different with the FORM rulings.

The average SoR score of the FORM type is almost as high as the overall average SoR score of the *substantial unconstitutionality* type (SUBST). These ruling types are the driving forces for strong decisions (Figure 4.15). Are there typical

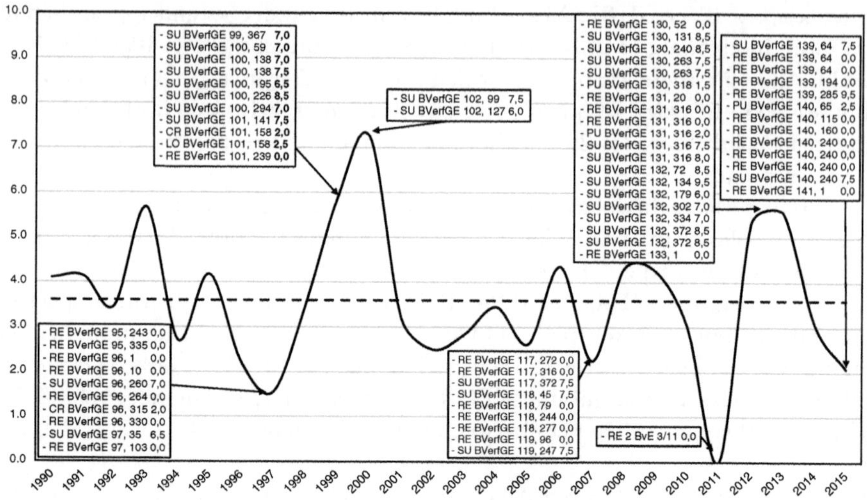

Figure 4.15 Annual peaks and lows in aggregated average strength of rulings (FCC)

fields of jurisdiction/policy in which the FCC has delivered particularly strong rulings? To answer this question, every ruling with a SoR score of ≥ 9.0 is sampled and categorized by the main constitutional articles and key principles that carry the rulings. This sample includes 21 rulings in total, which allows for a systematization of at least three categories.[29]

1 *Welfare state* (8 rulings out of 21): This category contains at minimum a third of the sample, depending, of course, on the scope (e.g. inclusion of labour law and law regulating industrial conflict). It becomes quite clear that one element that potentially strengthens the FCC's rulings is linked to social protection (1b, 1g–h), especially if children are concerned (1d–f).

   a BVerfGE 93, 37 – Co-Determination Act Schleswig–Holstein
   b BVerfGE 99, 165 – Student benefits (BAföG)
   c BVerfGE 99, 300 – Civil service pay
   d BVerfGE 106, 166 – Child benefit
   e BVerfGE 111, 160 – Child benefit
   f BVerfGE 115, 259 – Maternity leave
   g BVerfGE 132, 134 – Asylum Seekers' Benefit Act
   h BVerfGE 134, 1 – Tuition fee

2 *Equality* (5/21): In addition to the idea of social protection, the FCC seems to be willing to develop the concept of equal treatment, especially if minorities are involved (2b, 2d). Another "push-factor" is related to the (lack of) performance of the legislator (2e).

   a BVerfGE 84, 9 – Family name
   b BVerfGE 115, 1 – Transsexual Law

 c BVerfGE 122, 210 – Commuter tax relief payment
 d BVerfGE 133, 59 – Child adoption
 e BVerfGE 139, 285 – Real estate transfer tax

3 *Constitutional Politics* (5/21): Finally, the FCC feels obliged to enter the arena of judicial governance if the Court faces the challenge of setting the course in terms of constitutional politics. This covers a broad range of issues. However, among them the EU (1e) seems to trigger time and again strong rulings by the FCC.

 a BVerfGE 83, 238 – 6. Broadcasting
 b BVerfGE 100, 1 – GDR History of members of Parliament
 c BVerfGE 103, 111 – Scrutiny of election
 d BVerfGE 121, 30 – Broadcasting of Hesse
 e BVerfGE 123, 267 – Lisbon

4.7 Politically important cases

One premise of this study is the analytical distinction between a powerful Court and strong jurisdiction. This distinction has proven to be important in the case of the FCC. To be sure, the Court has the power to issue very hard-hitting decisions affecting the key political actors, and it has certainly used the power to restrain the legislator on many occasions during the last twenty-five years. At the same time, the judges have demonstrated their capacity to restrain themselves and to refrain the FCC from becoming a policymaker at the cost of the legislator. This is an assumption based on quantitative-structural analysis, which, of course, may be in many ways enriched by, for example, case studies or legal analysis.

4.7.1 Design and case selection

So far, these kinds of qualitative approaches have been used to determine the list of landmark decisions. The final step of the present study on the FCC is now an attempt to contribute to the sampling of such a list of landmark or major decisions. Since the research question is focused on the relationship between the FCC and the legislator, the scope is restricted to "politically loaded" cases. In this light, the contribution of this study aims at sampling "politically important" decisions in the sense that the role of political institutions, mainly related to the function of policy-making, is affected – and with that excluding important cases in the field, for example, of civil rights. Defined in this way, the focus on "politically important" decisions relates to the two-fold premise:

- The *first* premise is that strong rulings restrain the legislator. The strength refers, of course, to the index of the SoR. However, to achieve compatibility with other studies, the single unit of this analysis is *case*-based and no longer *ruling*-based. This gap is bridged by transforming the SoR index into a "strength of cases" index (SoC) by using the mean of the SoR scores in those cases with more than one ruling per decision.

- The *second* premise is that the rulings are part of an apparent consensus on their importance within the community of legal scholars as candidates for a list of "politically important" cases decided by the FCC. For the purpose of this second premise, this analysis makes use of three existing samples: a sample of the constitutional court itself (FCC), a list of decisions compiled by Grimm, Kirchhof and Eichberg (GKE), and another compilation by Menzel and Müller-Terpitz (MMT).

Taken together, these three different compilations list altogether 199 "important" cases since 1951, and 113 of the years between 1990 to 2015:[30]

- *FCC.* The constitutional court itself has provided a list of 39 decisions that it considers to be of relevance, mainly with respect to its own history and institutional development (Bundesverfassungsgericht 2016).
- *GKE.* Some time ago, two former judges of the FCC, Grimm and Kirchhof, started a compilation of 121 major decision addressed to students of constitutional law (Grimm et al. 2007). The case selection is based on an attempt to present the "core" of those cases which are necessary for every student to know.[31]
- *MMT.* Among the many valuable study books on German constitutional law, all of which discuss important decisions of the FCC, there is one collection in particular that aims to provide an overview of all the important cases embedded in a short synopsis of the decisions and their merits (Menzel and Müller-Terpitz 2016). This compilation contains 130 cases. In his attempt to "rationalize" the compilation, Müller-Terpitz names the following criteria: the "classics", a balanced overview over the time and of the various fields of constitutional law.

For the purpose of identifying and ranking politically important cases during the time under scrutiny, the focus excludes the individual complaints ($n = 68$). Of the remaining 45 "important" cases, the JUDICON sample has a share of roughly 75 percent.

4.7.2 Ranking

Based on the two-fold premise, Table A.2 presents the list of thirty "politically important" cases. Each case has, at least, one "hit" as being "important" by one of the three compilations "FCC", "GKE" and "MMT". The ranking depends on the SoC, indicating the strength and impact of the FCC's decision.

One-third of these cases (the "top ten") are above the SoR score.[32] These cases match the two criteria of being politically and legally important. In addition, they are the result of a strong FCC ruling. This is different with the cases at the bottom of this ranking. As rejections, they are a result of judicial self-restraint, yet they are in most cases obviously of (high) political relevance, and in addition, they have also been of considerable importance to the legal community. This also holds true, even more so, for the cases (highlighted in grey in Table A.2) that have more than one "hit" of the different compilations. With two exceptions,[33] these cases include rulings with a high SoR score. However, the ranking shows that political importance does not equal high SoC. Instead, strong and weak rulings seemed to be rather balanced.

4.8 Conclusions

Since its implementation in 1951, the FCC has been pursuing institutional interest to make the Court's competences count, especially the instrument of judicial review. Backed by high levels of trust, it has succeeded in becoming one of the most powerful constitutional courts in Europe and beyond. However, as the empirical findings of this chapter show, the FCC has resisted translating its power into judicial activism. No doubt, the FCC has made use of the manifold opportunity structure to render strong rulings, but it has also found time and again the power to restrain itself. Major trends that demonstrate a growing imposition of power on the legislator are not discernible, nor do we find a sequence of strong rulings that relates significantly to a particular political government over a longer period of time. Instead, the judges seem to have established a rather refined way of delivering rulings depending on the constitutional matter, the political situation or a specific policy field (e.g. in the field of welfare policies). Sometimes these rulings can be seen as a hard punch; sometimes they have more the character of issuing a warning; and sometimes it may be even more a matter of policy-making, compensating the ineffectiveness of the political system and their actors. Without doubt, the combination of politically important case rulings together with a high SoC is the fabric out of which judicial activism is made. And there are marks of it within the jurisdiction of the FCC. However, based on the empirical findings of the index, the FCC's rulings, viewed over a period of twenty-five years, lack the structure, consistency and intention that ultimately transform the power-sharing structure of the German political system.

Appendix

Table A.1 Frequency of ruling types II (in %) (FCC)

	CIIA – EX (*n*=0)	*REJ (n=122)*	*OM (n=4)*	*PROC (n=19)*	*CR (n=22)*	*SUB (n=122)*	*CIIA – RES (n=1)*	*Sum (in %)*
1990	–	3.2	0.0	15.8	4.5	6.6	0.0	5.5
1991	–	2.4	0.0	10.5	4.5	4.1	0.0	3.8
1992	–	6.5	0.0	21.1	13.6	6.6	0.0	7.9
1993	–	0.8	0.0	0.0	9.1	5.0	0.0	3.1
1994	–	6.5	0.0	0.0	0.0	3.3	0.0	4.1
1995	–	2.4	0.0	0.0	13.6	4.1	0.0	3.8
1996	–	3.2	0.0	0.0	4.5	1.7	0.0	2.4
1997	–	5.6	0.0	0.0	4.5	1.7	0.0	3.4
1998	–	6.5	25.0	0.0	18.2	5.0	0.0	6.5
1999	–	0.8	25.0	0.0	4.5	8.3	0.0	4.5
2000	–	0.0	0.0	0.0	0.0	1.7	0.0	0.7
2001	–	4.8	0.0	0.0	0.0	3.3	0.0	3.4
2002	–	5.6	0.0	10.5	0.0	1.7	0.0	3.8
2003	–	2.4	25.0	5.3	0.0	0.8	0.0	2.1
2004	–	3.2	0.0	10.5	0.0	3.3	0.0	3.4
2005	–	3.2	0.0	5.3	4.5	1.7	0.0	2.7
2006	–	2.4	25.0	0.0	0.0	2.5	0.0	2.4
2007	–	5.6	0.0	0.0	0.0	2.5	0.0	3.4
2008	–	4.8	0.0	0.0	0.0	5.8	0.0	4.5
2009	–	2.4	0.0	0.0	0.0	1.7	100.0	2.1
2010	–	5.6	0.0	5.3	9.1	5.0	0.0	5.5
2011	–	0.8	0.0	0.0	0.0	0.0	0.0	0.3
2012	–	4.0	0.0	10.5	0.0	10.7	0.0	6.9
2013	–	1.6	0.0	0.0	4.5	4.1	0.0	2.7
2014	–	8.1	0.0	0.0	4.5	5.0	0.0	5.8
2015	–	7.3	0.0	5.3	0.0	4.1	0.0	5.2
Sum (in %)	–	**100.0**	**100.0**	**100.0**	**100.0**	**100.0**	**100.0**	**100.0**

Table A.2 Ranking of "politically important" cases (FCC)

	BVerfGE	*Title*	*Hits*	*SoC*
1.	121, 30	Media Participation	1	9.0
2.	125, 175	Hartz IV	1	8.5
3.	138, 136	Inheritance Tax	1	8.0
4.	83, 37	Foreigner's Suffrage	2	7.5
5.	88, 87	Transsexuals	2	7.5
6.	135, 259	European Elections	1	7.5
7.	88, 203	Induced Abortion II	1	5.8
8.	123, 267	Lisbon	2	5.0
9.	101, 158	Financial Equalization Scheme IV	1	4.5

(continued)

Table A.2 Continued

	BVerfGE	*Title*	*Hits*	*SoC*
10.	92, 26	Seamen Register	2	3.8
11.	83, 238	6th Broad Casting Decision	1	3.7
12.	82, 60	Tax Exempt Margin of Subsistence	2	3.5
13.	93, 37	Codetermination Law of Schleswig–Holstein	1	3.3
14.	136, 9	Interstate Treaty on ZDF	1	3.2
15.	85, 264	Party Finance V	2	3.0
16.	106, 310	Immigration Law	2	3.0
17.	112, 226	Tuition Fees	1	2.5
18.	2BvL 17/09	Judge's Salary	1	2.5
19.	140, 65	Childcare Supplement	1	2.5
20.	82, 322	All-German Election	1	2.2
21.	112, 118	Conciliation Committee	1	2.0
22.	84, 304	PDS	1	1.5
23.	92, 365	Short-Term Allowance	2	1.0
24.	87, 1	Rubble Women	1	0.0
25.	105, 313	Civil Partnership Law	3	0.0
26.	95, 335	Overhang Seats III	1	0.0
27.	105, 197	Party Donations Inquiry Commission	1	0.0
28.	132, 195	European Stability Mechanism	1	0.0
29.	137, 185	Arms Sales	1	0.0
30.	140, 160	Libya Intervention	1	0.0

Notes

1 See the first decision by the Second Senate on 9 September 1951 (2 BvQ 1/51 – BVerfGE 1, 1).

2 The most visible examples are Spain (Pagio 2016), Portugal (Amaral and Pereira 2016), South Africa (Petersen 2015), South Korea (Kokott 1999) and, in some important ways, also the Czech Republic and Hungary (see Sipulova and Pócza et al. in this volume). For more detailed country reports, see: Battis et al. (1990), Starck and Weber (1986), Bogdandy et al. (2016) and Sólyom (2016). Moreover, the constitutional courts of the *Bundesländer* in East Germany reflect to a large degree the FCC (Reutter 2017, 5). As for the organizational structure, however, the unified one-chamber model is much more common than the two-Senate model of the FCC (Hönnige 2008, 134; Wahl 2015).

3 As for the *Bundestag*, the election of the constitutional judges had been delegated to a special committee of the parliament. This practice has been the subject of criticism for years, before it was ultimately changed by a recent reform in 2015. Now the judges are elected by the members of the *Bundestag* at the plenary joint session.

4 This is different with constitutional courts of the *Bundesländer*. Here the judges are appointed to an honorary office; and in some cases not only trained lawyers but also legal laymen are part of the bench (Reutter 2017).

5 As for the Adenauer era (Lembcke 2015, 231), some of the most prominent examples are BVerfGE 1, 281 – Rearmament, BVerfGE 12, 205 (1st Broadcasting Decision), BVerfGE 6, 309 (*Reichskonkordat*) and BVerfGE 8, 51 (Financing of Political Parties).

During Brandt's chancellorship (Grigoleit 2015, 245), it was among other topics BVerfGE 36, 1 (The Basic Treaty), BVerfGE 35, 79 (University Decision).

6 Consider only the (in)famous word of the "eight a***holes" coming from Brandt's kitchen cabinet (see, for example, Der Spiegel 10/1975, 62–67).

7 These findings of the ALLBUS polls (GESIS 2016) has been confirmed in two polls by infratest dimap on the trust in the media in general (Infratest 2016) and on trust in the media coverage of the Ukraine conflict (Infratest 2014).

8 In accordance with this assessment, it should come as no surprise that the decisions of the FCC are generally studied by many office holders in a scrupulous way. What matters is not restricted to the operative part of a ruling laying out the binding consequences of a decision (*Tenor*), but also that the various arguments are usually treated as legally relevant, even if these parts belong to the *obiter dicta* of the Court. In a similar fashion the headnotes (*Leitsätze*) of the FCC's rulings have become a subject of interest. They are perceived as judicial instruments signalling the main message of the FCC.

9 According to a public opinion poll by *Institut für Demoskopie Allensbach* (2014), 91 percent of respondents answered that they believe or even strongly believe in the *Grundgesetz*.

10 The type of average substantive unconstitutionality rulings is, empirically speaking, not relevant.

11 In terms of rulings stating qualitative partial unconstitutionality: pro futuro 20 percent and broad remedy 40 percent; in the case of complete unconstitutionality: pro futuro 21 percent, broad remedy 47 percent.

12 As for the interpretation power of the FCC, see Lembcke (2007), Jestaedt et al. (2011) and Hailbronner (2014).

13 This thesis deserves further research by contrasting the FCC's rulings of this research period with the ones of the Adenauer era. In a similar fashion, this might also be a starting point for an explanation of the relatively high number of constitutional requirements that have been applied by the judges from 1990 to 1999 (about 75 percent of all constitutional requirements of the time period 1990–2015 have been declared in these nine years. See Table A.1 in the Appendix).

14 To put things into perspective, it should be taken into consideration that the high peaks and sharp drops of this "line of strength" (Figure 4.8) are influenced by the relatively low number of rulings (Figure 4.5).

15 The data set covers the FCC's rulings only until 2015.

16 The highest peak with 7.1 (2010) was during the centre-right coalition with the Liberal Party (FDP).

17 The absolute numbers refer to the "votes", defined as the individual participation of a judge in a decision (of the Senate) and its rulings.

18 There are exceptions, but these exceptions themselves do not amount to a sufficient data set. In recent years there have been attempts trying to overcome this lack of data: Hönnige (2006); Brouard and Hönnige (2017).

19 For an overview of the dissenting opinions, see Lembcke (2007, 247). The methodological approach suggested by Jäger (1987) is noteworthy.

20 For dissenting opinions in the context of integration (and disintegration), see Lembcke (2007, 379).

21 The documented voting record underlines the fact that the collection of individual data is difficult in the case of the FCC. Of the cases in the data set, 68 percent are without any documentation of this kind. Another approach for evaluating the process of comprehensive deliberation at the Court involves measuring the amount of time that each Senate takes to reach a conclusion and ultimately to render a decision.

22 The contestation index (quotient of the division minority vote/majority per ruling) supports this observation. This index displays the average of the votes per ruling (in cases in which there is more than one vote; N = 82): According to this index, the quota of the consensus is even higher (50 percent).

23 This is the rare case of a once formal norm turned into an informal but still powerful one. Dissenting opinions were introduced in 1971 (Table 4.1) after some lengthy discussions, among others at the German Legal Association's Annual Meeting in Nuremburg in 1968 (Lembcke 2007, 134). Before that, the publication of dissenting opinions was widely viewed (including by judges of the FCC) as endangering the Court's authority. Seen in this light, the consensus of the judges toward the public was the official norm, supported by the idea of "unity" – a unified jurisdiction as an important condition of the FCC's authority. This idea has changed and transformed itself into a more pluralist understanding of FCC in general. However, the consensus orientation is still held to be of high importance among the judges of the FCC, but today it is much more related to the notion of integration inside the Court than to the outside appearance as an authoritative institution in the public realm.

24 See Fn 9 in Chapter 2.

25 See Möller and Limpert (2013) and Wimmel (2014). Related legislation: Gesetz über die Zusammenarbeit von Bundesregierung und Deutschem Bundestag in Angelegenheiten der Europäischen Union (EUZBBG) from 4 July 2013 (BGBl. I S. 2170); Gesetz über die Zusammenarbeit von Bund und Ländern in Angelegenheiten der Europäischen Union (EUZBLG) from 12. March 1993 (BGBl. I S. 313), last changed by Art. 1 of the law from 22 September 2009 (BGBl. I S. 3031).

26 This deviation, at least in part, from the general logic of the research focus might be taken as an opportunity to rethink the SoR coding with cases like the Lisbon decision.

27 For a detailed account of the dogmatic context and the consequences, see the article by a former FCC judge: Rupp-von Brünneck (1970).

28 On the difference between procedural unconstitutionality and substantive unconstitutionality based on formal grounds, see Fn 9 in Chapter 2.

29 Three rulings do not fit into any of these categories: BVerfGE 91, 1; BVerfGE 135, 1; BVerfGE 138, 1.

30 After 1991, double/multiple entries have been deleted.

31 The GKE sample is restricted by the publication date 2007; the FCC covers only 39 decisions in toto.

32 In general, the SoR is distinctively higher compared to the SoC score due to the transformation of the ruling scores into case scores. Take the example of the Lisbon case, which contains two rulings: one ruling displays the SoR score 10, the other the score 0. Both results amount to an SoC score of 5.

33 BVerfGE 105, 313 and 92, 365.

References

Alizivatos, Nicos. 1995. "Judges as Veto Players". In *Parliaments and Majority Rule in Western Europe*, edited by Herbert Döring, 556–589. Frankfurt/New York: Campus/St Martin's.

Amaral, Maria L. Mar, and Ravi Afonso Pereira. 2016. "Das portugiesische Verfassungsgericht" ["The Portuguese Constitutional Court"]. In *Ius Publicum Europaeum, Vol. VI: Verfassungsgerichtsbarkeit in Europa* [*Ius Publicum Europaeum, Vol. VI: Constitutional Jurisdiction in Europe*], edited by Armin von Bogdandy, Michael Huber and Christoph Grabenwarter, 519–572. Heidelberg: C.F. Müller.

Battis, Ulrich, Ernst Gottfried Mahrenholz, and Dimitris Tsatsos. 1990. *Das Grundgesetz im internationalen Wirkungszusammenhang der Verfassungen: 40 Jahre Grundgesetz. Schriften zum öffentlichen Recht* [*The Grundgesetz in the Context of International Interrelationship of Constitutions: The Grundgesetz's 40th Anniversary. Series on Public Law*]. Berlin: Duncker und Humblot.

Beyme, Klaus von. 2017. *Das politische System der Bundesrepublik Deutschland: Eine Einführung* [*The Political System of the Federal Republic of Germany: An Introduction*]. 12th ed., Wiesbaden: Springer-Verlag.

Bogdandy, Armin von, Michael Huber and Christoph Grabenwarter, eds. 2016. *Ius Publicum Europaeum, Vol. VI: Verfassungsgerichtsbarkeit in Europa* [*Ius Publicum Europaeum, Vol. VI: constitutional jurisdiction in Europe*]. Heidelberg: C.F. Müller.

Brouard, Sylvain, and Christoph Hönnige. 2017. "Constitutional Courts as Veto Players: Lessons from the United States, France and Germany". *European Journal of Political Research* 56 (3): 529–552.

Bundesverfassungsgericht. 2016. "Meilensteine in der Geschichte des Bundesverfassungsgerichts" ["Landmarks in the History of the Federal Constitutional Court"]. Bundesverfassungsgericht. Accessed September 23. www.bundesverfassungsgericht.de/DE/Das-Gericht/Geschichte-des-Bundesverfassungsgerichts/geschichte-des-bundesverfassungsgerichts.html.

Farahat, Anuscheh. 2016. "Das Bundesverfassungsgericht" ["The Federal Constitutional Court"]. In *Ius Publicum Europaeum, Vol. VI: Verfassungsgerichtsbarkeit in Europa* [*Ius Publicum Europaeum, Vol. VI: Constitutional Jurisdiction in Europe*], edited by Armin von Bogdandy, Michael Huber and Christoph Grabenwarter, 81–158. Heidelberg: C.F. Müller.

Garoupa, Nuno, and Tom Ginsburg 2015. *Judicial Reputation: A Comparative Theory.* Chicago: University of Chicago Press.

GESIS – Leibniz-Institut für Sozialwissentschaften. 2016. *Allgemeine Bevölkerungsumfrage der Sozialwissenschaften ALLBUS – Kumulation 1980–2014* [*Cumulated German General Social Survey 1980–2014*]. ZA4582 Data file Version 1.1.0. Cologne: GESIS Datenarchiv. doi:10.4232/1.12646.

Green, Craig. 2009. "An Intellectual History of Judicial Activism". *Emory Law Journal* 58 (5): 1195–1263.

Grigoleit, Klaus Joachim. 2015. "Bundesverfassungsgericht und sozialliberale Koalition unter Willy Brandt" ["The Federal Constitutional Court and the Social–Liberal Coalition under Willy Brandt"]. In *Handbuch Bundesverfassungsgericht im politischen System* [*Handbook Federal Constitutional Court in the Political System*], edited by Robert Chr. van Ooyen and Martin H. W. Möllers, 245–259. 2nd edition, Wiesbaden: Springer VS.

Grimm, Dieter, Paul Kirchhof, and Michael Eichberger. 2007. *Entscheidungen des Bundesverfassungsgerichts – Studienauswahl* [*Decisions of the Federal Constitutional Court – Case Selection for Studies*]. 3rd edition, Tübingen: Mohr Siebeck.

Hailbronner, Michaela. 2014. "Rethinking the Rise of the German Constitutional Court: From Anti-Nazism to Value Formalism". *International Journal for Constitutional Law* 12 (3): 626–649.

Häußler, Richard. 1994. *Der Konflikt zwischen Bundesverfassungsgericht und politischer Führung: ein Beitrag zu Geschichte und Rechtsstellung des Bundesverfassungsgerichts* [*The Conflict between the Federal Constitutional Court and the Political Leadership: A Contribution to the History and Legal Position of the Federal Constitutional Court*]. Berlin: Duncker & Humblot.

Hönnige, Christoph. 2006. "Die Entscheidungen von Verfassungsgerichten – ein Spiegel ihrer Zusammensetzung?" ["Constitutional Courts' Decisions – A Mirror of the Courts' Composition?"] In *Jahrbuch für Handlungs- und Entscheidungstheorie* [*Yearbook for*

Action and Decision Theory], edited by Thomas Bräuninger and Joachim Behnke, 179–214. Vol. 4., Wiesbaden: VS.

Hönnige, Christoph. 2008. *Verfassungsgericht, Regierung und Opposition: Die vergleichende Analyse eines Spannungsdreiecks* [*Constitutional Court, Government and Opposition. Comparative Analysis of a Triangle of Tension*]. Wiesbaden: Springer-Verlag.

Infratest dimap. 2014. Vertrauen in Medien-Berichterstattung über den Ukraine-Konflikt. Eine Studie von infratest dimap für das Medienmagazin ZAPP. Tabellarische Übersichten [Credibility of the Media Coverage of the Ukraine Conflict. A Study by infratest dimap on Behalf of the Media Magazine ZAPP]. https://www.ndr.de/fernsehen/sendungen/zapp/inffratest102.pdf (accessed 15 June 2017).

Infratest dimap. 2016. Glaubwürdigkeit der Medien. Eine Studie im Auftrag des Westdeutschen Rundfunks. December 2016 [Credibility of the Media. A Study on Behalf of the Public-Broadcast Service Westdeutsche Rundfunk. December 2016]. https://www1.wdr.de/unternehmen/der-wdr/unternehmen/studie-glaubwuerdigkeit-download-100.pdf (accessed 15 June 2017).

Institut für Demoskopie Allensbach. 2014. *Das Grundgesetz als eine der größten Errungenschaften der Bundesrepublik* [*The Grundgesetz as One of the Greatest Accomplishments of the Federal Republic*]. https://www.ifd-allensbach.de/uploads/tx_reportsndocs/PD_2014_09.pdf (accessed 30 August 2018).

Jäger, York. 1987. "Entscheidungsverhalten und Hintergrundfaktoren der Bundesverfassungsrichter" ["Decision Behaviour and Background Factors of the Federal Constitutional Court Judges"]. *Zeitschrift für Rechtspolitik* [*Journal of Legal Policy]* 20: 360–363.

Jestaedt, Matthias, Oliver Lepsius, Christoph Möllers and Christoph Schönberger. 2011. *Das entgrenzte Gericht: Eine kritische Bilanz nach sechzig Jahren Bundesverfassungsgericht.* [*The Unbounded Court: Striking a Critical Balance of 60 Years of the Federal Constitutional Court.*] Berlin: Suhrkamp.

Kelemen, Katalin. 2018. *Judicial Dissent in European Constitutional Courts: A Comparative and Legal Perspective.* Abingdon /New York: Routledge.

Kokott, Juliane. 1999. "From Reception and Transplantation to Convergence of Constitutional Models in the Age of Globalization". In *Constitutionalism, Universalism and Democracy: A Comparative Analysis*, edited by Christian Starck, 71–134. Baden-Baden: Nomos.

Lamprecht, Rolf. 2011. *Ich gehe bis nach Karlsruhe: Eine Geschichte des Bundesverfassungsgerichts* [*I Will Go All the Way to Karlsruhe: A History of the Federal Constitutional Court*]. München: DVA.

Lembcke, Oliver W. 2006. *Über das Ansehen des Bundesverfassungsgerichts. Ansichten und Meinungen in der Öffentlichkeit 1951–2001* [*On the Reputation of the Federal Constitutional Court. Views and Opinions in the Public 1951–2001*]. Berlin: BWV.

Lembcke, Oliver W. 2007. *Hüter der Verfassung: Eine institutionentheoretische Studie zur Autorität des Bundesverfassungsgerichts* [*Guardian of the Constitution: A Study of the Federal Constitutional Court's Authority Based on Institutional Theory*]. Tübingen: Mohr Siebeck.

Lembcke, Oliver W. 2013. "Autorität der Verfassungsgerichtsbarkeit – eine Skizze in vergleichender Absicht" ["Authority of the Constitutional Court – A Framework for Analysis"]. In *Politik des Verfassungsrechts. Interdisziplinäre und vergleichende Perspektiven auf die Rolle und Funktion von Verfassungsgerichten*, edited by Christian Boulanger and Michael Wrase, 34–62. Baden-Baden: Nomos.

Lembcke, Oliver W. 2015. "Das Bundesverfassungsgericht und die Regierung Adenauer – vom Streit um den Status zur Anerkennung der Autorität" ["The Federal Constitutional Court and the Adenauer Administration – From the Dispute Over Status to the

Recognition of Authority"]. In *Handbuch Bundesverfassungsgericht im politischen System* [*Handbook Federal Constitutional Court in the Political System*], edited by Robert Chr. van Ooyen and Martin H. W. Möllers, 231–243. 2nd edition, Wiesbaden: Springer VS.

Lijphart, Arendt. 2012. *Patterns of Democracy. Government Forms and Performance in Thirty-Six Countries.* 2nd edition, New Haven/London: Yale University Press.

Majone, Giandomenico. 2001. "Two Logics of Delegation: Agency and Fiduciary Relations in EU Governance". *European Union Politics* 2 (1): 103–122.

March, James G., and Johan P. Olsen. 2006. "The Logic of Appropriateness". In *The Oxford Handbook of Public Policy*, edited by Robert E. Goodin, Michael Moran and Martin Rein, 689–708. Oxford: Oxford University Press.

Menzel Jörg, and Ralf Müller-Terpitz. 2016. *Verfassungsrechtsprechung* [*Constitutional Jurisprudence*]. 3rd edition, Tübingen: Mohr Siebeck.

Meyer, Hans. 2015. "Bundesverfassungsgericht und Wahlrecht" ["Federal Constitutional Court and Electoral Law"]. In *Handbuch Bundesverfassungsgericht im politischen System* [*Handbook Federal Constitutional Court in the Political System*], edited by Robert Chr. van Ooyen and Martin H. W. Möllers, 511–524. 2nd edition, Wiesbaden: Springer VS.

Moench, Christoph. 1977. *Verfassungswidriges Gesetz und Normenkontrolle – Die Problematik der verfassungsrechtlichen Sanktion, dargestellt anhand der Rechtsprechung des Bundesverfassungsgerichts* [*Unconstitutional Law and Judicial Review – The Issue of Constitutional Sanction, Illustrated with the Federal Constitutional Court's Jurisprudence*]. Baden-Baden: Nomos.

Möller, Franz, and Martin Limpert. 2013. "Die Parlamentarisierung der politischen Willensbildung in europäischen Angelegenheiten" ["The Parliamentarization of Political Decision-Making in European Affairs"]. *Zeitschrift für Gesetzgebung* [*Journal of Legislation*] 28 (1): 44–59.

Pagio, Juan Luis Requejo. 2016. "Das spanische Verfassungsgericht" ["The Spanish Constitutional Court"]. In *Ius Publicum Europaeum, Vol. VI: Verfassungsgerichtsbarkeit in Europa* [*Ius Publicum Europaeum, Vol. VI: Constitutional Jurisdiction in Europe*], edited by Armin von Bogdandy, Michael Huber and Christoph Grabenwarter, 639–704. Heidelberg: C.F. Müller.

Petersen, Niels. 2015. *Verhältnismäßigkeit als Rationalitätskontrolle: Eine rechtsempirische Studie verfassungsrechtlicher Rechtsprechung zu den Freiheitsgrundrechten* [*Proportionality as Control of Rationality: An Empirical Study of Constitutional Jurisprudence Concerning Civil and Political Rights*]. Tübingen: Mohr Siebeck.

Pilz, Frank. 2015. "Das Bundesverfassungsgericht und der Sozialstaat" ["The Federal Constitutional Court and the Welfare State"]. In *Handbuch Bundesverfassungsgericht im politischen System* [*Handbook Federal Constitutional Court in the Political System*], edited by Robert Chr. van Ooyen and Martin H. W. Möllers, 713–734. 2nd edition, Wiesbaden: Springer VS.

Reutter, Werner, ed. 2017. *Landesverfassungsgerichte: Entwicklung – Aufbau – Funktionen* [*Constitutional Courts of the Bundesländer: Development – Design – Functions*]. Wiesbaden: Springer VS.

Rode, Karlheinz. 2012. *Verfassungsidentität und Ewigkeitsgarantie – Anmerkungen zu einem Mythos der deutschen Staatsrechtslehre* [*Constitutional Identity and Guarantee of Perpetuity – Comments on a Myth of German Constitutional Law Doctrine*]. Frankfurt am Main: Lang.

Rupp-von Brünneck, Wiltraut. 1970. "Darf das Bundesverfassungsgericht an den Gesetzgeber appellieren?" ["Is the Federal Constitutional Court Allowed to Appeal to the Legislature?"] In *Festschrift für Gebhard Müller*, edited by Theo Ritterspach, 355–378. Tübingen: Mohr.

Sachs, Michael. 2016. *Verfassungsprozessrecht* [*Constitutional Procedural Law*]. 4. Aufl., Tübingen: Mohr Siebeck.

Schlaich, Klaus, and Stefan Korioth. 2015. *Das Bundesverfassungsgericht – Stellung, Verfahren, Entscheidungen.* [*The Federal Constitutional Court – Position, procedures, decisions*] München: C.H. Beck.

Schreiber, Werner. 2014. *Das Sozialstaatsprinzip des Grundgesetzes in der Praxis der Rechtsprechung* [*The Welfare State Principle of the Grundgesetz in the Jurisprudence's Practice*]. Berlin: Duncker & Humblot.

Sólyom, László. 2016. "Das ungarische Verfassungsgericht" ["The Hungarian Constitutional Court"]. In *Ius Publicum Europaeum, Vol. VI: Verfassungsgerichtsbarkeit in Europa* [*Ius Publicum Europaeum, Vol. VI: Constitutional Jurisdiction in Europe*], edited by Armin von Bogdandy, Michael Huber and Christoph Grabenwarter, 705–794. Heidelberg: C.F. Müller.

Starck, Christian and Albrecht Weber, eds. 1986. *Verfassungsgerichtsbarkeit in Westeuropa, Teilband I: Berichte* [*Constitutional Jurisdiction in West Europe, Vol. 1: Reports*]. Baden-Baden: Nomos.

Stone Sweet, Alec. 2007. "The Juridical Coup d'État and the Problem of Authority". *German Law Journal* 8 (10): 915–928.

Vorländer, Hans. 1989. "Verfassungsverehrung in Amerika. Zum konstitutionellen Symbolismus in den USA" ["Constitutional Worship in America. On Constitutional Symbolism in the USA"]. *Amerikastudien* [*American Studies*] 34: 69–82.

Wahl, Rainer. 2015. "Das Bundesverfassungsgericht im europäischen und internationalen Umfeld" ["The Federal Constitutional Court in the European and International Context"]. In *Handbuch Bundesverfassungsgericht im politischen System* [*Handbook Federal Constitutional Court in the Political System*], edited by Robert Chr. van Ooyen and Martin H. W. Möllers, 825–844. 2nd edition, Wiesbaden: Springer VS.

Wimmel, Andreas. 2014. "Die Mitwirkungsrechte des Bundestages in der Euro-Krise. Eine machtpolitische Analyse" ["The Bundestag's Participation Rights in the Euro Crisis. An Analysis of Political Power"]. *Zeitschrift für Staats- und Europawissenschaften* [*Journal of State and European Studies*] 12 (4): 484–506.

Wöhrmann, Gotthard. 1987. "Reformvorschläge zum Verfahren des Bundesverfassungsgerichtes" ["Reform Proposals for the Federal Constitutional Court's Procedure"]. In *Festschrift für Wolfgang Zeidler*, edited by Walther Fürst, Roman Herzog and Dieter C. Umbach, 1343–1360. Berlin/New York: de Gruyter.

Zuck, Rüdiger. 2015. "Die Wissenschaftlichen Mitarbeiter des Bundesverfassungsgerichtes" ["The Constitutional Court's Scientific Staff"]. In *Handbuch Bundesverfassungsgericht im politischen System* [*Handbook Federal Constitutional Court in the Political System*], edited by Robert Chr. van Ooyen and Martin H. W. Möllers, 443–457. 2nd edition, Wiesbaden: Springer.

5 The Hungarian Constitutional Court

A constructive partner in constitutional dialogue

Kálmán Pócza, Gábor Dobos and Attila Gyulai

5.1 Introduction

Although the Hungarian Constitutional Court (HCC) was only the second established in the CEE region after the democratic transformation, its Polish predecessor suffered some deficiencies concerning its legitimacy. In contrast to Poland, where constitutional supremacy and judicial review had historical precedents, constitutional review was completely missing from the Hungarian constitutional tradition. Furthermore, in contrast to the Polish Constitutional Tribunal, which was established as early as 1986 when the fall of Communism was certainly not on the horizon, the HCC was an outcome of roundtable negotiations on democratic transition held in 1989 (Sadurski 2002; Luchterhandt et al. 2007; Sadurski [2008] 2014). This means that, in effect, the HCC was the first constitutional court established with almost complete democratic legitimacy during a democratic transformation process.[1]

5.2 Origins and structure of the Hungarian Constitutional Court

5.2.1 Origins of the Court

The democratic legitimacy of the Hungarian Constitutional Court, however, was only almost complete. Since the Hungarian democratic transformation embraced not a decade, as its Polish counterpart, but only one year, establishment of the HCC had a less troublesome heritage rooted in the Communist past. The National Round Table (*Nemzeti Kerekasztal*, NKA) negotiations between the Communist leaders and the democratic opposition began in June 1989 and showed a dynamic nobody expected at the beginning of the transformation process. At the beginning, it aimed only to elaborate the most important rules of the first democratic elections, leaving all important questions to be resolved for the first democratically elected parliament.[2] Nevertheless, at the end of the process, in October 1989, the old Communist constitution from 1949 was so heavily amended that, according to the contemporary *bonmot*, it was only the name of the capital of Hungary which had not been changed. Establishing a constitutional court was not a priority of the democratic opposition – at least not at the beginning of the transformation process. It was initiated rather by the Communist leaders, mainly to have another institution into which the Communist elite could parachute their comrades.[3] Due to the special dynamics of the negotiations in the summer of 1989, the democratic opposition was getting more and more willing to accept the establishment of a constitutional court, but only on condition that (1) the Court's decisions should be final, so not subject to the possibility of being overridden by the parliament, (2) the scope of the potential applicants should be as wide as possible (introduction of the so-called *actio popularis*) and (3) election of the 15 judges should occur in a staggered way (first five judges elected by the last Communist parliament, but based on an agreement with the democratic opposition; the next five in the first and the last five in the second parliamentary term after the democratic transformation) (Bozóki 2002, 107–191). Although the first judges of the HCC were elected by the last Communist parliament, two former ordinary judges were nominated by the democratic opposition, two law professors by the Hungarian Socialist Workers' Party (*Magyar Szocialista Munkáspárt*, MSZMP) and one in consensus of the two sides.

5.2.2 *Structure of the Court*

The HCC with five judges on its benches started to work on 1 January 1990, four months before the first democratic elections took place and approximately half a year before the first democratic parliament was summoned. In the summer of 1990, five more judges were elected by the parliament to the HCC, which sat with 9–10 judges from then on (Brunner 2000, 65). Originally the last five judges should have been elected by the second parliament after the democratic transformation process, but due to the lack of agreement about candidates, the missing members were never elected. Filling the empty chairs in the HCC caused serious problems later as well (the HCC was continuously on the brink of its quorum) since double-nomination (one right-wing and one left-wing candidate) became the informal standard. Thus, filling the vacant seats often took several months, sometimes directly risking the functioning of the Court. Election of the judges was a highly politicized process, since it was the unicameral parliament which nominated and elected them with a two-thirds majority (Körösényi et al. 2009, 34). Prior to the election procedure at the plenary session of parliament, an *ad hoc* committee was established with one representative of each parliamentary party. It was essential for the candidates to be backed by a two-thirds majority, not only in the plenary session but also in this *ad hoc* committee, which implied that without the consent of the opposition parties no successful election was conceivable until 2010. Consequently, this committee served as a formal instance and as a barrier even for governments backed by a two-thirds majority in the plenary session (e.g. between 1994 and 1998). Since the *ad hoc* committee had to approve the candidates, opposition parties could prevent the election of judges by simply not approving the candidates in the *ad hoc* commission. After 2010, the transformation of this *ad hoc* committee based on parity to an *ad hoc* committee based on proportional representation of parliamentary parties opened the way for one-party candidates, since the right-wing Fidesz-KDNP government had a two-thirds majority in parliament from 2010 to 2015 (Sonnevend et al. 2015, 44).

Between 1990 and 2010, judges were elected for a term of nine years, renewable once (which certainly did not serve their independence). Until 2012, the President of the HCC was elected by the HCC itself for three years, but this mandate was renewable several times (Schwartz 2000, 78). Since the president of the HCC designated the "reporter judge" (who prepared the first draft of the decision), internal election of the President increased the autonomy of the Court – at least until 2012, when the rules of the election of the President were changed, after which parliament has elected the president of the HCC.

The structure of the HCC between 1990 and 2010 was a quite simple one. Although there had always been chambers of three judges, most important decisions were exclusively taken by the full bench. There were no senates or chambers of equal rank to the full bench. There were no specific rules about decision-making, meaning that the Court made its decisions by a majority of the judges. According to the Act on the Constitutional Court of 1989, a law on the rules of procedures of the HCC should have been adopted by the parliament, which was continuously delayed until 2001, when the HCC adopted its own standing orders. This means that from 1990 to 2001, the HCC worked in a quite non-transparent way: general rules were determined by the 1989 constitution and the Act of HCC from 1989, but specific rules regarding procedures were generated (but officially never published!) through the praxis of the Court (Brunner 2000, 65).

As for the competencies or powers of the HCC, all forms of constitutional review but the "real" constitutional complaint were introduced in 1989 (Dezső et al. 2010, 184). *A priori* and *a posteriori* norm control, constitutional complaint against the law applied by ordinary courts in concrete cases and constitutional interpretation *in abstracto*, but no constitutional complaint against the decision of ordinary courts could be filed (until 2012, when the respective rules were changed).[4] This implied, for example, that real conflicts between ordinary courts and the HCC were very rare. Since the *actio popularis*, the right of all citizens to submit a petition to the Court without the requirement of having been affected directly by the challenged law, guaranteed that all critical issues landed on the Court's table, and it was almost irrelevant who else was specifically allowed to submit a petition to the Court (Dupré 2003, 37). All relevant political issues ended up being reviewed by the HCC. It is, however, of utmost importance that the Secretary General of the HCC filtered the petitions with respect to their formal adequacy. This kind of preselection ensured that the HCC, in contrast to its Romanian or Polish counterparts, would not have to struggle with formally inadequate petitions or with the bulk of petitions which ought to be simply refused on formal grounds. Some public hearings took place in the first months of its functioning, but otherwise the Court dealt in private with the issues on the table.

5.2.3 Changes after 2010

The Court functioned in this way until 2010, when political circumstances and legal regulations concerning its functioning changed dramatically.[5] After the landslide victory of Fidesz-KDNP, the party achieved a two-thirds constitutional majority in parliament. In one of the first sessions of the new parliament, the rules for the election of judges were changed (as delineated above). In the next two years, an intense clash between the constitutional majority and the HCC determined the fate of the Court. Heavy measures were deployed on both sides (constitutional amendments vs. threatening to review the unconstitutionality of constitutional amendments), which ended up with court-packing, cutting its competence and constraining its autonomy. Since the summer of 2010 the HCC has been deprived of its competence to review legislation concerning public finances, except when they are related to human dignity, the protection of personal data, Hungarian citizenship, or the freedom of conscience and religion. This shrinking of competences was incorporated into the new Fundamental Law of Hungary, which has been in force since 1 January 2012. Further changes concerned the structure of the HCC: since 2012 the HCC has consisted of 15 judges, elected by a two-thirds majority of parliament for 12 years, but without the possibility of renewing the term. On the other hand, the autonomy of the HCC has also been constrained to some extent, since the president of the new HCC is no longer elected by the members of the Court but by parliament. The range of potential applicants has been increased concerning *a priori* abstract review,[6] but drastically reduced with respect to *a posteriori* abstract review: while the institution of *actio popularis* has been abolished, the range of potential applicants has been restricted to the government, 25 percent of the MPs, the President of the Supreme Court, the Prosecutor General and the ombudsman. While nobody urged the first change, some scholars, and even the former president of the HCC, argued that abolishing the *actio popularis* (and introducing the real constitutional complaint) could serve the depoliticization of the HCC (Bragyova 2010, 59–61; Paczolay 2010, 44).

As for the functioning of the HCC, one critical juncture was the 2010 parliamentary election and the staggered election of several new judges (backed exclusively by the right-wing majority). This reshuffle of the Court led to a thin majority of the judges nominated by the right-wing parties as early as the autumn of 2010 (four judges nominated by the left-wing parties, one in consensus and five nominated by the right-wing parties). The enlarged HCC from 1 January 2012 consisted of 15 judges with a clear right-wing majority (four left-wing nominations, one consensus and ten right-wing judges) but the "old" judges elected in pairs before 2010, i.e. in some kind of compromise, were still in majority (eight to seven). It was following a new wave of elections of judges in the spring of 2013 when new judges elected only by the right-wing majority after 2010 formed the majority (eight to seven) in the Court.[7] For several reasons, many commentators argue that this was the crucial point for the Court: from 2010 until May 2013 the Court struggled with and resisted the constitutional majority in several ways, while deference (with several dissenting opinions) became the dominant behavioural model of the Court's majority after May 2013.[8]

5.3 General characteristics: a Court of outstanding performance?

Taking a look at the HCC's 25 years of functioning from a bird's-eye perspective, some myths about the HCC, and especially the Sólyom presidency, should be dispelled, while other topoi will be reinforced by findings of the present country study. In the legal scholarship, it is almost a commonplace that the Hungarian Constitutional Court played a decisive role in the democratic transformation and consolidation process.[9] This reputation of the Court among legal scholars was established very early and, according to the legend, was considered mainly as a "result" of the activity and authority of the first president. Less general findings focus on the activism of the Court in fundamental rights issues, but these activities also contributed to the highly positive image of the HCC in general, and its first presidency in particular (Halmai 2002). Whether these pretensions could be proved by systematic empirical exploration remains a research puzzle, since no systematic empirical research has been conducted to clarify the question of to what extent the HCC, and the Sólyom Court in particular, has contributed to the consolidation of democracy and the rule of law in Hungary.

Such voices of scientific doubt do not neglect or deny the Court's virtues and achievements concerning fundamental rights issues, but highlight the need for a comparative project which puts the question: in which form and to what extent have CCs of the CEE countries contributed to the consolidation of democracy? While the political science literature on consolidation of democracy is vast enough,[10] research on the exact role of the CCs in the democratic consolidation process is rather underexplored; however, this is not the place where we could answer this question fully.[11] Nevertheless, some parts of the question can be addressed. It is a commonplace in the political science literature that the more the parliament keeps the executive under control, the more likely it is that the democratic transformation and consolidation process will be successful (Andrews 2014, 647). Similarly, one could derive from the literature the hypothesis that the more CCs keep the legislature under control the more likely it is that the democratic transformation and consolidation process will be successful.[12] Keeping under control means that CCs should be able to constrain the legislature in an appropriate way to comply with the basic rules of the (democratic) game. Hence, the question emerges: how could we measure whether CCs are able to keep the parliaments under control?

In accordance with these general accounts of hypothesis about consolidation of democracy, on the one hand, and with the general assessment of the HCC in the legal scholarship, on the other, we expected that the HCC had placed heavy burdens on the political actors in Hungary because it emerged very early as a key player in salient political issues from 1990 to at least 1996. According to the general assumption, the HCC played a key role in strengthening the constitutional culture, respect for the rule of law and, in general, democracy by influencing (in this context: constraining) the legislature. This image of a very stringent and weighty Court which kept parliament under strict control, should, however, be corrected in light of the analysis of the Hungarian data of the JUDICON project.

5.3.1 A Court of average performance

Taking the data of the JUDICON project into account, one could argue that the first three years, and especially the first year, of the HCC showed a noteworthy performance concerning its role in keeping the legislature within the borders of constitutionality. In contrast to the general hypothesis and advice of the political science literature, the HCC proved to be pretty dauntless in annulling or correcting the legislation in any form in its early years. Nevertheless, by putting its performance in the context of other CEE constitutional courts, the JUDICON dataset shows that it was rather the first year of the HCC which differed strongly from its Polish, Czech and Romanian counterparts, while the Slovak Constitutional Court proved to be astonishingly and with distance more severe throughout the 1990s than the HCC – not to mention that the first year of the HCC was rather a half year, with 13 cases altogether, which might distort the comparison to some extent.[13] By putting aside this half year of activity, one could observe that the HCC performed in a very similar way as its regional counterparts. This means that there are no radical differences between the Hungarian and other constitutional courts in the region concerning the question to what extent have the courts constrained the legislature. In this regard, and we must emphasize that we deliberately limit ourselves to the specific question of measuring the constraint constitutional courts put on the legislature, the HCC showed no outstanding performance.

Nevertheless, we must remind the reader of two factors which should be kept in mind when talking about demystifying the legend of the HCC. As was elucidated in the methodological chapter of this volume, we have not selected the politically salient decisions but have conducted the research by including all relevant decisions of the CCs.[14] Another approach, which would be sensible to the case selection and would focus on politically significant cases, might produce a significantly different result. Since our project kept its eyes on the general performance of the constitutional courts, the results of the project pertain to the general performance of the courts and not to (politically relevant) specific cases.

Furthermore, in evaluating the performance of the HCC one should also keep in mind that the HCC was in several ways a path-breaker. There were no other regional examples of functioning constitutional courts with democratic legitimacy in 1990 which could have served as a model for institutional learning for the HCC. Of course, we do not deny that there were models from which the HCC could learn a lot. The German Federal Constitutional Court (FCC) served as a model, but the FCC provided inspiration rather than any institutional learning due to the highly different political contexts in which the FCC and other CEE courts operated.[15] Getting inspired from a well-functioning constitutional court in an established democracy (Germany) could certainly not guarantee the success of the constitutional adjudication during and after the democratization process.

Thus, it was rather the HCC which served as a model for other CEE courts, particularly since other courts were first established in 1992 (Romania) or in 1993 (Poland, Czech Republic, Slovakia) after the HCC had already engaged in highly intransigent activity in the first two years of its functioning. Two years of functioning and taking very restrictive decisions on politically salient issues without having any counterparts in the region should be very much appreciated. This is why we should note once again that the HCC certainly played a path-breaking role in the democratic transformation of the CEE region and served as a model for other courts (Prohacka 2002, 58). In the light of this context, the comparatively limited performance of the HCC in constraining the legislature, i.e. in controlling the activity of the parliament with respect to its constitutionality, certainly takes on a different meaning.

As a third factor, the phenomenon of self-restraint of the parliament should be also mentioned. In the scientific literature, it is a commonplace, most frequently with respect to the relationship between the German *Bundestag* and the FCC, that legislative majorities might presume what kind of decision the constitutional court would take and correct or change a bill in this sense before its adoption.[16] Taking the previous praxis of constitutional adjudication of the CC as a basis, parliamentary majorities try to figure out how the court would decide on the bill and legislators prevent the eventual annulment of the law by correcting it in advance. In the Hungarian context, we can also legitimately assume that such an effect might have played a role in the "not so outstanding" performance of the HCC in constraining the legislature. Since there are no tools in our hands to measure the extent of self-restraint of the legislators, this assumption remains an assumption, but a quite plausible one in the case of the HCC.[17] Since the HCC was quite severe in its first year and still found several critical points in the legislative acts in its second year of functioning, it is easily conceivable that the political actors frequently tried to avoid a clash with the CC.

In sum, as a first general impression one should note that the practice of the HCC, and in particular the first Court under the Sólyom presidency, did not confirm the hypothesis we formulated above by leaning on the general assumptions and findings of the legal scholarship. The HCC showed no outstanding performance in constraining the Hungarian legislature.

5.3.2 A Court of consistent performance

As a second general impression, one could assess that the HCC's practice showed astonishing consistency concerning the average strength of its rulings on a yearly basis. There are no ups and downs, neither long-run trends nor radical oscillations from one year to another. The only general trend is a very slight, almost insignificant decrease in average strength of rulings (Figure 5.1). Beyond that, the average strength has varied between 2.5 and 3.5 points which, compared to the Slovak or the German cases, could not be described as high. The standard deviation from the mean values decreased over time, which means that extreme rulings (extremely strong and extremely weak) became more and more infrequent. To put it another way, the simultaneous presence of highly restrictive and highly permissive rulings in the same year characterized the first years of the HCC (1990–1993). However, the strength of rulings converged over time.

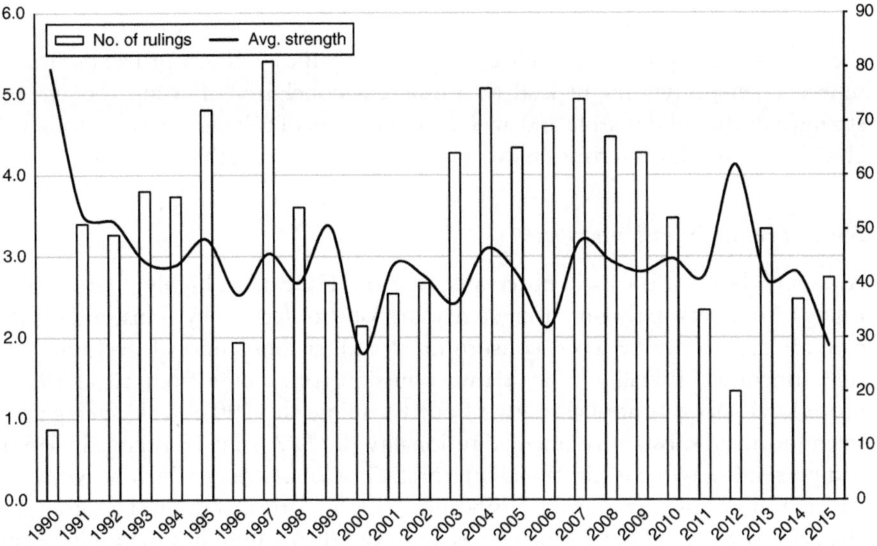

Figure 5.1 Number and average strength of rulings (HCC)

5.3.3 A Court of sophisticated rulings and growing polarization

Third, we can also say that the HCC greatly differentiated its rulings from very early on. While three-quarters of its rulings fit into the classical dichotomous model (finding the case before the Court unconstitutional or constitutional), approximately one-quarter of its rulings was legislative omission, procedural unconstitutionality, constitutional requirements or constitutional interpretation *in abstracto*. Furthermore, it has frequently taken the opportunity to differentiate in the temporal effect and completeness of rulings, not to mention the prescription several times found in the rulings. In sum, the HCC used the tools at hand in many ways, which led to a highly sophisticated constitutional adjudication.

Fourth, although no dominant trends in majority rulings of the HCC could be assessed, some kind of periodization of the Court's activity might be traced. This periodization is related not to the majority rulings but rather to the dissenting opinions. While the Sólyom Court (1990–1998) rarely published dissenting opinions (DOs), rulings with at least one dissenting opinion as well as the total number had already increased two years after the end of the Sólyom presidency and remained constant until 2010. The third period of the Court (2010–2015) is characterized once again by an "overnight" increase of rulings with at least one dissenting opinion and of the total number of dissenting opinions. This also means that while polarization of the Court was not symptomatic for the Sólyom period, the post-Sólyom Court experienced a clear leap in the number of dissenting opinions, and DOs sky-rocketed after 2010 in comparison to the previous period.[18]

5.4 Trends in majority rulings

While no general trends of majority rulings are discernible, if we have a look at the average strength of the rulings, approaching the question of trends from a different perspective might lead to a different conclusion. Putting the average strength of the rulings aside and analyzing the types of rulings the HCC took will elucidate some characteristics hidden by the average strength of rulings.

5.4.1 Trends in ruling types

As noted above, it is clearly observable that the HCC took highly differentiated rulings from very early on. It created some kind of leeway by transcending the classical dichotomy between constitutional and unconstitutional decisions and ruled unconstitutionality by legislative omission (one ruling from 13 in 1990), procedural unconstitutionality (two from 13 rulings in 1990), weak, average and strong form of substantive unconstitutionality (2/1/3 from 13 rulings in 1990) and presenting two constitutional interpretations *in abstracto* which heavily constrained the legislature. This diversification of rulings turned out to be a constant characteristic of the HCC, which it has preserved throughout its functioning from 1990 up to today (Figure 5.2). While the vast majority of all rulings between 1990 and 2015 were either rejection (43.9 percent on average per year) or substantive unconstitutionality (32.1 percent on average per year), approximately one-quarter of the rulings differed from this classical dichotomy and were either unconstitutionality by legislative omission, procedural unconstitutionality, constitutional requirement (CR) or constitutional interpretation *in abstracto* (CIIA).

Constitutional interpretation *in abstracto* both restricting and extending parliament's room to manoeuvre was more characteristic of the Sólyom presidency

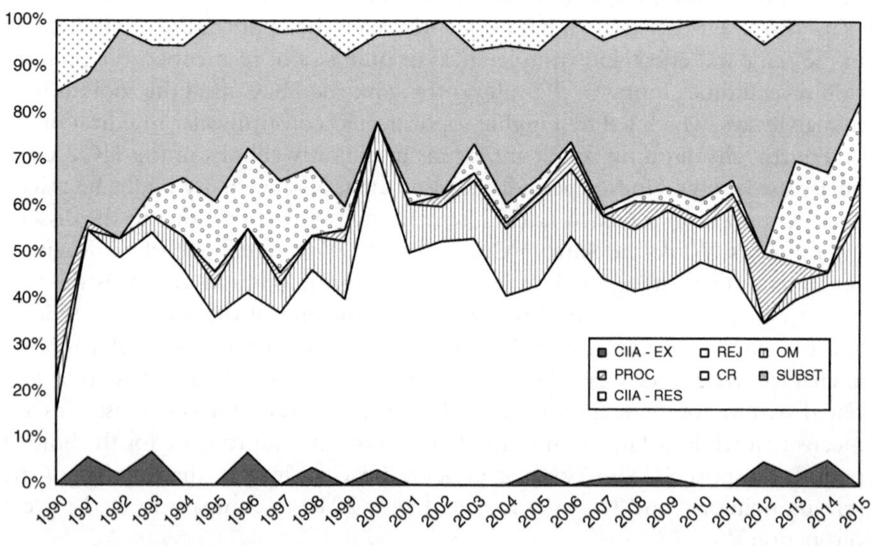

Figure 5.2 Frequency of ruling types I (HCC)

(respectively 45 percent and 43 percent of all CIIA of the Court from 1990 to 2015 were issued between 1990 and 1998), and determining constitutional requirements also became a frequent tool applied by the Sólyom Court (52 percent of all CR between 1990 and 2015 were issued between 1990 and 1998). While declaring legislative omissions was not unknown during the Sólyom period, it was more favoured in the post-Sólyom era from 2003 to 2009 (54.3 percent of all omissions from 1990 to 2015). The Sólyom Court made use of declaration of omission in the second half of its functioning, but even from 1994 to 1998 omissions accounted for only 8.3 percent of all rulings per year on average. It was also during the second half of its term (1994–1998) that declaring constitutional requirements became more frequent (49 percent of all CR from 1990 to 2015 had been declared between 1994 and 1998; 15.9 percent of all rulings involved CR on average per year). The second half of the Sólyom presidency was also the time period when the number of rejections fell from 47.4 percent per year on average (1991–1994) to 37.6 percent per year on average (1995–1998).

On the other hand, the second half of the Sólyom presidency exhibits further refinement of the adjudication. While in the first half of the term if the Court declared substantive unconstitutionality it mainly declared it *ex nunc* and as a quantitative partial annulment, between 1995 and 1998 the distribution of various forms of substantive unconstitutionality was more even. This means that in the second half of the Sólyom presidency rulings became highly differentiated, not only concerning the main types of rulings (see Table A.1 in the Appendix) but also among subtypes (like weak, average or strong form of omission, of procedural or substantive unconstitutionality) (see Figure 5.3). A clear shift might be detected in the second half of the Sólyom presidency in favour of weak and strong substantive forms of unconstitutionality, which means that the Sólyom Court expressed its opinion in an even more differentiated manner by declaring strong rulings of substantive unconstitutionality (annulling legislative acts *ex tunc* or complete laws, or even providing some remedy) or weak unconstitutionality (*pro future* quantitative partial annulment).

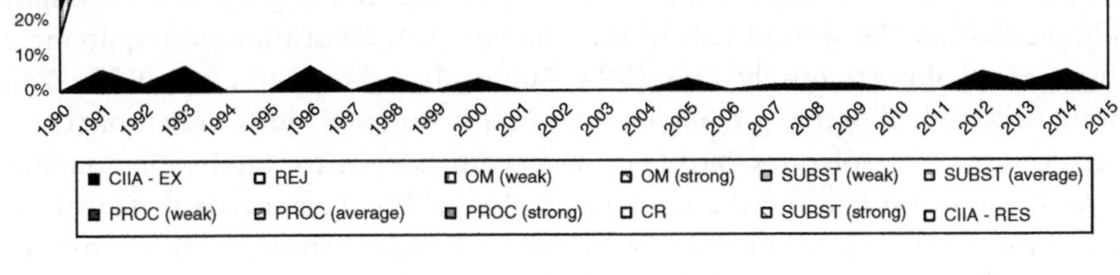

Figure 5.3 Frequency of ruling types II (HCC)

This means that the Sólyom Court became more active and was more willing to indicate some kind of unconstitutionality, rather than finding everything constitutional in the second half of its term. It is of utmost importance, however, that this increasing activity wasn't related to any increasing rigour: the average strength of rulings does not reflect this advanced activism in the time period between 1994 and 1998. This, in turn, means that while the Sólyom Court intervened more frequently from 1994 on, it adopted rather milder forms of rulings, such as declaring constitutional requirements or legislative omissions instead of declaring substantive unconstitutionality. The Sólyom Court became more active but less severe in the second half of its term.

After 1998, not only did CR disappear from the instrumentarium of the Court, omissions became more uniform (mainly a strong form of omission), and the Court also embraced fewer variants of substantive unconstitutionality. If it declared substantive unconstitutionality, it was the average form of it. It was only in 2012 and 2013, during the clash with the constitutional majority, that the Court "reinvented" not only the CR but also the strong form of substantial unconstitutionality. For these two years (2012 and 2013), approximately 15 percent of all rulings declared a strong form of unconstitutionality.

After two transitional years (1999 and 2000), declaration of constitutional requirements dropped from 15.9 percent to 2.5 percent per year on average (2001–2012) until the Court "reinvented" it in 2013 (20.2 percent per year on average, 2013–2015). By contrast, omissions became quite constant elements of the Court's rulings (12 percent per year on average from 1999 to 2011). There are, however, differences in what kind of omissions were declared by the Court. During the Sólyom era, some kind of balance was found between weak and strong omissions. This means that the Sólyom Court transformed itself (with the exception of the year 1996) rather rarely into a positive legislator by declaring omission and giving some kind of positive prescription. After the Sólyom era, however, the most frequent form of omission turned out to be the "strong omission", meaning that the HCC was strongly inclined to include in its rulings positive prescriptions on how unconstitutionality should be remedied, or it gave a strict deadline for unconstitutionality to be corrected. This engagement was interrupted by a short period of the Holló presidency when weak omissions dominated, i.e. the Court was satisfied by declaring the omission without prescribing any deadline or positive ruling on how unconstitutionality could be remedied.

In sum, while declaring constitutional requirements was common in the second half of the Sólyom Court and both weak and strong omissions became conventional forms of rulings from 1994 on (leading to a more active but milder adjudication in the second half of the Sólyom era), constitutional requirements disappeared almost entirely after 1998, only to be reinvented after 2012. While in the second half of the Sólyom era weak and strong omissions were more or less balanced, i.e. the Sólyom Court became a positive legislator rarely, the dominant form of omission became the strong one after 1998. This means that, with the exception of the Holló presidency, which was rather passive in this sense, the HCC not only declared legislative omissions but also determined more and more frequently a deadline for unconstitutionality to be remedied. This means that even if the HCC chose a milder form of declaring unconstitutionality (legislative omission), it quite often pressured the legislature by determining deadlines for correcting unconstitutionality.

5.4.2 Significant years

As noted in the previous section, it would be an overstatement to delineate sweeping trends in the average strength of majority rulings, while some kind of trend is discernible in the types of rulings the HCC took. While trends in average strength of rulings are lacking, there were remarkably strong as well as weak years which are worth scrutinizing. Accordingly, this section highlights those years in which the HCC performed in an especially strong or even weak manner. The three main periods in the history of the HCC will be considered – the Sólyom Court, the post-Sólyom era and recent years when the competences and the composition of the Court were significantly changed.

1990: the formative decisions

The HCC was established months before the first free and competitive election in 1990. However, in this research only those decisions were considered that were made after June 1990, since the activity of the Court is scrutinized with respect to the democratic legislature. Partly, this explains the low number of rulings (13) which, however, resulted in the strongest rulings in the 25 years after the regime change. Until 2012, the HCC did not approximate the strength of its first-year rulings, when the average strength of majority rulings peaked at 5.31 points. What could be the explanation for this unusually high level of strength?

Before considering the empirical evidence, it is worth mentioning that the political and institutional context of the regime change might have contributed to the strong rulings. On the one hand, the regime change brought about a new institutional setting, in which all players attempted to shape their specific role within the limits of the constitutional framework. The HCC was expected to guard the new regime against every possible majority in the legislature. To put it simply, the HCC set the limits and the "rules of the game" through decisions which interfered in the terrain of parliament. On the other hand, it followed from the nature of the regime change that the legislature needed to regulate fundamental rights and duties, which sparked sharp legal and political debates to be settled by the HCC that was seen as an institution standing above the political parties. In short, the HCC attempted to establish its authority *vis-à-vis* the legislature by strongly intervening in its affairs. (Later in this section, it will be seen that the first President of the HCC, László Sólyom, was also a key factor in the early self-empowerment of the Court.)

The activism of the early Court is reflected by the extremely low share of rejections, but more apparently by the (restrictive) constitutional interpretations *in abstracto* regarding such important issues as privatization and land properties.

The high level of this latter type of ruling remained important in the following years, too, but restricting the legislature through interpreting the constitution occurred only rarely in the following decades. A further characteristic of the strength of the early HCC is the relatively high level of rulings declaring substantive unconstitutionality. Although this type of ruling has been a recurring one for 25 years, in the first two years its proportion was above the average of the period analyzed in our research. However, it should be noted that already in its first year the HCC adopted a wide range of possible configurations of rulings. Beside rulings on substantial unconstitutionality at different strengths, the HCC developed a strategy in which legislative omission, procedural unconstitutionality and later constitutional requirement allowed the Court to weigh the level of influencing and constraining the legislature. Although the trends of the dissenting opinions will be analyzed in more detail later, it should be noted here that even if low in number, a few judges of the first Court would have even been more constraining towards the legislature than the majority.

After the first two years of the HCC, the strength of its rulings decreased somewhat and varied between more moderate intervals. However, it might be argued that in the first decade after the transition, the legislature, recognizing that the HCC is prone to constrain its room for manoeuvre, was actually constrained by a separation of powers between the two institutions. Thus, no especially strong rulings were needed by the HCC to keep the parliament between the limits set by the Court at the beginning of the 1990s.

1999–2000: the start of the post-Sólyom period

During the first decade after the transition, the HCC established its strong position *vis-à-vis* the legislature by making decisions that, albeit somewhat weaker compared to the first year analyzed above, allowed the Court to significantly constrain the legislature. The HCC became a key player in the Hungarian political system, often intervening in even the core issues of government policies. To name one of the most controversial, in 1995, invoking procedural as well as substantial standards, the HCC partly blocked the left-liberal government's austerity measures (the restrictive package of finance minister Lajos Bokros).

By the end of the decade, however, the composition of the Court had gradually changed. The mandate of the judges of the Sólyom Court terminated, and within an increasingly polarized political context, new judges were elected. As the election of the judges depends on a two-thirds majority, the Hungarian parliament developed an informal strategy of nominating judges in pairs or larger packs, in which the blocks of the political spectrum had their own nominees and their election was guaranteed by reciprocity. Formally, this nomination process was about electing consensual judges; however, signs of polarization were apparent even in the period when the remaining old and some of the incoming new judges served together in the Court. For example, in 1999 the number of dissenting opinions rose dramatically and, after a brief setback in the next year, that new level became a new standard for the following years. While during the Sólyom era on average every tenth ruling was supplemented with a dissenting opinion, in

1999 that proportion rose to 27.5 percent, signifying a steady increase up to 70.7 percent by 2015. That change is remarkable, even if it might be supposed that during its first decade it was an obvious strategy on the part of the HCC to reduce the number of dissenting opinions in order to represent a strong constitutional court as homogenously as possible.

The changing patterns in the practice of the post-Sólyom Court first became apparent in 2000, when the HCC reached its lowest strength value in the whole period our research investigated. By the middle of the first (right-wing) Orbán government (1998–2002), the composition of the Court leaned to the left, while the total strength of the majority rulings was only 1.8 (a similarly low value occurred only in 2015 after the competences of the Court were curtailed significantly). The weak rulings might be explained by the fact that the Court decided about laws that were accepted by the previous left-wing parliamentary majorities and only four rulings concerned legislation of the current right-wing majority.

Examining the rulings themselves, however, the weak value is the result of their specific types. The share of rejections has never been higher than in that year. While the overall average of rejections for the 25 years is slightly below 40 percent, in 2000 68.8 percent of all rulings belonged to that type. It is important that among the relatively few rulings there was one constitutional interpretation *in abstracto*, which actually extended the legislative's room for manoeuvre (while no such ruling was made in either the previous or the following year). In addition, the share of the stronger types of rulings, such as omissions with stricter conditions and restrictive constitutional interpretation, decreased.

Thus, one might argue that the record low strength of the rulings in 2000 was due to the subject of the petitions (legislation from previous periods), the composition of the Court (a left-leaning majority) and the specific pattern of rulings, which taken together reflect a Court not friendly towards the government and which understood its own role as a passive player in the political system.

2012: the Court's last stand?

Except for 2006, when the value of the strength of the rulings hardly went over 2 points, for the next decade the practice of the HCC resembled the moderate years of the Sólyom Court, at least considering the average strength of the rulings. This does not mean, however, that the most frequent ruling types were also similar, as will be seen below.

The systemic change for the HCC was brought about by the parliamentary supermajority Fidesz-KDNP gained in 2010. Using its power, the governing party gradually transformed the Hungarian political system into a process that peaked (albeit by no means ended) in adopting a new constitution. The HCC was one of the first institutions of the Hungarian political system to be affected by the changes. First, the competences were curtailed, then the formal rules of nomination and the composition were changed. By 2013 the Court was packed with judges that were expected to be loyal to the ruling party, as some of them left the parliamentary group for a seat at the HCC.

It needs to be explained, then, how the year 2012 turned out to be the second strongest year of the HCC after the transition considering the average strength of its rulings (4.13), while the number of rulings was almost the lowest (20). Furthermore, in 2012 5 percent of the rulings involved extending constitutional interpretations *in abstracto*, which – according to our model – significantly reduces a year's average strength. Thus, it means that some of the rulings of that year meant especially strong constraint for the legislature. To begin with the opposite type, 5 percent of the rulings were restrictive constitutional interpretations – also over the 25-year average; no higher proportion of this type occurred after 2005. Furthermore, only in 1990 were fewer petitions rejected by the HCC; the 30 percent proportion in 2012 remains well below the average (43.9 percent) of the whole period. At the same time, the HCC adopted procedural standards in an almost unprecedented proportion to declare unconstitutionality. Again, only in 1990 did the proportion of that ruling type reach 15 percent, while the average was only 2.3 percent per year. Finally, it was the share of rulings declaring substantial unconstitutionality that strongly increased the yearly average strength.

Looking at the subjects of the rulings, it is apparent that the HCC affected the core issues of the right-wing government. To name only a few, the HCC made decisions about the provisional regulations of the new constitution (Fundamental Law), the laws on labour strikes, ethnic minorities, local government authorities and personnel of the judicial system.[19] The composition of the Court might serve as an explanation for the extraordinary performance of the Court in 2012. While there were a few new judges nominated and elected by government majority alone, these new members of the Court formed only a minority. The majority was, however, not homogeneous politically; there were right-leaning judges among them. The main cleavage in this year was between the old and the new, and the latter group seemed to defend the Court itself against the parliamentary two-thirds majority of Fidesz. By 2013, however, the new judges were able to form a majority, which resulted in significantly weaker rulings in the following years.

5.4.3 *The role of the presidents*

Usually, during their mandates presidents of constitutional courts shape the institution they lead.[20] In the Hungarian case, the competences of the President in managing the HCC have always been strong. Regarding the President, the constitutional changes after 2010 brought about one significant modification: since then, the President has been elected by parliament and not by the judges themselves, as before. Therefore, the legislature now not only has a say in the composition of the Court but might influence its main directions and strategy in a more direct way. Presidents have informal competences as well. As already mentioned, it was an apparent strategy of the Sólyom Court to reduce the number of dissenting opinions to emphasize the role of the Court as a unified institution in the political system and not only as a random group of individual judges. Certainly, understanding different presidencies as different periods of the Court would be an overestimation of the Court's leadership. The composition of the Court is to some extent more important when it comes to the strength of the rulings. Furthermore, as the question here is how the legislature is constrained by the Court, the changing parliamentary majorities as well as the political background of the judges are also fundamental factors.

Considering these institutional and contextual factors, two main questions need to be addressed here. The first concerns the relative strength of the presidencies, while the second looks for any deviations between the strength of the rulings of the presidents and the Court's average. The first problem simply divides the examined period into more meaningful units than the yearly analysis. Explaining the second issue, however, might point to the individual characteristics of the presidents and their relations to the Court they led.

Following from the above analyzes, it is not surprising that the Sólyom Court had the strongest rulings. However, as mentioned earlier, contrary to the myths and superficial opinions, the difference between the Sólyom presidency and the subsequent Courts is far from striking (Figure 5.4). While the HCC led by László Sólyom had an average strength of 3.11 points, the following Németh Court had 2.52 points, and this value already includes the lowest value of the whole period. Similarly, it follows from the average of all majority rulings that the second strongest Court was the one led by Péter Paczolay, which started before 2010 and ended in 2015. As has been shown, the second strongest year, what we have called the Court's last stand, fell under his term. The presidencies of János Németh, András Holló and Mihály Bihari varied between slightly above 2.5 points but under 3 points. Further differences will be seen below, however, related to the individual values of the presidents. Finally, the Court with the lowest value is the last one our research investigated. Once the judges elected solely by Fidesz secured the majority in the Court, under the presidency of Lenkovics the value decreased to 1.88 points.[21]

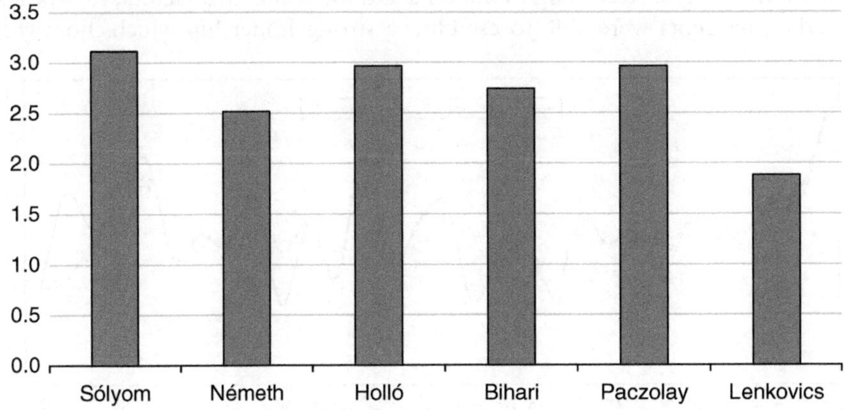

Figure 5.4 Average strength of rulings (by presidents) (HCC)

Turning to the second question, meaningful differences can be seen on closer inspection, since the presidents hardly diverged from the average of the whole Court. The reason for this might be either that the presidents were able to form and lead the majority of the judges and thus the Court's average represented the president's opinion, or that the presidents attempted to fit in with the judges (even if their average followed from polarized opinions). As the debates of the HCC are not public, there are no reliable sources to enable us to elaborate on these or further possibilities.

Starting with the differences between entire presidential terms and the majority averages of the Court, the highest value falls under the mandate of Mihály Bihari who – based on his dissenting opinions – proposed weaker constraints on the legislature by 0.30 points (Figure 5.5). In contrast, Péter Paczolay was a president of the HCC whose rulings would have been stronger than the majority average by 0.17 points. As these values do not imply significant deviations from the Court majority, it is worth looking at the same data on a yearly basis. From this aspect, it becomes apparent how the years with the highest average strength depended on the current presidents. The especially constraining early years of the Sólyom Court show no meaningful differences between the majority of the judges and the president. However, the other peak in 2012 shows that the sitting president, Péter Paczolay, started to differ from the majority opinion, and by 2015 the highest difference between the president and his court emerged. Presumably due to the increasing presence of the new judges elected solely by Fidesz, the president's rulings would have been constantly stronger (from 0.33 to 1.75 points). It is worth mentioning here that, before elected to the Court, in the 1990s President Paczolay served as a secretary of the HCC under Sólyom and even followed him to the office of the head of state when Sólyom was elected President of the Republic in 2005. As a contrast to these two presidencies, it was Mihály Bihari in 2008 who made the weakest rulings compared to the majority of the Court (–1.05 points).

Altogether, the presidents of the HCC were in line with the prevailing composition of the judges. According to our data and the contextual factors, this means that the presidents were able to establish a strong leadership which, however,

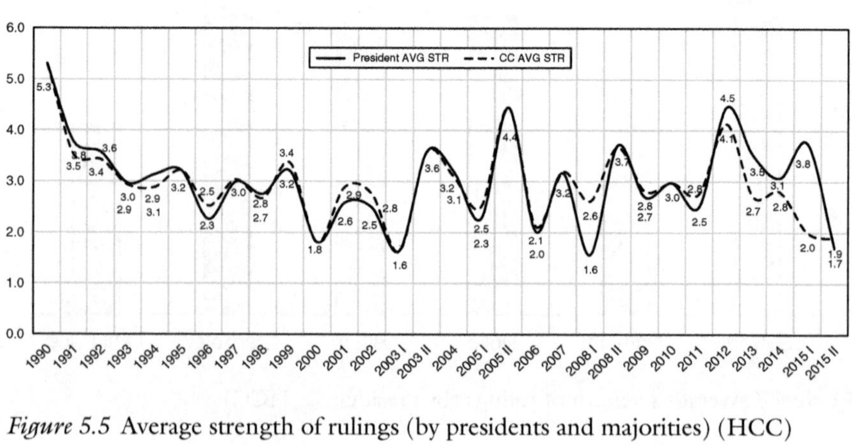

Figure 5.5 Average strength of rulings (by presidents and majorities) (HCC)

was gradually but only weakly eroded due to the increasing polarization within the Court, which will be seen from the general trends in the dissenting opinions.

5.5 Trends in dissenting opinions

Whereas in the case of the HCC the strength of the majority rulings does not offer an unambiguous explanation for the 25 years our research investigated, it is worth looking closely at how the individual and minority opinions were formed. Analyzing dissenting opinions can explain the individual behaviour of judges. Within the framework of our research, dissenting opinions are signs of a possible weaker or stronger constraint on the legislature which, however, did not gain a majority among the judges. In the Hungarian case, sometimes it is possible to identify the political parties behind the nomination and election of a given judge, while in other cases it is possible to infer their political background (assessing media information or statements given by the judges themselves). Therefore, through dissenting opinions it becomes possible to compare their position to the position of the political party that supported a certain judge.[22] Furthermore, beyond individual behaviour, the inner dynamics of the Court also becomes visible, as judges often adhere to a dissenting opinion written by another judge; groups and coalitions and the strength of their proposed rulings thereby become measurable.

There is an obvious trend in the number of dissenting opinions. During its first years the Court was seemingly highly cohesive and published dissenting opinions very rarely. However, from 1999 on the number of rulings with at least one dissenting opinion increased more or less steadily (Figure 5.6). The next level of changes occurred after 2010, as the number of rulings with at least one

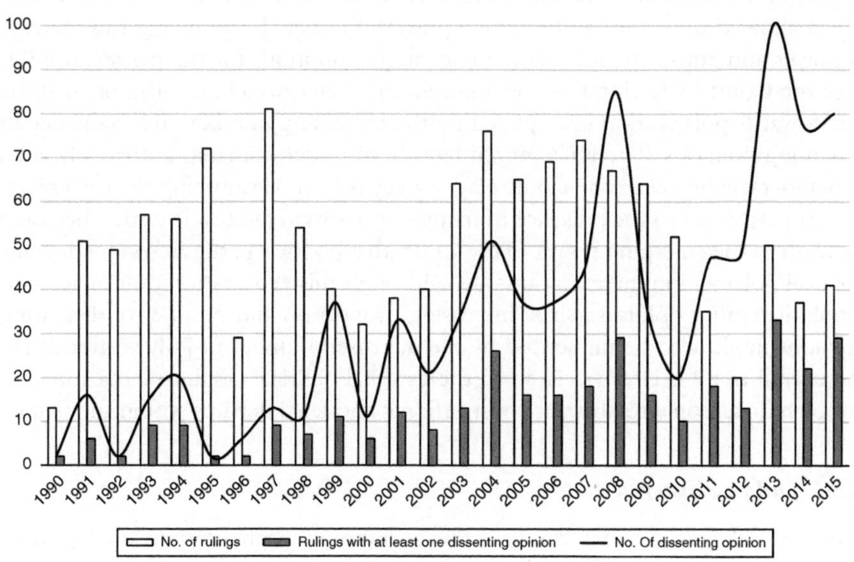

Figure 5.6 Number of rulings and dissenting opinions (HCC)

dissenting opinion increased to more than 20 per year on average.[23] Additionally, the total number of dissenting opinions also massively increased: while in the first eight years of the Court there were altogether ten dissenting opinions per year on average, this increased to 38 dissents per year between 1999 and 2010 on average, and to 62 per year between 2010 to 2015 on average.

These trends might help also in discerning three different periods of the Court, namely the first period of the Sólyom presidency, the second or "post-Sólyom era" and a third one which started directly after the Fidesz gained a two-thirds parliamentary majority in 2010. This periodization is commonplace in Hungary, connected to the myth around the first President of the Court and partly based on the facts concerning the number of dissenting opinions presented above.

The trends in dissenting opinions reinforce that periodization. Their frequency differs significantly in the three periods. An increasing number of rulings were accompanied by dissenting opinions and the absolute number of them also increased. During the Sólyom presidency only 5–15 percent of the rulings were published with dissenting opinions; their overall average was 10.4 percent, the yearly average number being 5.3. Later, in the post-Sólyom era (1999–2009), 20–30 percent of the rulings were published with a dissenting opinion; the average was 27.2 percent and the average total number rose to 15.5. The steady increase in the number of dissenting opinions continued in the third period (2010–2015). Dissenters added their opinions to 50–70 percent of the rulings during those years, which means that more than half the rulings of the HCC were disputed (57.2 percent on average per year).

A possible explanation for this apparent increase concerns the interplay between internal and external factors. In the first period, it was the intention of the president to keep the number of dissenting opinions low. László Sólyom attempted to establish the HCC as a unified institution *vis-à-vis* other elements of the political system, which allowed the Court to become a powerful player. Recognizing this increase in power and authority, it became increasingly important for the parties to influence the Court by having their own nominees elected which, in turn, opened the way towards polarization exemplified by the increasing number and frequency of dissenting opinions. The HCC might have been underestimated in the early years of democracy; however, the Court played a key role in constraining the legislature, at least partly due to the presence of many non-partisan judges. It came, then, as a backlash to the emerging power of the Court that political parties responded, while political polarization increased anyway. Although this explanation cannot account for all dissenting opinions, since increasing proportion and number of dissenting opinions might also be influenced by the increased number of judges after 2010, the overall trend is clearly related to the external political circumstances and cannot be reduced only to abstract constitutional and legal debates within the Court.

5.5.1 Judges clustered

The data allowed for determining the average strength of individual judges' rulings, which can be compared to the average strength of those majority rulings to which a judge did not add a dissenting opinion. Although the average value of the strength of dissenting opinions might obscure a few trends otherwise discernible in a yearly breakdown (to which we will return below), it might yet reveal something about the judges at the two extreme ends of the scale (Figure 5.7). Barnabás Lenkovics and Mária Szívós, to name two examples, were consistent in adding a dissenting opinion to the majority ruling only in cases when they would have rejected the petition, which means that they would not have constrained the legislature at all. Lenkovics's practice is especially interesting; as a constitutional judge from 2007, his dissenting opinions already suggested consistently fewer constraining rulings before 2010. All his dissenting opinions proposed a rejection. Mária Szívós proved to be similarly consistent, although she fulfilled her position only after 2010; her dissenting opinions suggesting rejection regarded legislative acts adopted by the same majority that elected her as a judge. At the other end of the scale, however, Ágnes Czine added a dissenting opinion to rulings in which she would have been more constraining against the legislature.

Figure 5.8 shows the activity of the judges: their share and the strength of their dissenting opinions. It is clearly discernible that Mária Szívós was a dissenting judge in at least every fourth ruling in which she participated, and according to the strength of her dissenting opinions, she would not have constrained the legislature at all.

It is also apparent that judge Lenkovics expressed his disagreement with the majority more infrequently as he added a non-constraining dissenting opinion to only 8 percent of the rulings. Considering Figure 5.7 and Figure 5.8 together, a group of judges becomes visible who were elected after 2010 and added a non-constraining or almost non-constraining dissenting opinion to every fourth or fifth majority ruling. Within this group, however, there are significant differences regarding the absolute number of their dissenting opinions. Whereas Mária Szívós wrote 46 dissenting opinions and Egon Dienes-Oehm added 42 dissents to the majority rulings, András Varga Zs. participated in only nine rulings in which he disagreed the majority of the judges. The position of Ágnes Czine in Figure 5.9 reveals that she was a frequent dissenter when she was participating in

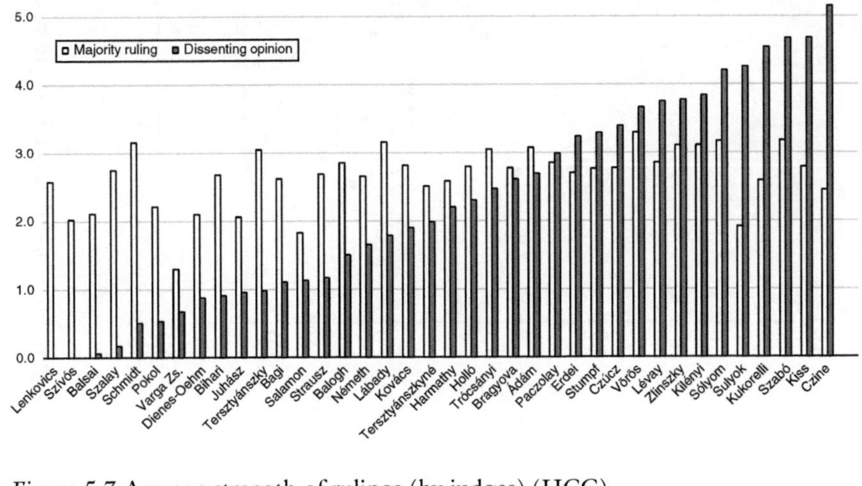

Figure 5.7 Average strength of rulings (by judges) (HCC)

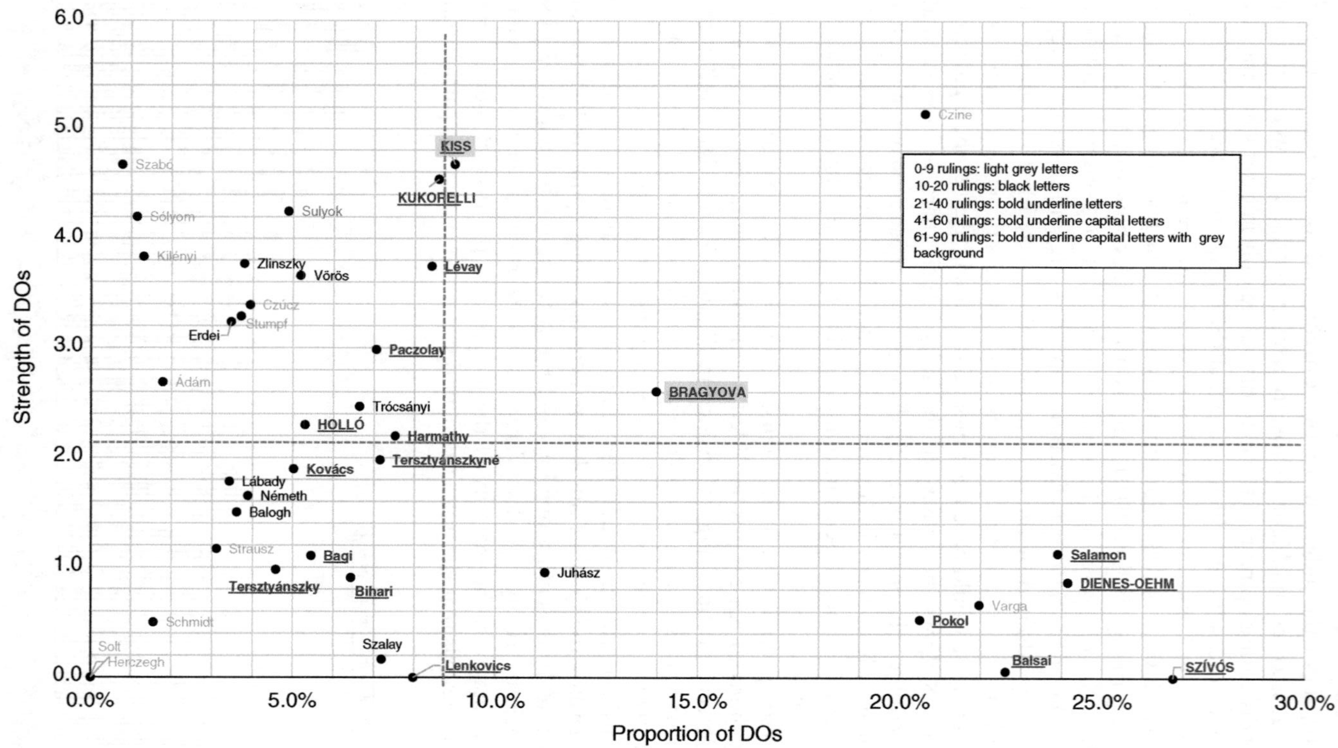

Figure 5.8 Proportion and strength of dissenting opinions (HCC)

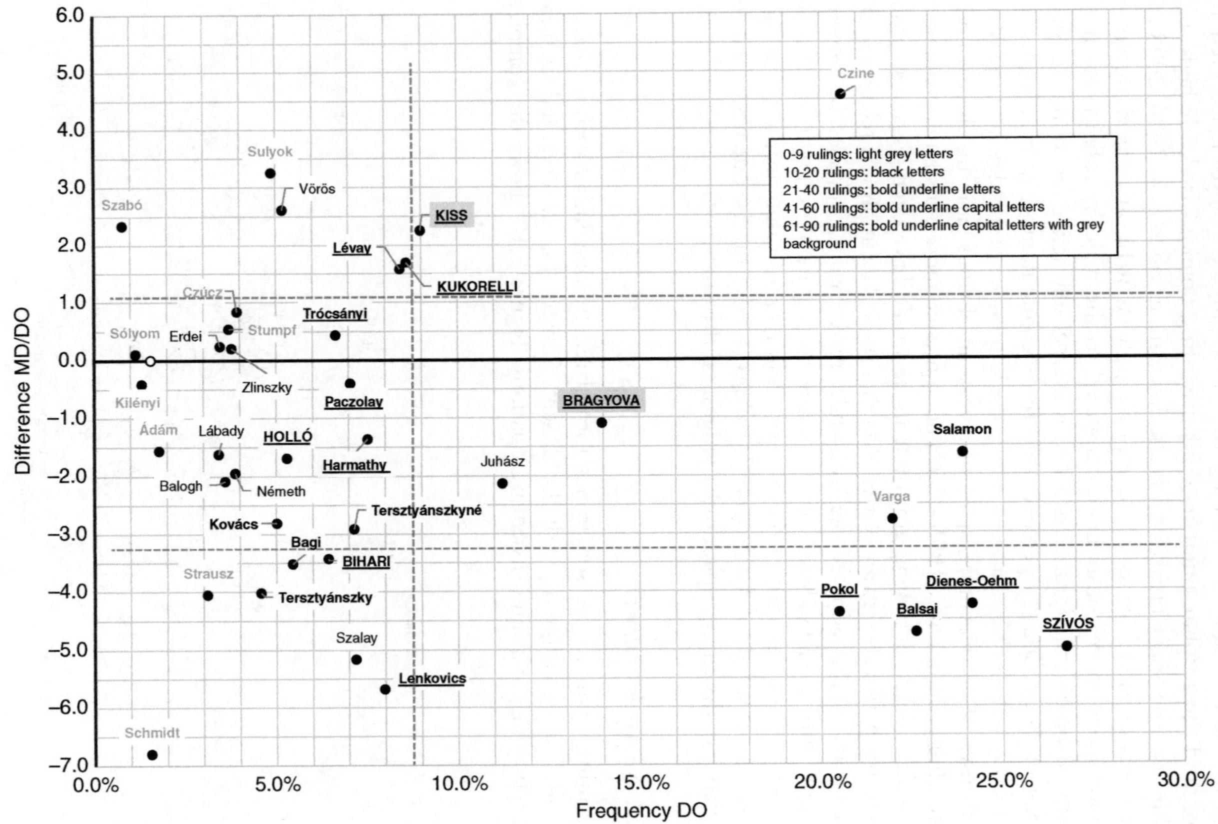

Figure 5.9 Average difference to majority rulings and frequency of dissenting opinions (HCC)

a ruling in 2015; she consistently suggested a more constraining stance towards the parliament. However, it is the result of nine rulings altogether. It is also worth highlighting two judges sitting longer on the benches of the court: András Bragyova and László Kiss. Among the older judges, Bragyova dissented the most, and the absolute number of his dissenting opinions is clearly high (67). In his case, the yearly breakdown is also interesting: whereas in 2006, 2008 and 2010 he suggested fewer constraining rulings, from 2012 onwards his dissenting opinions were more constraining compared to the majority rulings. From the group of the older judges, László Kiss was especially active regarding the share of dissenting opinions (9 percent), and the absolute number of his dissents was clearly the highest (82). László Kiss was the longest-serving judge, and the yearly breakdown of his dissenting opinions reveals an obvious pattern: whereas under right-wing governments (1998–2002) he suggested more constraining rulings in his dissents, under left-wing governments he would have been less constraining against the parliamentary majorities. Whether these data imply any relation to the actual majority that adopted the laws under review will be revealed by applying the attitudinal model in future research. Anyway, Figure 5.9 shows the difference between average strength of the majority ruling (zero value on the y axis) and the average strength of the dissenter's rulings (y axis), on the one hand, and the frequency of dissenting opinions by judges, on the other.

5.5.2 *Network analysis*

Dissenting opinions are sometimes formulated by one judge without having any other judges aligning with the dissent. Sometimes, however, judges make a coalition in publishing dissenting opinions. Figure 5.10 shows the complete

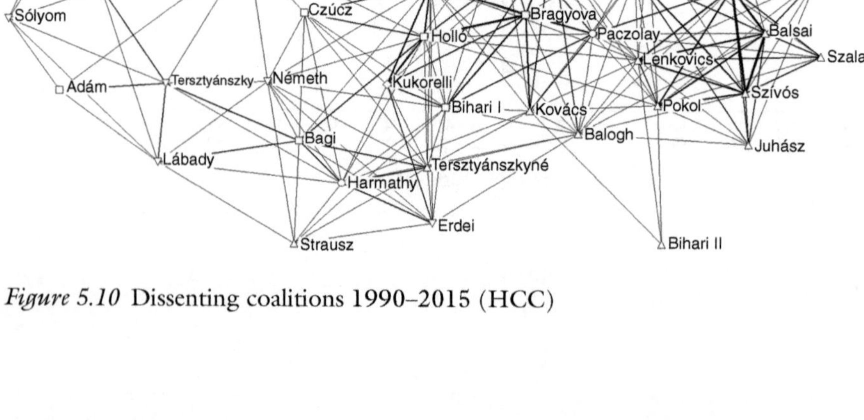

Figure 5.10 Dissenting coalitions 1990–2015 (HCC)

network of 38 judges who served between 1990 and 2015 at the Hungarian Constitutional Court.[24] There were no completely isolated judges who formulated exclusively solo dissenting opinions. Each judge formed a coalition with another judge at least once. The thickness of the lines between judges shows the strength of coalition, while the size of the nodes indicates the total number of dissenting opinions formulated by the judge; the colour indicates the party which nominated the judge.[25]

On the left-hand side of the figure, judges from the first Court can be discerned. They formulated dissenting opinions quite rarely (very small nodes and thin lines between the judges). The only stable coalition seems to have been between Tamás Lábady and Ödön Tersztyánszky. In those few occasions when judges of the Sólyom Court published a dissent jointly (or formulated one with the same strength), they formed both "cross-party" and "one-party" coalitions, i.e. they joined to judges nominated by a different party as many times as to judges nominated by the party they had been nominated by. Imre Vörös wrote dissenting opinions with almost all other judges, but only very few with each judge. In sum, we could argue that "party affiliation" played no role in the issue of who judges formed dissenting coalitions with, and that judges of the first Court were less inclined to form dissenting opinions in any way.

On the right-hand side of the figure, we can find judges nominated exclusively by the right-wing party after 2010. They have strong ties among themselves, which means that they very frequently formulated dissenting opinions and formed coalitions exclusively with judges nominated by the same party (Szalay, Varga Zs., Dienes-Oehm, Balsai, Szívós and Juhász). Other right-wing judges nominated after 2010 are heavily connected to this core group but very rarely also formed a coalition with left-wing judges (Salamon, Lenkovics and Pokol). Furthermore, there are three outlier judges nominated after 2010 who formed a coalition, with either both right-wing and left-wing judges in balance (Tamás Sulyok and István Stumpf) or even more frequently with judges from a different political camp (Czine).

Judges elected between 1999 and 2010 are located between the two poles. Seemingly, four judges nominated by the left-wing parties (Holló, Lévay, Kiss and Bragyova) form a very strong and highly cohesive group. They published dissenting opinions pretty often and joined with each other quite frequently. Based on the dataset, we can also say that this core group had been established well before 2010, which means that party affiliation played a decisive role in their case before they strengthened their cooperation after 2010 in order to resist the pressure from outside (constitutional majority and government) and inside (new judges elected by the right-wing majority). Judges Bihari and Kukorelli also joined this core group several times (although they have somewhat looser ties to this inner circle).

Even more interesting are judges nominated by the right-wing parties between 1999 and 2010, since they have not constituted a cohesive group. Balogh, Kovács and Trócsányi have several connections almost in balance with left-wing and right-wing judges. A small, not very cohesive and not very strong group of judges is formed by Erdei (right-wing consensus), Tersztyánszkyné (right-wing), Harmathy (consensus), Strausz (right-wing) and Bagi (left-wing). Seemingly, this is a rather colourful group with several connections to a left-wing outlier (Bihari). Interestingly enough, among the left-wing judges it was István Bagi who joined predominantly right-wing judges when he formulated a dissenting opinion. Furthermore, it can also be seen that judges elected in consensus are willing to form a dissenting coalition with both sides, left-wing and right-wing judges.

As a general characteristic of dissenting opinions between 1990 and 2010, we can assess that (well before the Court had been packed with judges of the right-wing constitutional majority from 2010 on) partisan dissenting coalitions had become a regular phenomenon among some left-wing judges (Figure 5.11). This means that, in contrast to the Sólyom Court, the Court was not fully immune to partisan voting behaviour; a small group of left-wing judges showed a strong affinity to join with other judges nominated by the same political camp. In contrast, such cohesive partisan behaviour was less discernible among right-wing judges sitting on the benches of the HCC between 1999 and 2010. This seems to be a new finding, since the general assessment of the Court reflects a different standpoint. According to the general evaluation of its pre- and post-2010 activity, the HCC worked quite well before 2010, and rulings and dissenting opinions did not reflect the "party affiliation" of judges. It was only after 2010 that the new judges showed consistent deference towards their nominating party. In contrast to this general account, we argue that partisan behaviour had been manifested before 2010 in dissenting opinions of a small group of left-wing judges, while right-wing judges were more immune to (even if not completely free from) this kind of judicial behaviour.

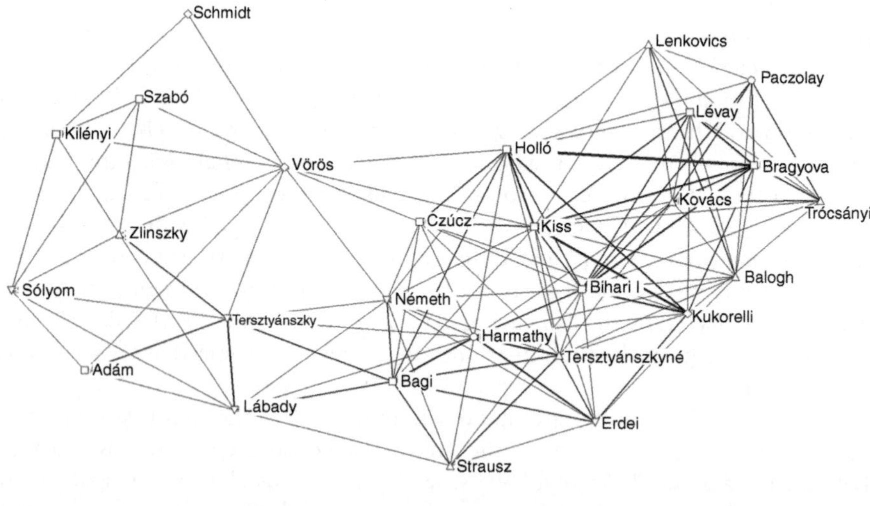

Figure 5.11 Dissenting coalitions 1990–2010 (HCC)

5.6 Conclusions

Although common knowledge suggested earlier that the Hungarian Constitutional Court was a strong and inexorable actor of the Hungarian political system, an in-depth analysis of the JUDICON dataset seems to disprove, at least partly, this general thesis. As the strength values of the rulings show, the HCC started its work with powerful "punches", but political players respected both the institution and the individual judges soon after the political transformation process. The rapidly emerging authority of the HCC was also fostered by the cohesive attitude of the Court itself: dissenting opinions were published only rarely and even when they did appear judges formed cross-party coalitions, which clearly contradicted the expectations of the attitudinal model of judicial behaviour. Due to this enormous authority, the HCC didn't have to make use of its strong "muscles", leading to a decrease in the strength of its rulings; with the exception of some years, these became stabilized for the rest of the time period under scrutiny. In general, we can argue that the HCC did not constrain the legislature very heavily.

On the other hand, political actors not only respected the Court but also realized that it had become a strong player on the political stage. Thus, it seemed worth influencing its practice by selecting and electing judges who were deemed to be more reliable in political terms. This led to the clear polarization of the Court well before the court-packing after 2010. Network analysis of the dissenting opinions reveals that the HCC gave up its cohesiveness and transformed itself into a court polarized in terms of political and ideological cleavages. Left-wing judges formed frequently strong dissenting coalitions before the shock of 2010.

However, the HCC's performance might also be evaluated from a third perspective, i.e. from the perspective of diversity of rulings. In this respect the HCC presented a unique practice, which is certainly one of the main findings of this chapter. While other courts of the region were not really engaged in softening or hardening their rulings, the HCC made use of its instrumentarium and produced a wide range of ruling types. The first Court was especially keen to say something, i.e. declare some kind of unconstitutionality, while dampening its provisions by relying on soft elements of rulings, such as constitutional requirements or legislative omissions, *pro futuro* and partial annulments. This might be read as some kind of "constitutional dialogue", even if this term has been popularized in another way. Signalling that something went wrong but avoiding deep interference with the competences of the legislators, this strategy of the first Court seems to be more than obvious. Yet the heritage of the first Court is rather mixed. While the cohesiveness faded away over time, the practice of declaring highly diverse rulings survived the three waves of its transformations as far as its composition is concerned. In this regard, the HCC tried to be a constructive partner in a constitutional dialogue with the legislature, even in hard times when the legislative majority was rather interested in a political battle over the question of "who has the last say". Taking all these findings together, we can conclude that the general narrative of the political actors accusing the HCC of unduly entering the political field should be certainly revised. The HCC has been a constructive partner in correcting unconstitutionality, rather than a militant actor on the political stage.

Appendix

Table A.1 Frequency of ruling types III (in %) (HCC)

	CIIA – EX (n=22)	*REJ (n=582)*	*OM (n=129)*	*PROC (n=30)*	*CR (n=96)*	*SUB (n=426)*	*CIIA – RES (n=41)*	*Sum (in %)*
1990	0.0	0.3	0.8	6.7	0.0	1.4	4.9	**1.0**
1991	13.6	4.3	0.0	3.3	0.0	3.8	14.6	**3.8**
1992	4.5	4.0	1.6	0.0	0.0	5.2	2.4	**3.7**
1993	18.2	4.6	1.6	0.0	3.1	4.2	7.3	**4.3**
1994	0.0	4.5	3.1	0.0	7.3	3.8	7.3	**4.2**
1995	0.0	4.5	3.9	6.7	11.5	6.6	0.0	**5.4**
1996	9.1	1.7	3.1	0.0	5.2	1.9	0.0	**2.2**
1997	0.0	5.2	3.9	6.7	16.7	6.1	4.9	**6.1**
1998	9.1	4.0	3.1	0.0	8.3	3.8	2.4	**4.1**
1999	0.0	2.7	3.9	3.3	2.1	3.1	7.3	**3.0**
2000	4.5	3.8	1.6	0.0	0.0	1.4	2.4	**2.4**
2001	0.0	3.3	3.1	0.0	1.0	3.1	2.4	**2.9**
2002	0.0	3.6	2.3	3.3	0.0	3.5	0.0	**3.0**
2003	0.0	5.8	6.2	3.3	4.2	3.1	9.8	**4.8**
2004	0.0	5.3	8.5	3.3	3.1	6.1	9.8	**5.7**
2005	9.1	4.5	9.3	3.3	2.1	4.2	9.8	**4.9**
2006	0.0	6.4	7.8	10.0	1.0	4.2	0.0	**5.2**
2007	4.5	5.5	7.8	0.0	1.0	6.3	7.3	**5.6**
2008	4.5	4.6	7.0	13.3	1.0	5.6	2.4	**5.1**
2009	4.5	4.6	7.8	3.3	2.1	5.2	2.4	**4.8**
2010	0.0	4.3	3.1	3.3	2.1	4.7	0.0	**3.9**
2011	0.0	2.7	3.9	3.3	1.0	2.8	0.0	**2.6**
2012	4.5	1.0	0.0	10.0	0.0	2.1	2.4	**1.5**
2013	4.5	3.3	1.6	6.7	11.5	3.5	0.0	**3.8**
2014	9.1	2.4	0.8	0.0	8.3	2.8	0.0	**2.8**
2015	0.0	3.1	4.7	10.0	7.3	1.6	0.0	**3.1**
Sum (in %)	**100.0**	**100.0**	**100.0**	**100.0**	**100.0**	**100.0**	**100.0**	**100.0**

Notes

1 The Polish Constitutional Tribunal not only had an undemocratic origin but also lacked the competence to have the final say. The Communist parliament could override its decisions and even the democratically elected Sejm had this competence until 1997. The first fully democratically elected judges sat from 1993 in the Polish Constitutional Tribunal.

2 On the democratic transition in Hungary, see: Bozóki et al. ([1992] 2016) and Tőkés (1996).

3 On the inclination of the old elite to preserve its hegemony by creating new institutions or parachuting its members to old institutions, see: Ginsburg (2003, 19) and Hirschl (2004, 50).

4 Further competences included constitutional review of (1) international agreements, (2) legal regulations with respect to international agreements and (3) referenda processes. Furthermore, the HCC had the competence to dissolve local municipality councils in the case of their unconstitutional activity. Nevertheless, these competences are irrelevant from the perspective of our research project, since we are focusing on the legislative–judicial relations.

5 On the changes after 2010 in general, see: Sonnevend et al. (2015).

6 Before 2012 it was only the Head of the State; after 2012, the Head of the State, government and Speaker of parliament could file a petition.

7 On this process, see: Vincze (2014, 92). For a general overview of the critiques from various European organs, see: Kelemen (2017).

8 Though it is beyond the time frame of the present research, it is worth noting that, up to now, the last round of judge election in November 2016 turned out to be more consequential than previously, since the right-wing Fidesz lost not only several by-elections from early 2015 on but also its constitutional (two-thirds) majority in parliament. This implied that the governing party had to make a deal with the opposition to be able to elect new judges to the HCC. Due to vacancies, four new judges were elected in November 2016 with the support of the small (green) opposition party (LMP, Politics Could Be Different). This might bring fresh impulses into the Court, since all four judges came either from the academic sphere or higher courts. Whether this could lead to a rebalancing and (after a short deferential period) revival of the Court remains a question to be answered in the near future.

9 For recent assessments on the role of the court in democratic transformation, see: Lembcke and Boulanger (2012); Kovács and Tóth (2011, 185). For a personal account of the first president: Sólyom (2003).

10 For a general account, see: Schneider (2009). For recent trends of deconsolidation, see: Howe (2017).

11 On that question in general, most recently see: Daly (2017, 27–66).

12 See the path-breaking piece by Lee Epstein et al. (2001) on that hypothesis. For more recent accounts, see: Chavez (2008, 63); Ginsburg (2013, 47); and Smulovitz (2014, 731). For a more sceptical take on the issue, see: Gardbaum (2015, 307).

13 For data of other CEE countries, see the comparative chapter (Chapter 9).

14 See also: Pócza et al. (2017).

15 On the German influence, see: Tatham (2013, 41–64).

16 On the "Karlsruhe astrology", see: Beyme (2002, 110) and Vissier (2014, 35).

17 In the theoretical literature this assumption is formulated by Shapiro (1999).

18 For a qualitative assessment of the dissenting opinions at the HCC, see: Kelemen (2018).

19 It is worth noting that in the previous year, similarly crucial issues were sent to the Court – media law, law on electoral process, law on churches – however, the strength of the rulings was significantly lower. The explanation for this difference is that these latter issues were packed among many lesser ones, while in some important cases the Court restricted itself – all factors behind a weaker yearly average.

20 For the role of the presidents in general, see: Kelemen (2017).

21 It should be mentioned, however, that to keep to the time frames of the comparative research, we did not investigate the whole mandate of President Lenkovics.

22 For the methodology of assessing the party nominating the judges of the HCC, see: Pócza et al. (2017).

23 Number of rulings with at least one dissenting opinion: 1990–1998: 5.3 per year; 1999–2010: 15.5 per year; 2010–2015: 20.3 per year.

24 Two judges (Pál Solt and Géza Herczegh) never formulated DOs, since they were members in the very early years of the HCC when DOs were absolutely rare (and Pál Solt left the HCC after a few months to become the first President of the Supreme Court). Judge Mihály Bihari has been enumerated twice, since first he was nominated by the left-wing parties, but after having left the HCC in 2008 he was nominated once again, this time by the right-wing parties.

25 Red – left-wing nomination; pink – left-wing / consensus nomination; blue: judge nominated in complete consensus of left-wing and right-wing parties; light orange: right-wing / consensus nomination; orange: right-wing nomination.

References

Andrews, Josephine T. 2014. "Legislatures in Central and Eastern Europe". In *The Oxford Handbook of Legislative Studies*, edited by Shane Martin, Thomas Saalfeld, and Kaare W. Strøm, 647–675. Oxford: Oxford University Press.

von Beyme, Klaus. 2002. "The German Constitutional Court in an Uneasy Triangle between Parliament, Government and Federal Länder". In *Constitutional Justice East and West*, edited by Wojciech Sadurski, 101–118. The Hague/London: Kluwer Law International.

Bozóki, András, ed. 2002. *The Round Table Talks of 1989: The Genesis of Hungarian Democracy*. Budapest: CEU Press.

Bozóki, András, Körösényi András, and Schöpflin György, eds. ([1992] 2016). *Post-Communist Transition. Emerging Pluralism in Hungary*. London: Bloomsbury.

Bragyova, András. 2010. "Az alkotmánybíráskodás jövője". *Fundamentum* 1: 59–74.

Brunner, Georg. 2000. "Structure and Proceedings of the Hungarian constitutional Judiciary". In *Constitutional Judiciary in a New Democracy: The Hungarian Constitutional Court*, edited by Sólyom, László, and Georg Brunner, 65–102. Ann Arbor: University of Michigan Press.

Chavez, Rebecca Bill. 2008. "The Rule of Law and Courts in Democratizing Regimes". In *The Oxford Handbook of Law and Politics*, edited by Keith W. Whittington, 63–80. Oxford: Oxford University Press.

Daly, Tom Gerald. 2017. *The Alchemists: Questioning our Faith in Courts as Democracy-Builders*. Cambridge: Cambridge University Press.

Dezső, Márta, Bernadett Somody, Attila Vincze, Eszter Bodnár, Nóra Novaoszádek, and Beatrix Vissy. 2010. *Constitutional Law in Hungary*. Austin: Kluwer Law International.

Dupré, Catherine. 2003. *Importing the Law in Post-Communist Transitions. The Hungarian Constitutional Court and the Right to Human Dignity*. Oxford: Hart Publishing.

Epstein, Lee, and Shvestova, Olga. 2001. "The Role of Constitutional Courts in the Establishment and Maintenance of Democratic Systems of Government". *Law & Society Review* 35 (1): 117–164.

Gardbaum, Stephen. 2015. "Are Strong Constitutional Courts Always a Good Thing for New Democracies?" *Columbia Journal of Transnational Law* 53 (1): 286–320.

Ginsburg, Tom. 2003. *Judicial Review in New Democracies*. Cambridge: Cambridge University Press.

Ginsburg, Tom. 2013. "The Politics of Courts in Democratization: Four Junctures in Asia". In *Consequential Courts: Judicial Roles in Global Perspective*, edited by Diana Kapiszewski, Gordon Silverstein, and Robert A. Kagan, 45–66. Cambridge: Cambridge University Press.

Halmai, Gábor. 2002. "The Hungarian Approach to Constitutional Review". In *Constitutional Justice East and West*, edited by Wojciech Sadurski, 189–212. The Hague/London: Kluwer Law International.

Hirschl, Ran. 2004. *Towards Juristocracy. The Origins and Consequences of New Constitutionalism*. Cambridge: Harvard University Press.

Howe, Paul. 2017. "Eroding Norms and Democratic Deconsolidation". *Journal of Democracy* 28 (4): 15–29.

Kelemen, Katalin. 2017. "The New Hungarian Constitution: Legal Critiques from Europe". *Review of Central and East European Law* 42 (1): 1–49.

Kelemen, Katalin. 2018. *Judicial Dissent in European Constitutional Courts. A Comparative and Legal Perspective*. London: Routledge.

Körösényi, András, Csaba Tóth, and Gábor Török. 2009. *The Hungarian Political System* Budapest: Hungarian Center for Democracy Studies Foundation.

Kovács, Kriszta, and Gábor Attila Tóth. 2011. "Hungary's Constitutional Transformation". *European Constitutional Law Review* 7 (2): 183–203.

Lembcke, Oliver, and Christian Boulanger. 2012. "Between Revolution and Constitution: The Roles of the Hungarian Constitutional Court". In *Constitution for a Disunited Nation: On Hungary's New Fundamental Law*, edited by Gábor Attila Tóth, 269–299. Budapest: CEU Press.

Luchterhandt, Otto, Christian Starck, and Albrecht Weber, eds. 2007. *Verfassungsgerichtsbarkeit in Mittel- und Osteuropa*. Baden-Baden: Nomos Verlag.

Paczolay, Péter. 2010. "Nekünk az a feladatunk, hogy az alapjogok pártját fogjuk, és ne a társadalomirányítás általános szempontjait vegyük figyelembe". *Fundamentum* 1: 41–50.

Pócza, Kálmán, Gábor Dobos, and Attila Gyulai. 2017. "How to measure the strength of judicial decisions? A Methodological Framework". *German Law Journal* 18 (6): 1558–1586.

Prohacka, Radoslav. 2002. *Mission Accomplished. On Founding Constitutional Adjudication in Central Europe*. Budapest: CEU Press.

Sadurski, Wojciech, ed. 2002. *Constitutional Justice East and West*. The Hague/London: Kluwer Law International.

Sadurski, Wojciech, ed. (2008) 2014. *Rights Before Courts. A Study of Constitutional Courts in Postcommunist States of Central and Eastern Europe*. Dordrecht/New York: Springer.

Schneider, Carsten. 2009. *The Consolidation of Democracy*. London: Routledge.

Schwartz, Herman. 2000. *The Struggle for Constitutional Justice in Post-Communist Europe*. Chicago: University of Chicago Press.

Shapiro, Martin. 1999. "The Success of Judicial Review". In *Constitutional Dialogues in Comparative Perspective*, edited by Sally Kenney, William M. Reisinger, and John C. Reitz, 193–220. New York: MacMillan.

Smulovitz, Catalina. 2014. "Law and Courts' Impact on Development and Democratization". In *The Oxford Handbook of Empirical Legal Research*, edited by Peter Cane and Herbert M. Kritzer, 729–752. Oxford: Oxford University Press.

Sólyom, László. 2003. "The Role of Constitutional Courts in the Transition to Democracy. With Special Reference to Hungary". *International Sociology* 18 (1): 133–161.

Sonnevend, Pál, András Jakab, and Lóránt Csink. 2015. "The Constitution as an Instrument of Everyday Politics: The Basic Law of Hungary". In *Constitutional Crisis in the European Constitutional Area. Theory, Law and Politics in Hungary and Romania*, edited by Armin von Bogdandy, and Pál Sonnevend, 33–110. Oxford and Portland: Hart Publishing.

Tatham, Allan F. 2013. *Central European Constitutional Courts in the Face of EU-Membership. The Influence of the German Model in Hungary and Poland*. Leiden: Brill.

Tőkés, Rudolf. 1996. *Hungary's Negotiated Revolution*. Cambridge: Cambridge University Press.

Vincze, Attila. 2014. "Wrestling with Constitutionalism: The Supermajority and the Hungarian Constitutional Court". *ICL Journal* 8 (1): 86–97.

de Vissier, Maartje. 2014. *Constitutional Review in Europe: A Comparative Analysis*. Oxford: Hart Publishing.

6 The Polish Constitutional Tribunal

Deference beyond the veil of activism

Artur Wołek and Iga Kender-Jeziorska

6.1 Introduction

The Polish Constitutional Tribunal (PCT) has been a hot political topic since 2015. However, when the present research project was conceived, the PCT had been everything but an attractive issue for a mainstream political scientist. It was not only securely pigeonholed as a part of "legal studies", but due to the "mostly apologetic, smoothing and supportive character of Polish legal-constitutional thought", to quote Wojciech Sadurski (*Sąd czy ustawodawca* 2009, 31), it seemed to be uncontroversial, if not boring. The prevailing opinion was that in the 1990s the PCT was an important actor in the democratic transformation process, but with the consolidation of Polish democracy, its political significance ceased to be so vital. It simply became a low-profile part of the obligatory institutional package of democracy (O'Donnell 1996, 12), politically important only in a crisis situation, as in 2006–2007 when populists came to power and the PCT turned out to be an effective barrier to their political ambitions encroaching constitutional order.

All these assumptions ceased to be valid in 2015. First, the centre-right ruling coalition of the Civic Platform (*Platforma Obywatelska*, PO) and the Polish People's Party (*Polskie Stronnictwo Ludowe*, PSL), sensing a debacle in the coming elections, decided to elect three judges "in advance", well before their predecessors' term would end.[1] Then, after the October 2015 elections, the new parliamentary majority of the Law and Justice party (*Prawo i Sprawiedliwość*, PiS) not only ignored all five judges elected by the previous parliament but also changed the Constitutional Tribunal Act to take full control of the institution. By the end of 2017, the PCT was effectively defunct: packed with judges fully obedient to the new parliamentary majority, inefficient in terms of the docket handling and with its legitimacy in shreds.[2] However, this development meant that apparently the PCT had not been as unproblematic an institution as it seemed to legal scholars and much more of interest to politicians than to political scientists.

The following study addresses the question concerning to what extent the PCT has been an important political actor in Poland. As an indicator, we examine the scope and means by which the PCT restricts the *Spielraum* of the parliament, empirically analyzing the data on judicial behaviour collected in the JUDICON project. The examination is restricted to the period 1993–2015; therefore, it terminates once the present PCT crisis had commenced, but indirectly it hints at the factors overlooked by the scholarship, factors which triggered the fall of the PCT in 2015–2016.[3]

This chapter does not take for granted the received wisdom about the PCT's political neutrality and examines whether partisan politics might be a variable explaining the judicial behaviour in the Polish Constitutional Tribunal. Therefore, after sketching the historical development and institutional setup of the PCT, the article reconstructs the Tribunal's political trajectory. The existing scholarship on the issue is highly flawed; thus, we try to reuse the existing data and draw some new conclusions based mainly on the data collected by the JUDICON project.

The analysis suggests that, since the political process of PCT judges' nomination was highly partisan, party politics was a major factor behind the institutional strategy of the PCT in relation to both parliament and the adjudication. The PCT was activist when there was no clear majority in parliament and more deferential when a parliamentary majority succeeded in electing judges more amenable to the requirements of political governance. For most of the period under scrutiny, the PCT acted as a Kelsenian negative legislator, following its legitimation doctrine, but its political neutrality was questionable, especially during the crisis situation and the period of bi-polar politics in Poland (2005 to date). When it came to politically divisive issues, the judges acted in line with the preferences of the parties which selected them, and in other cases they at least took into account political–partisan considerations.

6.2 Origins of the court and institutional setup

6.2.1 Origins of the court

Unlike constitutional courts in all other Central and Eastern European countries, the PCT was not a product of the democratic transformation, or to be more precise, it was a product of the transformation of the communist regime that began in the early 1980s. The change of political and intellectual climate which resulted in the Solidarity (*Solidarność*) revolution of 1980–1981 emboldened law professors and legal professionals. Even though they generally remained supporters of communist rule, they started to raise ideas of establishing communist power more on legal rules than political will, not to say open violence. The first result of this new thinking was the re-establishment of the administrative courts in 1980. Quite paradoxically, military suppression of the Solidarity movement in 1981–1982 created a legitimacy vacuum, which legal proceduralization of the communist rule promised to fill. In this atmosphere of an acute legitimacy crisis, the Constitutional Tribunal was created by the constitutional amendment of 1982. It took communists another three years to clarify the details of the new institution and to select judges for the PCT, so the first ruling was delivered only in May 1986 (Czeszejko-Sochacki 2001; Garlicki 2003).

The delay was telling. If the Tribunal were to deal with the deep legitimacy deficit, the institution had to be endowed with real powers; the judges could not simply be another set of communist apparatchiks. On the other hand, the whole communist legal system was based on the assumption of the unrestricted sovereignty of the "working people" embodied in the parliament (the Sejm). As a result of this dilemma, the newly created PCT could strike down parliamentary legislation, but such rulings had to be accepted or dismissed by the Sejm with a two-thirds majority. A general perception was that the PCT should act as a counsel and not an opponent of parliament, and its real field of activity should be secondary legislation, where the Tribunal had a final say. In the period 1986–1988, the PCT dealt with four acts of parliament and 22 substatutory acts, in which only one statute was declared unconstitutional (Garlicki 1999, 283). At the same time, the PCT gained some authority within the legal profession – if not among the general public. Among the 12 judges elected by the Sejm in December 1985, dominated by law professors and former Supreme Court judges, only a few had a direct political involvement. On the other hand, half the judges were elected for a short, four-year term.

Thanks to this back-door arrangement secured by the communists in case the Tribunal became too independent, the PCT played an instrumental role when the political transformation gained momentum after the round-table talks (spring 1989), partly free parliamentary elections (June 1989) and the appointment of the first non-communist prime minister (September 1989). When the term of six judges expired in December 1989, the new Sejm elected five judges clearly linked to the Solidarity movement (plus a former Supreme Court judge). One of the new judges became the president of the Tribunal, a position crucial for the day-to-day functioning of the PCT (including allocation of judges to cases), and the institution gained a completely new dynamic. Not only was the Tribunal more assertive towards the parliament, declaring the unconstitutionality of half the statutes it dealt with, it also developed an extensive jurisprudence based on the new constitutional definition of the state. Article 1 of the 1952 Constitution amended in December 1989 pronounced Poland to be "a democratic state ruled by law realizing the principles of social justice" (henceforth the *Rechtsstaat* clause). This clause was often referred to in rulings presenting an abstract authoritative binding interpretation of statutes, a competence taken over from the communist-era collective Presidency of the Republic and used extensively during the political transition – 29 such rulings in 1990–1992, and 101 up to 1997 (Czeszejko-Sochacki 1996).

In one such ruling the Tribunal further strengthened its position *vis-à-vis* parliament when it declared that the statutes deemed unconstitutional by the PCT ceased to be binding law, even if the Sejm would not accept or dismiss the ruling (W 6/93). When the Sejm is passive, it is the President of the PCT who pronounces in the official gazette the abrogation of the act. This ruling, delivered in 1994, was a visible sign of the strong self-confidence of the PCT stemming from the substantial legitimacy capital it accumulated in the period of transition. For the legitimacy of the PCT it was not irrelevant that in February 1993 the first democratically elected Sejm selected its own judge (after one of the old judges resigned) and Solidarity judges effectively were a majority of the court. Changes in the composition of the PCT following the elections of 1993, which were disastrous for the post-Solidarity camp, did not change the general outlook of the institution, even though they changed its adjudication strategy.[4] It was held in high esteem among legal professionals, respected by politicians and legitimized by the general public. As such, it definitely had its say in the legislative–political process leading to the preparation of the new constitution.

6.2.2 Institutional setup

The new constitution of 1997 (in force from 17 October 1997), followed by the new Constitutional Tribunal Act in the same year, strengthened the position of the PCT and stabilized it for almost 20 years. The new legal framework upheld the competences of the PCT: deciding on the conformity of statutes with the constitution, deciding on the conformity of the secondary legislation issued by national executive organs with the constitution and statutory law, resolving disputes between state organs and vetting the constitutionality of goals and activities of political parties. It also retained the relatively long list of actors entitled to petition the PCT: parliament, a group of 50 members of the Sejm or 30 senators, the government, the President of the Republic, courts of law, the ombudsman. Local authorities, trade unions and churches were also eligible if they perceived their legal interests were infringed by legislation, and only in these cases did the PCT have the power over its docket authorized to dismiss any application as inadmissible. A new institution introduced in 1997 was the constitutional complaint, defined in a rather restrictive way as a grievance against a legal regulation which was the basis for a final court decision infringing rights or freedoms of the applicant. The PCT also retained the competence of the *a priori* review of statutes before their promulgation on the motion of the President of the Republic (Garlicki 2016, 406–429).

The big change in the new legal framework concerned the final character of the PCT decisions. This applied to statutory and substatutory legal acts, *a priori* and *a posteriori* review, competence disputes and all other forms of procedures.[5] At the same time, the PCT was deprived of the competence of issuing *in abstracto* binding interpretations of statutes, a competence vehemently contested by the Supreme Court in the 1990s.

Only minor changes took place concerning the Tribunal's composition and *modus operandi*. The number of judges was increased from 12 to 15, and the term of their office was expanded from eight to nine years without the possibility of re-election. They are elected by the Sejm in a strictly political procedure: candidates are proposed by groups of deputies (*de facto* by political parties) and an absolute majority of those present is needed. The only real threshold for candidacy is the requirement to have worked at least ten years in a legal profession. In practice, the candidates of the ruling majority almost always are elected, and broader coalitions or non-partisan candidacies are extremely rare. This does not mean that politicians elect politicians. Out of 40 judges elected between 1993 and 2015 there were 17 active politicians and 33 law professors who constantly dominated the bench.[6] There were also 12 judges originating from courts of law, but they were also sponsored by a political party.

A peculiar feature of the PCT involves decision-making by benches (councils) created *ad hoc* for each case. The five-member bench is a basic mode of operation of the PCT, and minor cases are decided by the bench of three. The only exceptions are matters previously adjudicated by the full Tribunal and as such reserved by the law for full Tribunal and "especially complicated cases" (as decided by the PCT President). Thus, it is clear that a crucial power involves the allocation of judges to respective cases. Before and after 1997 this was a competence of the Tribunal's President, who was selected by the President of the Republic from two candidates proposed by the PCT judges. Before 2006, the Tribunal's President could allocate judges at his/her will, even though a practice of more or less stable benches evolved. On the other hand, in 1993 when the ratio of Solidarity to old judges was 6:6, Andrzej Zoll, the leading Solidarity-nominated judge (and the Tribunal's President after November 1993) sat on benches which delivered 20 out of 25 rulings. Since 2006, the internal rules and regulations of the PCT have required the Tribunal's President to allocate cases according to the alphabetical order of judges. This provision definitely restricts the power of the President, but it should be stressed that he/she is also the sole employer and superior of all clerks serving the Tribunal, so the space for the informal influence of the President is still very broad.

6.2.3 Caseload

If the importance of an institution in the political system is measured by its output, the PCT role was steadily growing all through the 1990s and the first decade of the new millennium. The number of cases it took a substantive decision was in the single digits in its first years of its operation and reached 173 in 2015. The political weight of the PCT decisions also grew. In the early years, an essential part of its activity was secondary legislation, with only a few statutes probed by the judges (one in 1986 and 1988, two in 1987). It was only in 1992 that the number of statutes under PCT consideration exceeded the number of substatutory acts. Since that time, the PCT has dealt on average with more than four times as many statutes as secondary legislation (and for the last ten years the proportion has been 9:1). As for the subject of the PCT activities, there are three more very distinct trends: first of all, the number of statutes questioned before the Tribunal has been more or less stable since 1997 (between 30 and 40 on average). The second trend has been the rising number of "questions of law" addressed to the PCT by courts of law: they were single-digit until 1999, but after 2000 became more and more popular (60 cases in 2009). The third tendency was a growing popularity of the constitutional complaint between when it was introduced in 1997 and 2009, when it was quite abruptly cut (65 PCT final decisions in 2008, 49 in 2009 and 31 in 2010). These trends are mirrored to a great extent by the statistics of decisions and rulings qualified for the JUDICON database: steady growth till 2006, a drop and a stabilization since 2010 (Figure 6.1).

A drop in the total number of constitutional complaints received by the PCT is partly responsible for the smaller caseload after 2008, but even more than this is the growing number of complaints refused at a preliminary stage of the proceedings. The number of constitutional complaints grew from 168 in 1998 to 405 in 2008; then they dropped to 321 in 2009 and 351 in 2010. During the first three years of this new instrument of constitutionality control, between 11 and 17 percent of motions passed through the preliminary stage and were considered by the Tribunal on merit. In the period 2001–2006, the percentage grew to 34; in 2007, it suddenly dropped to 16 percent and down to 9 percent in 2010. Allegedly potential claimants noticed this change in the PCT policy and became less eager to petition the Tribunal. The astonishing difference between the number of decisions and the number of rulings in Figure 6.1 is a result of strategies taken by both claimants and the PCT itself. The petitioners seemed to believe that the argument about unconstitutionality of several clauses of an act was more legally persuasive than attacking the act wholesale. The PCT most often felt obligated to address all the grievances one by one, but it also took the opportunity to kill the whole act by invalidating several of its crucial clauses. This strategy allowed a relatively low political profile to be kept and the achievement of the PCT's goals, as in the case of the lustration act decision (K 2/07), composed of 77 rulings including 40 declarations of unconstitutionality.

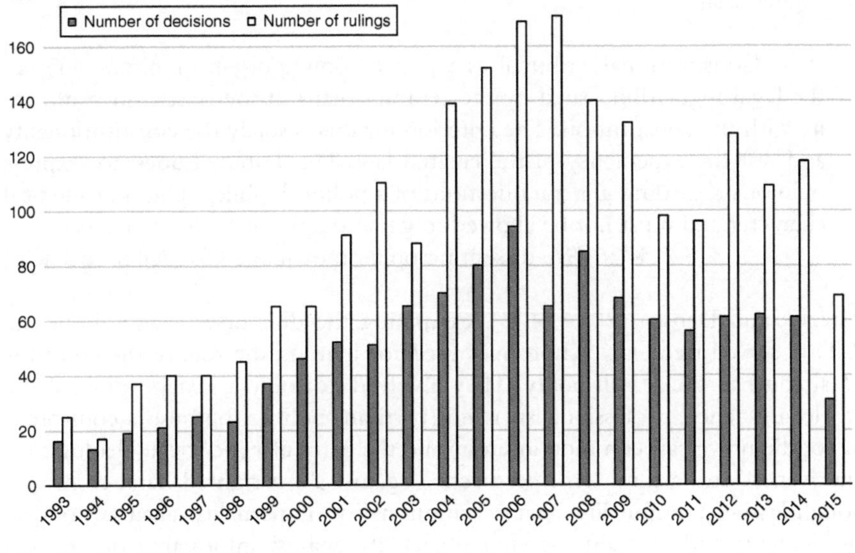

Figure 6.1 Number of decisions and rulings (PCT)

6.3 General observations: a barrier for politics or a part of it?

The dominating narrative about the PCT and its relationship with the realm of politics embodied by parliament was rather apologetic before 2015 (Sulikowski 2016). For legal scholars – and they effectively monopolized the research on the PCT – it was obvious that the PCT was a barrier for politics and not a part of politics. Hanna Dębska (2015), studying the legitimacy production of the PCT, argues that in the early communist period of the Tribunal this ostentatious detachment from politics was a deliberate strategy, given that the new institution was to fulfil the expectations of its designers, namely to strengthen the legitimacy of the whole regime. It proved to be useful during the transition period, as the PCT was eager to play the role of a neutral, professional facilitator of the legal changes leading to the *Rechtsstaat* construction in Poland. The PCT could claim to be neutral because judges had a strong cultural capital perceived as independent from the political capital of the old communist guard: they were law professors, law professionals with few immediate political links. This was a stable tendency among the PCT judges: in the period 1989–2015, 70 percent held a professorial degree and 64 percent had engaged in a legal profession during their career, while 43 percent combined both types of capital: they were both law professors and law professionals (Dębska 2015, 35–37; Dębska 2015a, 204–217).

High prestige and an image of political neutrality were apparently transferred from law professors to the institution of the PCT. Dębska (2015, 36) claims that "the constitutional court, similarly to the supreme court, is located on Poles' mental maps close to universities and not the law or politics". The Tribunal itself took care of strengthening its image as a neutral "negative legislator". It repeatedly argued that

> [t]he Constitutional Tribunal as a judicial power organ monitors whether the legal regulation issued by the central organs of the state is in conformity with the constitution. The criterion for this is solely the constitutionality and not the expediency of the created law. The Tribunal does not express opinions regarding general questions of a political, philosophical or medical character and must not be allowed to get entangled in those conflicts.
>
> (K 26/96, dissenting opinion by judge Czeszejko-Sochacki)

Warczok and Dębska (2014, 472), examining the discourse of and about the PCT, observed frequent dichotomies used for framing the role of the constitutional court in the Polish polity. They involved not only a juxtaposition of the law (legal science, professionalism) and (partisan) politics, but also a confrontation of the universal (common interest) and the particular (political, ideological); reflexiveness and a long-term perspective against short-sighted hand-to-mouth thoughtlessness; rationality against emotionality; impartiality against political engagement; and formality serving objectivity against informality on services of subjectivity.

This kind of "it's the law, stupid" legitimacy ideology was for a long time an effective deterrent when it came to empirical studies about the role of the PCT in Polish politics. For a long time "the power of the Constitutional Tribunal [became] a 'denied power', an apolitical legal professionalism denying politics" (Warczok and Dębska 2014, 472), not only for political actors and legal scholars, but also for social scientists. It is quite paradoxical that even the researchers drawing from critical social studies without much empirical examination are ready to claim that "despite the fact that politicians appoint the judges for the Tribunal, it does not mean that they are directly politicised" (Dębska 2015, 38; Sulikowski 2016). They might be entangled in power processes, they might even have political views, but being first of all professionals they "leave them in the cloakroom of the Tribunal", as the popular sound bite went. Unlike the scholars dealing with the United States Supreme Court, we cannot simply examine this claim empirically because of the secrecy of the most important parts of the Tribunal's proceedings; we are left with a black box model with "politics" on the input side and the "neutral law" claim on the output side, a model constructed by the legal community for their own use (Stone Sweet 1992, 115–116).

However, some light into this box is provided by the judges themselves. Marek Safjan, the President of the PCT in 1998–2006, writing about constitutional courts as positive legislators, quite openly admits that adding new normative content in relation to the existing legal situation "remains somewhat concealed, never being openly proclaimed or clearly expressed in a legal solution, as doing so would transgress the boundaries of the ethos and ideology of constitutional justice" (Safjan 2013, 703). He recalled the sole case when the PCT directly told parliament what deputies should do, ordering the restoration of a provision that had been in force before the statute eliminated by the PCT was accepted by the Sejm (K4/99). Safjan acknowledges, however, that during the transition "when adequate constitutional norms were still missing, [the PCT was] practically pushed toward substantial creativity, which consisted in decoding the standards of rights and freedoms – which were not directly expressed in the constitutional norms – from the axiology of a new democratic system" (710), which apparently means from some extra-legal sources. He argued that "social and political revolution justified such an attitude" but continued that after the new constitution of 1997 was accepted "the scale and direction of judicial activism changed, the nature of the phenomenon of creation of norms of constitutional significance did not"; this consisted in the "process of decoding rules (and, *de facto*, their creation) and finding a new normative content" (712).

Moreover, Safjan not only discloses an insider's view about the procedural dimension of the decision-making process in the PCT but also comments on its content. The PCT avoids statements that would lead to imposing a certain vision on the sphere of social and economic policies which would direct the Sejm toward specific legal solutions, but a "modern European state and member of the EU has strongly determined directions in relation to social and economic solutions" (Safjan 2013, 712). The PCT under Safjan's presidency was ready to remind the Sejm what these "determined directions" are.

There have been few openly political statements made by the PCT judges, but they are often ready to admit that they might have struck a statute down because it was obviously unconstitutional, yet did not do so because of some prudential/political reasons. Judge Biruta Lewaszkiewicz-Petrykowska recalled "Act 203" of December 2000, in which parliament raised the salaries of medical staff without allocating extra money for their employers. "We had to do a lot of balancing and stretching in order to keep the act. It was all about weighing different values, and the act itself was very badly written". It could have been easily deemed unconstitutional as encroaching "principles of correct legislation", a part of the *Rechtsstaat* principle often cited by the PCT (*Sąd czy ustawodawca* 2009, 22).

If judges themselves admit (though not in rulings) that they make policy choices based on some extra-legal considerations, it opens the field for empirical research. Without going into a discussion on the nature of the constitutional court's activities (Segal 2010; Lax 2011; Sadurski 2008, 27–63; Smekal and Pospíšil 2013), we can ask how judges' policy choices restrict parliament: how often they contradict the will of deputies, how far they go and what patterns of interaction between the institutions exist temporally. Moreover, we can bracket the legitimation ideology of the PCT and disaggregate both the world of politics and the PCT itself, asking which parliamentary majorities were restricted by which majorities in the PCT. In the following sections, we propose such an analysis for the period 1993–2015, marked by the election of the first PCT judge by the first democratically elected parliament in 1993 and the change of the Constitutional Tribunal Act – the beginning of the still unfinished conflict in 2015 over the PCT.

6.4 Trends in majority rulings

6.4.1 Trends in ruling types: the Tribunal's political trajectory

In view of the short history and prevailing legitimation ideology of the PCT we have just presented, it is clear that using the attitudinal model of judicial politics is hardly possible in the Polish environment (Dyevre 2010, 300–302). Therefore, the student of judicial politics in Poland is left with some kind of institutionalist model based on an assumption that judges are policy-seekers, but in pursuing their policy goals they are severely constrained by the institutional environment (Dyevre 2010, 304–311). An advantage of this approach is that it corresponds to a degree with the legal scholarship on constitutional courts, and its accomplishments can be used for judicial politics explanations. A disadvantage of most of the institutionalist models is that they tend to lose politics from their sight, ignoring the partisan dimension of institutional games judges and politicians allegedly play. In the argument that follows we will try, insofar as possible, to supplement a basically institutionalist reasoning with elements of an attitudinal approach to present convincing data on judicial behaviour.

The presumed watershed: 1997

For legal scholarship, but also for lay commentators and the Tribunal itself, it is uncontroversial that the year 1997 was a watershed for the workings of the PCT. The new (post-)transitional constitution was adopted and the whole approach of the PCT to social reality was able to change. There was no need to fill the gaps in the constitutional system; the new basic law was founded on an assumption of completeness. The institutional position of the PCT in relation to parliament also changed substantially, as the rulings of the Tribunal became final and could not be overridden by the Sejm.

An analysis of the judicial rulings included in the database of the JUDICON project confirms to some extent this common knowledge. If we compare the period 1993–1997 to the whole sample of the rulings and to the later period of the PCT behaviour, there is a real difference. The average rate of rejections of motions was 47.6 percent for the period 1993–1997 and 56.3 percent for the whole 22 years under research, while for the period 1998–2015 it was 57.7 percent. Conversely, a substantive unconstitutionality was found in 44.2 percent of the statutes questioned before the PCT from the 1993–1997 period and 37.5 percent of 1998–2015 rulings. A milder form of restricting the *Spielraum* of the parliament – the constitutional requirement/interpretation in harmony with the constitution – was also used much more frequently in 1993–1997 (6.6 percent of rulings) than in 1998–2015 (2.1 percent of rulings) (Figure 6.2).

These results fit somehow the narrative of the PCT, which was activist when it was needed because of the numerous lacunae in the legal system that had to be filled with PCT decisions, but once the constitution was in place (1997) the PCT could afford some self-restraint. On the other hand, they contradict to a degree

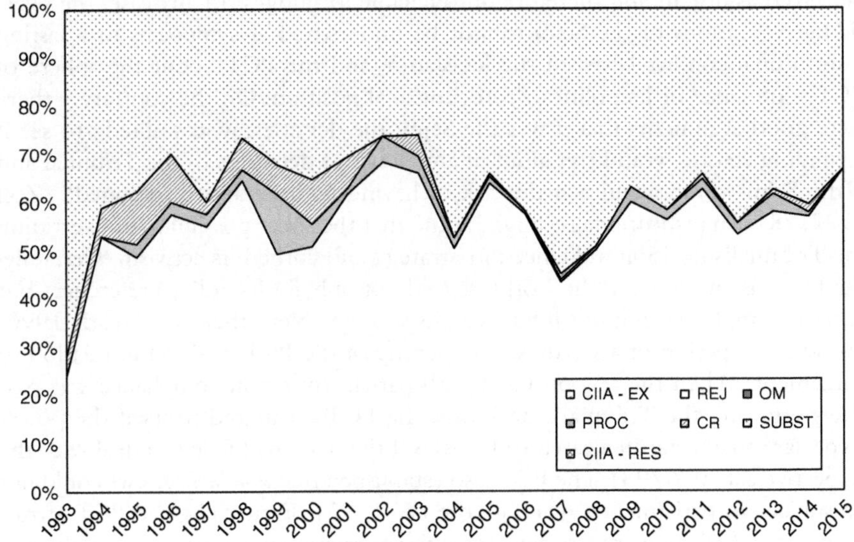

Figure 6.2 Frequency of ruling types I (PCT)

the crucial role of the final character of the PCT rulings. If the new 1997 constitution's finality for PCT decisions was "a final victory of the Constitution over politics and acknowledgment that nothing can justify keeping unconstitutional legal provision in the legal system" (Safjan 1999), it apparently was not capitalized duly, as might have been expected.

Overridings by parliament between 1993 and 1997

The analysis of the frequency of PCT decisions overridden by the Sejm shows, however, that this competence of parliament was not an important barrier for the PCT in having a final say in the period 1986–1999.[7] During these 13 years, parliament overrode 11 PCT decisions, some of them only in part, which constituted 11.3 percent of all decisions declaring the unconstitutionality of a statute (Garlicki 1999, 283–289). It would be difficult to argue that any of these "restored" acts were important from the constitutional point of view. Many of them were statutes concerning financial matters, and the Sejm majority managed to convince the opposition (a two-thirds majority was required) that acceptance of the PCT decision would be disastrous for the state budget. Other decisions overridden by parliament dealt with social rights, and it was a strong interest group that stood behind the prevailing majority. What they all had in common was a fairly random selection of the decisions that the Sejm succeeded in overriding. No pattern could be traced, and in fact, the result of the chamber vote was always uncertain.

Some of the overridden decisions of the PCT contained sound legal reasoning and the PCT valued them positively, referring to them in its later jurisprudence; others probably did not. Nevertheless, it was not the legal arguments that caused the decision of deputies; most often, it was simply the subject matter politicians perceived as urgent and therefore untouchable for judges. In any case, the overriding resolutions of the Sejm cannot be understood as symptoms of a lasting institutional conflict between the legislature and the PCT about the sphere of PCT's influence or its political/constitutional position. On the contrary – there were good arguments that it was the Sejm, the deputies, who wanted "to see if a pending statute would run afoul of any previous decisions of the Tribunal and if the Sejm would again run the risk of having its legal acts questioned" (Zoll 1997, 78). An institutionalist might argue that the sheer possibility of overriding the Tribunal's decision influenced its strategy and curbed its activism. Certainly, the PCT, as any court in the world, strived not only for its policy preferences but also for compliance and this influenced its strategy. Nevertheless, the early 1990s was rather a period of a steady strengthening of the PCT position in relation to parliament. When the real problem with parliament's non-compliance was passively ignoring the Tribunal's decisions, the PCT attributed to itself the power to declare that a statute ceased to be valid if the Sejm had failed to deal with the respective act (W 6/93). The PCT also established that *a priori* reviews could not be subject to parliament's reversal vote (W 1/95). Eventually, the PCT attributed to itself the power to review not only international agreements but also the standing orders of parliament (Procházka 2002, 89–91).

In terms of Vanberg's model (2005), Poland in the early 1990s would probably be close to the "judicial supremacy" situation, with legislative self-censorship, a powerful or rather steadily strengthening constitutional court and strong public support for the PCT.[8] The formal constitutional framework restraining the PCT proved to be of secondary importance. It was the extreme fragmentation of parliament that was significant. During the first democratic elections of 1991, 28 groupings received seats in parliament; there were 18 parliamentary factions in the Sejm in 1993 when the chamber was dissolved, and early elections followed. The deputies could hardly arrange a simple majority to support a cabinet, so the two-thirds majority required for overriding a ruling of the Tribunal was normally beyond their reach.[9]

The real watershed: 1994

This extreme fragmentation was abruptly discontinued by the second free election (1993), leaving representatives of more than 30 percent of the voters outside parliament (due to the electoral threshold) but returning a six-party parliament and a stable two-party, post-communist governing coalition. In late autumn 1993, the coalition elected half the PCT and in May 1994 the seventh judge, all of them linked to the governing parties. Two newly elected judges were members of parliament for the (post-)communist party and one ran on the junior coalition party ticket to the Senate. One was a public prosecutor but also a high official of the Justice Ministry, and two judges were law professors engaged previously as party experts. The professional authority of the new judges could not be questioned, but their links to partisan politics were definitely stronger than those of previous judges; no candidate of the opposition parties was accepted.

The new composition of the PCT was reflected in a change of judicial behaviour, as represented by the data in the JUDICON database. There was a prevailing majority of Solidarity-nominated judges in 1993. Of 25 rulings taken by the PCT in 1993, 16 were decided by a bench where Solidarity judges were in majority (64 percent). By contrast, in 1994 58 percent and in 1995 76 percent of rulings were taken by benches with the new coalition-nominated judges in the majority. Interestingly, the first dissenting opinions ever in the PCT were submitted in 1995, and they were authored almost exclusively by the Solidarity-nominated judges.

The changes of personnel had a clear influence on the relationship between the PCT and parliament. Whereas in 1993 the PCT declared 72 percent of the statutes it dealt with unconstitutional, in 1994 it was only 41.2 percent and on average 37.3 percent yearly by 1997.[10] In 1993 the PCT rejected only 24 percent of motions, and in the 1994–1997 period it was 53.5 percent on average. It should be noted, however, that there was no major difference in behaviour of benches with a majority of post-Solidarity or left-nominated judges. The year 1994 marks more a change of the PCT culture in general than a simple change of political majorities.

This change is apparently reflected in the PCT jurisprudence. The presumption of constitutionality is obviously a dogma in the "negative legislator" model of constitutional courts. This had always been a working assumption of the PCT, but more elaborate consequences of this principle resulting in deference to parliament appear as late as 1994 (Oniszczuk 1998, 36–37; Sadurski 2008, 99–100). The principle that the PCT is limited to the scrutiny of constitutionality and is not interested in "the wisdom" of legal acts (K 19/96, K 18/95) or the principle of parliamentary freedom to choose any constitutionally acceptable policy (K 2/94, K 6/94, K 12/94) and the very self-definition of the PCT as "the negative legislator" (K 13/95) were formulated by the Tribunal with a majority of judges elected by the first strong parliamentary majority after 1989.

Despite the dominant legal scholars' narrative, empirical data suggest that the breaking point for the early PCT was 1994 and not 1997. Apparently, there was a continuity of the strong and still strengthening position of the PCT in relation to parliament in the period 1989–1993 and a pronounced change in 1994 – a 29 percentage-point drop in unconstitutionality rulings and a 29 percentage-point rise in rejections. There is no such clear discontinuity in 1997–1998, despite the change of the constitutional framework, even though the tendency beginning in 1994 was reinforced after 1997. The most obvious explanation of these facts would be politics. After the 1993 election a strong parliamentary majority took the opportunity to elect judges who would be more responsive to the troubles of everyday governing and leave more space for politicians. This argument does not contradict a more general interpretation of the PCT of the 1990s as a "constitutional emergency-unit [...] fixing the gap-ridden texture of Poland's pre-1997 constitutional law", constructing missing rules instead of evading hard cases. Thus, the PCT was generally more activist and positively creative, while at the same time understanding that particular needs of the systemic transition needed to be taken into account in its decision-making (Procházka 2002, 87, 206). The PCT was ready "to exhibit considerable self-restraint in reviewing transition-related policies" (84), but only after the first parliamentary majority succeeded in electing friendly judges. Earlier, the judges were ready much more often to "fix the gaps" according to their own vision of the new democracy; this is especially valid for post-Solidarity judges mustering a working majority in the Tribunal in 1993.

Weak substantive unconstitutionality as dominant ruling type

This evolution explains also why weak and average substantive unconstitutionality are dominant ruling types. They make together 38.7 percent of all rulings, and if we take into consideration that 56.3 percent are rejections, it means that only in 5 percent of cases does unconstitutionality mean something different than weak and average substantive unconstitutionality.

Behind this extremely high number there is a combination of several factors. First is the self-image of a negative legislator, which most often means two default options: either constitutionality or unconstitutionality on substantive grounds.

Weak and average forms of the latter ruling were first of all consequences of the PCT institutional setup: no *ex tunc* rulings were admissible in the Polish legal system, and due to the PCT's origins, prescriptions or positive policy directives in rulings were unthinkable.[11] These circumstances narrowed the options available to judges, but they narrowed them themselves even more when they tried to be more compassionate and therefore more deferential to the requirements of governance in the period of transition.

The PCT almost never used the tool of complete annulment of an act of parliament (16 cases during 22 years, 12 of them in the *a priori* procedure). The Tribunal more frequently found some parts of an act unconstitutional (45.5 percent quantitative partial annulment) but most frequently (52.8 percent qualitative partial annulment) declared unconstitutionality of specific usage or application of some parts of regulations.

Moreover, the new constitution introduced a new measure for judicial self-restraint (effective since 1999) by allowing rulings with *pro futuro* temporal effect. One might say that before 1999 all rulings had been *pro futuro* as they needed to be confirmed by the parliament, and it took the Sejm some time to cope with the PCT output. Formally, however, the rulings were *ex nunc*, and courts might have taken the "suspended" ruling as binding or at least have suspended their own proceedings. Between 1991 and 2015 there were 28.2 percent *pro futuro* substantive unconstitutionality rulings; this explains to a degree why the weak rulings started to dominate over rulings of an average strength. Only once (2002) were there more average than weak substantive unconstitutionality rulings after 1999; this trend was especially evident after 2011 (Figure 6.3). On the other hand, the "weakness" of ruling is in the case of the PCT most often a combination of the partial character of a ruling and the time it leaves to the legislator for finding an alternative to the questioned policy.

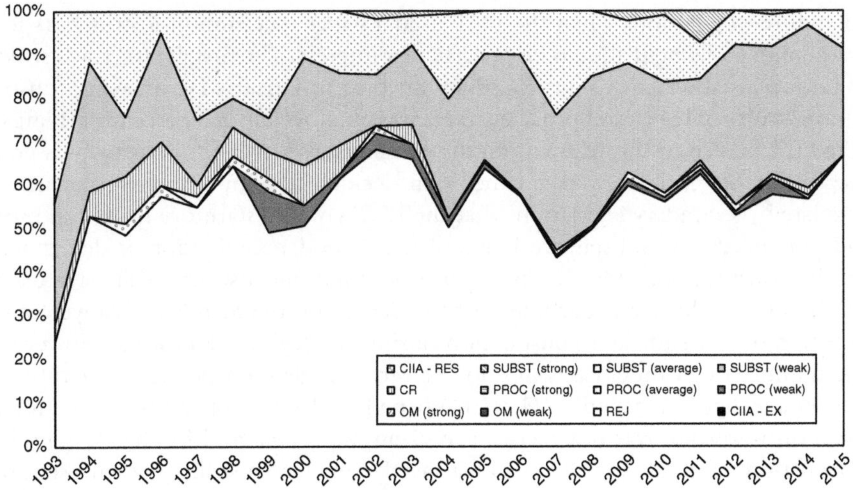

Figure 6.3 Frequency of ruling types II (PCT)

The data about the domination of weak and average substantive unconstitutionality rulings in the PCT's adjudication practice may also be read through the lens of the extensive research about PCT jurisprudence undertaken by Stawecki et al. (2008). The authors were interested primarily in the models of legal reasoning empirically detectable in PCT jurisprudence and its influence on the courts of law and lawmaking in Poland. The authors found that the PCT is devoted to the "model of rules", using Robert Alexy's (2002) conceptual framework. In this model, a constitution is composed of standards that allow for a conclusive qualification of actions as fulfilling or infringing respective standards. Rules are based on the logic of all or nothing and, unlike "principles", cannot be realized partially, to a greater or lesser degree. This corresponds with the Kelsenian vision of the constitutional court as a negative legislator eliminating "unlawful" statutes which do not fulfil constitutional standards. Stawecki et al. (2008, 21) observed that 70 percent of the PCT arguments were based on the interpretation of the constitutional norms as rules. In this context it is understandable why the PCT rarely reaches for instruments other than substantive unconstitutionality and positively renounces using tools known to other Central European courts, such as the unconstitutional legislative omission, for instance.

The above analysis has shown that the PCT, following its legitimation doctrine most of the period under research, really was a negative legislator and used more nuanced measures in its interactions with the Sejm very rarely. It is particularly evident if compared to some other Central European constitutional courts. The Hungarian Constitutional Court delivered 24 percent other rulings; in the Slovak case it was 8.1 percent; and after 1990 the German Federal Constitutional Court delivered 15.8 percent of rulings other than belonging to the two categories.

Procedural unconstitutionality

Therefore, the periods when the PCT used a wider spectrum of instruments for restraining parliament should be of particular interest. The first measure was striking down a statute due to its procedural unconstitutionality, i.e. breaking constitutional rules of legislative process, and it was employed in 2.3 percent of rulings. The PCT perceived this restraint on the parliament's activity in a narrow way and used it almost exclusively when the Sejm decided to allow the government to regulate by secondary legislation what the PCT saw as a statutory matter and/or did not specify the substantive limits of the secondary legislation as demanded by the constitution. Other cases when procedural unconstitutionality was used by the PCT include encroachment of the Senate on the Sejm's legislative competences or not sufficient consultation during the legislative process. However, the number of all these cases did not exceed a single digit per year, even if the percentage figure reached 12.3, as happened in 1999. Apparently, procedural unconstitutionality was not recognized as an important tool by the PCT itself. One reason was a critique that the PCT faced, namely that striking down a statute based on the procedural requirements of the legislative process was a comfortable way for not taking a position in a controversial case. Sometimes the PCT itself provoked this kind of charge when an inconsistency between the operative part of the decision and its justification was more than noticeable. Adjudicating on the state budget (K 16/93) and land management and property expropriation (K 18/95), the PCT declared a violation of legislative procedures, but in the justification the Tribunal referred extensively to substantive constitutional standards such as the principles of proportionality and clarity.

The PCT quite often phrased its reservations in relation to the formal quality and not substance of the legislative production in terms of the *Rechtsstaat* requirements, e.g. "proper legislative technique" (P 1/94), "definiteness of legal regulations" (K 11/94, K 17/93). They were contested less and still allowed the PCT to avoid taking positions in divisive cases. The JUDICON database records 27 such rulings during the 22 years of PCT activity under "formal unconstitutionality/principle of rule of law".[12] This includes, however, only those rulings which explicitly cited the formal *Rechtsstaat* clauses in the operative parts of the decision. It is not infrequent that only while reading the justification can this approach of the PCT be reconstructed. In any case, it may be concluded that the PCT refrained from an excessive use of procedural clauses to strike down legislation and was ready to face a substantive assessment of the challenged laws.

Constitutional requirements

Much more consequential is an analysis of the rulings which include conditionality in relation to a PCT ruling on constitutionality: an act is constitutional if understood in such and such a way. Polish legal scholars call these decisions interpretive rulings, and the JUDICON project uses the term "constitutional requirement". They seem to be less intrusive in relation to parliament's legislative decisions, as they declare that only a particular way of interpreting the act would be unconstitutional and all other interpretations are permissible.

The PCT has also used the opposite way, though extremely rarely, outlining the only interpretation permissible from the constitution's point of view.[13] Such an approach seems to be as restraining *vis-à-vis* parliament's decision as a fully-fledged declaration of substantive unconstitutionality, or even maybe more, as it makes explicit which solution of a problem is permissible from the PCT point of view. Adjudicating on the Act on House Rents and Housing Allowances, the PCT obliged the Sejm to adopt a state budget which would guarantee full funding for the expenses borne by the municipalities with regard to housing allowances funded from the state budget and, subsequently, the Tribunal defined the notion of "full funding" (K 4/95). Another two cases of this type included lustration laws. In both decisions (K 39/97; K 2/07), the statutory notion of "cooperation with the state security organs" was questioned as not sufficiently specified. Nevertheless, instead of declaring the act unconstitutional due to the unsatisfactory precision of legal regulations, the PCT itself defined five specific characteristics of "cooperation" to be used when applying the act. The PCT highlighted that if in the future the courts contradict this interpretation and it becomes a widely established practice, the PCT will (upon a new application) again examine the statute, as the *ne bis in idem* principle will no longer apply. This approach can hardly fit the negative legislator model as it positively points to the single policy option constitutionally admissible, according to the judges.

Interestingly, constitutional requirement rulings were relatively numerous until 2001 (6.9 percent of all rulings), and then they almost completely disappeared from the PCT toolbox (0.7 percent on average). Moreover, the 1990s rulings including constitutional requirement were inversely proportional to the rulings on substantive unconstitutionality: when the latter instantly fell in 1994, the former started to rise and grow further in the two following years (Figure 6.2). This observation supports the thesis defended earlier that the personnel change in the PCT which took place in 1994 influenced the adjudicative strategy of the Tribunal, which was taken over by a parliamentary coalition-friendly majority of judges, who preferred milder restrictions on their parliamentary colleagues.

The disappearance of rulings including a constitutional requirement could be explained by a widespread critique the PCT faced. This was precisely targeted at the legitimation doctrine of the PCT as a negative legislator. Interpretive rulings involved more than just removing unconstitutional regulations from the legal system. They directed the courts (and administration) how to interpret and apply the law and were perceived especially by the judges of ordinary courts as an intrusion of their domain (Woś 2016; Mikołajewicz 2010). This critique was taken seriously, not least because of the personnel changes in the PCT described above. The renewed PCT of the beginning of the new decade had no clear majority, was no longer bi-polar and apparently worked more consensually.

An extreme year: 2007

This ceased to be true by 2007, a year which witnessed the climax of the divided PCT, with a strong anti-PiS majority of left and centre-right-nominated judges and PiS-nominated minority explicit about its disagreement with the majority. The PiS-led coalition government (2005–2007) was perceived by most political and professional elites as a danger to the achievements of the democratic transformation, and many of its controversial policies were deemed unconstitutional by the PCT (Sadurski 2007). Basic statistics show how strong the PCT could be when it decided to restrain the populist majority in parliament: 55 percent of the rulings declared unconstitutionality and 43.3 percent of petitions were rejected, both representing the extreme values for the period 1994–2015. In 2008 the PCT still struggled with the legislative after-effects of the short-lived PiS-led government, which lost power after the early elections of October 2007, and the percentage of substantive unconstitutionality rulings was 49.3.

Nevertheless, the following years showed a trend towards a more deferential attitude, which was probably reinforced by the choice of seven new judges proposed by the Civic Platform (PO) after 2008. Almost all of them were either law professors or judges with no distinctive track record in politics. In the period 2009–2015, on average 38.5 percent of the rulings declared substantive unconstitutionality and 59 percent of petitions were rejected. These results are very similar to the period 1994–1997, when an at that time left-wing parliamentary majority succeeded in nominating a friendly majority in the PCT.

6.4.2 *Trends in five-member benches' rulings: partisanship and non-divisive rulings*

The PCT adjudicates in three modes: whole Tribunal for the *a priori* review and "notably complicated cases", five-member benches for petitions concerning statutory law and three-member benches for secondary legislation. It is the President of the Tribunal who decides about adjudication by the whole Tribunal.[14] In practice, highly publicized and divisive issues are most often decided by the whole Tribunal, which also means that a majority of dissenting opinions concerned decisions taken by the whole Tribunal. In the period of high partisanship in divisive rulings (2007–2015), out of 1,061 rulings there were 333 (31 percent) decided by the whole Tribunal; 217 (65 percent) of them were accompanied by at least one dissenting opinion. If we deduct from this number the special case of the lustration act of 2007 (K 2/07, with 77 rulings and 160 dissenting opinions), it turns out that the whole Tribunal is a relatively rare procedure reserved mostly for highly visible and divisive cases (16 percent of all rulings, but 69 percent of rulings with dissenting opinions) (Table 6.1).

On the other hand, the daily activity of the PCT is undertaken by five-member benches: between 2007 and 2015, 69 percent of the rulings (728 instances) were decided by five-member benches. Even though only 8.6 percent of them were accompanied by at least one dissenting opinion, the sheer number suggests that these could not be politically irrelevant matters only. Indeed, politically salient issues like the establishment of the special service Central Anti-Corruption Bureau (K 54/07), (il)legality of communist and fascist propaganda (K 11/10), (un)constitutionality of shooting down a hijacked passenger aircraft (K 44/07), (un)constitutionality of compensatory redistribution payments incurred on richer municipalities (the so-called Robin Hood tax [K 14/11]), conditional annulment of court decisions delivered during the Stalinist era (P 8/11) and different aspects of the act on higher education (K 40/12, SK 61/12, K 16/13, K 35/11) were decided by five-member benches between 2007 and 2015.

Table 6.1 Number of rulings decided by the full bench 2007–2015 (PCT)

	With lustration act (K 2/07)	*Without lustration act (K 2/07)*
Total number of rulings	1061	984
Decided by the full bench	333 (31%)	256 (26%)
Dissent	217 (65%)	57 (22%)

The adjudicating benches are created *ad hoc*, and since 2006, as a rule, the cases are assigned to judges in alphabetical order; therefore, there is a high probability of a random allocation of cases to judges. This means that there should be a sizeable group of rulings where the judges nominated by PiS in 2005–2006 were in majority. In fact, they formed a majority in 221 rulings, which was 30 percent of all rulings delivered by five-member benches. Our hypothetical reasoning, then, is as follows: if we assume that the partisanship in judicial decision-making is strong, the PiS-nominated minority takes the opportunity to achieve its policy preferences whenever it becomes a majority in a five-member bench. This means that there should be a robust difference between rulings by PiS-dominated benches and all other benches, and especially that PiS-nominated judges should declare statutes accepted by the PO-dominated Sejm unconstitutional more often, and more often reject petitions concerning statutes from the period of the PiS rule.

Analysis of the JUDICON database generates a few surprising observations. First of all, only 28.6 percent of the rulings by five-member benches were on an act accepted by the parliaments with either PiS or PO majority. Almost all constitutional complaints and petitions by courts of law concerned earlier legislation, and astonishingly few "fresh" statutes were referred to the PCT by numerous actors authorized by the constitution. The relatively small number of instances not only makes our observations dubious in terms of statistics rules but also indicates that politics relatively rarely has access to the docket, mostly due to the time-lag. Once it appears on the docket, it is channelled through the full Tribunal path.

Nevertheless, the analysis of one-third of five-member rulings discloses interesting trends. There were relatively more cases of PiS-sponsored legislation (99 rulings for the two-year period of PiS majority) than PO-sponsored legislation (109 rulings for almost eight years of PO–PSL government). And PiS legislation was declared unconstitutional much more frequently: 40 percent as opposed to the PO's 30 percent.

Benches with a majority of PiS-nominated judges adjudicated in 38.5 percent of PO-sponsored legislation cases and delivered 36 percent of unconstitutionality rulings. This result, damaging for the hypothesis of judges' partisanship, gives a good context for the next observation: PiS-nominated majorities adjudicated only in 11 percent of PiS-sponsored legislation. The only explanation is that the sequence of incoming cases was manipulated in order not to allow PiS-nominated judges to adjudicate over PiS legislation. Confirmation for this explanation might be the fact that more numerous PiS-nominated majority benches started to appear after 2011 when the PiS–PO conflict seemed to be over. This date also overlaps with the election of the new PCT President, Andrzej Rzepliński. The percentage of rulings on unconstitutionality of PiS legislation delivered by PiS-nominated judges (54.5 percent) cannot lead to any conclusions when we speak about 6 out of 11 rulings.

This data hints at the conclusion that non-PiS judges (led by the non-PiS President) preferred not to take the risk that PiS-nominated judges would try to achieve their partisan political preferences and decided to adjudicate themselves, even if it involved bending PCT procedures. Once they got the PiS legislation into their hands, they did not seem to be excessively partisan. The ratio of unconstitutionality rulings (40 percent) is on a par with the averages of such rulings for the consecutive years of 2007–2015 for all PCT rulings.[15] This strategy precludes verification of the partisanship hypothesis, but it strongly supports the argument that when it comes to politics it is the political/partisan logic that is a primary point of reference for the judges. It is striking especially when juxtaposed with roughly 60 percent of the PCT work – adjudicating over the legislation from the period before the PiS–PO divide. Here there are no differences in behaviour of PiS-nominated and non-PiS judges.

6.4.3 Trends in strength of majority rulings

When a constitutional court is a negative legislator and almost all of its rulings either declare a law in accordance with the constitution or strike it down as unconstitutional, it is difficult to follow trends in such an undifferentiated mass of rulings.

When a crude average strength is taken into account, PCT rulings are not only weak but also fairly undifferentiated in terms of changes over time (Figure 6.4). On a ten-point scale, the average for the PCT is 2.7 points, with Slovakia at 3.71 points, Germany at 3.59 points, the Czech Republic at 2.94 points, Hungary at 2.89 points and Romania with its procedural specificity at 1.1 points. If we ignore the highly untypical years 1993 and 2007, the average strength of PCT rulings falls to 2.55 points. This is mostly due to the high number of rejection rulings (56.3 percent of the total) weighted zero on the scale. Apart from the rejections, the PCT rulings score most frequently 6.5 points (22.5 percent) and 7 points (13.3 percent), which is nearly on a par with the Czech and Slovak Constitutional Courts. In all three of these countries, the dominating groups of non-rejections

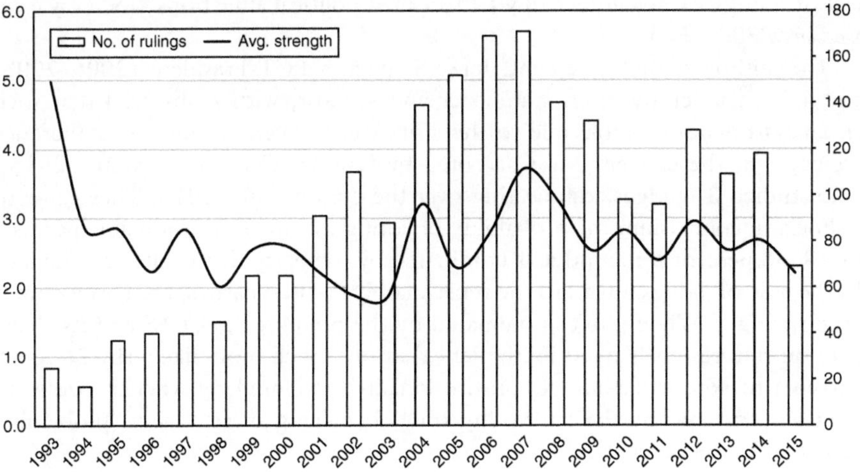

Figure 6.4 Number and average strength of rulings (PCT)

are weak and average versions of substantive rulings. The PCT has the biggest share of weak substantive rulings in the whole region (25.5 percent of total rulings) and almost no strong rulings (16 instances, or 0.7 percent). Other Central European constitutional courts generally prefer stronger rulings: either average (Czech Republic, Slovakia) or strong (Germany).

It is also quite interesting that these tendencies seem to be stable. If we exclude the untypical years of 1993 and 2007, the average strength of PCT rulings remains between 1.86 points and 3.27 points, and again this is the smallest amplitude among the countries under research (Figure 6.4).

6.5 Trends in dissenting opinions

6.5.1 Dissenting opinions and partisanship

If we want to analyze the trends in dissenting opinions, it should be stressed, first of all, that the election of PCT judges on a brute majoritarian principle became a stable rule during the period under research. During those 22 years, there were only two cases when a majority elected a candidate not from its ranks. Not only were the candidates formally proposed by the party factions in the Sejm, but also, out of 40 judges elected by the parliament after the first democratic elections (1992), there were only 13 with weak political links, and eight of them were elected after 2007. Twelve judges jumped into the robe directly from politics (Wiaderek 2016; Bojarski et al. 2016).

This type of pedigree made proving lack of partisanship in judges' behaviour an acute legitimacy demand. Polish legal scholarly literature and journalism is full of solemn exclamations that a "constitutional judge never feels a member of a [political] grouping. If one would analyze the judicial behaviour [...] one would be surprised how often the cleavages in substantial issues that are the subject of rulings are absolutely athwart so-called political affiliations" (*Sąd czy ustawodawca* 2009, 53).

The author of this statement, Jerzy Stępień, a PCT President (2006–2008) and a former deputy interior minister and senator, wittily observed that such an analysis is not possible due to the strict rule concerning judges' conference secrecy, but the challenge was accepted by Kantorowicz and Garoupa (2016), who studied 31 judges adjudicating over the period 2003–2013. They came to a shocking conclusion: the probability of voting for unconstitutionality increases by 18–38 percent if the judge is nominated by the party that challenges the law. In the case of judges linked to the most sharply focused parties, the correlation is even stronger. When judges nominated by the populist right (PiS and its allies) vote on statutes challenged by the left, they are much more likely (by 26 to 48 percent) to vote in favour of constitutionality, and similarly when it comes to judges nominated by the left voting on PiS-challenged legislation (probability grows to 14–63 percent).

These results would be ground-breaking, but alas they are methodologically flawed. Authors facing the basic problem of how to learn about judges' actual voting when it is kept secret simply ignore it, assuming that "the absence of the dissenting opinion indicates that a judge, even if initially s/he voted differently than the majority, eventually s/he agrees with the decision of the adjudicating bench" (Kantorowicz and Garoupa 2016, 76). This is, first of all, a strongly counter-intuitive assumption, as being outvoted does not mean agreeing with the winning majority decision. Apart from this, judges may be as dissent-averse or simply as lazy as any other human being. Moreover, this assumption goes against sound theoretical models, which the authors themselves acknowledge to a degree. If we frame judicial decision-making as a collegial game, we may assume that an explicit dissent is strongly discouraged. Similarly, if judicial decisions are a function of interactions between the court and other players on the field of politics, an explicit dissent weakens the institution and is perceived as harming legitimacy.

Fortunately, the authors pay special attention to a sphere where these reservations are less valid – decisions with at least one dissenting opinion. In such a restricted sample, the odds that a judge would vote in congruence with the stance of the nominating party are twice as high as in the whole sample. If the petitioner challenging a law and the judge were from the same party, in 66.7 percent of instances the judge voted against constitutionality, and if they were from different parties the percentage was 38.9. The differences between the whole sample and non-unanimous decisions may be a result of the flawed methodology, but at the same time they indicate a sound argument: if the collegial and/or strategic constraints do not bind judges, or bind them less (at least one judge decided to disclose his/her opposition), the default logic is partisanship.

Now, the big question concerns the degree of importance regarding what Kantorowicz and Garoupa established, when and how often the logic of partisanship dominates. The most obvious answer is: when the subject under consideration is strongly politicized and the divisions are too strong to pretend a consensus is attainable. The majority of media-covered cases fit this pattern: lustration process (K 2/07), pensions of former secret service agents (K 6/09), relationship between the state and the Catholic Church (K 3/09), financing Catholic universities by the state (K 55/07), allotment gardens – post-communists' darlings (K27/95) and regulation of the credit unions linked to the PiS party (Kp 10/09).

The judicial decisions (cases) with at least one dissenting opinion account on average for 15 percent of all decisions, but the annual results vary from 3 percent (2006) to 33 percent (2012), and if rulings are counted they vary from 1.8 percent (2006) to 49.7 percent (2007) and 37.5 percent (2012). What is probably most striking is that dissenting opinions come in waves. First of all, they appear only in 1995 and until 2000 they are at the level of just over a dozen. Then there is the period 2001–2006 with almost no dissenting activity of the judges, with scores between 1.8 and 4.6 percent of rulings with a dissenting opinion. The period between 2008 and 2015 was characterized by a nearly linear growth trend of the share of rulings with dissenting opinions, with an annual average of 22.3 percent. A special case was 2007, when the lustration laws package (K 2/07)

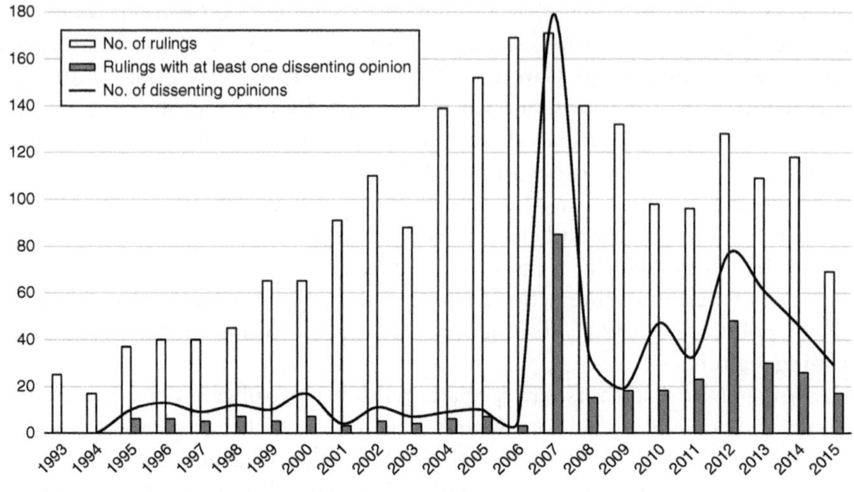

Figure 6.5 Number of rulings and dissenting opinions (PCT)

was dissected by the Tribunal into 77 rulings and accompanied by 160 dissenting opinions, making 2007 a strongly deviant, highly unrepresentative case (Figure 6.5).

These crude statistics suggest that an explanation for the fluctuating character of dissent-aversion is again politics. The dissenting opinion as a practice appears when a group of judges nominated by the first strong (post-communist) majority sits on the bench. Even though they were elected in December 1993, they dominated the adjudicating benches absolutely only in 1995. The need to demonstrate a dissent to the prevailing majority became apparently acute among Solidarity-nominated judges, who authored nine out of ten dissenting opinions in 1995. Once the practice became acceptable, the political origin of judges ceased to play a role.

The fall in the number of dissenting opinions in 2001 is also explainable in political categories. Not only were the Solidarity-nominated judges replaced in 1997 by the nominees of the weak centre-right coalition of Solidarity Electoral Action (*Akcja Wyborcza Solidarność*, AWS) and Freedom Union (*Unia Wolności*, UW) without a strong ideological identity or high political profile, but the post-communist judges also dispersed as their terms came to an end. The situation created by a lack of a clear majority in the PCT took place in the context of a weakened parliament, where the majority was first unstable and then hardly existed. The latter changed after the 2001 election, but at that time the PCT was already a multi-player game and not a bi-polar competition. The new left-wing coalition elected six new judges, but due to the total number of judges being increased by the new constitution, they were a minority, even if one could not identify a coherent majority.

6.5.2 Network analysis of dissenting opinions

The network analysis of the dissenting coalitions clearly illustrates this new mode of operation of the PCT in relation to divisive cases with an explicit disagreement. The opinions indeed may differ in many aspects, but by the very fact of disclosing a disagreement and proposing an alternative, judges question the legitimating ideology of decision-making by professional consensus and disclose a conflict, as well as parties involved. Figure 6.6 identifies two fairly strong centres of post-communist judges jointly dissenting in the periods 1995–2001 (top left corner: Garlicki, Sokolewicz, Jaworski, Wierzbowski, Czeszejko-Sochacki and Trzciński) and 2001–2010 (centre: Grzybowski, Jamróz, Mazurkiewicz, Zdziennicki, Wyrzykowski and Łętowska). But between them there is a group of centre-right-nominated judges (Mączyński, Stępień and Safjan) well connected to both centres, i.e. building dissenting coalitions with the left.

This picture is radically different if compared to the period 2007–2015, when again there are two centres or rather poles, but there are very few connections between them: left-wing judges (centre: Grzybowski, Jamróz, Mazurkiewicz, Zdziennicki, Wyrzykowski and Łętowska), whose term ended in 2010, and PiS judges elected in 2006/2007 (right side: Gintowt-Jankowicz, Liszcz, Cieślak, Hermeliński, Kotlinowski and Granat). The latter clearly formed a distinct group in the PCT, with not only the largest number of joint actions ever but with the largest numbers of dissenting opinions in general. The six PiS-nominated judges are in the top seven producers of dissenting opinions in the history of the PCT.[16] The weakening of the tensions in the PCT after 2008 apparently enabled cooperation between PiS-nominated judges and centre-right nominees. Figure 6.6 clearly shows a network of interactions in setting up dissenting coalitions between several PiS judges and the PCT president after 2010, Andrzej Rzepliński, or judges Wronkowska-Jaśkiewicz, Zubik and Wróbel.

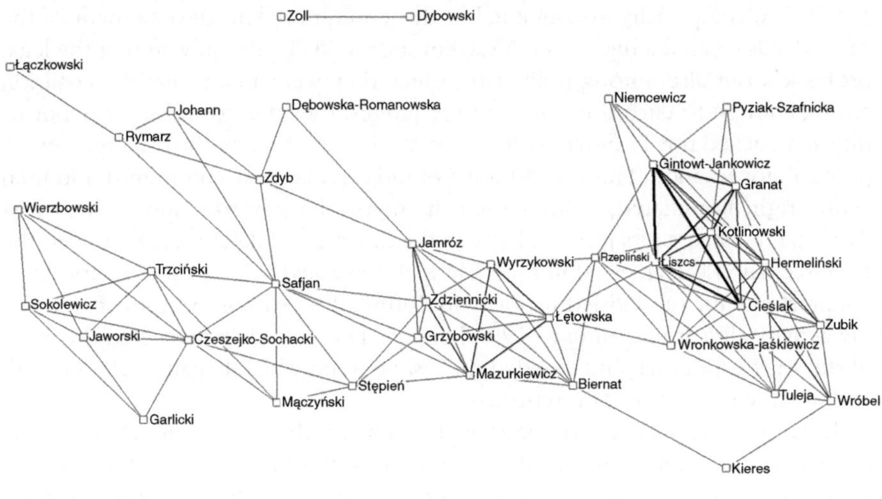

Figure 6.6 Dissenting coalitions 1993–2015 (PCT)

To sum up, the partisan logic behind judicial decision-making in the situation of an open conflict (as indicated by dissenting opinions) can hardly be applied to the pre-2003 (or in fact pre-2007) PCT activities. Before 1994, as well as over the periods 1994–1997 and 2001–2006, open disagreements played a marginal role, but apparently 2007 marks the real beginning of the "if a divisive issue, then vote partisan" reasoning.

6.6 Conclusions

Stawecki et al. (2008) argued that the model of legal reasoning accepted by the PCT had far-reaching consequences for the influence of PCT jurisprudence on other actors of the legal–political field. Neither courts of law, nor administrative courts, nor parliament draw from the PCT jurisprudence as "it is difficult to reconstruct [from the PCT interpretative practice] an axiological system" (Kozak 1997, 66). References to PCT jurisprudence are ornamental or symbolic and do not determine the way the legal reasoning of the courts is conducted. The adjudicative activity of different judicial organs is self-contained, and the legislators also rarely take into account the PCT jurisprudence. "There is no 'central organ' of the legal order which would be able to decide about the way other organs act" (Stawecki et al. 2008, 76), and the PCT cannot aspire to such a role. Even though these conclusions refer to the legal field and are based on the analysis of the PCT adjudicative activity in 1997–2007, they characterize well an ambiguous role the Tribunal played in the Polish political system in the period 1993–2015.

On the one hand, it did function as a serious restraint on parliament, especially in the early period of the democratic transition. The PCT quickly established its authority over a fragmented parliament and effectively co-authored the legal framework of Polish democracy, filling the gaps created by a pace of change too fast for the Sejm. The multi-layered doctrine of the *Rechtsstaat* developed by the PCT was especially instrumental in this enterprise. This development of the early 1990s created a high level of esteem for the PCT, not only among the legal profession but also among politicians. Once they were able to build a coalition strong enough to curb this power of the judges, they did not miss the opportunity and packed the Tribunal with judges more responsive to the requirements of political governance. This second wave of judges, first post-communist and then centre-right-nominated, skilfully used the myth of a powerful and fairly activist Tribunal but steered its jurisprudence in the direction of deference. However, the resources the PCT amassed in the early 1990s enabled it to become a very active counterforce for the PiS-led majority in 2005–2007, with indicators of restraining activity almost returning to 1993 heights. This episode rejuvenated the myth of the strong Tribunal and clouded the visible trend which began in 1994/1995 and to which the PCT soon returned.

Deference or a weak court might be the name for this trend, since the restraints on parliament created by the PCT seem to be the weakest out of all Central European constitutional courts (except, perhaps, for the Romanian court). Nevertheless, despite the weakness of PCT rulings its authority was high, and it was targeted as a main pillar of the Polish version of *impossibillismo*, a doctrine or maybe a practice prohibiting any radical changes in the post-transitory *status quo* (Kaczyński 2005). The Stawecki et al. (2008) study offers a useful hint concerning how to solve this apparent contradiction. The PCT jurisprudence was not weakened, but once the Tribunal decided to stay in its niche of the negative legislator and refrain from encroaching on the field of politics, it was "encysted" by politicians and also (as Stawecki et al. suggest) by courts of law. The PCT might issue whatever ruling it wished, but parliament (and the courts) developed methods to circumvent the barriers the Tribunal built. They did not question the authority of the PCT, but its jurisprudence had a meagre influence on lawmaking or law execution. The diminishing number of openly partisan nominations to the Tribunal in the period 2008–2015 probably proved best that politicians had learnt how to live with the PCT. Becoming fully predictable, the PCT became harmless for politicians.

Harmless, that is, for those politicians who were ready to maintain this *status quo*. However, the predictability combined with a legitimacy doctrine based on neutral legal professionalism was dangerous for politicians, whose aim was to change radically the post-transition order. Dangerous, because – as this research has established – when an issue was politically divisive the judges followed the partisan logic. Then, the new majority elected in 2015 could not miss the opportunity supplied by the previous majority to paint the judges as simply a transmission belt of the outgoing governing coalition and summarily get rid of the restraining institution.

Notes

1 Simultaneously, two more judges were elected to replace those finishing their terms.

2 In 2016, a year of struggle between old and new government-nominated judges, the PCT was petitioned only 360 times (57.8 percent of the 2015 number) and issued 99 final substantive decisions (57.2 percent of the 2015 number, the lowest number since 2003). In 2017, the numbers were even lower, though official data was not available in January 2018 (official data for 2016 was disclosed only in December 2017; see Trybunał Konstytucyjny 2017). On the ongoing conflict over the PCT, see Sadurski (2018) and Młynarska-Sobaczewska (2017).

3 The timeframe of the research is marked by the election of the first PCT judges by the first democratically elected parliament (1993) and the coming into force of the PCT Act amendments that triggered the period of the present turmoil around the Tribunal. The beginning date was arbitrary to a certain degree as there was a clear continuity of the PCT operation in the pre-democratic and democratic period. Even though the 1993 caesura is necessary in order to have comparative data from different countries, we often refer to the earlier PCT strategies and adjudication lines since they continued after 1993.

4 Terms "post-Solidarity" and "post-communist" are widely used to describe political scene of Poland in the 1990s. Whereas it was easy to define the post-communist side as parties directly descending from the old regime communist party and its allies, the post-Solidarity camp was composed of myriad parties with different ideological profiles, changing their organizational forms and names. It is generally agreed that the

2005 elections mark the end of this distinction and the beginning of the new, current phase in Polish party politics.

5 Temporarily, until 1999, the Sejm could overrule decisions concerning pre-1997 legislation.

6 Sometimes the two categories overlapped.

7 A two-year transitional clause was included in the constitution.

8 Seventy-six percent of respondents agreed that it was needed and 59 percent assessed its functioning as good or very good (CBOS 1995, 2–4).

9 Nevertheless, they actually succeeded twice.

10 The year of the next election and the next wave of judicial nominations was 1997.

11 Parliament's assent was needed for the binding force of ruling.

12 For the phenomenon of formal unconstitutionality as distinguished from procedural unconstitutionality, see Fn 9 in Chapter 2.

13 As explained in Chapter 2 "[c]onstitutional requirement [...] is suitable [...] for both declaring a particularly weak or strong provision which constrains the legislative branch seriously or just barely. This means that the court might be a mild or a very rigorous positive legislator". See: Chapter 2, Section 2.4.

14 Unless the issue was previously decided by the whole Tribunal, in which case this procedure becomes obligatory.

15 There are only four years with an average less than 40 percent.

16 The number one dissenter was judge Zdziennicki, who delivered 77 dissenting opinions to the aforementioned lustration decision deviant case, though apart from this he was a moderate dissenter.

References

Alexy, Robert. 2002. *A Theory of Constitutional Rights.* Oxford: Oxford University Press

Bojarski, Łukasz, Katarzyna Furman, and Krzysztof Riedl. 2016. *Wybory pod społeczną kontrolą. Wybory sędziów Trybunału Konstytucyjnego, Generalnego Inspektora Ochrony Danych Osobowych, Rzecznika Praw Obywatelskich, Prokuratora Generalnego. Raport z monitoringu* [*Elections Under Social Control. The Election of Constitutional Tribunal Judges, General Inspector of the Personal Data Protection, Ombudsman, Prosecutor General. A Report from Monitoring*]. Warsaw: Instytut Prawa i Społeczeństwa INPRIS

CBOS. 1995. *Opinie o najwyższych organach władzy sądowniczej. Komunikat z badań BS/37/31/95* [*Opinions on Highest Organs of the Judicial Power. Survey BS/37/31/95 Press Release*]. Warsaw: CBOS

Czeszejko-Sochacki, Zdzisław. 1996. "O niektórych problemach powszechnie obowiązującej wykładni ustalanej przez Trybunał Konstytucyjny" ["On Selected Problems of Generally Binding Interpretation by Constitutional Tribunal"]. In *Konstytucja i gwarancje jej przestrzegania. Księga pamiątkowa ku czci prof. Janiny Zakrzewskiej* [*Constitution and Guarantees for Its Enforcement. A Festschrift for Janina Zakrzewska*], edited by Janusz Trzciński, Adam Jankiewicz, 39–54. Warsaw: Wydawnictwa Trybunału Konstytucyjnego

Czeszejko-Sochacki, Zdzisław. 2001. "Trybunał Konstytucyjny w PRL (zagadnienia wybrane)" ["Constitutional Tribunal in PPR (Selected Issues)"]. *Państwo i Prawo* 56 (6): 3–15

Dębska, Hanna. 2015. "Trybunał Konstytucyjny w poszukiwaniu legitymizacji" ["Constitutional Tribunal in Search of Its Legitimacy"]. *Studia Prawnicze* (4) 204: 23–40

Dębska, Hanna. 2015a. *Władza–Symbol–Prawo. Społeczne tworzenie Trybunału Konstytucyjnego* [*Power–Symbol–Law. Social Construction of Constitutional Tribunal*]. Warsaw: Wydawnictwo Sejmowe

Dyevre, Arthur. 2010. "Unifying the Field of Comparative Judicial Politics: Towards a General Theory of Judicial Behaviour". *European Political Science Review* 2 (2): 297–327.

Garlicki, Lech. 1999. "Odrzucanie orzeczeń Trybunału Konstytucyjnego przez Sejm" ["Rejection of the Constitutional Tribunal Rulings by the Sejm"]. In *Państwo prawa, administracja, sądownictwo: prace dedykowane prof. dr. hab. Januszowi Łętowskiemu w 60. rocznicę urodzin* [*Rechtsstaat, Administration, Judiciary: A Festschrift for Professor Janusz Łętowski on the Occasion of the 60th Birthday*], edited by Adam Łopatka, Andrzej Wróbel, Stefan Kiewlicz, 281–293. Warsaw: Scholar.

Garlicki, Lech. 2003. "The Experience of the Polish Constitutional Court". In *Constitutional Justice, East and West. Democratic Legitimacy and Constitutional Courts in Post-Communist Europe in a Comparative Perspective*, edited by Wojciech Sadurski, 265–282. The Hague: Kluwer

Garlicki, Lech. 2016. *Polskie prawo konstytucyjne. Zarys wykładu* [*Polish Constitutional Law. An Outline*]. Warsaw: Wolters Kluwer

Kaczyński, Jarosław. 2005. "Ponoszę odpowiedzialność polityczną. Wywiad z Jarosławem Kaczyńskim" ["I Take the Political Responsibility. An Interview with Jarosław Kaczyński"]. *Tygodnik Solidarność* December 20 (9)

Kantorowicz, Jarosław and Nuno Garoupa. 2016. "An Empirical Analysis of Constitutional Review Voting in the Polish Constitutional Tribunal, 2003–2014". *Constitutional Political Economy* 27 (1): 66–92.

Kozak, Artur. 1997. "Rodzaje wykładni prawa w uchwałach Trybunału Konstytucyjnego" ["Different Types of Legal Interpretation in the Adjudication of the Constitutional Tribunal"]. In *Z zagadnień wykładni prawa. Acta Universitatis Wratislaviensis No 2032* [*Legal Interpretation Issues*], edited by Stanisław Kaźmierczyk, 59–71. Wrocław: Wydawnictwo Uniwersytetu Wrocławskiego

Lax, Jeffrey R. 2011. "The New Judicial Politics of Legal Doctrine". *Annual Review of Political Science* 14: 131–157.

Mikołajewicz, Jarosław. 2010. "Orzeczenia zakresowe i interpretacyjne Trybunału Konstytucyjnego jako przejaw kryzysu legitymizacji legalnej" ["Interpretive Rulings of the Constitutional Tribunal as a Symptom of Legal Legitimacy Crisis"]. In *Normalność i kryzys. Jedność czy różnorodność. Refleksje filozoficzno-prawne i ekonomiczno-społeczne w ujęciu aksjologicznym* [*Normalcy and Crisis: Unity or Diversity. Legal–Philosophical and Socio-economic Reflexions from an Axiological Perspective*], edited by Jerzyniszczuk, 233–238. Warsaw: OW SGH

Młynarska-Sobaczewska, Anna. 2017. "Polish Constitutional Tribunal Crisis: Political Dispute or Falling Kelsenian Dogma of Constitutional Review". *European Public Law* 23 (3): 489–506

O'Donnell, Guillermo. 1996. "Another Institutionalization: Latin America and Elsewhere". Working Paper no. 222, The Helen Kellogg Institute for International Studies.

Oniszczuk, Jerzy. 1998. *Orzecznictwo Trybunału Konstytucyjnego w latach 1986–1996* [*Jurisprudence of the Constitutional Tribunal 1986–1996*]. Warsaw: Wydawnictwo Sejmowe

Procházka, Radoslav. 2002. *Mission Accomplished: On Funding Constitutional Adjudication in Central Europe*. Budapest: CEU Press

Sadurski, Wojciech. 2007. "Porządek konstytucyjny" ["Constitutional Order"]. In *Demokracja w Polsce 2005–2007* [*Democracy in Poland 2005–2007*], edited by Lena Kolarska-Bobińska, Jacek Kucharczyk, Jarosław Zbieranek, 13–72. Warsaw: Instytut Spraw Publicznych.

Sadurski, Wojciech. 2008. *Rights Before Courts: A Study of Constitutional Courts in Postcommunist States of Central and Eastern Europe*. Dordrecht: Springer

Sadurski, Wojciech. 2018. "How Democracy Dies (in Poland): A Case Study of Anti-Constitutional Populist Backsliding". Sydney Law School Research Paper no. 18/01.

Safjan, Marek. 1999. "Epitafium dla nieostatecznych orzeczeń" ["An Epitaph for Non-final Rulings"]. *Rzeczpospolita*, October 4.: C-2

Safjan, Marek. 2013. "Poland. The Constitutional Court as a Positive Legislator". In *Constitutional Courts as Positive Legislators. A Comparative Law Study*, edited by Allan R. Brewer-Carías, 701–720. Cambridge: Cambridge University Press.

Segal, Jeffrey. 2010. "Judicial Behavior". In *The Oxford Handbook of Law and Politics*, edited by Keith Whittington, 19–32. Oxford: Oxford University Press.

Smekal, Hubert and Ivo Pospíšil, eds. 2013. *Soudcokracie, nebo judicializace politiky? Vztah práva a politiky (nejen) v časech krize* [*Rule of Judges or Judicialization of Politics? The Relation between Law and Politics (Not Only) in Times of Crisis*]. Brno: MUNI Press

Stawecki, Tomasz, Wiesław Staśkiewicz, and Jan Winczorek. 2008. *Między policentrycznością a fragmentaryzacją. Wpływ Trybunału Konstytucyjnego na polski porządek prawny* [*Between Polycentrism and Fragmentation: The Influence of the Constitutional Tribunal on the Polish Legal Order*]. Warsaw: Ernst&Young

Stone Sweet, Alan. 1992. *The Birth of Judicial Politics in France: The Constitutional Council in Comparative Perspective*. Oxford: Oxford University Press

Sulikowski, Adam. 2016. "Trybunał Konstytucyjny a polityczność. O konsekwencjach upadku pewnego mitu" ["Constitutional Tribunal and the Political. On Consequences of the Fall of a Myth"]. *Państwo i Prawo* 71 (4): 3–14

Sąd czy ustawodawca? Legitymizacja sądownictwa konstytucyjnego we współczesnej Polsce i Europie. Trzecia debata Tocqueville'owska. 2009. [*A Court or a Lawgiver? The Legitimacy of Constitutional Courts in Contemporary Poland and Europe. 3rd Tocquevillean Debate*]. *Łódź: Centrum Myśli Polityczno-Prawnej im. Tocqueville'a.*

Trybunał Konstytucyjny. 2017. *Informacja o istotnych problemach wynikających z działalności i orzecznictwa Trybunału Konstytucyjnego w 2016 roku* [*Information on Important Problems Resulting from Activities and Adjudication of the Constitutional Tribunal in 2016*]. Warsaw: Wydawnictwa Trybunału Konstytucyjnego.

Vanberg, Georg. 2005. *Constitutional Politics in Germany*. Oxford: Oxford University Press.

Warczok, Tomasz, and Hanna Dębska. 2014. "Sacred Law and Profane Politics. The Symbolic Construction of the Constitutional Tribunal". *Polish Sociological Review* 4 (188): 465–478.

Wiaderek, Grzegorz, ed. 2016. *Procedury nominacji na wybrane stanowiska publiczne – przejrzystość, standardy, rekomendacje* [*Nomination Procedures for Selected Public Positions: Transparency, Standards, Recommendations*]. Warsaw: Instytut Prawa i Społeczeństwa INPRIS

Woś, Tomasz. 2016. "Wyroki interpretacyjne i zakresowe w orzecznictwie Trybunału Konstytucyjnego" ["Interpretive Rulings in the Adjudication of the Constitutional Tribunal"]. *Studia Iuridica Lublinensia* 25 (3): 985–995

Zoll, Andrzej. 1997. "Interview with Professor Andrzej Zoll, Chief Justice of the Polish Constitutional Tribunal", by Irena Grudzinska-Gross. *East European Constitutional Review* 6 (1): 77–79

7 The Romanian Constitutional Court

Muddling through democratic transition

Csongor Kuti

7.1 Introduction

Romania's first democratic constitution entered into force towards the end of 1991, while the Romanian Constitutional Court (RCC) began its activity the following year, issuing its first decision on 30 June 1992. It is envisaged as a political institution that is not part of the judicial system, although only legal professionals might be appointed as judges. Regarded with distrust by politicians, who perceived it as an undemocratic political authority, as well as by the judicial system, which feared that the new court was an assault on their powers, the RCC attempted to position itself as a guardian of rules, ensuring that the boundaries of lawmaking set by the constitution were not overstepped. It has to be added, in fairness, that it did not have many choices left: as will be discussed below, the initial institutional arrangement was set up so as to bar the Court from taking away politics from the legislator. In *a priori* review procedure, unconstitutionality decisions of the RCC could have been overridden by the parliament with a qualified majority, while the effects of *a posteriori* review decisions were not clearly established. Consequently, in the early years, the major challenge for the Court was to impose itself as ultimate arbitrator of constitutional issues in front of the regular courts, and to ascertain that its decisions were recognized as mandatory by the judicial system.

From this perspective, the 2003 revision of the Constitution of Romania represented a watershed, bringing significant changes to the Court's institutional arrangements, which to some degree enhanced its powers with respect to both the legislature and the ordinary courts. Since then, the RCC has become involved in political conflicts more often, and therefore its activity attracted more attention from political actors and the general public as well. This shift is reflected in the Court's activity by the growing number of dissents, a noticeable increase of the rulings' strength and a polarization within the RCC. In this context, it is not entirely surprising that the past decade has seen a political backlash against the Court, accused of trespassing into the field of politics and assuming too much power over the legislature, constraining in an illegitimate way their room for manoeuvre.

This study argues that, contrary to the political narrative of the most recent years, the RCC was reluctant to become a "positive legislator"; hence, it generally refrained from offering consistent remedies, leaving it up to parliament to decide how to correct faulty legislation. On the basis of the present analysis, it appears far-fetched to speak about a constitutionalization of the political environment in Romania. The explanation for the perceived strengthening of the rulings of the RCC seems to rest in contextual factors, which are presented in detail below.

The research covers the first 24 years of the Court's functioning, from 1992 to 2015. This time span might be divided in different periods, according to various factors. For instance, on the basis of the changes made in the institutional arrangements of the RCC, one may distinguish the 1992–2003 and the 2004–2015 periods. Another distinction might be made from the perspective of the docket of the Court: in the period between 2007 and 2012, the Court issued more than 1,000 decisions per year.[1] This study focuses on two time periods in which the average strength of the Court's rulings produced the lowest degree of variation: 2001–2004 and 2009–2012. It will analyze the trends in the strength of the rulings in order to determine whether and how the influence of various factors is reflected by the Court's activity. The enquiry concludes that the RCC has never been a strong check upon parliament. In the past decade, during which tensions between government and/or parliament and the presidency have escalated, the Court has on several occasions had to become an arbitrator, a role that it was not particularly enthusiastic to interpret.

This chapter begins with some historical background to familiarize the reader with the context of Romanian constitutionalism, continues with a presentation of the institutional arrangements of the Court and, after a brief overview of methodological and country-specific issues, turns to the analysis of the trends in the strength of rulings, which contains a discussion of the contextual factors that might determine these trends and also touches upon details such as the performance of the presidents of the RCC and the analysis of dissenting opinions.

7.2 Historical background and institutional arrangements

7.2.1 Historical background

It might seem harsh, but it can be safely stated that genuine democracy never existed in pre-communist Romania, not even in the "golden years" of interwar Greater Romania: there was merely a succession of more or less authoritarian regimes. Thus, after the fall of communism in 1989, when a new democracy had to be drafted, there was nothing to return to, no healthy democratic or constitutional tradition to build upon. In this context, the absence of any control of constitutionality was a natural consequence. Indeed, after the adoption of the first constitution (of 1866), for almost 60 years no meaningful attempts to review the constitutionality of a legislative act were recorded.

The 1923 Constitution legitimized judicial review, but at the same time restricted it to the exclusive competence of the united chambers of the Supreme Court, regular courts retaining only the power to examine the formal constitutionality of laws. It has also been specified that the effects of a constitutionality review decision extended only to the specific case in question. Complaints of unconstitutionality were to be decided only when the parties had exhausted all possible remedies. However, under this system of judicial review, only a single decision of unconstitutionality was passed (Benke n.d., 7).

Amongst the Central and East European regime changes in 1989/1990, the Romanian case proved to be the most violent, claiming several hundred lives and culminating with the execution of Nicolae Ceausescu and his wife, Elena Ceausescu. This violent toppling of the communist dictator suggested a profound rupture with the past. Yet in reality, a significant continuity could have been observed: second- and third-ranking members of the communist *nomenklatura* stepped up to seize power and dominate Romanian politics for years to come. The post-communist National Salvation Front (*Frontul Salvării Naționale*, FSN), which gained a majority of more than two-thirds in the 509-member Constituent Assembly following the election in May 1990, dominated the constitution-drafting process. Hence, there were shallow debates on the constitution's text, and the voting procedure allowed the victors to impose their vision without any meaningful opposition.[2] The ensuing referendum, which took place on 8 December 1991 as a final step in the constitution-making process, was merely a legitimating exercise (Lungu 2002, 12).

This does not mean that the 1991 Romanian Constitution was an utterly bad construction. Just like their nineteenth-century predecessors, the post-communist drafters attempted to import and engender contemporary democratic institutions – of course tailored to their particular interests, which resulted in a few shortcomings, partly corrected by the 2003 revision. Arguably, it was less the text of the Constitution *per se* and more the circumstances of its adoption that exerted a negative effect on the development of Romanian constitutionalism. Due to the huge majority of the former communist *nomenklatura*, which allowed it to draft the Constitution as it pleased and cement their supremacy for years to come, a significant moment was wasted. The shortness of the passage from a single-party dictatorship to a democratically elected Constituent Assembly (in less than six months) meant that no serious political forces could assemble, and no relevant civil movements could crystallize. Consequently, there was no serious political or social debate about constitutional principles, ideas and institutions, whereas such a debate would have been essential for the development of a modern constitutional (and democratic) culture.

Judicial review powers were carved out by Romanian courts in the first half of the twentieth century and later formalized by the 1923 Constitution, while the institution of constitutional review was unknown in Romanian constitutional tradition. According to a former president of the RCC, in 1990 there was hardly a consensus in the Constituent Assembly about the necessity of a constitutional court (Mungiu-Pippidi 1997). Many perceived it as an undemocratic political authority, while the judicial system feared that the new court was an attempt to limit its powers since the Supreme Court attempted to perform judicial review on several occasions before the adoption of the new constitution (Tănăsescu 2013).

Perhaps as a consequence of this distrust, the RCC was not credited as final arbiter: it could not decide about conflicts between public institutions, and parliament could override its *a priori* review rulings with a two-thirds majority.[3]

Unfortunately, for more than a decade the Court maintained "a marginal, almost irrelevant" stance, and the language and logic of constitutionalism was absent from public debates (Iancu 2009). While authors heavily criticized the RCC for its "silence and ignorance" (Weber 2002), it has to be admitted in fairness that it managed to pass a small number of significant decisions. For instance, in 1992 it imposed separation of powers as a constitutional standard, even if until the 2003 revision this fundamental principle was missing from the Constitution's text; and in 1994 it found unconstitutional the executive's practice of adopting delegated legislation (ordinances) to circumvent decisions of unconstitutionality. In the late 1990s the Court's case law focused mainly on individual rights and it even managed to identify new fundamental rights previously not enshrined in the Constitution, such as the right to positive discrimination, inferred from the principle of equality (Tănăsescu 2013, 20).

The 2003 revision of the Constitution managed to correct some of the constitution's ambiguities (notably after the adoption of the *acquis communautaire*, under the pressure of the imminent EU accession), such as a clear reference to the separation of powers, the consolidation of the RCC as final arbiter, express provisions on equality and access to culture and to fair trial (Blokker 2012, 4). On the other hand, important provisions were introduced concerning the equality of chances, electoral rights of EU citizens and the organization and functioning of the Superior Council of Magistracy, as a guarantor of the independence of the judiciary.

Taking it all together, however, up to the mid-2000s the RCC was rather passive, meddling discreetly in the background of the democratization process. Unlike some of its counterparts from the region – such as the Hungarian or Polish bodies – it was largely absent from the transition process. A contrary view – in a stunning display of instrumentalism – explains the Court's passivity by the Constitution's alleged role as a motor of transition and precondition for the creation of democratic institutions. Accordingly, the Court's role was simply to enforce the Constitution, without any need for "creativity" or activism (Tănăsescu 2013, 20). However, beyond the elements of institutional design of the 1991 Constitution, which support this theory, there are also indications that the RCC's passive attitude was consciously assumed, with perhaps the most obvious of them being the often restated concern about not becoming a "positive legislator".

7.2.2 Institutional arrangements

As has already been mentioned, the specific settings of the RCC are contained in the Constitution and the relevant law for the organizing and functioning of the Court. Both norms have been amended over the years, altering to some degree the initial institutional arrangements of the Court. Provisions pertaining to the appointment of judges and their term of office have remained unchanged. The RCC is composed of nine judges, six appointed by the parliament (each chamber appointing three judges) and the rest by the President of the Republic. Judges enjoy a nine-year, non-renewable mandate, and the first Court was appointed in such a way as to ensure the renewal of one-third of its composition every three years. The President of the RCC is elected by the judges and holds office for three years. Judges must hold a law degree, enjoy a "high degree of professional competence" and have at least 18 years of professional experience, as either practitioners or academics. Interestingly, several members of the first Court had also been members of the constitution drafting committee in 1990, and it has been a constant practice to appoint members of parliament as judges, while it is less common for members of the judiciary to become constitutional judges.

Initially, the Court's review powers comprised the *a priori* review of bills, the review of parliaments' rules and regulations, the *a posteriori* review of laws and governmental ordinances and the *ex officio* review of constitutional revision bills.[4] *A priori* review motions could have been lodged by the President of Romania, the presidents of the two chambers of the parliament, members of parliament (at least 50 deputies or 25 senators), the government and the President of the Supreme Court. For the review of parliament's rules and regulations, the presidents of the two chambers of the parliament, members of parliament (in the same numbers as above) or a parliamentary group might file a complaint.

A posteriori review of laws or governmental ordinances was possible only by way of "exception of unconstitutionality" (as procedural defence, similar to the French *exception d'inconstitutionnalité*) raised before ordinary courts of justice during regular litigation proceedings by the parties, the prosecutor or by the court.[5] While in the first two cases (*a priori* review and review of parliament's rules and regulations) decisions had to be taken by the full court, with no possibility of appeal, in the case of *a posteriori* review motions, decisions were taken by a panel of three judges appointed by the President of the RCC with the possibility of appeal to a panel of five judges, chaired by the President of the RCC.[6] Decisions of the Court were mandatory and had effect only from the moment of their publication in the Official Gazette.

The first important alteration of the initial institutional arrangement took place in 1997, through the amending of the law for the organization and functioning of the RCC.[7] The most important modifications concerned *a posteriori* review proceedings: the system of panels was abolished and from then on, all decisions were taken by the full court. The possibility of appeal was also abandoned; after that proceedings before regular courts were mandatorily halted until the RCC decided about the "exception of unconstitutionality".

The 2003 constitutional revision brought further significant changes to the Court's functioning and jurisdiction.[8] It extended the sphere of persons considered to have standing to bring a complaint directly before the Court, so as to include the President of the Superior Council of Magistracy,[9] the prime minister, the President of Romania and the presidents of the two chambers of parliament, in the case of constitutional conflicts between public institutions (constitutional conflict complaints or *Organstreitverfahren*); the Ombudsman (*a priori* and *a posteriori* complaint); and a number of at least 50 deputies or 25 senators in cases of constitutionality of treaties and international agreements signed by Romania.[10] Furthermore, the Court's jurisdiction included juridical conflicts of constitutional nature between different public institutions (parliament, executive, presidency), treaties and other international agreements. "Exceptions of unconstitutionality" could from now on also be invoked before commercial arbitration tribunals. Finally, but perhaps most importantly, the Court's decisions became generally binding in both *ex ante* and *ex post* review procedures (eliminating parliament's power to veto its decisions).

As for what concerns the RCC's special *a priori* mandatory review powers over constitutional revision bills, these were introduced in the current form by an amendment to Law no. 47/1992 on the organizing and functioning of the RCC in 2004. Until then, the RCC mandatorily reviewed such constitutional revision bills *ex officio* only prior to their adoption. (The 2003 revision bill's second reading therefore took place according to the ordinary *a priori* proceeding, upon the request of several MPs.)[11]

Significantly, in *a posteriori* review proceedings, the constitutional revision from 2003 introduced a 45-day term from the date of the publication of the Court's decision, within which the parliament (or the government, in case of ordinances) might "correct" the provisions ruled unconstitutional so as to bring them into line with constitutional requirements. For this period of 45 days, the provisions at stake are suspended, and if the aforementioned actors fail to act, they will be annulled. Seemingly, according to the Court's own – partial – statistics, the lawmakers were not especially keen on respecting this constitutional deadline (Constitutional Court of Romania Statistics, 2009–2017). These modifications of the institutional settings enhanced the Court's review powers, which created the possibility of phrasing more debates or conflicts in a constitutional context, made it more accessible and generally strengthened its potential to become an arbitrator, or at least a more significant player in the complicated relationship between the various public powers.

Nevertheless, probably as a part of the political bargain that allowed for the above mentioned modifications, parliament retained a trump card to compensate for the loss of its power to override the RCC's decisions. That is to say, the Constitution's article dedicated to the Court's jurisdiction was appended with the phrase "other duties stipulated by the organic law of the Court" – hence allowing a certain degree of legislative control over the Court's jurisdiction, with the parliament being able to alter (or at least to add to) the Court's sphere of competence. The legislature played this card the first time in 2010, when the organic law of the RCC was revised.[12]

Arguably, these changes to the RCC's functioning and jurisdiction rapidly placed it at the heart of embittered political conflicts and constitutional crisis, especially due to its new competence in solving conflicts of a constitutional nature between public institutions and the enlarged sphere of persons enabled to lodge a complaint. At the same time, its visibility increased significantly, and public debates were often carried out within "constitutional parameters" (Blokker 2012, 13; Iancu 2009).

7.3 Methodological peculiarities and caseload

7.3.1 Methodological peculiarities

This chapter is based on the research carried out for the JUDICON project, using its data collection and evaluation methodology. However, there are a few specific features – due to the characteristics of Romanian constitutional adjudication – which demand explanation. It must be noted that the Romanian Constitutional Court (also) has the power to adjudicate *ex ante* on the constitutionality of laws. This is not an unknown practice in Europe; for instance, the French, Portuguese or in certain circumstances the Hungarian and Polish constitutions also create the possibility to review the constitutionality of laws before their entry into force. Nevertheless, the *a priori* review powers of the Romanian Constitutional Court and the circle of persons who may lodge a motion with the Court are both larger than in the case of other post-communist countries. First, in the case of bills, referral can be made, as in Hungary and Poland, by the President of the Republic. But, unlike in Hungary, it can be either of the presidents of the two chambers of the legislature, or a group of MPs (at least 50 deputies or 25 senators, i.e. members of the opposition) who may address the Court as well. In addition, the government, the Ombudsman and the President of the High Court of Cassation and Justice are all entitled to lodge an *a priori* review request with the Court. As regards international treaties and agreements, the Court might review their constitutionality before being ratified by parliament upon the request of either of the presidents of the two chambers, or of a group of MPs (at least 50 deputies or 25 senators). Finally, as regards constitutional amendments, the Court has *ex officio*, mandatory review powers, and it reviews each amending proposal twice: first before the legislative procedure is initiated within the parliament and second after their adoption.[13]

As constitutional scholars have observed, the *ex ante* approach might bring stability to the legal system, strengthening the law and protecting it from future challenges. However, when *ex post* review is also made possible within the same system, the stability feature diminishes, and the *ex ante* review becomes more or less a political tool for obstructing the legislative procedure (Sadurski 2011). Interestingly, even if the Court recently came under severe criticism, being depicted as intensely politicized and unable to transcend political disputes (Perju 2010; Gilia 2012), the problematic coexistence of *ex post* and *ex ante* review was not really questioned. However, a commission for the analysis of the political and constitutional regime, set up by the Presidential Administration, came up with a proposal, recommending a possible solution for the rationalization of constitutional justice. The commission envisaged a system of dual competence, in which the RCC should retain the power to adjudicate *ex ante*, while regular courts should exercise *ex post* review powers over the constitutionality of laws (Presidency 2008).

Beyond these, one more specific feature of Romanian constitutionalism requires some explanation. In this system, parliament is named as the sole legislative authority of the state, albeit the Constitution creates significant objections to this rule. First, the government has the option to engage its responsibility for a programme, a political declaration or a bill. In this case, if the government is not dismissed via a vote of no confidence within three days' time, the bill must be considered passed and the political declaration or programme as mandatory.[14] Second, through the institution of legislative delegation, parliament can mandate the government to enact ordinances within a specified domain and period of time. Parliament has the option to impose through the delegation act a subsequent approval procedure for these ordinances. Third, the government also has the possibility to enact emergency ordinances, in extraordinary and urgent situations, without any parliamentary mandate, but without affecting the domains reserved to constitutional laws, the fundamental institutions of the state, constitutional rights, liberties and duties, electoral rights and the regime of expropriations. All emergency ordinances must undergo the subsequent parliamentary approval procedure.[15] Alas, governmental lawmaking via emergency ordinances became a common practice, amounting, in the first decade of the new millennium, to one-third of the number of laws enacted by parliament (Cogitus 2011). Taking into consideration the fact that the most important pieces of legislation of recent years – including the Penal Code, the Civil Code, the Codes of Penal and Civil Procedure – were forced through the legislature by the engagement of responsibility procedure, one might speak about a significant erosion of parliament's powers (Kuti 2013). The JUDICON research project covers decisions issued in both *ex ante* and *ex post* review procedures; however, it focuses solely on the review of the acts of the parliament, excluding judicial decisions passed on the constitutionality of governmental ordinances. Government-made normative acts appear in the dataset only in those cases in which either the Court reviewed a law approving, rejecting, amending or supplementing a governmental ordinance, or provisions of ordinances are addressed inseparably, together with various articles of law, in the very same judgement.

Furthermore, as individual complaints can reach the RCC solely by way of "exceptions of unconstitutionality" raised before regular courts, regarding the constitutionality of the legal norms applicable in a given case, the Court might be facing recurring complaints regarding the same issue. In addition, as the RCC has no preliminary screening mechanism, all complaints are currently decided upon by the full court. This in practice leads to a large number of rejection decisions, creating a distorted image of the relative power of the constitutional court. Therefore, recurring complaints have not been taken into consideration, unless the Court has changed its jurisprudence and implemented a different solution. Similarly, judgements on the constitutionality of treaties or other international agreements, as well as decisions concerning disputes of constitutional nature between public authorities other than parliament, have also been disregarded.[16]

As to what concerns the consequences of the Court's decisions, the Constitution has explicitly established a deadline since the 2003 revision, until which point provisions found unconstitutional may be revised accordingly. Parliament, or in the case of governmental ordinances, the executive, has 45 days after the publishing of the decision to remedy problems of unconstitutionality. During this period, the application of the normative act in question is suspended.[17] If no action is taken, the provision in question shall cease its legal effects. Technically, the RCC has no powers to abrogate unconstitutional legislation; nevertheless, decisions of unconstitutionality can produce similar effects.[18] Finally, according to the fundamental law, decisions of the RCC are generally binding from their publication and take effect only for the future.[19] Consequently, unconstitutional provisions become inapplicable from the day the decision is published and thus rulings of the Court may have only an *ex nunc* effect.

7.3.2 Workload of the Court

The RCC had quite a stunning workload, as has already been mentioned above. According to its own official statistics, in the time span covered by this research (1992–2015), the RCC received a total of 33,771 complaints, of which 288 were *a priori* review (including mandatory review of constitutional revision bills), 42 regarded rules and regulations of the parliament, 30 concerned conflicts of constitutional nature between organs of the state, and a stunning 33,411 represented objections raised previously during litigation before ordinary courts – i.e. *a posteriori* review. In the same period, the RCC issued a total of 16,300 decisions, of which 246 were *a priori* review, 38 regarded rules and regulations of the parliament, 27 concerned conflicts of a constitutional nature and 15,989 were *a posteriori* review decisions.

The number of *a priori* review claims did not present dramatic deviations over the years, generally gravitating around 10–20 claims per year, but there was clearly a low number of claims in the 1998–2004 period (three to eight claims per year), the clear peak being 24 claims in 2010. The number of *a posteriori* review claims demonstrated a steadily growing tendency from 24 in 1992 to 2,458 in 2006, with a smaller peak in 1997 (570 claims). After 2006, the tendency was more erratic, fluctuating from 888 in 2012 to almost ten times more with 8,823 in 2009. It must be noted that the methodology elaborated by the JUDICON project uses rulings as the unit of analysis instead of decisions, as in a single decision the courts may address more than one legal provision and can offer various solutions (see Section 2.3 of Chapter 2). As for what concerns the RCC, the analysis did not lead to a dramatic difference between the number of rulings and the number of decisions, the former usually exceeding the latter by a narrow margin (Figure 7.1).

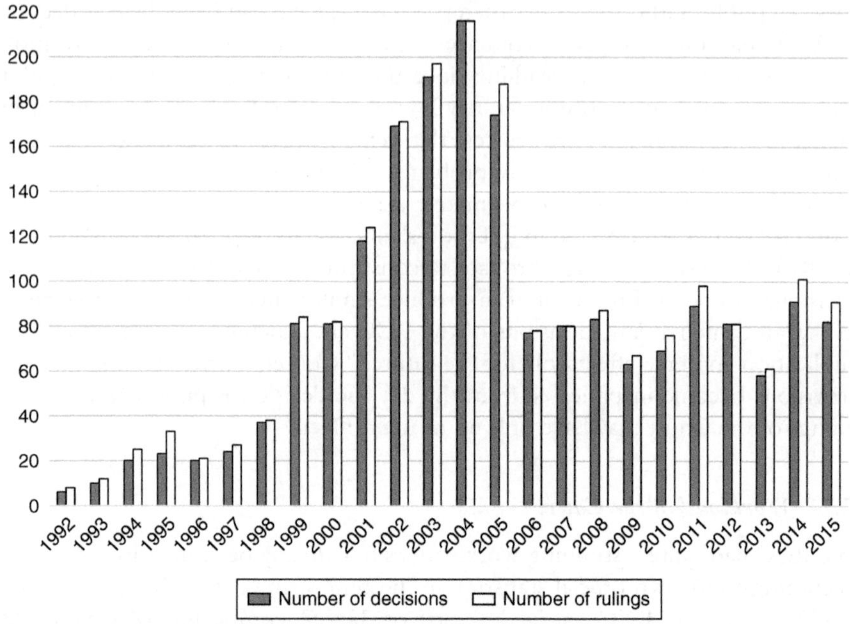

Figure 7.1 Number of decisions and rulings (RCC)

7.4 Trends in the strength of majority rulings

On the basis of the variation in the average strength of rulings per year, the entire period under scrutiny (from 1992 to 2015) might be divided into three periods: from 1992 to 1998, when the average strength of rulings remained over 1.0 point and varied from 1.0 to 3.98 points; from 1999 to 2006, with an average strength falling under 1.0 point and varying from 0.13 to 0.82 points; and from 2007 to 2015, when the average strength was again above 1.0 point and varied from 1.44 to 3.16 points. The watershed represented by the 2003 constitutional revision is also noticeable in these trends, as after a constant weakening from 1994 to 2003, rulings started strengthening from 2004 on, leading to a relatively stable 2007–2013 period, while the last two years of the timespan present a prominent strength (Figure 7.2).

From the entire period, the first five and the last two years stand out as representing the highest average strength of rulings, with peculiarly high values for 1994 and 2015. For the first five years, the explanation for the high values and the high variation in strength might be identified in several factors. First, in the early years, the workload of the RCC was insignificant in comparison with the rest of the analyzed period. The number of complaints received per year (except for the year 1997) remained under or around 300 until the turn of the millennium.[20] The number of rulings coded is accordingly low, too, varying from eight in 1992

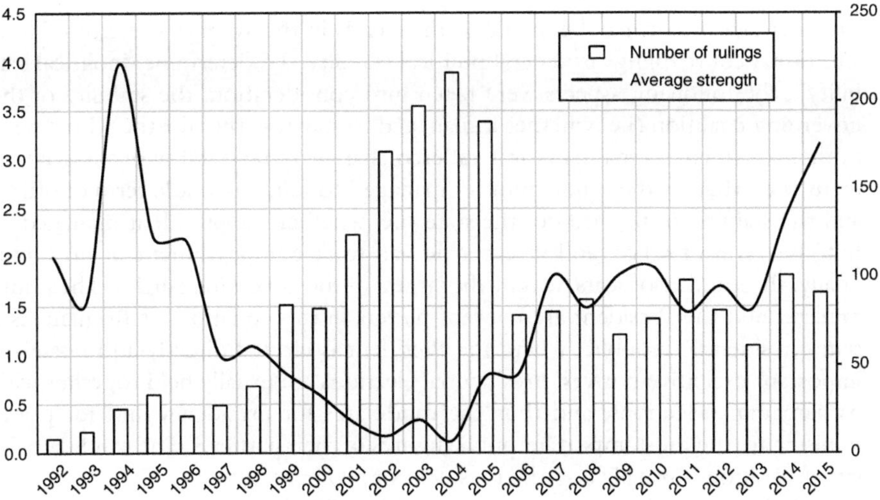

Figure 7.2 Number and average strength of rulings (RCC)

to 38 in 1998. Comparatively, the lowest number of rulings coded in the rest of the period dropped only once under 70 (61 rulings in 2013). Second, especially in the first four years, the relative proportion of ***a priori*** review motions – which, as it will be shown later, have an incomparably better success rate than ***a posteriori*** review motions – was high (more than 10 percent of all motions, a rate that has not been achieved since) (Constitutional Court of Romania 2017c). Under these conditions, even a relatively small number of rulings declaring unconstitutionality could lead to a peculiarly high average strength.[21] For the last two years, the factors that explained the relatively high average strength of the first five years were no longer present: the workload of the RCC was high (more than 5,000 complaints received in those two years) and the number of rulings coded was also significantly higher (192 for the two years) while the rate of ***a priori*** review motions was less than 1 percent.

Nevertheless, in order to be able to identify the factors that might be linked to trends in the average strength of rulings, this chapter proposes a comparison between two longer periods in which the rulings present a constant difference in average strength (constantly low and constantly high, at least in comparison to the Court's own average). Consequently, in the following this chapter focuses on the periods 2001–2004 and 2009–2012, which present a relatively small degree in variation over a longer period of time but significant difference in average strength. Both periods have been selected so as to fall between two parliamentary elections.[22] By choosing a timeframe for the analysis that is significantly larger than a year, the analysis attempts on one hand to reduce the possibility of alteration of the results by extreme rulings and, on the other, to address the fact that in the case of ***a posteriori*** review rulings, the RCC usually does not constrain the parliament in office at the date of the issuance of the RCC decision.

7.4.1 The first factor: political stability

The first factor that may be linked to the trends in the average strength of constitutional court rulings is general political stability. To determine "political stability", the following aspects were taken into consideration: the stability of the governing coalition (i.e. whether it managed to stay together for the whole term of the parliamentary mandate or it suffered changes), the stability of the government (i.e. whether the prime minister managed to fulfil his whole term of office) and the stability of the head of the state (i.e. whether the president managed to fulfil his term of office, and whether he had to face impeachment or not) and, finally, the number of seats held by the largest of the governing parties. The prime minister and the President are relevant players in this equation, as Romania is a semi-presidential republic, where the President is elected directly and possesses important executive powers. Presidential elections are usually held together with parliamentary elections, and thus the candidates for presidency and for prime minister are the most important public figures of their parties.[23] The candidate for either position is usually also the president of his/her party.

In light of the above, considering the 2009–2012 period, when the smallest degree in variation paired with a relatively high average strength of the rulings, one may find a low degree of political stability. The two parliamentary elections, in 2008 and 2012, led to a change in the governing parties. However, in addition, the governing coalition that came to power in 2008 suffered major alterations in almost each year of its mandate, the prime minister resigned in early 2012 and the new government was dismissed after merely three months of office through a vote of no confidence. In the meantime, the president managed to survive a second impeachment procedure in 2012 (the first taking place in 2007, during his first mandate).[24] The main governing parties held in the given period only 34.4–38.8 percent of the total number of seats.[25] Comparatively, in the 2001–2004 period, which featured an almost equally low degree in variation of the average strength of rulings paired with the lowest average strength, one may find a high degree of political stability – arguably the highest in the entire period of the functioning of the RCC. The governing coalition suffered only minor alterations during its mandate. The prime minister and the President fulfilled their mandates, and the main governing party enjoyed a comfortable 44.9 percent relative majority in the parliament.

Apparently, there is a connection between general political stability and the strength of RCC rulings, in the sense that in politically more stable periods the rulings tend to be weaker, while in periods of political unrest, they tend to become stronger. This argument might hold scrutiny even for the early years of the RCC (1992–1996), when the social democrats governed in minority (27.7 percent of the seats) with informal support from smaller far-right and leftist parties, gathering merely 48 percent of the seats in the upper house, which made government bills difficult to pass. However, for this early period there are other significant aspects that must also be taken into consideration, such as the very low number of rulings and the relatively high percentage of *a priori* review rulings.

7.4.2 The second factor: political affiliation of the judges

A second factor that might be considered – also in relationship to the first one – is the position of the judges' nominating party within the parliament. At the outset, the first nine judges were appointed for terms of three, six and nine years, so as to allow – theoretically – a renewal of one-third of the Court every three years. In practice, however, judges did not always fulfil their entire mandate for various reasons (health, age and other personal or political reasons).[26] There was even a case when a judge was first appointed for a part of the mandate and subsequently for an entire nine-year mandate.

Regarding the appointment of judges, during the first 15 years of the Court, an unwritten convention was formed, according to which in the case of vacancy, the political family or party that nominated the judge whose mandate had expired was able to nominate the new judge, too. This convention has been more or less observed until 2004 and allowed for instance the discrete party of the Hungarian minority, which holds roughly 6 percent of the seats, to almost continuously have a judge appointed to the Court. However, this also meant that the Court has been dominated by the political left.[27] Beginning with 2006, the sharpening of political power struggles disrupted the above custom and majorities tried to impose their candidates on the Court. When talking about Romanian political left and right, it must be noted that the left is traditionally monolithic, being represented by a single large Social Democratic Party (*Partidul Social Democrat*, PSD), while the centre-right is fragmented in a varying number of smaller parties. Occasional break-away groups from the PSD always attempt to position themselves centre-right, never to the left.

In the 2009–2012 period, there were 11 judges involved in the analyzed rulings. In 2009–2010, four of them were nominated by the left, four by the right and one by the Democratic Alliance of Hungarians in Romania (*Romániai Magyar Demokrata Szövetség*, RMDSZ), which – due to its ethnic determination – can be considered centrist. In 2010 a judge nominated by the left was replaced by one nominated by the right. Of course, being nominated by a party does not necessarily mean that the nominated judge is affiliated with the given party, and this is especially true in the case of judges appointed by the President of the Republic (except for the cases in which a member of parliament is nominated or appointed).[28] This relative equilibrium of right-wing and left-wing judges, combined with the frequent change of majorities in parliament and the relatively fragile general political stability, can be considered as contributing towards the high average strength and low degree of variation of rulings. A politically more balanced and, consequently, more polarized Court coupled with an increased political instability enhances the opportunities for gathering the necessary majority in the Court for rulings declaring unconstitutionality. Furthermore, more frequent and intense political conflicts in the legislature seemingly contribute to a decreasing concern of the RCC judges towards rules and procedures of the legislative processes; consequently, the proportion of procedural unconstitutionality rulings were significantly larger for the 2009–2012 than for the 2001–2004 period.[29]

In comparison, during the 2001–2004 period, there were 16 judges involved in the analyzed rulings; however, in this case nine of them were nominated by the left, three by the right and one by the centrist RMDSZ, while in the case of the remaining three judges, unfortunately no relevant record can be found about their nominating parties.[30] This permanent and strong leftist influence, combined with a high degree of general political stability under left-wing government, can be considered as a factor contributing towards a low average strength and low degree of variation of rulings.

Scholars criticized the Court's deferential, passive attitude, especially during the first two decades of its existence, arguing that even if decisions concerning delicate and socially important issues were taken by a minimal (five to four) majority, that majority was always made up of justices appointed by the then governing parties (Gilia 2012). This argument, however, is not necessarily supported by the findings of the present analysis. As voting patterns of the judges are not publicly available, the best indicators are dissenting opinions. In the dataset used for this inquiry, there are only 13 rulings which produced at least four dissents. These might be considered as the most debated rulings of the Court, since all the minority judges considered it necessary to formally express their disagreement with the majority decision in the form of a dissenting opinion. Nevertheless, in only one single case out of 13 can the four dissenting judges be linked with the same nominating party (coalition), and even in that case they had all been nominated by parties which formed the then governing coalition.[31] Furthermore, there was only a single ruling where all four dissenting judges were nominated by opposition parties.[32]

We might extend the analysis also to those cases where at least three dissents were formulated, which can also be regarded as betraying a strong disagreement between the judges, especially given that in five of the analyzed cases the Court was made up of only eight judges; thus, the rulings were taken by the narrowest possible majority (5–3).[33] In the entire analyzed period, the dataset contains 27 rulings with three dissenting judges. There was a single case in which all three dissenting judges had been nominated by the governing party,[34] and eight cases in which all three dissenting judges had been nominated by the opposition parties.[35] Cumulatively, out of 40 rulings with at least three dissents, there are only eight cases in which all dissenting judges had been nominated by opposition parties. Therefore, on the basis of the present analysis, it can be stated that in the most debated rulings (taken with a minimal majority) the Court was, as a rule, not split according to the affiliation of the judges (at least not according to their nominating parties) and the majority was not, as a rule, formed by judges appointed by the then governing parties.

7.4.3 *The third factor: a priori or a posteriori review*

The third factor, which is worth taking into consideration, is the character of the constitutional review, namely whether it is an *a priori* or *a posteriori* review. A superficial look at the frequency of ruling types (Figure 7.3) and trends of

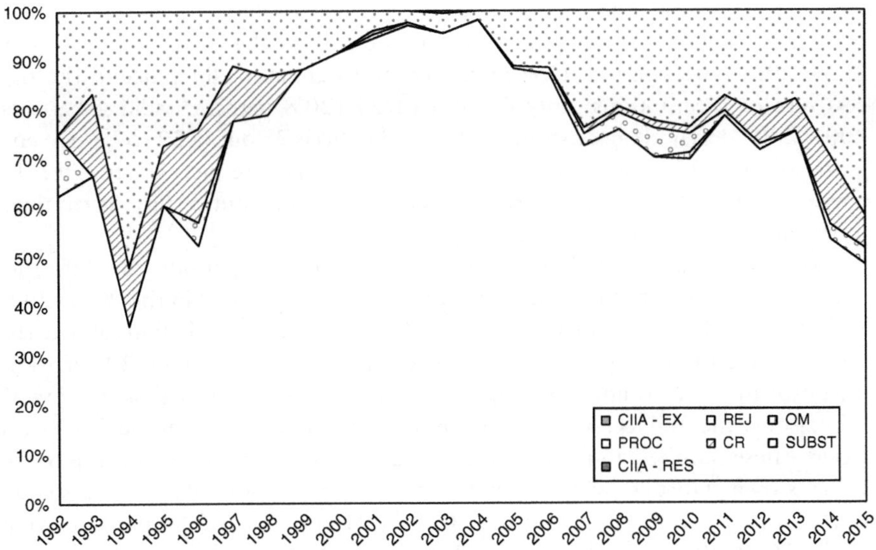

Figure 7.3 Frequency of ruling types I (RCC)

the average strength of rulings (Figure 7.2) might suggest an obvious answer for the puzzle of this chapter: there is a relationship of direct proportionality between the number of rejections and the average strength of rulings, i.e. more rejections mean lower average strength of rulings. But on closer examination, the situation is more nuanced. If the rulings are clustered according to whether they were issued in an *a priori* or in an *a posteriori* review, the results become more intriguing.

The *a priori* review procedure enables the Court to adjudicate on the constitutionality of bills before their promulgation. The *a priori* motion, as mentioned above, might be lodged by the President of the Republic, either of the presidents of the two chambers of the parliament, the President of the High Court of Cassation and Justice, the Ombudsman and at least 50 deputies or 25 senators, but the bulk of the motions comes from MPs. In fact, in the 1992–2015 period, they lodged 208 out of 281 *a priori* review motions (Constitutional Court of Romania 2017a). This data is of special importance, since MPs usually translate into members of the opposition.

The total number of *a priori* review rulings in the analyzed dataset is low: only 252 out of 2,046, but their success rate is stunning: 106 of the rulings have been in favour of the complainant. This is almost three times higher than the success rate of the *a posteriori* review motions. It must be noted, as mentioned above, that until the 2003 revision of the Constitution, parliament had the possibility of overriding the Constitutional Court's *a priori* review decisions with qualified majority vote. Although it never made use of this power, nevertheless it might have been perceived as a chilling factor.

Narrowing the analysis to the two periods in question, it can be found that there is no dramatic difference between the strength of the *a priori* review rulings declaring unconstitutionality: 5.6 points in the 2001–2004 period and 6.5 points in the 2009–2012 period. However, there is a significant difference in the success rate of the motions: only five out of 24 (20.8 percent) rulings between 2001–2004 declared unconstitutionality, while this is 35 out of 52 (67.3 percent) in the 2009–2012 period. Even more outstanding than the success rate is the difference between the number of rulings declaring unconstitutionality: seven times more such rulings in the 2009–2012 period.

Comparing the *a posteriori* review rulings of the same periods, the difference is also considerable, but less dramatic: 2.9 percent success rate in the 2001–2004 period versus 19.2 percent in the 2009–2012 period, but this translates better into concrete rulings, where the difference is just above two times: 20 versus 52 unconstitutionality rulings. Taking into consideration the fact that, for practical reasons, the JUDICON project covers only a fraction of the docket of the Court, these numbers must be tested against the full case law. According to the Court's own statistics (which operates with decisions, not rulings), the success rate of *a priori* review claims in the 2001–2004 period was 22.9 percent, while in the 2009–2012 period it was 52.3 percent, which translates into five versus 32 unconstitutionality decisions. Even more interesting is the difference in the *a posteriori* review claims, where the success rate was 2.8 percent in the 2001–2003 period and 2.4 percent in the 2009–2012 period, which translates into 44 versus 65 unconstitutionality decisions (Constitutional Court of Romania 2017b).

Finally, this finding must also be tested against the relevant data from the two outstanding years (from the perspective of the average strength of rulings): 1994 and 2015. If the presumption announced at the outset of this chapter is correct, then in these years the clustering of rulings according to their character should produce an outcome similar to the 2009–2012 period. Indeed, in 1994 the success rate of *a priori* review rulings according to the JUDICON database was 46.1 percent, while in 2015 it was 71.4 percent, translating into six versus five unconstitutionality rulings. However, the success rate of *a posteriori* reviews was 83.3 percent versus 50 percent , producing an average strength of rulings by year of 3.98 points in 1994 and 3.16 points in 2015.

What follows from the above is that a clustering of the rulings according to the character of the constitutional review (i.e. *a priori* or *a posteriori*) can offer a valid explanation for the trends in the strength of RCC rulings. At least in the case of the Romanian Constitutional Court, *a priori* review rulings are of paramount importance, as in most cases they are generated by motions filed by members of the opposition. Consequently, a low degree of success rate (for instance, in 2004 five out of five such rulings were rejections) will result in a lower average strength of rulings; this effect is more prominent than in the case of *a posteriori* review rulings.

Analysts have noted this distortion between the success rate of *a priori* and *a posteriori* reviews and have proposed the elimination of the *a priori* review powers of the Court, arguing that *a priori* motions are in essence the expression of political conflicts and are used by the opposition as an alternative means of political dispute, after being defeated in the parliamentary voting procedures (Perju 2010). This view finds some degree of support in the present analysis, as data show that the relative rate of *a priori* review motions has been the highest when the general political stability has been low (52 of the total of 252 rulings, that is, 20.6 percent, being issued in the 2009–2012 period), while their success rate has also been significantly higher in comparison with periods of high general political stability (67.3 percent versus 20.8 percent). The fact that *a priori* review motions might be an expression of political conflicts is also supported by the fact that claims coming from the office of the President of Romania have been extremely low in the periods of general political stability (two motions filed in the 2001–2004 period), while they became regular in the politically less-stable periods (13 motions filed in the 2009–2012 period) (Constitutional Court of Romania 2017a).

7.5 Trends in the strength of unconstitutionality rulings

When faced with a constitutional complaint, constitutional courts typically come up with two solutions: they either refuse/reject the complaint or admit it. Refusal usually means that the court will not hear the case for various reasons, while rejection occurs when the court, after a hearing (discussion on the merits), finds no breach of the constitution. The Romanian Court has yet to develop a clear-cut, unambiguous and unitary wording for its decisions.[36] For instance, the Court does not distinguish at the level of language between refusal and rejection; it uses the same word – "rejects" (*respinge*) – for both situations. Key phrases in rejections might contain further hints ("rejects as inadmissible" or "rejects as unfounded"), but this is a rule of thumb rather than a matter of consistent phrasing. An extremely high proportion of the Court's rulings from the dataset used for this research qualify as refusals or rejections (81.8 percent). The bulk of the rulings declaring unconstitutionality are represented by substantive unconstitutionality rulings (14.1 percent), while constitutional requirement and procedural unconstitutionality rulings represent a marginal quantity (see Table A.1 in the Appendix).

However, it must be noted that the Court is seemingly more likely to issue constitutional requirements in periods of lower general political stability: such rulings were regularly present in the Court's case law in the 1993–1998 period, disappeared from 1999 to 2006 (one single ruling in 2001) and have been, again, a constant presence since 2007 (Figure 7.3). In the 2009–2012 period there were 14, while in the 2001–2004 period merely one such ruling can be found out of 56 in total.

Constitutional interpretation *in abstracto* or legislative omissions are absolutely rare, as the dataset contains only one ruling from each of these two categories (see Table A.1 in the Appendix). The omission ruling referred to the electoral law's provisions, which, according to the Court, omitted to regulate the participation of independent candidates in intermediate elections; this resulted in the exclusion of this type of competitor, which amounted to a breach of the fundamental right of being elected.[37] The constitutional interpretation *in abstracto* ruling was part of a large decision on the *ex officio* review of a constitutional revision bill.[38] One ruling of this decision formulated a set of observations about various provisions of the bill – from a technical rather than a constitutional perspective – and recommended the legislature take the observations into consideration. Turning to the procedural unconstitutionality rulings, one may find that these types of rulings were rare in the first but increased in the last decade of the Court. In the 2009–2012 period, there were nine, while in the 2001–2004 period there were two such rulings out of 26 in total. An explanation for these figures might be that, as already argued above, in periods of greater political instability less attention is paid to procedural rules of the legislative processes.

From the above data it can be seen that the Court's rulings are less differentiated. To some extent in line with the instrumentalist view cited above (Tănăsescu 2013), the Court seems comfortable in the classical dichotomy of constitutional and unconstitutional decisions, perfectly fitting the image of the "enforcer of the constitution". Hence, the bulk of its rulings are either rejection or substantive unconstitutionality (Figure 7.4).

7.6 Analysis of the presidents' performance

The presidents of the Court are elected by the judges with a secret majority vote for a three-year renewable term: theoretically, the president's term is connected with the periodical renewal of one-third of the Court. In practice, once elected, presidents kept their office until the end of their mandate. In the period covered by this research, the Court had six presidents: Gionea, Muraru, Mihai, Popa, Vida and Zegrean. Of these, only Mihai did not fulfil his term as president: he resigned from the Court after only four years.

Presidents have strong formal competencies and are presumed to put their mark on the functioning of their institution. From this perspective, their background cannot be neglected. Interestingly, and presumably not by chance, three

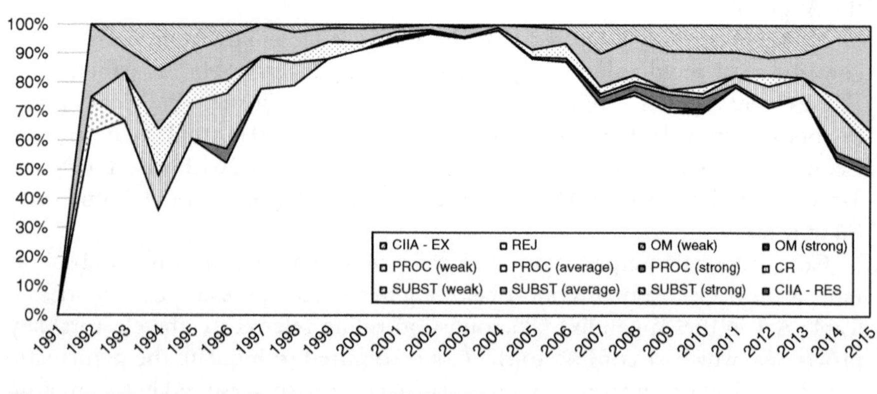

Figure 7.4 Frequency of ruling types II (RCC)

of the six presidents have been members of the drafting committee that elaborated the Constitution in 1990 (Gionea, Muraru and Vida). As to what concerns their political affiliation, three of them had no formal affiliation (Muraru, Mihai and Vida), two of them were MPs (Gionea for the former Christian Democrat Peasant Party and Zegrean for the Democratic Party), while Popa has been counsellor for the President of Romania, which can also be considered as an indication of political preference.

Comparing the average strength of the presidents' rulings, significant differences can be found. However, their rulings did not significantly differ from those of the Courts they led. Still, a few points of divergence can be detected: President Gionea in 1993 produced an average strength of rulings 0.5 points lower than the Court's average, while in 1995, before the end of his mandate, he was involved in rulings that were 0.6 points stronger than the average of his Court. Furthermore, President Muraru in his first year of presidency (1995) managed to produce an average strength 0.5 points lower than the Court. Finally, President Zegrean in 2013 showed a trend that went completely opposite to his Court, resulting in an average strength that was higher by 0.49 points. Yet these divergences are too few to be considered as decisive.

More interesting is a comparison between the dissenting opinions of the presidents (Figure 7.5). Here President Gionea and President Zegrean stand out, with zero and 19 dissenting opinions, respectively. The other presidents were closer to the average (four dissents): Muraru and Vida wrote five, Popa six and Mihai seven. In fairness, it must be noted that Gionea had a mandate of three years and Mihai resigned after only four years. Nevertheless, it is surprising that, except for Gionea, the presidents produced an above-average rate of dissents, with Mihai and Zegrean being the remarkable performers. This amount of dissent might be an indicator of the presidents' efforts to impose their hallmark on the Court, or it might be a sign of their failure to do so (materializing in an outstanding number of minority opinions) as well.

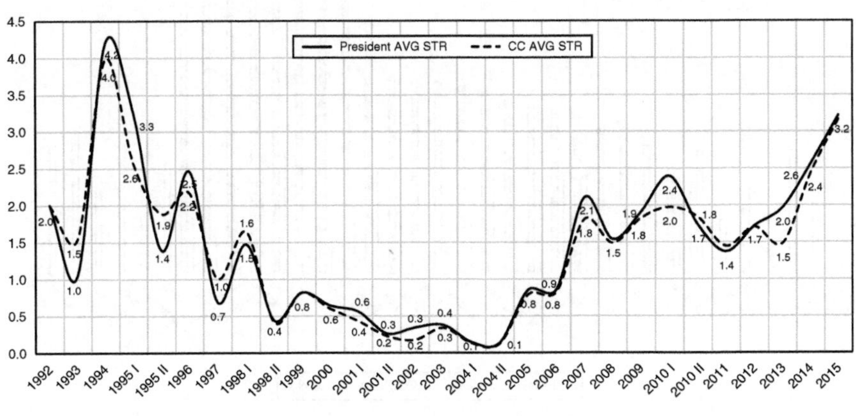

Figure 7.5 Average strength of rulings (by presidents and majorities) (RCC)

7.7 Analysis of dissenting opinions

7.7.1 Trends in dissenting opinions

In the entire period covered by the dataset that forms the basis of this analysis, there were 35 judges involved in the rulings passed by the Court. Of these, there were six judges who did not formulate a single dissenting opinion from the analyzed rulings.[39] All six performed their activity in the first decade, five of them as members of the initial composition of the Court. Besides them, there were seven other judges for whom the average strength of their dissenting opinions was lower than the average strength of the majority rulings.[40] In the case of the remaining 22 judges, the average strength of their dissenting opinions exceeded the average strength of their majority rulings, usually with quite an appreciable margin (Figure 7.6).

Generally, the number of dissenting opinions from the rulings of the Court is relatively modest. In the first five years of the Court there were only two dissents registered in the dataset used for the present research. This number increased moderately over the years and peaked in 2010 with 42 dissents (Figure 7.7).

The outstanding number of dissents in 2005 can be explained by the relatively large number of *a priori* review rulings (30) passed in that year, generating 16 dissents. These data might be linked to the fact that the 2004 December elections produced a right-wing parliamentary majority and government, while the RCC was still dominated by leftist judges, up until 2006, after which the composition of the Court started to become more balanced.

Another exceptional case was in 2010, when a larger number of *a priori* review rulings (28) produced 13 dissents. Again, the larger number of *a priori* reviews and dissents might be linked to an increasingly unstable political context: the

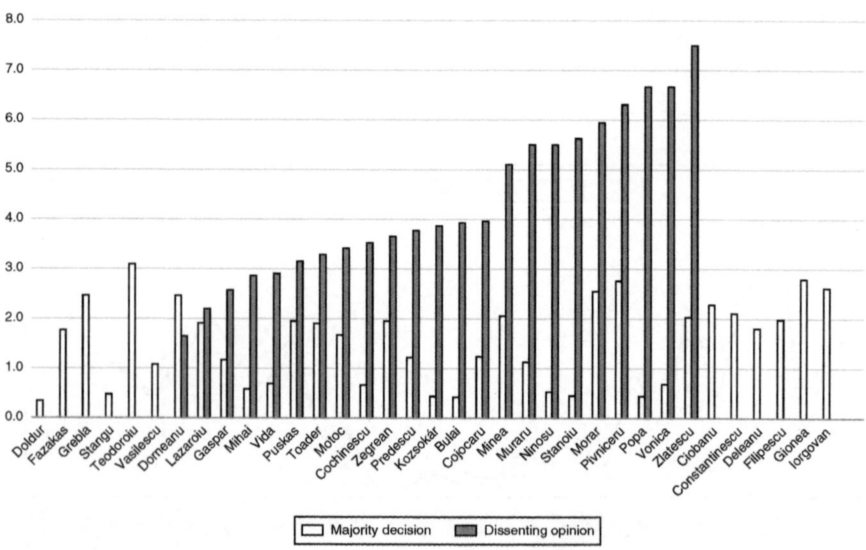

Figure 7.6 Average strength of rulings (by judges) (RCC)

grand coalition that came to power in December 2008 fell apart less than a year later, and in October 2009 the government was dismissed (for the first time in post-communist Romania) after a vote of no confidence but remained in place as an interim government until the presidential elections (December 2009). After the right-wing President of the Republic obtained his second mandate, he re-appointed the interim (previously dismissed) prime minister, who obtained the necessary support from the legislature.

It can generally be observed that from 1992 to 1998, an extremely low number of dissenting opinions was published (5), and while the percentage of *a priori* review rulings was relatively high, a single dissent was formulated from these rulings. It is also noticeable that in case of *a priori* review rulings this tendency continued until 2004, as only two dissents were published to such rulings from 1992 till 2004. Starting from 2005, the number of *a priori* review rulings and of dissents from such rulings was boosted. Also, it appears that after 2005, the number of dissenting opinions from *a priori* review rulings amounted to at least 50 percent of the number of such rulings in each year following parliamentary elections: 53.3 percent in 2005, 50 percent in 2009 and 56.6 percent in 2013.[41]

Conclusively, it can be argued that in the initial years, the Court was more unanimous – or at least attempted to convey such an image – which can be explained by the fact that it had to assert its own legitimacy, and by the fact that it was less diversified and polarized than in the later years. Furthermore, since the political environment became less stable and more polarized, after parliamentary elections political actors increasingly attempted to counter the new parliamentary majorities via constitutional review, leading to more disputed *a priori* review rulings visible from the increased number of dissenting opinions to such rulings.

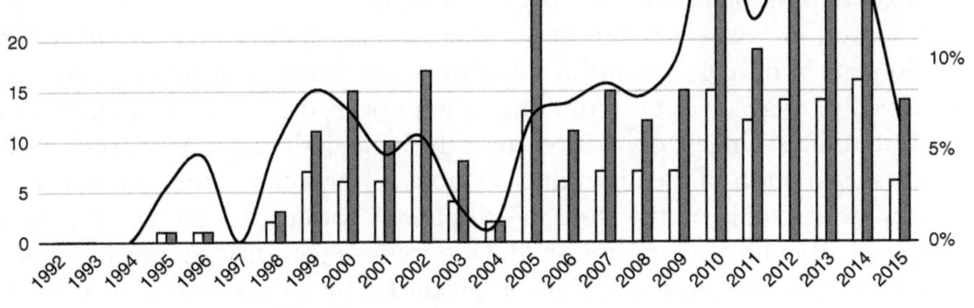

Figure 7.7 Number of rulings and dissenting opinions (RCC)

This does not mean to say that the number of dissenting opinions determines the direction and strength of majority rulings. But it can be taken as indicative of the fact that in periods when the Court is (at least seemingly) more balanced and there is a lower degree of general political stability rulings are more disputed, producing a larger number of dissents. In the 2009–2012 period, the proportion of dissenting opinions varied from 10.4 percent to 19.7 percent, while in the period of general political stability and lowest average strength of rulings (2001–2004) the proportion of dissents varied from 0.9 percent to 5.8 percent. The total number of dissenting opinions in the 2009–2012 period was 101, out of 322 rulings. There were six rulings issued with a minimal (five to four, or five to three) majority from which all minority judges formulated dissenting opinions, but in only one of these rulings had the minority judges all been nominated by the same party or coalition. In comparison, in the 2001–2004 period there were only 37 dissenting opinions out of 708 rulings, but the difference is even greater with regard to the other indicators: there were zero rulings taken with a minimal majority and all minority judges dissenting.

From the above numbers, it might be inferred that in periods when the Court is (seemingly) more balanced and the general political stability is lower, it is more likely to meet minimal majority rulings with all minority judges dissenting. Furthermore, in the case of intensely disputed rulings (with at least three dissenting judges) the average strength of the majority rulings is the highest, while the average strength of dissents from such rulings peak, on the contrary, in periods when the Court is (seemingly) less balanced and the general political stability is higher.

7.7.2 Network analysis of dissenting opinions

Amongst the individual judges there is also a high variation with regard to dissenting opinions. In the 1992–2015 period, 35 judges were appointed to the Court, and their individual record ranges from none to a couple of dozens of dissents. Nevertheless, 12 judges distinguished themselves from the rest, producing together an impressive 206 out of a total of 299 dissents (Figure 7.8). Interestingly, the average strength of these dissents is only 3.39 points, which hints towards the fact that the judges who dissent more rarely tend to formulate a stronger opposition towards the majority opinion.

Moreover, in this select club of 12, there are five judges who formulated at least 50 percent of their dissents in a coalition with at least two other judges and thus arguably were involved more often than not in the groups of judges who constituted the strongest opposition towards the majority opinion. Surprisingly, the average strength of the dissenting opinions of these five judges is lower than the average strength of the dissenting opinions formulated by all 12 judges (3.07 vs. 3.19 points). Conclusively, the numbers suggest that the strongest dissenting opinions are most likely to be produced by judges who dissent more rarely, and/or when they do so, they rather formulate their views alone.

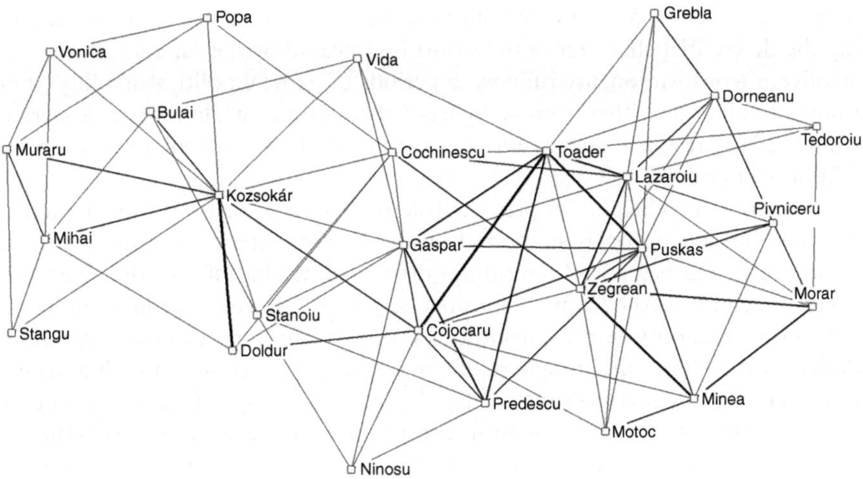

Figure 7.8 Dissenting coalitions 1992–2015 (RCC)

A similar conclusion might be reached by taking into consideration the judges with the highest average strength of dissents. There are also twelve judges whose dissents produced an average strength of at least 4.0 points (from 4.07 to 7.5 points). Amongst them, there are only three who also appear on the list of judges with the highest frequency of dissenting opinions, albeit all of them formulated most of their dissents alone or together with a maximum of one other judge (13 out of 22, 21 out of 29 and 10 out of 16).

7.8 Conclusions

The Romanian Constitutional Court has never been a strong check on parliament. In the past decade, during which tensions between government and/or parliament and the presidency have escalated, the Court had several opportunities to become an arbitrator, a role that it was not particularly enthusiastic to interpret. The Court is deferential, as the rate of refusal/rejection rulings is high: 81.8 percent in the entire period. Moreover, the success rate of *a posteriori* review claims is significantly lower than the success rate of *a priori* review claims: 14.9 percent vs. 42 percent. A further indicator of the Court's deferential attitude towards the legislator is the relatively low rate of dissenting opinions: only 7.5 percent of the rulings generated at least one dissent in the entire period under analysis.

Perhaps an even more telling fact is that the relative rate of *a priori* review motions has been the highest when the general political stability has been low (52 of the total of 252 rulings, that is, 20.6 percent, being issued in the 2009–2012 period), while their success rate has also been significantly higher in comparison with periods of high general political stability (67.3 percent versus 20.8 percent).

Further weight is added to these data by the fact that most of the *a priori* review motions are filed by MPs (i.e. the opposition parties). A further argument regarding the deferential character of the Court is indicated by the variation in the substantive unconstitutionality rulings: in periods of general political stability, these rulings tend to be rather average or weak than strong, while less stable periods (2009–2012) result in strong and average rather than weak substantive unconstitutionality rulings.

The Court is reluctant to play the role of arbitrator or to assume an activist stance. This conclusion is supported by the low occurrence of remedies in the rulings: only 5.2 percent of the rulings offered some kind of remedy. The Court is very careful not to become a "positive legislator"; it avoids grounding its rulings on reasons outside the constitutional text. Moreover, even the institutional design of the Court and its sphere of competence is conceived in such a manner to preserve as much as possible the legislators' lawmaking supremacy: norms are not abrogated by the effect of an unconstitutionality decision; instead, the legislator has a limited period of time to correct the faulty provisions (or abrogate the norm). This cautiousness is also reflected by the fact that in constitutional requirement rulings, the Court constantly seeks to offer such an interpretation for the contested norm that is in line with constitutional provisions, instead of declaring it unconstitutional.

It can also be considered a specific feature that constitutional requirement rulings have been more frequent in periods of lower general political stability. Furthermore, *a priori* review rulings generate the highest frequency of dissenting opinions: 14.2 percent of all *a priori* rulings have produced at least one dissenting opinion, while in the case of *a posteriori* reviews this rate is only 6.5 percent. This means that motions submitted by political actors generate far greater debates and controversies than motions claiming a breach of individual rights. In the 2009–2012 period, 22.9 percent of *a priori* review rulings generated at least one dissent, while in the 2001–2004 period this type of ruling did not register a single dissent. Procedural unconstitutionality and constitutional requirement rulings also generate a high rate of dissent (10.97 percent compared to 7.5 percent for all rulings) in the entire period.

Finally, in the case of the rulings with at least three dissenting opinions, the average strength of the majority rulings is 2.60 points for the entire period and 2.66 points for the 2009–2012 period, while the average strength of dissents is 3.32 points for the entire period and 3.64 points for the 2009–2012 period. However, in the 2001–2004 period, the average strength of majority rulings is 1.25 points and the average strength of dissents is 5.66 points. Here, the larger degree of variation suggests that in periods of higher general political stability, combined with a less balanced composition of the Court, rulings tend to be the least strong in the arguably most disputed cases (at least three minority judges dissenting), while proportionally, the dissenting coalitions of judges tend to produce the strongest opinions.

Appendix

Table A.1 Frequency of ruling types III (RCC)

	CIIA – EX (n=0)	*REJ (n=1673)*	*OM (n=1)*	*PROC (n=26)*	*CR (n=56)*	*SUB (n=289)*	*CIIA – RES (n=1)*	*Sum*
1992	0	5	0	1	0	2	0	**8**
1993	0	8	0	0	2	2	0	**12**
1994	0	9	0	0	3	13	0	**25**
1995	0	20	0	0	4	9	0	**33**
1996	0	11	0	1	4	5	0	**21**
1997	0	21	0	0	3	3	0	**27**
1998	0	30	0	0	3	5	0	**38**
1999	0	74	0	0	0	10	0	**84**
2000	0	75	0	0	0	7	0	**82**
2001	0	117	0	1	1	5	0	**124**
2002	0	166	0	1	0	4	0	**171**
2003	0	188	0	0	0	8	1	**197**
2004	0	212	0	0	0	4	0	**216**
2005	0	166	0	1	0	21	0	**188**
2006	0	68	0	1	0	9	0	**78**
2007	0	58	0	2	1	19	0	**80**
2008	0	66	0	3	1	17	0	**87**
2009	0	47	0	4	1	15	0	**67**
2010	0	53	1	3	1	18	0	**76**
2011	0	77	0	1	3	17	0	**98**
2012	0	58	0	1	5	17	0	**81**
2013	0	46	0	0	4	11	0	**61**
2014	0	54	0	3	14	30	0	**101**
2015	0	44	0	3	6	38	0	**91**
Sum	**0**	**1673**	**1**	**26**	**56**	**289**	**1**	**2046**

Notes

1 Out of the 16,338 rulings of the analyzed period, more than half, specifically 8,755, were issued in the years 2007–2012. In the rest of the period, the number of the decisions surpassed 900 only twice (in 2006 and 2015).

2 Rules prescribed a simple majority on articles and two-thirds majority on the final text of the constitution.

3 It must be noted, however, that parliament has never managed to make use of this power.

4 Regarding the review of constitutional revisions, the RCC has a double *a priori* review competence: first, revision bills must be reviewed before being presented to the parliament. Second, after their adoption, such bills must be presented to the RCC for a second *a priori* review. The RCC made use of this power several times after 2003, frequently finding the constitutional revision bills constitutional but striking down

provisions on the first reading on two occasions: Decision no.148/2003, published in the Official Gazette no.317/2003 and Decision no.799/2011, published in the Official Gazette no.440/2011. It has yet to review a revision bill on the second reading (after being adopted by the Parliament). Apart from these, the Court had the power to supervise the election procedure of the President of Romania and to confirm the results of the elections, to ascertain the existence of the circumstances justifying the interim in the exercise of the position of President of Romania, to issue an advisory opinion on the suspension from office of the President of Romania, to supervise the organization of referendums, to verify citizens' legislative initiatives and to decide on motions which contest the constitutionality of political parties.

5 The referring court could but did not necessarily have to suspend litigation until the objection was decided upon by the RCC.

6 If procedures had not been halted before the referring court, decisions declaring unconstitutionality constituted cause for retrial upon the request of the party which raised the exception in civil litigation and *ex officio* in penal litigation, if the conviction had been passed on the basis of a provision declared as unconstitutional.

7 Law no.138/1997 on amending and supplementing of Law no.47/1992 on the organization and functioning of the Romanian Constitutional Court, Official Gazette no.187/1997.

8 Constitution Review Act 2003 and Law no. 232 of 2004, amending and supplementing Law no. 47 of 1992 on the organization and functioning of the Romanian Constitutional Court.

9 The Superior Council of Magistracy is a representative body of the judicial authority, the guarantor of the independence of judiciary, which oversees the careers of magistrates, prepares and keeps professional records of the magistrates, coordinates the activity of the National Institute of Magistracy and of the National School of Clerks of the Court and exercises various powers with regard to the organization and functioning of the courts of law and the public prosecutors' offices. It has 19 members: nine judges and five public prosecutors elected by the magistrates, two representatives of civil society elected by the Senate, the Ministry of Justice, the President of the High Court of Cassation and Justice and the General Public Prosecutor. The President of Romania can attend meetings of the plenum of the Superior Council of Magistracy. In these situations, he/she is chairing these meetings, without a right to vote.

10 *A priori* complaint standing: President of the Republic, Presidents of the two chambers of the Parliament, President of the High Court of Justice and Cassation, Ombudsman. *A posteriori* complaint standing: Ombudsman. Constitutional conflict complaint ("Organstreitverfahren") standing: President of the Republic, President of the two chambers of Parliament, Prime Minister, President of the Superior Council of Magistracy.

11 Law no. 232/2004 on amending and supplementing of Law no.47/1992 on the organizing and functioning of the Constitutional Court, Official Gazette no. 502/2004; Decision no.356/2003, published in the Official Gazette no.686/2003.

12 Law no. 177 /2010 for the revision of Law no. 47 of 1992, Official Gazette no.672/2010, of the Code of Civil Procedure and of the Code of Criminal Procedure.

13 Art. 15–23, Law no.47/1992 on the organizing and functioning of the Constitutional Court, as amended by Law no.138/1997 on amending and supplementing of Law no.47/1992, Official Gazette no.187/1997.

14 Constitution of Romania, Art. 114.

15 Constitution of Romania, Art. 115.

16 Disputes of constitutional nature are resembling the *Organstreitverfahren* before the Federal Constitutional Court of Germany.

17 Art. 147 sect.(1), Constitution of Romania (2003 revision).

18 Decision no.1039/2012, published in the Official Gazette, no.61/2013.

19 Art. 147 sect. (4) Constitution of Romania.

20 A reason for this could rest in an alteration of the Court's institutional setting (art.23 para. (6) of Law no. 47/1992 on the organization and functioning of the Constitutional Court, introduced by Law no.138/1997 on amending and supplementing of Law no.47/1992 Official Gazette no.187/1997), according to which, from 1997, in the case of objections, proceedings before regular courts were halted until the objection of unconstitutionality was decided upon by the Court. In 1997, the number of *a posteriori* review motions almost doubled (570 v. 292 in 1996), and although this figure dropped in the next year, it kept on growing for a good decade, peaking at 8,823 in 2009. In 2010, the parliament adopted a novel amendment to Law no.47/1992 (Law no. 177/2010, Official Gazette no.672/2010), abrogating the mandatory halting of proceedings. In the following years, the number of objections dropped dramatically to 888 in 2013 and managed to climb again to a high of 1,887 in 2015. For details see: Constitutional Court of Romania 2017c.

21 For instance, in 1994 there were 14 unconstitutionality rulings, leading to an average strength of 3.98 points, while in 2005, 22 decisions resulted in an average strength of merely 0.78 points.

22 General elections framing the first period took place on 26 November 2000 and 28 November 2004, while the second period was framed by parliamentary elections on 30 November 2008 and 9 December 2012.

23 As an exception to this rule, between 2004 and 2014 the Romanian president had a term of five years, so as to allow the separation of presidential from general parliamentary elections.

24 The impeachment procedure consists of a vote in the united chambers of the parliament and an ensuing referendum, which must either confirm or reject the decision of the parliament. In both cases the president managed to obtain popular support against the decision of parliament.

25 It has to be noted that this general political instability exceeds the analyzed period: in the preceding years the President of the Republic had to face an impeachment procedure, which saw him suspended from office until reconfirmed by a referendum (April to May 2007), and further deepened his conflict with the executive, which at that time lost its majority in the legislature. Moreover, in preparation for the 2008 parliamentary elections, the electoral laws were revised so as to introduce a hybrid majority voting system. Similarly, after the 2012 elections, 2013 started with a grand coalition government, which only lasted until 2014, while the conflicts between the conservative president and the left-wing prime minister continued. At the 2014 presidential elections a liberal candidate defeated the social-democrat prime minister, whose government fell after a vote of no confidence towards the end of 2015.

26 One judge was forced to resign after corruption charges were brought against him; but there was also a case when a judge resigned in order to accept a mandate at the European Court of Human Rights.

27 The initial Court had been appointed just months before the first general elections organized according to the new Constitution, and the leftist coalition held at that point 66.4 percent of the seats in the parliament.

28 In the 2001–2004 period there were five judges with clear indication of their political position: Gaspar, Ninosu, Predescu and Vonica had all previously been MPs of the Social Democratic Party (PSD), while Kozsokar had been an MP for Democratic Alliance of Hungarians in Romania (RMDSZ). A further three judges (Vasilescu, Popa and Stângu) had been counsellors of the President of Romania (Iliescu, PSD),

which was a strong indication of their ideological orientation. In the 2009–2012 period there were five judges with clear political affiliation: Gaspar, Predescu and Dorneanu were previously MPs of the PSD, Puskás had been an MP of RMDSZ and Zegrean (president of the Court from 2010) was a former MP of the Democratic Party (*Partidul Democrat*, PD). One more judge had held the position of ministry of justice under the governments Ponta I.–II. (PSD), which might be also considered a strong hint of ideological preference.

29 The equilibrium and polarization of the Court can also be detected in the increased number of dissenting opinions and of rulings with more than one dissent, an aspect which will be also addressed later.

30 Five judges were active in both periods, four of them being nominated by the left, one by the right.

31 Decision no.1431/03.11.2010, published in the Official Gazette no. 758 / 12.11.2010.

32 Decision no.1237/06.10.2010, published in the Official Gazette no. 785 / 24.11.2010.

33 Decisions no. 1414/04.11.2009, published in the Official Gazette no. 796 / 23.11.2009; 1415/04.11.2009, published in the Official Gazette no. 796 / 23.11.2009; 53/25.01.2011, published in the Official Gazette no. 90 /03.02.2011; 511/12.12.2013, published in the Official Gazette no. 75 /30.01.2014; 662/11.11.2014, published in the Official Gazette no. 47 /20.01.2015.

34 Decision no. 71/05.03.2002, published in the Official Gazette no. 309 / 10.05.2002.

35 Decisions no. 279/22.03.2006, published in the Official Gazette no. 323 / 11.04.2006; 657/09.10.2006, published in the Official Gazette no. 890 /1.11.2006; 321/29.03.2007, published in the Official Gazette no. 330 /16.05.2007; 2/04.01.2011, published in the Official Gazette no. 136 /23.02.2011; 334/26.06.2013, published in the Official Gazette no. 405 /05.07.2013; 449/06.11.2013, published in the Official Gazette no. 784 /14.12.2013; 471/14.11.2013, published in the Official Gazette no. 754 /04.12.2013; 417/03.07.2014, published in the Official Gazette no. 535 /18.07.2014.

36 This is also reflected in the editing of decisions: certain decisions may contain numbered paragraphs, while *a priori* and *a posteriori* review decisions have a different style of editing.

37 Decision no. 503/20.04.2010, published in the Official Gazette no. 353/28.05.2010

38 Decision no. 148 /16.04.2003, published in the Official Gazette no. 317 / 12.05.2003

39 Viorel Ciobanu, Mihai Constantinescu, Ion Deleanu, Ion Filipescu, Vasile Gionea and Antonie Iorgovan have never published dissenting opinions.

40 It must be stressed that on the basis of the dataset used, the voting pattern of individual judges cannot be determined, except for those situations in which the judges formulated dissenting or concurring opinions.

41 From this perspective, 2006 and 2010 were special years as they produced comparable figures – 50 percent and 46.4 percent – but it has to be noted that 2006 represented the last year of significant left-wing dominance in the Court facing a right-wing parliamentary majority and government. Furthermore, 2009 ended with presidential elections and the appointment of a new executive after a vote of no confidence in the autumn.

References

Benke, Károly. n.d. "Provocări ale controlului de constituționalitate: trecut și viitor" ["Challenges for the Control of Constitutionality: Past and Future"]. Accessed 28 February 2018. http://www.ccr.ro/ccrold/events/conferinta/benke_vechi.pdf.

Blokker, Paul. 2012. "Romanian Constitutionalism: Form Without Content?" Accessed 22 May 2018. https://papers.ssrn.com/sol3/papers.cfm?abstract_id=2146568.

Cogitus. 2011. "Prea multe ordonanțe?" ["Too Many Ordinances?"] *Cogitus*, January 20. http://www.cogitus.ro/administratie/prea-multe-ordonante-numarul-initiativelor-legislative-ale-guvernelor-din-ultimii-10-ani.

Constitutional Court of Romania. 2017a. *Statistics on the Activity of the Constitutional Court from Its Establishment Until 31.07.2017.* Accessed 28 February 2018. https://www.ccr.ro/uploads/Statistica/2017/ActivitateRo_iul.pdf.

Constitutional Court of Romania. 2017b. *Statistics on the Acts of the Constitutional Court from Its Establishment Until 31.07.2017.* Accessed 28 February 2018. https://www.ccr.ro/uploads/Statistica/2017/SinRo_iul.pdf

Constitutional Court of Romania. 2017c. *Statistics on the Dynamics of Complaints.* Accessed 28 February 2018. https://www.ccr.ro/uploads/Statistica/2017/graficsesizariro_iul.pdf

Constitutional Court of Romania. 2009–2017. *Statistics on the Implementing of the Constitutional Courts' Decisions.* Accessed 25 May 2018. https://www.ccr.ro/Implementarea-deciziilor-Curii-Constituionale

Gilia, Claudia. 2012. "Curtea Constitutionala sub imperativul reformei" ["The Constitutional Court Under the Imperative of Reform"]. *Sfera Politicii* 20 (6): 21–34.

Iancu, Bogdan. 2009. "Constitutionalism in Perpetual Transition: The Case of Romania." In *The Law/Politics Distinction in Contemporary Public Law Adjudication*, edited by Bogdan Iancu, 187–211. The Hague: Eleven International Publishing.

Kuti, Csongor. 2013. "In Courts We Trust?" *Acta Iuridica Hungarica* 54 (4): 384–392.

Lungu, Ioana. 2002. "Romanian Constitutional Nationalism". *Polish Sociological Review* 140: 397–412.

Mungiu-Pippidi, Alina. 1997. "Interview with President of the Romanian Constitutional Court, Ion Muraru". *East European Constitutional Review* 6 (1): 78–83.

Perju, Vlad. 2010. "A sosit timpul pentru reformarea Curtii Constitutionale?" ["Has the Time Come for Reforming of the Constitutional Court?"] *Contributors.ro*, November 29. http://www.contributors.ro/idei-si-solutii/a-sosit-timpul-pentru-reformarea-curtii-constitutionale-partea-i.

Presidency. 2008. *Raportul Comisiei Prezidențiale de Analiză a Regimului Politic și Constituțional din România.* [*Report of the Presidential Commission for the Analysis of the Political and Constitutional Regime – To Consolidate the Rule of Law*]. Accessed 28 February 2018. http://old.presidency.ro/static/rapoarte/Raport_CPARPCR.pdf.

Sadurski, Wojciech. "Constitutional Review in Europe and in the United States: Influences, Paradoxes and Convergences." Legal Studies Research Paper no. 11/15, Sydney Law School, 2011. http://ssrn.com/abstract=1754209.

Tănăsescu, Simina. 2013. "Constitutional Review of Judicial Activism?" *International Journal of Law and Jurisprudence Law Review* 3 (2): 19–36.

Weber, Renate. 2002. "The Romanian Constitutional Court: In Search of Its Own Identity." In *Constitutional Justice, East and West. Democratic Legitimacy and Constitutional Courts in Post-Communist Europe in a Comparative Perspective*, edited by Wojciech Sadurski, 283–308. The Hague: Kluwer Law International.

8 The Slovak Constitutional Court

The third legislator?

Erik Láštic and Max Steuer

8.1 Introduction

The Slovak Constitutional Court (SCC) is commonly known as one of the Central European "guardians of constitutionalism", which successfully helped establish democratic standards through the division of powers and guarantees of fundamental rights. Yet there has been a lack of research on its decision-making since the accession of Slovakia to the European Union, and the differences between the three constitutional courts, divided in line with its three presidents so far. This paper uses the analytical framework of the "negative" and "positive" legislator to address whether and if so why the SCC acted as a legislator during the three court terms. For this purpose, it uses a new dataset (generated within the JUDICON project) that allows us to identify how the SCC positioned itself *vis-à-vis* changing legislative majorities between 1993 and 2015, and whether there has been a period in which it used its legislating capacities beyond the average standard. The analysis offers new findings about each of the three constitutional courts. During the period of the third, with a few exceptions, the SCC's rulings gradually shifted towards ones favourable to the parliamentary majority (2006–2010) and the head of state. Moreover, the recent emptying out of the bench due to the conflict over the president's authority regarding the appointment procedures (Steuer 2018) further exacerbated the resignation of the majority over the legislating function of the SCC and gave rise to some arguably unconstitutional decision-making practices (Drgonec 2017).

8.2 Origins and institutional design

There was not much discussion about whether to establish a constitutional court (CC) in Slovakia after the break-up of the Czech and Slovak Federal Republic in 1992.[1] The Federal Republic had its own, albeit short-lived constitutional court established in 1991 after the more than forty-year period of communist rule. Even though after 1968 a constitutional court for the federal Czechoslovak Socialist Republic was imagined in a constitutional act (Vodička and Cabada 2011), it was never set up, so the post-communist constitutional court was built up directly on the legacy of the first (interwar) Czechoslovak Constitutional

Court (Langášek 2011). The Slovak Constitutional Court, alongside the Czech Constitutional Court, is built on this legacy, and its structure and powers mirror the typical centralized model of judicial review.[2]

The Court has a broad range of powers, which encompass, among others, *ex ante* review of international agreements, review of constitutionality of referenda, review of electoral outcomes and decision on the impeachment of the head of state. Yet by far the majority of cases, as could be expected, concern individual complaints about alleged human rights violations. Since the constitutional amendment of 2001, the number of judges on the SCC increased from ten to thirteen. A majority decision in the plenum may pass only with a minimum of seven votes in favour (in the pre-2001 period, six votes were required). This is not influenced by the number of judges present or possible vacant positions at the Court. The judges are selected through a collaborative model, whereby the parliament elects twice as many candidates as there are vacant seats on the bench. Then, the president collaborates with the parliament by appointing judges to the vacant position(s) from this pool of candidates (Art. 134 sec. 2 of the Constitution). However, for several years the SCC has not been operating with the full number of judges due to the dispute between parliament and the head of state over the appointment of constitutional judges.

The SCC has a broad range of competences, including in electoral matters. As of summer 2017, there were sixteen types of proceeding that could unfold before the Court, although many have either never seen a concrete case or have been used only rarely.[3] The SCC decides in the plenum in proceedings which are explicitly listed in Art. 131 of the Constitution; in the remaining proceedings (including decisions about individual complaints), it decides in the senates. In both types of proceedings, which are subject to analysis here (constitutional review of legislative acts and constitutional interpretation *in abstracto*), the SCC decides in the plenum. There are four senates composed of three judges each, the composition of which changes on a regular basis in line with a work schedule adopted annually by the plenum of the Court.[4]

Since the early 2000s, the Slovak Constitutional Court has not been a popular subject of international scholarly analysis. All major analyzes (Procházka 2002; Schwartz 2002, 194–225; Malová 2010) have finished roughly with the first term of the group of constitutional judges. They covered the seven years following the creation of the Court in 1993 as one of the two successors of the briefly functioning Czechoslovak Federal Constitutional Court but have not captured the developments since the broadest amendment of the Slovak Constitution in 2001, which also impacted the formal powers of the Court[5] and the tenures of the new judges.[6] Yet it would be inappropriate to conclude that the SCC became a "boring institution" after 2001 – quite the contrary. The explanation that might rest in the more internationally followed developments of its Czech counterpart[7] and the generally low availability of English-language sources and translation of judgements makes it a useful and timely subject of investigation twenty-six years after its establishment as an independent institution.

The position of the SCC towards legislative power forms an even more visible gap in contemporary constitutional scholarship. While in Slovakia there are two legislators according to the Constitution (the people through referenda and the legislature as the representative decision-making body), the question arises as to whether and to what extent the SCC can be considered as the "third legislator", thereby limiting the powers of parliament and/or the people.[8] We examine this question with the help of the dataset generated in the JUDICON project with respect to judicial review of legislation, and constitutional interpretation *in abstracto* of the SCC since its establishment up to the end of 2015.[9] Thus, this case study helps us to understand not only some focal points and developments in the case law of the SCC after 2001 in an accessible format, but also the strength of its decision-making that can later be compared with its regional and European counterparts.

8.3 Three Courts

Slovak constitutional scholarship offers a useful distinction between the "three Courts" on the basis of the composition of the SCC. The first ran between 1993 and 2000 (under the presidency of Milan Čič), the second from 2000 to 2007 (under the presidency of Ján Mazák until 2006) and the third was established in 2007 and runs up to 2019 (under the presidency of Ivetta Macejková) (Drgonec 2010). If there is a relevant difference in various trends of judging among these periods, the sensible explanation rests in the change of the Court's composition and thus possibly the overall atmosphere on the Court. Yet one needs to be careful with such inferences, because in these periods the executives were changing rapidly as well. The first court, as documented in the aforementioned scholarship, was known as a barrier against the authoritarian tendencies of the government of prime minister Vladimír Mečiar. The second court started its functioning under the pro-reform government of prime minister Dzurinda with the core aim to ensure the accession of Slovakia to the EU (Malová et al. 2005), but it ended under the first government of Robert Fico, encompassing nationalist and populist parties of Mečiar's People's Party – Movement for Democratic Slovakia (*Ľudová strana – Hnutie za demokratické Slovensko*, ĽS-HZDS) and the Slovak National Party (*Slovenská národná strana*, SNS), led by anti-Hungarian politician Ján Slota. The third and current court continued from there and has largely operated under the centre-left governments of prime minister Fico, with the short break of the centre-right government of prime minister Iveta Radičová (2010–2012).

From a theoretical perspective, if constitutional courts are positive legislators, they are by definition strong. This argument is already implied in the writings of Hans Kelsen, the doyen of research on constitutional justice, when he contrasts the optimal role of constitutional courts as "negative legislators" with the risks entailed in courts protecting fundamental rights, which was his understanding of the "positive legislator" (Sweet 2007, 83–84). Since Kelsen, not only have human rights been codified in core international and regional conventions, but the concept of the positive legislator has broadened to encompass a variety of other trends, such as constitutional courts "interfering with the constituent power", "with existing legislation" or "declaring legislative omissions" (Brewer-Carías 2013, 893–923). It is in light of this broader understanding of the positive legislator that the most recent English analysis of the SCC answers the question of whether the SCC is a positive legislator in the affirmative (Svák and Berdisová 2013), albeit through highlighting a set of cases the selection criteria of which are not clearly determined. Our attempt at a more nuanced analysis thus provides the potential for a more refined answer about whether the SCC has been a positive legislator, though more in the Kelsenian conceptualization of the SCC as the protector of rights against the interference of the legislative power than the broader, more complex one of Brewer-Carías.

8.4 Methodological specifics of the Slovak case

This project assesses the strength of the CCs' rulings *vis-à-vis* the legislator. As a result, the main type of procedure under scrutiny is the constitutional review of legislation, according to Article 125 sec. 1 a) of The Constitution of the Slovak Republic. In addition, the SCC is also tasked with constitutional interpretation (Art. 128), which gives it a chance to influence the "room of manoeuvre" of the unicameral legislature (National Council). While only these two types of procedure were considered, it cannot be excluded that in specific cases handled within other procedures, such as the decision on the constitutionality of the subject of the referendum (Art. 125b), or an international treaty (Art. 125a, both as *ex ante* review), or even individual complaint procedure (Art. 127),[10] the verdict of the SCC has relevance for the scope of exercise of the legislative power.

Seven other specifics should be mentioned. Firstly, the SCC does not have the power to derogate legislation directly, since the Constitution grants a six-month period to the parliament to harmonize the provisions declared unconstitutional, which lost effect as a result of the SCC's decision, with the Constitution and with constitutional laws. Should it fail in this task, only then do the provisions lose their validity.[11] This mechanism could give rise to a more dynamic interaction between the two bodies, whereby the parliament can react in various ways, including changing the provisions in another way that is questionable from the point of view of their constitutionality, and may be challenged again by actors entitled to submit petitions to the Court on judicial review of legislation, at a later point.

The second specific feature that the Constitution provides is the SCC's competence to decide on suspending "the effect of challenged legal regulations, their parts or some of their provisions, if fundamental rights and freedoms may be threatened by their further application, if there is a risk of serious economic damage or other serious irreparable consequence".[12] The reluctance of the Court to use this provision upon request by the opposition parties might be one reason for the comparatively lower number of cases (Láštic 2012, 36; Čorba 2005). Furthermore, the eligible petitioners might have gradually given up on the capacity of the SCC to take swift action if – in their perception at least – it should be necessary for the protection of the constitutional order.[13]

Thirdly, on average, there have been one and a half rulings in each decision. A closer look shows that in fact many decisions have only one ruling, while a few decisions consist of a disproportionately high number of rulings. These are PL. ÚS 10/05 and PL. ÚS 102/2011, in which the Court dealt with a number of provisions concerning the method of selection of judges to Slovak ordinary courts; PL. ÚS 105/2011, which in a similar vein reacted to a set of amendments to the Act on prosecutors (see Figure 8.1 with the outlier year of 2014 when these decisions were delivered). Both latter sets of amendments passed during the Radičová government and were challenged by deputies of Direction–Social Democracy (*Smer–sociálna demokracia*, Smer–SD) (PL. ÚS 102/2011) and the acting attorney general (PL. ÚS 105/2011) in the subsequent period of the single-party government of Robert Fico (2006–2016). The former (challenged in the case PL. ÚS 10/05) was enacted by the second Dzurinda government (2002–2006) and decided by the SCC before the general elections in 2010 which stripped Robert Fico of the PM seat. While all decisions seem to concern the relationship within the judiciary or the "fourth, controlling power" of the prosecution, in fact they pose limits to the legislature as to what extent it can determine, for instance, the judicial competence in enforcement matters, removal of court presidents and the composition of judicial selection committees. Yet due to the structure of these decisions (comprising a high number of rulings), their influence on the final statistics may be disproportionately high and must be taken into account in the analysis of the strength of the third court.

Fourthly, the database of the decisions provided by the SCC, while improved in recent years, does not offer full guarantees against possible existing decisions

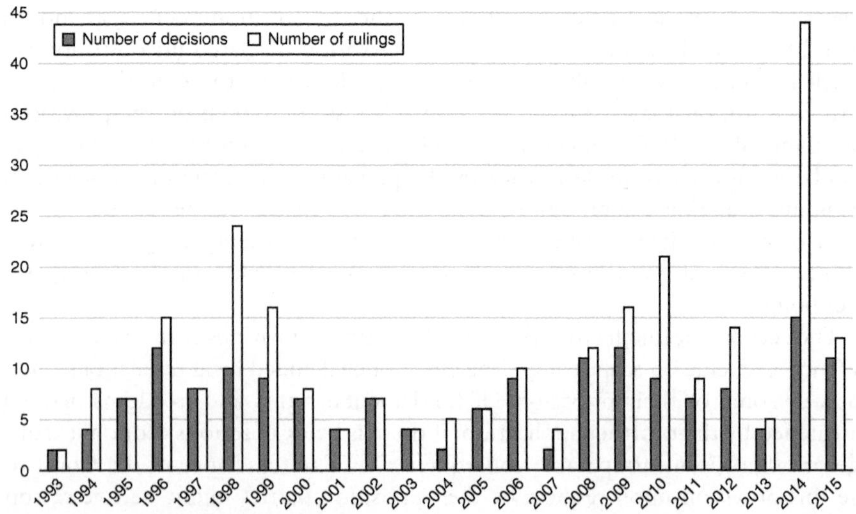

Figure 8.1 Number of decisions and rulings (SCC)

which might, however, not be displayed on the list. Neither is there an exhaustive printed collection of SCC decisions. To minimize such risks, the list was triangulated with some data from the two major commentaries on the Slovak Constitution (Drgonec 2015; Čič 2012), but a full guarantee cannot be established in this case, either.

Fifthly, the Act on the organization of the Slovak Constitutional Court (No. 38/1993 Coll.) introduces the preliminary proceeding for petitions, which allows them to be refused already at this stage. This increases the effectiveness of the proceeding, since manifestly ill-founded petitions can be refused. However, refusals at this stage may have a symbolic and political importance, and especially in the last years included in this analysis there have been concerns raised that some petitions have in fact been refused with a reasoning that materially equates a decision on the merits. This is why those cases which have been refused at this stage, but had one or more dissenting opinions issued arguing that the refusal was based on material review, have been included in the dataset. The most notable cases of this kind are the ones submitted by the Slovak Ombudswoman (PL. ÚS 40/2014, PL. ÚS 36/2015, PL. ÚS 44/2015) or a recent case concerning the Act on advocacy, more specifically, the status of lawyer trainees (PL. ÚS 53/2015). Since in several of these cases the dissenters did not propose a specific decision on the merits but objected towards refusing the petition in the preliminary proceeding, a separate code for these dissents has been used in the dataset but they were not included in the statistical evaluation.

Sixthly, publicly available statistics provide a picture about the SCC's workload and decision-making in selected proceedings, particularly in recent years (Table 8.1). They demonstrate that overall the workload of the court has been high, which has mainly been caused by individual complaints, and even within them, one particular legal person who submitted tens of thousands of complaints (Orosz 2014; Ústavný súd Slovenskej republiky 2010). Decision-making according to Article 125 and 128 (the two types of proceedings which have been examined) has only comprised a small portion of the Court's overall workload, although these cases have been overwhelmingly decided by the plenum. Therefore, each of these can be expected to have increased the workload of each individual judge more substantially than standard complaint cases.[14] The "rate of unconstitutionality" between 2009 and 2016 is quite high, but it should be read with the knowledge that (1) it includes cases pursuant to Art. 125 sec. 1 b) and c) which have not been the subject of this analysis (ministerial decrees and government ordinances), and (2) it does not include cases that have been procedurally disregarded for technical reasons or otherwise not considered. Nevertheless, it does include decisions of preliminary proceedings, which have normally not been included in the analysis.

Finally, the notion of "landmark cases" would need to be approached carefully if it were to be applied. While the higher number of dissents might signal an important debate reflecting the broader impact of one or more rulings of the decision (Kelemen 2013), the Act on the organization of the SCC (38/1993 Coll.) only allowed the publication of separate opinions after 2000 (§ 32 sec. 1). Before this

Table 8.1 Workload of the SCC

Year	*No. of petitions*	*No. of decisions*	*No. of decisions declaring unconstitutionality in proceedings pursuant to Art. 125 of the Constitution (number of all decisions in this type of proceeding)*
1993–2009	57826	57064	n/a (n/a) [206 petitions in 2002–2010]
2009	2365	2324 (41 plenary)	9 (17)
2010	7801	2728 (41 plenary)	8 (18)
2011	4277	2344 (116 plenary)	7 (16)
2012	16326	2455 (22 plenary)	7 (17)
2013	23915	2845 (19 plenary)	4 (10)
2014	17889	2848 (57 plenary)	12 (29)
2015	16847	2247 (90 plenary)	6 (21)
2016	15218	2543 (14 plenary)	6 (14)
Total	162464	75074	59 (142) SUCCESS RATE: 41.5

Source: Ústavný súd Slovenskej republiky and own calculations.

amendment, separate opinions could only have been "briefly included" in the "minutes from the voting", which is not a public document. Thus, the number of dissents can only be used for the post-2001 period, whereby a decision will need at least four dissents to be considered a landmark case in this analysis.[15]

8.5 Assessing the trends

In order to discern the influence of macro- and individual-level factors on the strength of the SCC's rulings, we break down the following analysis into a chronological overview followed by a closer look at individual judges' decision-making and then present a more in-depth explanation of possible influences of landmark cases as defined above. The results reveal (1) the decreasing strength of the SCC's majority rulings *vis-à-vis* the legislature, (2) the decreasing strength on the individual level, with the strength of the dissenting rulings mostly clearly outweighing the strength of the majority rulings and (3) the prevalent deep divide over a "judicial coalition and opposition" on the bench in a number of key cases, with some latter views framed even in terms of a possible "cold war on the Court".

8.5.1 Trends in majority rulings

There is a clear decrease in strength of the rulings after the defeat of the Mečiar government in the elections of 1998, which was further exacerbated after the selection of a new cohort of judges in 2000 (Figure 8.2). An intervening factor here might be the emphasis that was put on the EU accession, whereby it was more important to harmonize domestic legislation with EU treaties than to

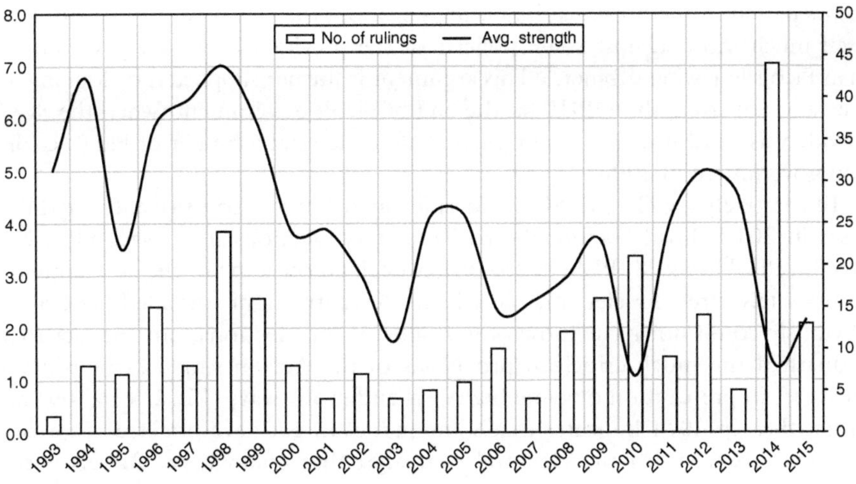

Figure 8.2 Number and average strength of rulings (SCC)

engage in domestic reforms of questionable constitutional nature. Moreover, the amending of the Constitution in 2001 incorporated many changes which were later reflected in ordinary legislation, such as the creation of the Judicial Council as an institution of judicial self-administration. The year before EU accession (2003) is among the lower points in the figure displaying the developments of overall strength of the rulings, and while there is a slight increase afterwards, it by far does not reach the pre-2000 levels. Perhaps the most important rulings in this period revolved around property rights, such as some provisions of the Act on the usage of land in established garden settlements and the settlement of their ownership (PL. ÚS 17/00).

Also, it is worth noticing that one of the first recognizable cases of decision by non-decision[16] can be identified during the second SCC (2000–2007): PL. ÚS 3/02 related to one of the evergreens of the 1993–2000 period, that is, the competences of the head of state. Examples of refusals on such grounds were to appear several more times in the era of the third SCC (post-2007). Yet the mere fact that there were comparatively fewer declarations of unconstitutionality during the second SCC compared to the first cannot allow us to infer that the authority of the Court was undermined. Rulings, even though the new tool of dissents was quite often used by some judges, revolved around factual matters, questions of legal theory and practice, as opposed to some rulings of the post-2007 period, to which we turn now.

The judges in 2007 were appointed by the President of the Republic, who two years later declared himself to be "a sort of member of Smer" (Tódová 2009), i.e. of the strongest party of the ruling coalition led by prime minister Fico. According to the results in the two types of proceedings, the strength of the SCC's rulings gradually increased in this period. It is important to note that since most cases decided in 2007 and the subsequent two years originated from legislative amendments passed in the previous right-wing coalition, the Court thereby positioned itself much more against some policies of the previous Dzurinda government than Fico's left-wing cabinet.[17] This argument is further supported by looking at the values of strength in 2010, at the end of Fico's government, when the SCC already was to deal with cases originated after the establishment of Fico's coalition government in 2006.

Illustratively, while the SCC did rule on the unconstitutionality in three cases in 2010 shortly before the parliamentary elections took place (PL. ÚS 13/09, PL. ÚS 3/08, PL. ÚS 23/06), it decided on some of the core amendments safely after the elections, in which the centre-right prevailed. The SCC obviously could not have known the results of the elections, but the fact that it quashed the much-criticized provisions of the Act on single extraordinary measures in preparation of some highways and motorways (PL. ÚS 19/09) no earlier than in 2011 indicates that some judges might have preferred to avoid any interference with the electoral campaign that could harm Robert Fico. Some suspicions arose that the judge rapporteur and Vice President of the SCC, Milan Ľalík, delayed the procedure of final voting on a decision (Jesenský 2011). In 2011, there was a general increase in the strength of other decisions on unconstitutionality of acts adopted during the Fico government as well, which signals that some judges might have felt less constrained by the new executive to declare unconstitutionality on some of the amendments adopted during Fico's first cabinet.

The year 2012 saw the peak of the post-2000 strength of the SCC's rulings. This was mainly due to the constitutional interpretation of the competence of the head of state to appoint the candidate for the attorney general (PL. ÚS 4/2012), as well as the case of the (un)constitutionality of some provisions of the Act on state aid (PL. ÚS 115/2011). The subsequent years were followed by a slight drop in the strength of the rulings; however, the overall measure becomes arguably less valid for these years as opposed to the earlier ones, due to a rapid increase in the "deciding via non-deciding" practice of the court. A prime example of this was the refusal of the review of constitutionality of the amendments to the Citizenship Act (PL. ÚS 11/2012), where neither of the draft judgements and justifications gained the support of the majority on the bench.

8.5.2 Ruling type frequency

The SCC's case does not allow us to demonstrate the full variation of the scale offered by the coding manual. In other words, the predominant types of rulings in the period and proceedings under study were rejections, declarations of substantive unconstitutionality and restricting constitutional interpretations *in abstracto*. This may indicate the reluctance of the court to set constitutional requirements in these types of proceedings and the reluctance to decide on unconstitutionality by legislative omissions, in contrast to some of its counterparts in the region.

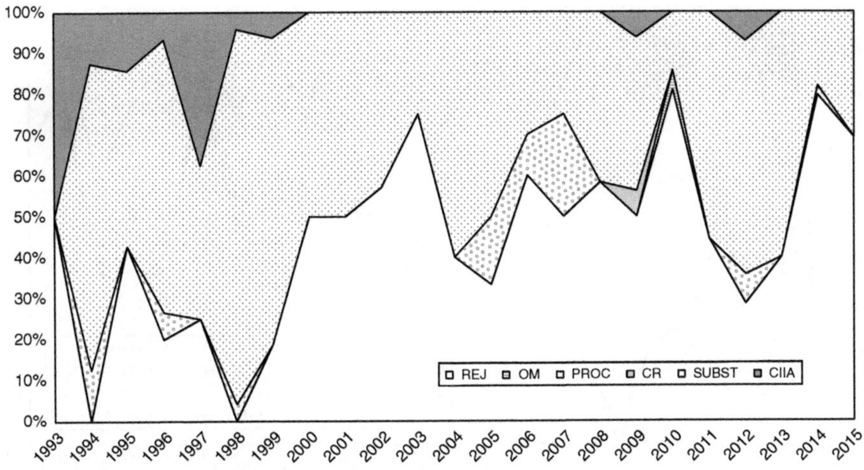

Figure 8.3 Frequency of ruling types I (SCC)

Table A.1 in the Appendix and Figure 8.3 demonstrate this trend, as well as confirm the 1990s as the years witnessing the struggle over constitutional interpretations, which the first Court usually decided in favour of a more restrictive competence of the legislature as opposed to other actors. The second Court, besides not having to deal with so many cases, rarely delivered rulings other than rejections or declarations of substantive unconstitutionality in these proceedings. In the third Court, the rejection rate has increased, although the specifically high rejection rates in 2010 and 2014 are, once again, caused by the few decisions with a high number of rulings.

As for the distribution of the ruling types with respect to their strength, when the SCC declared a procedural unconstitutionality, it was overwhelmingly of average strength. More interestingly, some kind of trends in the proportion of average and strong substantive unconstitutionality can be noticed (Figure 8.4). While there is at least one ruling declaring a substantive unconstitutionality with average strength in each year of the analysis, rulings declaring strong substantive unconstitutionality are more centred in certain periods, notably up to 2001 and then in the period 2009–2013. Therefore, in these periods there were several strong rulings declaring substantive unconstitutionality, potentially signalling a greater willingness of these courts to deliver such rulings, which could have also been influenced by the political context.[18]

8.5.3 The performance of the presidents

As Figure 8.5 displays, there is no fundamental difference between the trends of decision-making of the three presidents of the SCC, on the one hand, and the respective majorities, on the other hand. True, each president on average

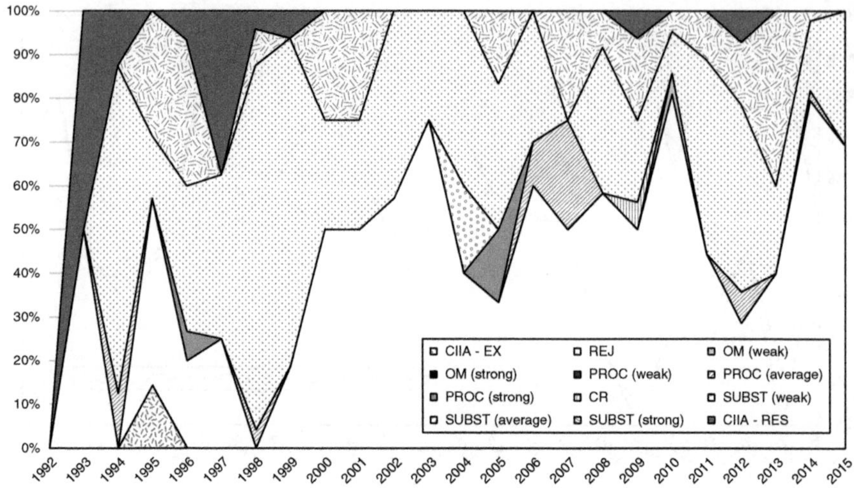

Figure 8.4 Frequency of ruling types II (SCC)

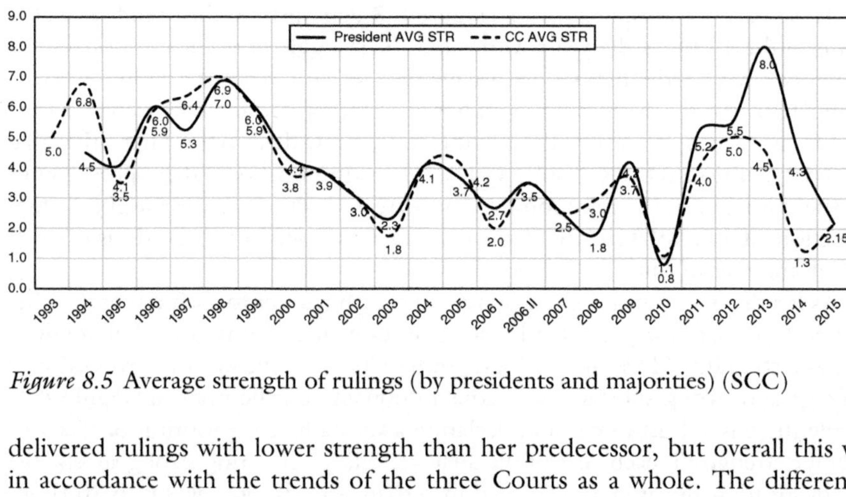

Figure 8.5 Average strength of rulings (by presidents and majorities) (SCC)

delivered rulings with lower strength than her predecessor, but overall this was in accordance with the trends of the three Courts as a whole. The differences displayed in the 1990s are caused by the fact that constitutional interpretations *in abstracto* were delivered in senates rather than by the plenum (which changed with the constitutional amendment of 2001) and, logically, the President of the SCC was not a member of each of these senates.

During his presidency, Ján Mazák delivered one notable dissent (together with judge Babjak) where he, in contrast to the majority, claimed that the National Council is entitled to establish special bodies, such as a parliamentary commission.[19] It is only under President Macejková that more significant differences can be observed, in that her opinions in several cases advocated for stronger rulings than the rulings of the majority. Cases in which this tendency manifested are the ones related to the legal regulation of the ordinary courts and the prosecution service, including appointments of judges and presidents of ordinary courts, as well as prosecutors, the institute of so-called court trainees (PL. ÚS 102/2011, PL. ÚS 105/2011). Essentially, President Macejková defended in these cases a stricter understanding of the separation of powers that gives fewer competences to the legislature. However, it should be noted that in these cases, the legislative provisions widened the powers of the executive, for instance in determining part of the composition of selection committees for judges and court presidents, or in allowing the minister of justice to submit petitions on disciplinary proceedings against prosecutors or to appoint some of the members of the selection committees for prosecutors (both, according to Macejková and Milan Ľalík in a co-authored dissent, were unconstitutional extensions of the powers of the minister of justice to interfere with the prosecution service). At the same time, the significant discrepancy, especially in 2013, is caused by these cases being broken down into a high number of rulings on concrete provisions, although the principles behind the dispute were close, if not in many rulings identical with each other. In the following section, we turn to the evaluation of rulings on an individual level and argue that the importance of dissenting opinions has grown in the third Court.

8.5.4 Individual judges and dissenting opinions

In this section, we evaluate the decision-making of the judges of the SCC in the analyzed types of proceedings, which adds to the picture of the overall performance of the Court *vis-à-vis* the legislature and also allows us to determine the main similarities and differences in the decision-making traits of the judges.

The aggregate evaluation of the strength of the majority rulings and dissents demonstrates that there is no outstanding judge among those serving at the court since Slovakia's independence up to 2015. Yet some trends might be cautiously recognized, bearing in mind that the number of rulings for the second Court is significantly lower than those for the first and third. In 2014, the number of dissenting opinions in the two types of proceedings was four times higher than in any other year of the period under scrutiny (see Figure 8.6). While many dissents were actually made to different rulings of the same decision (PL. ÚS 102/2011, PL. ÚS 105/2011), some significant ones related to, for example, the appointment of the Attorney General (PL. ÚS 4/2012) or the right of the Ombuds(wo) man to submit petitions to the SCC (e.g. PL. ÚS 40/2014, PL. ÚS 36/2015) can be identified precisely in this year.

Figure 8.7 shows the differences in the number of rulings by judges. However, it should not be interpreted as if the judges that delivered the most rulings have been the most active ones, since some judges have been at the bench for a substantially longer time than other judges. Ľubomír Dobrík seems to be an "extreme" judge in this regard since he delivered 190 rulings while serving at the court from 1997 to 2016. Furthermore, Figure 8.7 shows that the "main dissenters" were SCC President and Vice President Macejková and Ľalík, and to a lesser extent judge Dobrík (in few cases but with a high number of rulings) and judges Mészáros, Gajdošíková and Orosz.[20]

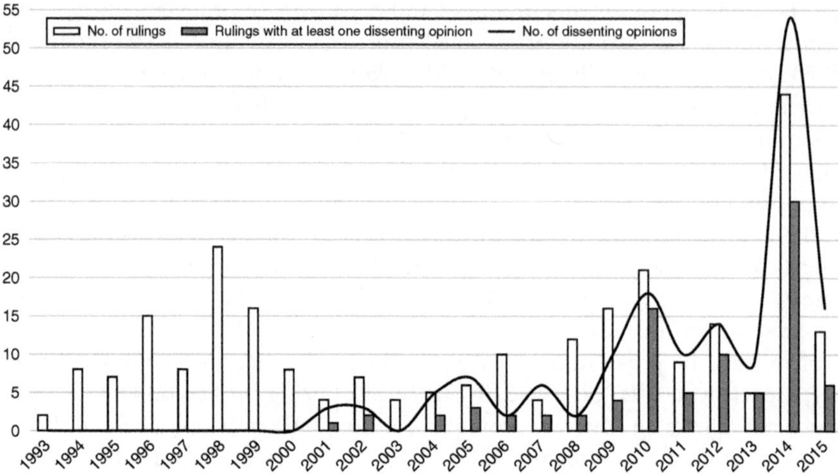

Figure 8.6 Number of rulings and dissenting opinions (SCC)

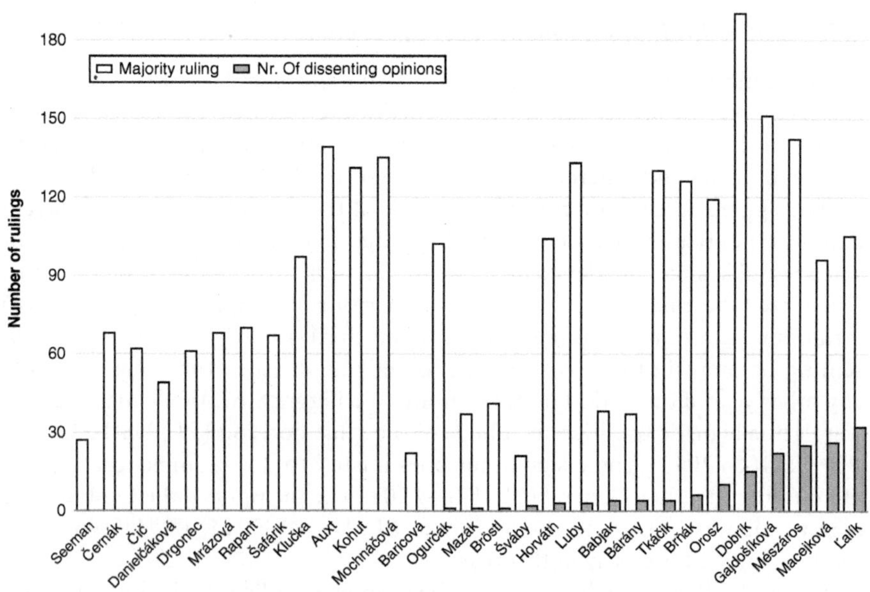

Figure 8.7 Number of rulings and dissenting opinions (by judges) (SCC)

The results of the network analysis based on the methodology of the project (Figure 8.8) show two enduring dissenting coalitions: Macejková–Ľalík–Dobrík (Coalition 1) and Gajdošíková–Mészáros–Orosz (Coalition 2). While all these judges were chosen by President Gašparovič, a strong supporter of Robert Fico and his party, from a pool of candidates submitted by a parliament in which Fico

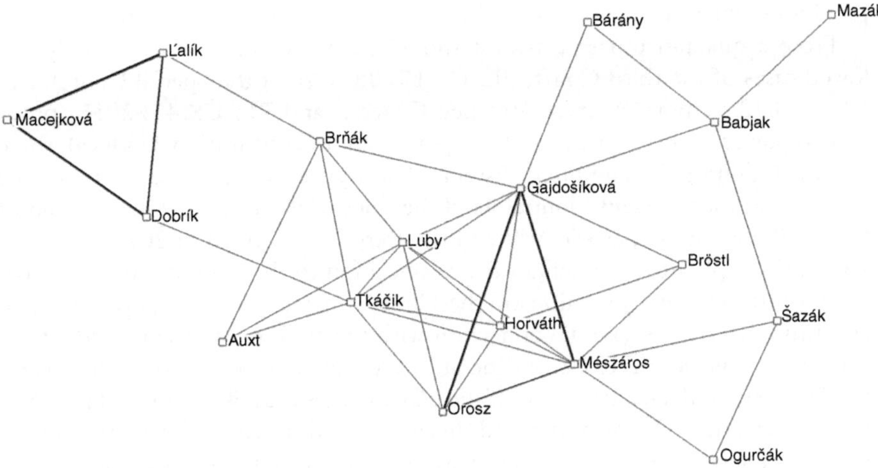

Figure 8.8 Dissenting coalitions (SCC)

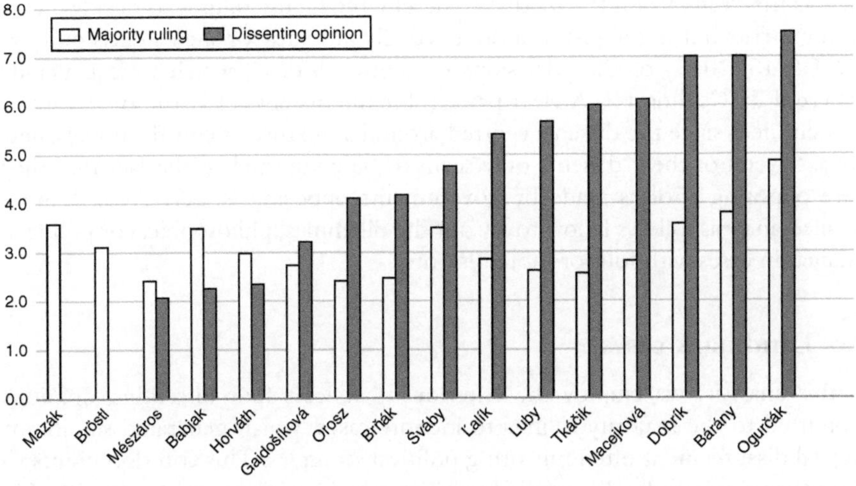

Figure 8.9 Average strength of rulings (by judges) (SCC)

and his coalition had a majority,[21] they gradually positioned themselves in opposition to each other in most cases, which indicates more than coincidental difference in their understanding of the role of the SCC and their reasoning. Possibly, political factors could have played a role in that Coalition 1 more frequently advocated invalidating pieces of legislation adopted by parties opposing Fico and his government.

Whether it was political or philosophical factors, or their combination, that played a role in the emergence of these two coalitions, there are noticeable differences in the strength of their dissenting opinions, as Figure 8.9 demonstrates.[22] While Coalition 1 on average more often advocated declaring unconstitutionality,

Coalition 2 was more permissive in this sense, suggesting the upholding of several provisions which the majority of judges decided were unconstitutional.

From a qualitative perspective, it should be noted that in three closely followed cases of the third Court, PL. ÚS 17/08 (case of the Special Court), PL. ÚS 4/2012 (appointment of Attorney General) and PL. ÚS 45/2015 (presidential powers in the context of the appointment of constitutional judges), three judges (Coalition 2) submitted dissents that argued along the same lines. The positions in these dissents contradicted the ones of the Fico government and of former President Gašparovič, while in the third case decided in 2015 they used several sharp phrases to highlight their opposition to the unconventional refusal of constitutional interpretation by the Court's majority in the appointment of constitutional judges case in connection with the abolition of the precedent the very same majority developed in the attorney general case. On the other hand, the President and Vice President of the SCC, judges Macejková and Ľalík (members of Coalition 1), also submitted dissents to various rulings, sometimes even jointly.[23] These are very imperfect measures, but they indicate that towards the end of 2015 the SCC was more polarized than ever before. This polarization seems to reflect some developments in the decision-making practices of the SCC, such as the "refusals on the merits", whereby the Court refuses to decide a case on the merits but in the justification it actually provides for such a decision (e.g. PL. ÚS 45/2015) or the "decisions by non-decisions", which were generally criticized by Coalition 2. A clear pattern for the dissents of Coalition 1 cannot be identified, since the dissents centred around a mixture of constitutional questions. Several of these dissents only seem to be connected to the fact that they were opposing choices made by governments opposing Robert Fico. A more detailed analysis follows below to lay out the dilemmas, philosophical or political, entailed in cases with four or more dissents.

8.6 Landmark cases

In this analysis, we employ the criterion of at least four dissenting opinions submitted to the majority rulings to identify cases, which generated significant judicial disagreement often mirroring political struggles. This criterion points to also otherwise broadly discussed cases, in particular of the third Court (PL. ÚS 17/08, PL. ÚS 4/2012, PL. ÚS 45/2015). At the same time, it is less suitable for the first Court because, as mentioned above, before 2001 there were no dissenting opinions. However, this does not mean that there was a lack of landmark cases back then. In fact, an evaluation of the dispersion of types of proceedings and the rulings shows that the proportion of unconstitutionality was higher during the first court. This means that from all the cases submitted to the SCC in the two types of proceedings, the SCC more often ruled on unconstitutionality in the period prior to 2000 than afterwards. Even in the pre-2000 period, however, it seems it acted more as a negative than positive legislator, as it did not issue broad remedies that constrained the legislature in future cases. One exception to such an interpretation is the position of the head of state, whereby the SCC extended her constitutional powers, for instance, declaring that it was not necessary for her to recall a member of the executive upon the request of the prime minister (I. ÚS 39/93), or reaffirming the breadth of the presidential veto powers (I. ÚS 5/94).

In most cases, however, it was the role of the negative legislator which seems to have prevailed, and without any substantial component of judicial activism as understood by, for instance, Kmiec (2004). Rather than being an activist or positive legislator, the Court simply confirmed some basic principles of a democratic constitutional order, which were more or less clearly included in the constitution as well. Among these was the ruling that declared unconstitutional an act on the annulment of some earlier decisions of the executive on privatization of companies and other assets through direct sale (PL. ÚS 16/95). The court referred broadly to the separation of powers, legal certainty and the prohibition of retroactivity when it stated that "the legislature is also bound by the constitution and its principles, and the constitution does not allow for any changes in those principles because of their constitutive importance for the democratic nature of the Slovak Republic". It is thus unconstitutional if an executive decision is annulled via a legislative act (Constitution Watch 1995, 29). Importantly, this is one of the three decisions in the whole database the validity of which is *ex tunc*.[24]

The SCC was also a negative legislator in another case, where it prohibited the National Council to approve a piece of legislation which would come into effect earlier than was deemed valid and published in the Collection of Laws. The SCC highlighted that

> no organ, not even the constitutional court, can resolve the discovered contradiction with interpretation. In a state [under the rule of] law, state organs strictly follow and respect the constitution, statutes, generally valid legal acts and decisions of the constitutional court. [...] Non-fulfilment of legal principles in the practical actions of state organs equates the contesting of legal certainty and trust of citizens in law.
>
> (PL. ÚS 17/96)

8.6.1 Landmark cases from the first Court

From the first Court, two other points need to be raised. Firstly, this period included some constitutional interpretations which have arguably not targeted the legislature at all but were rather sending a message to the executive *in lieu* of the continuing intra-executive conflict between the President of the Republic and the prime minister (see Malová and Rybář 2012). In its decision I. ÚS 7/96, the SCC declared a general obligation of mutual cooperation between constitutional bodies. The case concerned the reluctance of the executive to submit a report requested by the President, whereby the SCC ruled that such a request must be fulfilled. In effect, however, this hardly provides a substantial constraint on the legislator. Similarly, in the interpretation I. ÚS 61/96, the Court gave itself the power to continue with a proceeding despite the withdrawal of the petition in case "the grounds for [...] a dispute still exists". This was at best an indirect restriction of the legislature, in that the SCC could continue with the proceeding even though the legislature (e.g. in its changed composition after the election) or another eligible petitioner withdrew a petition that it had submitted earlier. Along the same lines are the rulings specifying the dates of term of the President of the Republic (II. ÚS 65/97) and the prohibition of the executive to change the President's decision on an amnesty (I. ÚS 30/99).[25] On the other hand, despite some of these cases posing a more minor (if any) restriction on the legislature than attributed in the coding process, it does not invalidate the conclusion about the SCC acting as a negative legislator in this period and frequently declaring the unconstitutionality of pieces of legislation it had been tasked to review.

Secondly, this period includes the closely followed decision on the 1997 Slovak referendum (II. ÚS 31/97), which was criticized from a number of perspectives (Drgonec 2010, 249–55; Láštic 2011). Yet from the perspective of the relationship between the SCC and the legislature, the ruling itself poses a clear constraint. Indeed, the construction of the SCC was that in case there is a positive decision in a referendum, the Slovak Constitution does not precisely stipulate that the result becomes a legally valid act. As a consequence, and because often referendum questions are not formulated as a legal text, it would be practically impossible for the referendum result to become legally binding. The only way to avoid this unconstitutional outcome is to bind the deputies to vote in favour of a piece of legislation that transforms the referendum result into law. Hence, the vote on a legally valid referendum result limits Art. 73 sec. 2 of the Slovak Constitution, which stipulates that MPs "shall be elected to exercise their mandates individually and according to their best conscience and conviction. They are bound by no directives". This conclusion can be contested by asking how it could be ensured that the "legal–textual version" of the referendum result would appropriately carry the citizens' will from the vote.

8.6.2 Landmark cases from the second Court

From the period of the second Court, there is only one ruling with four dissents.[26] The ruling (PL. ÚS 8/04) concerned the amendment of the Antidiscrimination Act (No. 365/2004 Coll.) with a provision stipulating that "in order to ensure equality of opportunities [...], it is possible to approve special compensatory measures to prevent unfair treatment related to racial or ethnic origins" (§ 8 sec. 8). The majority ruled that this provision contradicts the democratic nature and the rule of law in Slovakia (Art. 1 sec. 1), as well as the equality in rights and the prohibition of favouring anyone on the grounds of race, nationality and ethnic origin (Art. 12 sec. 1 first sentence and sec. 2), among others. The reason for this contradiction rested on a number of grounds, including the lack of temporality, the absence of determination of the methods to achieve the desired goal, the permittable subject of the compensatory measures and criteria to determine their content. In essence, the dissenting judges emphasized that the compensatory measures represent a constitutional principle, the details of which can be specified with sub-statutory regulations.

Interestingly, the judge with concurring opinion, who often dissented in favour of a more robust interpretation of social rights, agreed with the majority decisions for a more specific reason, i.e. that the realization of the provision in question would require evidence of persons according to racial and ethnic origin, which "is prohibited in the rule of law". Clearly, a cleavage appeared between a more principle-oriented judging and more positivist, textualist interpretation of the constitution.

While only "accompanied" by two dissents, the ruling in case PL. ÚS 6/04 from 2005 is of importance because of the National Council's response to it. In this case, the majority ruling of the SCC declared unconstitutional those provisions that gave parliament the power to create a special investigative commission allowed to deliver binding decisions. Subsequently, however, the National Council used its position as a constituent assembly and adopted virtually the same regulation into a constitutional act (254/2006 Coll.) (Nikodým 2014), with only nineteen out of the 129 voting deputies abstaining or voting against (National Council of the Slovak Republic 2006). Since the SCC had earlier refrained from ruling on the compatibility of two acts with the same position in the hierarchy of legal sources as derived from Art. 125 sec. 1 of the Constitution (Procházka 2011, 20), it would not have been able to declare this constitutional act unconstitutional without overruling its earlier approach.[27] Consequently, the Slovak parliament has the "last resort" at its disposal to grant an earlier unconstitutional provision constitutional status (provided it wins the necessary majority), thereby further limiting the role of the SCC as a legislator.[28] This is in accordance with Kelsen's concept of "the switchman" (Troper 1999, 93–94). It remains to be seen what the SCC will do if the parliament approves a constitutional law (as referred to e.g. in Art. 125 sec. 1 a) of the Constitution) that manifestly contradicts some of the basic values of the Constitution as interpreted by the SCC.

8.6.3 Landmark cases from the third Court

Moving on to the third Court, there is hardly any evidence to substantiate that the court would have moved beyond a negative legislator. On the other hand, polarization has apparently increased, if only because there were four cases with more than four dissents (out of those, one with five and one with six dissents) and numerous cases with two or three dissents. We now go through these four cases, demonstrating that while in two of them an effort to act as legislator is visible in the majority opinion, neither had relevant impact other than a certain degree of instability in the constitutional system, to which, in the latter case, the SCC itself contributed with an unconvincing and contradictory ruling on the President's appointment of constitutional judges.

The first case, decided in December 2007 (PL. ÚS 12/01), was the "SCC's own abortion ruling". The SCC basically allowed the legislature to implement its own preferred approach when stipulating that

> [t]he choice of twelve weeks as a limit for carrying out an abortion upon the request of a mother cannot be considered, according to the opinion of the Constitutional Court, as an arbitrary one. This period derives from the time of creation of sensibility in the foetus and is in accordance with prevailing European practice of relevant legislation of the states permitting abortion upon request.

While the formulation does give rise to the assumption that some decision types of the legislature could be contested by the SCC (e.g. the possibility to undergo abortion during any moment of the pregnancy without a specific reason), it is a largely deferential ruling. The dissenting opinions (by five male judges) were defending a more conservative standpoint, stressing the need for more substantial protection of human life before birth. From a methodological perspective, the dissent of Lajos Mészároš can be mentioned, since it attempted to conduct a proportionality test following the German model, trying to find the harmonious relationship between the right to life and right to privacy. In addition, the dissenting judge highlighted that a concrete determination of the conditions for the protection of life before birth would overstep the powers of the SCC.

The second case (PL. ÚS 17/08) was more conflictual and also unique in two ways. Firstly, it witnessed the highest number of dissents so far – six out of thirteen judges of the plenum. Secondly, it is the only one where a broad remedy (binding prescription) could be identified according to this project's methodology. The core ruling essentially invalidated the whole Act on the establishment of the Special Court (an independent judicial authority in the Slovak general court system of district courts, regional courts and the Supreme Court) because it was supposed to violate legal certainty by the "possibility of the National Security Authority to revoke the judge's security verification at any time, and thus to cause the dissolution of his activities at the Special Court in proceedings without clear and in advance predictable rules". Consequently, separation of powers was infringed upon, as well as judicial independence and judicial authority. The broad remedy rested in the possibility of the Special Court, which at that time was already functioning, to retain the validity of the proceedings and decisions which were already running at the time of the ruling. The dissents, which included the coalition of Gajdošíková, Mészároš and Orosz, objected primarily to the method of the analysis. They believed that the Special Court fulfilled the requirements "set for the establishment of a judicial institution in the Slovak judicial system". This set of dissents to some extent already predetermined a common pattern in later ones, characterized by objections towards the degree of care and attentiveness to detail the majority decision paid to justify the verdict.

The ruling received a decent amount of criticism. One scholar, for instance, argued that the SCC presented reflections which should be attributed to the legislative power, and hence cast doubts on the operative part of the decision (Nikodým 2009, 332). The SCC's president, who voted for the majority decision, defended the ruling, among other arguments, by rejecting the principle of "minimalization of interferences in the competences of other constitutional organs" (Macejková 2010, 1212–13). In the end, the National Council passed another act on the establishment of the Specialized Criminal Court, which did not differ from many of the core elements of the Special Court the SCC's majority decision had invalidated.

The third and fourth rulings, with four dissents each, manifest more explicitly the divide that is recognizable among the SCC's judges. The first of these, an *in abstracto* interpretation, broadened the President's powers by allowing her not to appoint the candidate for the Attorney General voted upon by the National Council in case of a

> substantial matter related to the personality of the candidate that justifiably casts doubt upon her capability to exercise her function in a way that does not disqualify the esteem of this function or the whole constitutional body or in a way that would not be in a conflict with the mission of this constitutional body, if as a consequence of this matter the regular operation of constitutional bodies could be disrupted.
>
> (PL. ÚS 4/2012)

While at first sight this seems another decision restraining the legislature *vis-à-vis* the head of state, attentiveness towards the electoral periods provides a more nuanced picture. The candidate for the Attorney General, Jozef Čentéš, was selected by parliament with a centre-right majority. The President of the Republic, however, was leaning to the party of the opposition leader, Robert Fico, as described above. After Čentéš was selected, the President refused to decide on his appointment until a group of deputies submitted a request to the SCC for a constitutional interpretation. The SCC's ruling, which served as grounds for the President to refuse Čentéš's appointment, thus helped him and Robert Fico, who eventually managed to have his former classmate from law studies elected to the position instead of Čentéš. It is worth noting that the SCC's ruling came after the parliamentary elections in 2012, which Fico's party won overwhelmingly and then formed a single-party government. While later the SCC declared in an individual complaint case that Čentéš's rights were indeed violated by the President's decision because there were no grounds for refusing him even based on the SCC's interpretation, such satisfaction did not change the fact that by then there was another individual occupying the position.

The dissents to this ruling should not be unanimously interpreted as favouring Čentéš as the candidate. Instead, they argued on procedural grounds that it is only by a constitutional amendment that the head of state can gain such an autonomous competence to review the candidates for the Attorney General, or at least, that the right to refuse a candidate should be a limited one and applied only in exceptional circumstances when the candidate clearly fails to fulfil the necessary conditions of respect towards constitutional principles. In effect, though, they could be perceived as "opposition standpoints" to (at that time again) prime minister Fico and the then President of the Republic, supporting the choice of the previous centre-right coalition government of prime minister Radičová.

Last but not least, in 2015 the situation mirrored the one in 2012 in that the SCC again received a request for constitutional interpretation as a result of a conflict between the new President Kiska, who ran as an independent candidate, and the single-party parliamentary majority of Fico's Smer regarding the appointment of constitutional judges. The Slovak Constitution stipulates: "The President shall, on the nomination of the National Council, appoint the judges of the Constitutional Court for a period of twelve years. The National Council shall propose a double number of candidates who are to be appointed by the President" (The Constitution of the Slovak Republic, Art. 134 sec. 2). However, in 2014 the President refused to appoint three judges to vacant spots out of the six candidates the parliament offered him. He appointed only one candidate and decided that neither of the five other candidates fulfilled the material qualification criteria for a constitutional judge, referring to the President's constitutional obligation to "[...] ensure the regular operation of constitutional bodies by his or her decisions" (Art. 101 sec. 1 second sentence). Unsurprisingly, this decision became the target of heavy criticism from political and legal representatives of Smer. To clarify his role in the process, the president submitted the request for constitutional interpretation to the SCC.

The Court's decision (PL. ÚS 45/2015) was much more surprising than the earlier criticism. Instead of delivering any decision on the substance, the SCC refused the case, arguing there was no dispute between the two constitutional bodies. In its justification, however, it basically prescribed the President to select from the double number of candidates, declining his right to refuse all of them. Moreover, it referred to an earlier senate decision on the individual complaints of some of the unsuccessful candidates, although such decisions are considered to be binding only *inter partes* (Drgonec 2013). Most importantly for this analysis, the decision broadened the powers of the parliamentary majority by obliging the President to select among the candidates offered to him.[29] Some of the four dissents to this ruling, as well as some commentators, used strong language, highlighting the unconvincing claim about the absence of a constitutional dispute when there had clearly been two sides with opposing interpretations of at least one element of the appointment procedure.[30] Dissenter judges also stressed the departure from the SCC's own earlier approach to the presidential powers in the case of the Attorney General, when it allowed the President to make a material review of the candidate's eligibility. In summary, these judges appear to have supported a restriction on parliament's powers; however, their criticism was primarily directed against the degree of detail and persuasive power of the justification of the majority decision.

8.7 Conclusions

We have reviewed the trends of decision-making of the SCC during twenty-two years of its operation with reference to two types of proceedings in relation to the legislature. The empirical analysis showed that the SCC has not been a positive legislator *vis-à-vis* parliament as the "second legislator". The analysis also highlights the need for a contextual examination of the relationship between the SCC and the legislature, which may be done by asking the question "what kind of legislature"? The parliament is not a monolithic body; there are shifting majorities and minorities in it that are manifest through the coalition–opposition dichotomy. This was well illustrated by the decision regarding the appointment of the Attorney General. From a formal perspective, the legislature was restrained as a result of the ruling of the SCC because its nominee could have been rejected by the President according to the SCC. Practically, however, the decision empowered the next parliament with a single party majority to appoint its own candidate, after which the President, who was sympathetic to this majority, rejected the previous one and, as was later announced, infringed upon his rights. This also points to a promising avenue of further research, namely, analyzing not only the relationship between the SCC and the legislators, but other political actors, such as political parties, coalitions or oppositions.

This institutional "playing with fire" may well be explained by the changes in the executive power and the head of state, as suggested by the overall trends in the strength of judicial rulings. After 2000, the SCC was strongest when it ruled on the constitutionality of provisions approved by a parliamentary majority during the term of the subsequent parliamentary majority, which was ideologically different from the one that had adopted the provisions in question. Similarly, the change in the position of the head of state in 2014, to whose powers one of the most important lines of the SCC's case refers, coincided with a shift in the SCC's jurisprudence from the direction of strengthening the President *vis-à-vis* other political actors. At the end of 2015, the thirteen-member Court had two vacant positions, which increased to three two months later. The identified "coalition of dissenters" thus gained proportionately more influence, since there had to be at least seven members of the plenum to vote for a valid majority ruling. On the other hand, such setting increases the risk that there will be more cases refused because of the inability of the court to agree on a majority ruling on the merits.

The polarization of the SCC seems to reflect a divide between Fico's supporters and his opponents, yet this might be significantly shaken up by the post-2016 coalition which "bridged" traditional opponents of Fico and the Slovak National Party with the civic Hungarian party Bridge (*Most-Híd*). Moreover, what seems to be a divide along partisan lines may well be one among those who vote in accordance with a party's political line and those who try to interpret the Constitution according to the principles of human rights, democracy and the rule of law. Such a conclusion cannot be made without a more in-depth review of the case law of the SCC, including more than the two proceedings, and a critical normative as well as empirical analysis of the quality of the justifications of judicial decisions. Thus, the SCC remains a fruitful object for further research.

Appendix

Table A.1 Frequency of ruling types III (SCC)

	CIIA – EX (n=1)	*REJ (n=123)*	*OM (n=1)*	*PROC (n=8)*	*CR (n=1)*	*SUB (n=118)*	*CIIA – RES (n=10)*	*Sum (in %)*
1993	0.0	0.8	0.0	0.0	0.0	0.0	10.0	**0.8**
1994	0.0	0.0	0.0	12.5	0.0	5.1	10.0	**3.1**
1995	100.0	2.4	0.0	0.0	0.0	2.5	0.0	**2.7**
1996	0.0	2.4	0.0	12.5	0.0	8.5	10.0	**5.7**
1997	0.0	1.6	0.0	0.0	0.0	2.5	30.0	**3.1**
1998	0.0	0.0	0.0	12.5	0.0	18.6	10.0	**9.2**
1999	0.0	2.4	0.0	0.0	0.0	10.2	10.0	**6.1**
2000	0.0	3.3	0.0	0.0	0.0	3.4	0.0	**3.1**
2001	0.0	1.6	0.0	0.0	0.0	1.7	0.0	**1.5**
2002	0.0	3.3	0.0	0.0	0.0	2.5	0.0	**2.7**
2003	0.0	2.4	0.0	0.0	0.0	0.8	0.0	**1.5**
2004	0.0	1.6	0.0	0.0	0.0	2.5	0.0	**1.9**
2005	0.0	1.6	0.0	12.5	0.0	2.5	0.0	**2.3**
2006	0.0	4.9	0.0	12.5	0.0	2.5	0.0	**3.8**
2007	0.0	1.6	0.0	12.5	0.0	0.8	0.0	**1.5**
2008	0.0	5.7	0.0	0.0	0.0	4.2	0.0	**4.6**
2009	0.0	6.5	0.0	0.0	100.0	5.1	10.0	**6.1**
2010	0.0	13.8	100.0	0.0	0.0	2.5	0.0	**8.0**
2011	0.0	3.3	0.0	0.0	0.0	4.2	0.0	**3.4**
2012	0.0	3.3	0.0	12.5	0.0	6.8	10.0	**5.3**
2013	0.0	1.6	0.0	0.0	0.0	2.5	0.0	**1.9**
2014	0.0	28.5	0.0	12.5	0.0	6.8	0.0	**16.8**
2015	0.0	7.3	0.0	0.0	0.0	3.4	0.0	**5.0**
Sum (in %)	**100.0**	**100.0**	**100.0**	**100.0**	**100.0**	**100.0**	**100.0**	**100.0**

Notes

1 This is clear from the explanatory statement regarding the proposal of the Slovak Constitution (Petranská Rolková 2012, 189–98) and the respective parliamentary debate (National Council of the Slovak Republic 1992). One relevant point in the explanatory statement is that the "judicial power is strengthened by the establishment of the constitutional court, which will to a significant extent influence the conformity of legislation with the constitution". There seems, therefore, to have been an intention to establish a rather strong model of judicial review.

2 Arguably, there is a stronger tradition to refer to this legacy in the Czech Republic. The Czech Constitutional Court archives the decisions of the Czechoslovak Constitutional Court and explicitly refers to it in its website (Ústavní soud České republiky n.d.), while the Slovak CC does not.

3 For instance, the most recent type of proceeding adopted explicitly (as it was justified) to deal with the so-called Mečiar amnesties was explicitly designed so that it can possibly be used only for this one case (since it refers to a decision-making process valid

under the Slovak Constitution before its amendment in 2001), and in this period there was only one set of decisions for which the proceeding can be (and was) invoked – the Mečiar amnesties. See PL. ÚS 7/2017 (not subjected to the analysis since the case was decided on 31 May 2017).

4 The President of the Court is conventionally the fourth member of one of the senates.

5 After 2001, the Court's powers were extended in several areas, such as reviewing the constitutionality of the questions proposed for referenda, individual complaints from natural and legal persons and reviewing the constitutionality of sub-statutory legislation in relation to international treaties ratified by Slovakia, as well as matters determining the scope of the control competence of the Supreme Audit Office in disputable cases. Art. 129 sec. 8 of the Constitution enshrined the general validity of the SCC's decisions for "all bodies of public authority, natural persons or legal persons whom they concern". In addition, the access to the Court was widened. Depending on the exact type of procedure, not only one-fifth of the MPs, the president, the executive, another court, the attorney general and individuals may become petitioners but also the Chair(wo)man of the Judicial Council, matters in connection with the Ombuds(wo)man or the Supreme Audit Office. At the same time, as demonstrated by several decisions of the SCC in which it ruled on petitions submitted by the Slovak Ombudswoman (e.g. PL. ÚS 40/2014, PL. ÚS 44/2015), the Court reserved room for interpretation on the eligibility to submit petitions in concrete proceedings.

6 Since the amendment, judges have been elected for twelve-year, non-renewable terms, while before that a judge could have been elected for a second seven-year term. Consequently, some judges elected for a first seven-year term in 2000 were eligible to be re-elected for a twelve-year term in 2007, making 19 the total number of years they could spend on the bench.

7 See, for example, the numerous analyzes of important judgements of the Czech CC on the relationship between the Czech and EU law in Komárek (2012); Bříza (2009); Anagnostaras (2013).

8 Note that theoretically a decision restraining parliament may enhance direct decision-making of the people, e.g. through elections, or legislating through referenda.

9 The total number of rulings is 262, and 145 rulings have included dissenting opinions.

10 Officially, decisions in this type of procedure are binding only on the parties concerned. However, their authority can be significant for future development of case law and thus potentially also for setting the limits to which the legislature can restrict fundamental rights.

11 In line with the methodological guidelines of the project, this has not been coded as a positive prescription. Yet it can be considered as a certain form of call on the legislature, which may or may not react by changing the quashed provisions. Further research could explore how often the legislature adopts an amendment as a result of the Court's decision. Moreover, there is no body of the parliament that would systematically be responsible for initiating such amendments.

12 The Constitution of the Slovak Republic, Art. 125 sec. 3.

13 Another explanation could be that the SCC never possessed the competence of the *actio popularis* as, for instance, the Hungarian Constitutional Court did (Sadurski 2014, 15–16). Without this competence, citizens cannot submit petitions for constitutional review of legislation, and thus their access to the SCC in this form was limited and one channel for submitting petitions was non-existent.

14 Each judge should optimally have studied the case to some extent before voting on a particular decision.

15 We chose this number to create a group of cases that can be analyzed qualitatively within the scope of this chapter. Moreover, in a thirteen-member court (where especially recently not all the seats are filled), four dissents signal there is more than just coincidental disagreement caused by a specific world view of a couple of judges. The pool of cases with four or more dissents can also be used in the future for a more in-depth analysis of the reasoning of these judges.

16 This term denotes refusal on procedural grounds due to the impossibility of reaching a majority for either of the proposals for decisions on the merits. In most of these cases, more proposals were submitted by the judge rapporteur and/or other judges, but none received the minimum of seven votes. The cause of this might have been more complex cases, in which more than two opposing positions could have been adopted; thus, if there were three or more groups of judges, the majority of them could not agree on a single outcome. It should be noted that such decisions do not add to the reputation of the court, so it also signals a lack of willingness to make compromises in the name of the broader image of the court, which may be linked to the polarization among its judges, especially in the most recent period.

17 In 2009, there were fewer cases from the period of the previous government, but the strength increased due to the almost unprecedented total annulment of the act which established the Special Court.

18 Courts during the well-known Mečiarist era in the 1990s and during the government of Iveta Radičová (2010–2012), where the judges predominantly were elected by the then-opposition party Smer–SD, seemed to have been more inclined to engage in this type of ruling.

19 This decision (PL. ÚS 6/04) became the one that was later overturned by the parliament through establishing the commission with a constitutional act.

20 For more on the cases in which they dissented, see "landmark cases".

21 Except Dobrík, who has been a judge since 1997 and was selected in 2004 for twelve years after the constitutional amendment in 2001.

22 It should be noted that thirteen judges (Seeman, Černák, Čič, Danielčáková, Drgonec, Mrázová, Rapant, Šafárik, Klučka, Auxt, Kohut, Mochnáčová, Baricová) have not published dissenting opinion at all, either deliberately or because it was still not allowed before 2001.

23 It is worth noting that the latter two judges overwhelmingly dissented either on provisions enacted during the centre-right governments of Dzurinda or Radičová, which were upheld by the majority, or between 2010 and 2012 when Radičová was in power (bearing in mind that a declaration of unconstitutionality could come with negative views of the parliamentary majority by the public regardless of the fact that the actual provision declared as unconstitutional might well have been enacted during the previous government composed of competing parties). For example, judge Ľalík would have declared unconstitutional no fewer than thirteen rulings on the amendment to the Act on judges and associate judges, enacted in 2005 (during the right-wing Dzurinda government). Both Macejková and Ľalík would have confirmed the constitutionality of the above-discussed provisions of the first Fico government's Act on single extraordinary measures in preparation of some highways and motorways, which was a quite blatant example of unconstitutional expropriation according to the other judges participating in this decision. In addition, they would have declared unconstitutional the public voting for the candidate of the Attorney General in 2011 and quashed the provisions enshrining the so-called three strikes principle into the Slovak criminal proceeding in 2011. Had Macejková won a majority, fourteen rulings on unconstitutionality of provisions related to the judicial reform of the right-wing Radičová government would have been delivered in 2014. Another six rulings on unconstitutionality would have

been delivered if the joint dissent by Macejková and Ľalík on the prosecutorial reform by the same Radičová government had become a majority opinion.

24 The other two decisions with *ex tunc* effects were PL. ÚS 3/01, whereby the SCC quashed a provision prohibiting multiple memberships in political parties, thereby reinstating those multiple memberships which had been considered illegal before, and PL. ÚS 8/2013 from 2014, which was part of a series of rulings connected to the case of the appointment of the Attorney General. In this case, the SCC declared that it was unconstitutional to amend the Act on the Organization of the SCC in a way that if a certain number of judges is exempted from decision-making on a concrete case because of biases, the composition of the plenum or the senate returns to the original format, disregarding all decisions or declarations on these biases. In effect, several judges remained excluded from the decision-making on the individual complaint of Jozef Čentéš, an unsuccessful candidate for the Attorney General, whom the President of the Republic refused to appoint and who subsequently claimed that his rights were violated due to this presidential decision. In the end, the SCC confirmed the violation of his right to access to a public office (I. ÚS 397/2014).

25 The provisions concerning the President's power to grant an amnesty were amended in 2001, so this ruling should not be read as directly relevant to the current provisions. In addition, the SCC had at the end of May 2017 confirmed the legislature's decision to abolish the controversial decisions on amnesties issued by prime minister Mečiar at a time when he executed some presidential powers due to the absence of a newly elected president. While this decision passed with a constitutional majority subsequently to a constitutional amendment in the National Council, it underlines that the SCC's interpretation from June 1999 should not be considered as a significant constraint on the legislature.

26 More precisely, one dissent was signed by three judges and in addition to this and one more dissent, there was a fourth opinion labelled "dissenting", but in fact was a concurring opinion and thus was excluded from the analysis.

27 This ruling of the decision PL. ÚS 8/94 is not part of the database because it concerned a different type of proceeding (review of a ministerial decree). Yet it shows how in some contexts even other types of proceedings may be relevant for assessing the relationship between the CC and the legislature.

28 This is the only apparent case when the legislature adopted an arguably unconstitutional provision as a constitutional act. However, there is a case where the legislature as the constituent assembly "constitutionalized" norms previously found as unconstitutional by amending the Slovak Constitution. The case concerned the issue of evidencing the origin of property, whereby an act excluding property obtained in violation of evidencing its origin (especially for public figures) was found unconstitutional (PL. ÚS 29/05), and then the National Council amended the Constitution in Art. 20 (right to property) (National Council of the Slovak Republic 2010) before adopting another, slightly modified act on evidencing the origin of property (101/2010 Z. z.).

29 Provided that we accept that it had legal effects despite being a refusal. This can, however, be contested (see Venice Commission 2017).

30 See references in: Steuer (2017).

References

Brewer-Carías, Allan R. 2013. *Constitutional Courts as Positive Legislators: A Comparative Law Study.* Cambridge: Cambridge University Press.

Čič, Milan, ed. 2012. *Komentár k Ústave Slovenskej republiky.* (*A Commentary to the Constitution of the Slovak Republic.*) Žilina: EUROKÓDEX.

"Constitution Watch". 1995. *East European Constitutional Review* 4 (2): 2–33.
Čorba, Juraj. 2005. "Ústavný súd v podmienkach zápasu o pravidlá hry". ("The Constitutional Court in the Context of the Struggle Over the Rules of the Game".) In *Spoločnosť a politika na Slovensku. Cesty k stabilite 1989–2004* (*Society and Politics in Slovakia. Roads to Stability 1989–2004*), edited by Soňa Szomolányi, 181–98. Bratislava: Univerzita Komenského.
Drgonec, Ján. 2010. *Ochrana ústavnosti Ústavným súdom Slovenskej republiky.* (*The Protection of Constitutionality by the Constitutional Court of the Slovak Republic.*) Žilina: EUROKÓDEX.
Drgonec, Ján. 2013. *Konanie pred Ústavným súdom Slovenskej republiky.* (*Proceeding before the Constitutional Court of the Slovak Republic.*) Šamorín: Heuréka.
Drgonec, Ján. 2015. *Ústava Slovenskej republiky: Teória a prax.* (*The Constitution of the Slovak Republic: Theory and Practice.*) Bratislava: C. H. Beck.
Drgonec, Ján. 2017. "Všetko, Čo by ste mali vedieť o tom, ako ústavní sudcovia prikázali Kiskovi konať". ("Everything that you Should Know about How Constitutional Judges Ordered Kiska to Act".) *Denník N*, 15 December 2017. https://dennikn.sk/972222/vsetko-co-by-ste-mali-vediet-o-tom-ako-ustavni-sudcovia-prikazali-kiskovi-konat/.
Jesenský, Mikuláš. 2011. "Ficov vyvlastňovací zákon je protiústavný". ("Fico's Expropriation Act Is Unconstitutional".) *Sme*, 26 January 2011. https://ekonomika.sme.sk/c/5738192/ficov-vyvlastnovaci-zakon-je-protiustavny.html.
Kelemen, Katalin. 2013. "Dissenting Opinions in Constitutional Courts". *German Law Journal* 14 (8): 1345–71.
Kmiec, Keenan. 2004. "The Origin and Current Meanings of Judicial Activism". *California Law Review* 92 (5): 1441–77.
Langášek, Tomáš. 2011. *Ústavní soud Československé republiky a jeho osudy v letech 1920–1948.* (*The Constitutional Court of the Czechoslovak Republic and Its Developments in 1920–1948.*) Plzeň: Aleš Čeněk.
Láštic, Erik. 2011. *V rukách politických strán: Referendum na Slovensku 1993–2010.* (*In the Hands of Political Parties: Referendum in Slovakia 1993–2010.*) Bratislava: Univerzita Komenského.
Láštic, Erik. 2012. "Opposition's Labour's Lost? Minority Rights in Slovakia, 1994–2012". SSRN Scholarly Paper ID 2567291. Rochester, NY: Social Science Research Network. https://papers.ssrn.com/abstract=2567291.
Macejková, Ivetta. 2010. "K otázke ústavnosti Špeciálneho súdu v SR". ("On the Question of Constitutionality of the Special Court in the SR".) *Právník* 149 (12): 1193–1217.
Malová, Darina. 2010. "The Role and Experience of the Slovakian Constitutional Court". In *Constitutional Justice, East and West: Democratic Legitimacy and Constitutional Courts in Post-Communist Europe in a Comparative Perspective*, edited by Wojciech Sadurski, 349–72. The Hague: Springer.
Malová, Darina, and Marek Rybář. 2012. "Slovakia's Presidency: Consolidating Democracy by Curbing Ambiguous Powers". In *Semi-Presidentialism in Central and Eastern Europe*, edited by Robert Elgie and Sophie Moestrup, 182–200. Manchester; New York: New York: Manchester University Press.
Malová, Darina, Marek Rybář, and Erik Láštic. 2005. *Slovensko ako nový členský štát Európskej únie: Výzva z periférie?* (*Slovakia as a New Member State of the European Union: A Challenge from the Periphery?*) Bratislava: Friedrich Ebert Stiftung.
National Council of the Slovak Republic. 1992. "Transcript of the Fifth Parliamentary Session". http://www.nrsr.sk/dl/Browser/DsDocumentVariant?documentVariantId=12491&fileName=zazn.pdf&ext=pdf.
National Council of the Slovak Republic. 2006. "Návrh skupiny poslancov na vydanie ústavného zákona o zriadení a Činnosti Výboru NR SR na preskúmanie rozhodnutí

NBÚ". ("Proposal of Several MPs to Issue a Constitutional Act on the Establishment and Activity of the Committee of the National Council on the Investigation of the Decisions of the National Security Authority".) http://www.nrsr.sk/web/Default.aspx?sid=zakony/zakon&MasterID=1900.

National Council of the Slovak Republic. 2009. "Vládny návrh zákona o Špecializovanom trestnom súde a o zmene a doplnení niektorých zákonov". ("Executive Proposal of the Act on the Specialized Criminal Court and on the Amendment of Certain Acts".) http://www.nrsr.sk/web/Default.aspx?sid=zakony/zakon&MasterID=2874.

National Council of the Slovak Republic. 2010. "Vládny návrh ústavného zákona, ktorým sa dopĺňa Ústava Slovenskej republiky v znení neskorších predpisov". ("Executive Proposal of a Constitutional Act Which Amends the Constitution of the Slovak Republic as Amended".) http://www.nrsr.sk/web/Default.aspx?sid=zakony/zakon&MasterID=3193.

Nikodým, Dušan. 2009. "K problematike súladu Špeciálneho súdu s Ústavou Slovenskej republiky". ("On the Question of the Constitutionality of the Special Court".) *Právny Obzor* 92 (4): 330–40.

Nikodým, Dušan. 2014. "Ústavná legislatíva a otvorené problémy". ("Constitutional Legislation and Open Problems".) *Právny Obzor* 97 (6): 555–62.

Orosz, Ladislav. 2014. "Ústavný súd Slovenskej republiky ako manufaktúra na ústavné sťažnosti". ("The Slovak Constitutional Court as a Manufacture on Constitutional Complaints".) In *Ochrana ľudských práv a základných slobôd ústavnými súdmi a medzinárodnými súdnymi orgánmi – III. Ústavné dni* (*Protection of Human Rights and Fundamental Freedoms by Constitutional Courts and International Courts*), edited by Ladislav Orosz and Tomáš Majerčák, 218–33. Košice: Univerzita P. J. Šafárika. http://www2.pravo.upjs.sk/ustavne-dni-2017/files/04_OchranaLudskychPrav.pdf.

Petranská Rolková, Natália. 2012. *Ústava Slovenskej republiky a jej dvadsaťročný vývoj (1992–2012)*. (*The Slovak Constitution and Its Twenty-Year Development (1992–2012)*.) Bratislava: Národná rada Slovenskej republiky.

Procházka, Radoslav. 2002. *Mission Accomplished: On Founding Constitutional Adjudication in Central Europe*. Budapest: CEU Press.

Procházka, Radoslav. 2011. *Ľud a sudcovia v konštitučnej demokracii*. (*The People and Judges in a Constitutional Democracy*.) Plzeň: Aleš Čeněk.

Sadurski, Wojciech. 2014. *Rights Before Courts: A Study of Constitutional Courts in Postcommunist States of Central and Eastern Europe*. Second edition. Dordrecht: Springer.

Schwartz, Herman. 2002. *The Struggle for Constitutional Justice in Post-Communist Europe*. Chicago: University of Chicago Press.

Steuer, Max. 2017. "Kto a ako vyberá strážcov? Legitimita výberu sudcov Ústavného súdu Slovenskej republiky v komparatívnej perspektíve". ("Who Selects the Guardians and How? Legitimacy of the Selection of Constitutional Court Judges of the Slovak Republic in a Comparative Perspective".) *Právník* 156 (4): 338–56.

Steuer, Max. 2018. "The Slovak Constitutional Court on Amnesties and Appointments of Constitutional Judges: Supporting Unrestrained Majoritarianism?" *Diritti Comparati*, March 26, 2018. http://www.diritticomparati.it/slovak-constitutional-court-amnesties-appointments-constitutional-judges-supporting-unrestrained-majoritarianism/.

Stone Sweet, Alec. 2007. "The Politics of Constitutional Review in France and Europe". *International Journal of Constitutional Law* 5 (1): 69–92. https://doi.org/10.1093/icon/mol041.

Svák, Ján, and Lucia Berdisová. 2013. "Constitutional Court of the Slovak Republic as Positive Legislator via Application and Interpretation of the Constitution". In

Constitutional Courts as Positive Legislators: A Comparative Law Study, edited by Allan R. Brewer-Carías, 767–81. Cambridge: Cambridge University Press.

The Constitution of the Slovak Republic. n.d. https://www.constituteproject.org/constitution/Slovakia_2014.pdf?lang=en.

Tódová, Monika. 2009. "Gašparovič: Som Člen Smeru". ("Gašparovič: I Am a Member of Smer".) *Sme*, 31 March 2009. https://domov.sme.sk/c/4373334/gasparovic-som-clen-smeru.html.

Troper, Michel. 1999. "'The Guardian of the Constitution' – Hans Kelsen's Evaluation of a Legal Concept". In *Hans Kelsen and Carl Schmitt: A Juxtaposition*, edited by Dan Diner and Michael Stolleis, 81–100. Gerlingen: Bleicher Verlag.

Ústavný súd Slovenskej republiky. 2010. "Tlačová informácia č. 5/2010". ("Press Release No. 5/2010".) https://www.ustavnysud.sk/documents/10182/1042665/TS_20100224.pdf.

Venice Commission. 2017. "Opinion on Questions Relating to the Appointment of Judges of the Constitutional Court, Adopted by the Venice Commission at Its 110th Plenary Session". http://www.venice.coe.int/webforms/documents/?pdf=CDL-AD(2017)001-e.

Vodička, Karel, and Ladislav Cabada. 2011. *Politický systém České republiky: Historie a současnost.* (*The Political System of the Czech Republic: History and Present.*) Prague: Portál.

9 Courts compared

The practice of constitutional adjudication in Central and Eastern Europe

Kálmán Pócza, Gábor Dobos and Attila Gyulai

9.1 Introduction

As noted in the Introduction to this volume, to date no scientific works have analyzed comprehensively, systematically and empirically the practice of constitutional adjudication in Central Europe. Certainly, the JUDICON research project cannot fill this huge research gap at once, but we have tried to map the diversity and measure the strength of judicial decisions in six Central and Eastern European (CEE) countries. The scope of our project is surely limited as far as the number of courts and the types of judicial decisions concerned, but we hope that we have made only the first steps and that by applying our methodology another research project could provide a comprehensive picture of constitutional adjudication in Europe.

Although the country studies of the present volume have analyzed Central European constitutional adjudication from several perspectives, they have not intended to make a comparative analysis of all data produced by the JUDICON project. Obviously, they had to focus on the data of individual countries to be able to say something about salient years or longitudinal trends in majority rulings, dissenting opinions, the role of the presidents and diversity of ruling types or strength of judicial rulings in each country. In contrast to these country studies, this chapter will deal with the 'big picture' by analyzing the dataset comparatively and, at the end of the chapter, assessing the practice of constitutional adjudication in six countries in general.

First, we will briefly compare the proportion of relevant rulings and decisions in the six countries (Section 9.2). Second, we will disclose the differences and similarities in the courts' practice of selecting various ruling types (Section 9.3). We will conclude that the Hungarian Constitutional Court (HCC) preferred to declare the most diverse rulings and that the German Federal Constitutional Court (FCC) became most frequently a positive legislator. The same holds true if we consider only the 'non-zero' rulings, i.e. rulings which declared any form of unconstitutionality. The distribution of strength values, as presented in Section 9.4, reflects similar differences among the six countries. While the German FCC was frequently inclined to include some kind of prescription in its rulings, which contributed to the relatively wide distribution of strength values, other courts, like the Czech or the Polish ones, preferred certain combinations of the elements of judicial rulings, leading to a relatively low variance of the strength values. While the Hungarian and the German courts have been frequently enumerated in the literature as the strongest courts in the world, it is certainly one of the most interesting findings of our research project that it was not the Hungarian or the German court which took the most powerful rulings, but rather the Slovak one. Furthermore, Section 9.5 below will also disclose that the HCC employed the softest combinations of the elements of judicial rulings, which led to the situation whereby the HCC has been ranked as last when we compare the average strength of 'non-zero' rulings of the six courts. The same section will also shed light on the differences among the six courts' practices concerning the longitudinal changes in the average strength of their rulings. In the last section (Section 9.6), we will explore the different strategies of the courts in relation to publishing dissenting opinions. While Germany is clearly an outlier in the sense that the FCC published as few as 35 dissenting opinions in total during the time period 1990–2015, a general tendency unfolded from the early 2000s in almost all other CEE countries under scrutiny. The number and proportion of majority rulings provoking at least one dissent steadily increased and even reached the maximum value in Slovakia in 2013, i.e. all majority rulings were opposed by some judges of the SCC in that year. While this last phenomenon might be illusory due to the low number of majority rulings, the general trend is undeniable. The courts became increasingly polarized as measured by the number and proportion of dissenting opinions. Several times this polarization had a political background (as in Slovakia, Poland or Hungary), while in other countries, such as the Czech Republic, polarization could not be linked to political circumstances.

9.2 Rulings and decisions

To start with, the reader should be reminded that we have included only those decisions of the constitutional courts which affected a law adopted by the legislature. No decisions on secondary legislation have been considered. Furthermore, we restricted our research to decisions which were published in the official gazette of the country. Refusals were coded only if there was a dissenting opinion to that specific refusal. Any statistical comparison below thus refers only to these 'filtered' decisions of the constitutional courts.

These and other restrictions heavily reduced the number of cases in some countries (as in Germany, where the vast majority of cases have usually been constitutional complaints without any effect on legislation), while keeping the number of relevant cases on a very high level in other countries (e.g. Romania or Poland). As explained in the relevant country studies, the Romanian Constitutional Court and the Polish Constitutional Tribunal do not have any preselection procedures; thus, these courts have to deal even with cases which could have been refused by an administrative organ of the court.[1] The institutional design, which determines who can file a motion/petition as well as the competences of the court, has a further impact on the number of relevant cases. While preselection by an administrative body is well known in Hungary, the institution of *actio popularis* greatly widened the range of potential applicants which, in turn, led to a quite high number of relevant cases. This is why we have three groups of countries considering the number of relevant rulings. Romania and Poland form a separate group, with their number of rulings clearly over 2000. Hungary stands alone with its 1326 rulings, while the constitutional courts of the Czech Republic, Germany and Slovakia 'produced' a significantly lower number of rulings (Figure 9.1).

It is also telling how many relevant decisions have been considered in the research project and how they are related to the number of rulings. As Figure 9.2 shows, there might be significant differences between the number of rulings and the number of decisions, which means that the courts of Hungary, Poland and

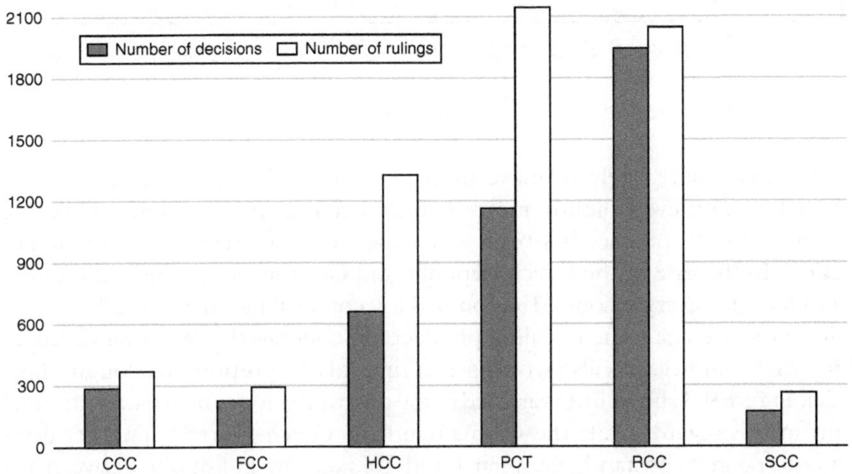

Figure 9.1 Number of decisions and rulings in comparison

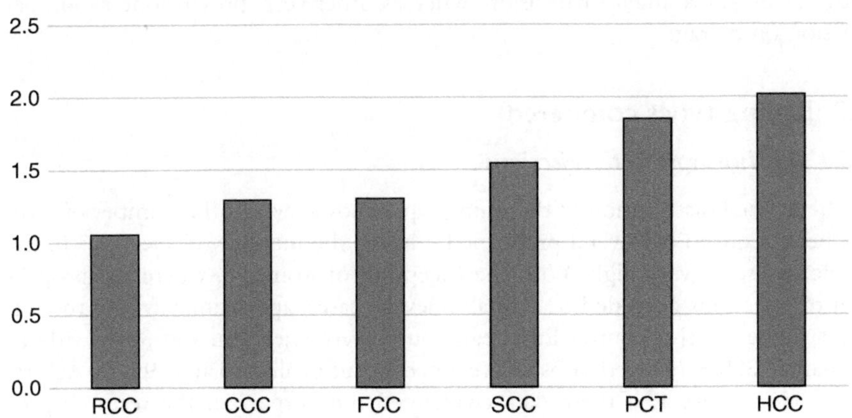

Figure 9.2 Ruling/decision rate of six courts

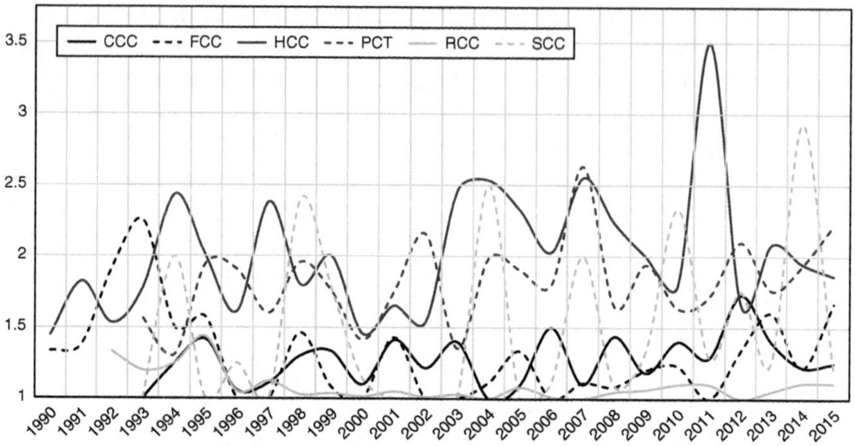

Figure 9.3 Ruling/decision rate of six courts (by years)

Slovakia were more likely to make more than one ruling per decision (in the case of Hungary even slightly more than two rulings per decision), while the Romanian court's practice has been very close to the average of one ruling per decision. In the case of the Czech Republic and Germany every third, and in the case of Slovakia every second, decision had a second ruling on average.[2]

Since the average value of ruling per decision conceals the temporal variances within each country, it is also worth presenting this proportion on a longitudinal model. Figure 9.3 shows little variance in the case of the Romanian Constitutional Court in this regard, while the German and the Czech courts' ruling per decision ratio ranged constantly between 1 and 1.5, and the Polish one between 1.5 and 2. The Hungarian court's performance varied between 1.5 and 2.5, while the Slovak court's practice is seemingly 'hectic' in the sense that there are years with 2.4 or 2.9 rulings per decision, whereas other years present one ruling per decision on average.

9.3 Ruling types compared

9.3.1 Ruling types with rejections

As the general distribution of the ruling types shows, even if the number of cases has been reduced by several predefined criteria, the number of rejections in the whole dataset is very high. With the exception of Romania, where the proportion of rejections exceeded 81% of all relevant cases, approximately half the relevant rulings of the Central European courts were rejection, and 30% (without Romania, 38%) involved substantive unconstitutionality (Table 9.1).[3] At first glance, it appears as if these data challenged the purport of the research project, since approximately 90% of the cases fit into the dichotomous approach of upholding or striking down statutes.

Table 9.1 Distribution of ruling types (full dataset with and without RCC)

	All countries		*Database without RCC*	
	N	%	*N*	%
CIIA – EX	23	0.4	23	0.5
REJ	3907	60.7	2234	50.9
OM	137	2.1	136	3.1
PROC	138	2.1	112	2.6
CR	226	3.5	170	3.9
SUBST	1952	30.3	1663	37.9
CIIA – RES	53	0.8	52	1.2
Sum	**6436**	**100.0**	**4390**	**100.0**

Table 9.2 Distribution of ruling types II (full dataset with and without RCC)

	All countries		*Database without RCC*	
	N	%	*N*	%
CIIA – EX	23	0.4	23	0.5
REJ	3907	60.7	2234	50.9
OM – weak	46	0.7	46	1.0
OM – strong	91	1.4	90	2.1
PROC – weak	44	0.7	43	1.0
PROC – average	44	0.7	39	0.9
PROC – strong	50	0.8	30	0.7
CR	226	3.5	170	3.9
SUBST – weak	754	11.7	705	16.1
SUBST – average	878	13.6	712	16.2
SUBST – strong	320	5.0	246	5.6
CIIA – RES	53	0.8	52	1.2
Sum	**6436**	**100.0**	**4390**	**100.0**

Although this highly simplified summary suggests that rejection was a quite dominant form of decision-making, it conceals two facts: that country-specific variances exist and that completeness, timing and prescription did in fact several times soften or exacerbate the ruling. Table 9.2 shows that the general distribution of ruling types is greater, if we also take into account completeness, timing and prescription. As explained in Chapter 2 (Section 2.5.2), weak, average and strong forms of ruling types also indicate the 'secondary intentions' of the courts by counting with not only the provision but also further elements of judicial rulings.

The general distribution of the data structured by refined ruling types obviously shows more variances and proves that judicial rulings in Central Europe clearly transcend the dichotomy of rejection/striking down. Even if not widespread, weak and strong forms of omission and procedural unconstitutionality are traceable, not to mention the ruling type 'constitutional requirement', which accounts for approximately one-tenth of all 'non-zero' rulings. Even more interesting is the distribution of weak, average and strong substantive unconstitutionality, which shows that constitutional courts in CEE have been ready to soften or exacerbate their rulings by varying completeness, timing or prescription of the ruling.

The country-specific data are also enlightening, since they show that some courts refined their practice by using various options in decision-making, while other countries' constitutional courts were more conservative and did not take the opportunity to diversify their practice. As Table 9.3 shows, the Hungarian Constitutional Court's practice proved to be highly diverse: by keeping rejections clearly under 50%, almost all forms of ruling types were employed – even constitutional interpretation *in abstracto* became a frequent tool in the hands of judges.

Similar diversity is discernible in the practice of the German Federal Constitutional Court, which rejected only 42% of the relevant cases, although constitutional interpretation *in abstracto* was very rare, while strong procedural and substantive unconstitutionality were very much favoured by the court. This means that the FCC, if it found a law or a bill procedurally or substantively unconstitutional, became very severe and annulled the law either *ex tunc* and/or instructed the legislation about how to remedy this unconstitutionality in almost half the cases (Table 9.4 and Table 9.5). This means that in comparison with other courts, the German court, as a powerful actor with a high reputation and strong authority, was more willing to make severe rulings if it found a law or a bill procedurally or substantively unconstitutional.

Other countries' courts show clearly lower variance concerning their ruling patterns. All forms of legislative omission were almost completely unknown in the Czech Republic, Poland, Romania and Slovakia. Some forms of procedural unconstitutionality are clearly traceable in the same countries, but they are certainly not dominant forms of decision-making, while the distribution of these kinds of ruling types is greater even in Germany and Hungary. Declaring

Table 9.3 Distribution of ruling types (by courts)

	CCC	*FCC*	*HCC*	*PCT*	*RCC*	*SCC*
CIIA – EX	0.0	0.0	1.7	0.0	0.0	0.4
REJ	54.0	42.6	43.9	56.3	81.8	46.9
OM – weak	0.3	0.0	3.3	0.0	0.0	0.4
OM – strong	0.3	1.4	6.4	0.0	0.0	0.0
PROC – weak	0.3	1.7	0.4	1.5	0.0	0.0
PROC – average	0.3	0.3	1.1	0.7	0.2	2.3
PROC – strong	1.1	4.5	0.8	0.0	1.0	0.8
CR	2.7	7.6	7.2	1.9	2.7	0.4
SUBST – weak	13.9	5.2	6.9	25.5	2.4	0.4
SUBST – average	24.5	3.1	17.9	13.2	8.1	35.1
SUBST – strong	2.7	33.3	7.4	0.7	3.6	9.5
CIIA – RES	0.0	0.3	3.1	0.0	0.0	3.8
Sum (in %)	100.0	100.0	100.0	100.0	100.0	100.0

constitutional requirements was more favoured by all courts (except Slovakia). A weak form of substantive unconstitutionality is very much characteristic of the Polish Tribunal (every fourth ruling was a weak substantive unconstitutionality), while average substantive unconstitutionality is dominant in Slovakia (every third ruling) and in the Czech Republic (every fourth ruling). Declaring legislative omission and both forms of constitutional interpretation *in abstracto* seems to be an entirely Hungarian peculiarity, albeit strong omission is present in Germany and the restrictive form of CIIA is quite frequent in Slovakia (Figure 9.4).

Generally speaking, we have the impression that the Hungarian and the German courts were more willing to utilize the full range of the available options of ruling types, while other courts neglected several possible combinations of decision-making and/or had their favoured ruling types. While the Polish Constitutional Tribunal quite frequently tried to soften its rulings by declaring a *pro futuro* annulment or a qualitative partial annulment (Table 9.6 and Table 9.7), the German court usually made the opposite move and tried to sharpen its rulings by annulling the law *ex tunc* (Table 9.5) or by giving guidance on how to remedy the unconstitutionality (Table 9.4).

9.3.2 *Ruling types without rejections*

Since nearly half the relevant rulings in our database were rejections, it is worth focusing on those rulings which were 'non-rejections' and asking how differentiated were the rulings of the courts when they did not reject the motion.

Table 9.4 Frequency of prescriptions (FCC)

	REF/REJ	*OM*	*PROC*	*CR*	*SUBST*	*CIIA*
No prescription	0.0%	0.0%	68.4%	0.0%	50.4%	0.0%
Non-binding prescription	0.0%	25.0%	0.0%	0.0%	9.1%	0.0%
Directive	0.0%	0.0%	26.3%	0.0%	18.2%	0.0%
Binding prescription	0.0%	75.0%	5.3%	0.0%	22.3%	0.0%
Constitutional requirement	0.0%	0.0%	0.0%	100.0%	0.0%	100.0%
Sum	0.0%	100.0%	100.0%	100.0%	100.0%	100.0%

Table 9.5 Frequency of temporal effects (FCC)

	REF/REJ	*OM*	*PROC*	*CR*	*SUBST*	*CIIA*
Pro futuro	0.0%	0.0%	5.3%	0.0%	20.7%	0.0%
Ex nunc	0.0%	0.0%	52.6%	0.0%	36.4%	0.0%
Ex tunc	0.0%	0.0%	42.1%	0.0%	43.0%	0.0%
Sum	0.0%	100.0%	100.0%	0.0%	100.0%	0.0%

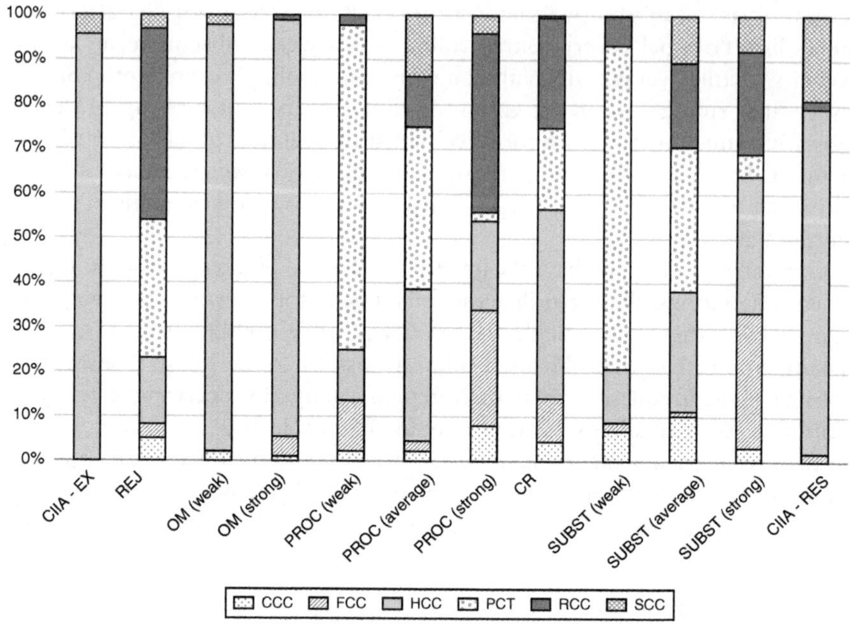

Figure 9.4 Distribution of ruling types (by courts)

Table 9.6 Frequency of completeness (PCT)

	REF/REJ	*OM*	*PROC*	*CR*	*SUBST*	*CIIA*
Partial	0.0%	–	16.3%	0.0%	52.8%	–
Complete	0.0%	–	81.6%	0.0%	45.5%	–
Total	0.0%	–	2.0%	0.0%	1.8%	–
Sum	0.0%	–	100.0%	0.0%	100.0%	–

Table 9.7 Frequency of temporal effects (PCT)

	REF/REJ	*OM*	*PROC*	*CR*	*SUBST*	*CIIA*
Pro futuro	0.0%	–	59.2%	0.0%	19.6%	–
Ex nunc	0.0%	–	40.8%	0.0%	80.3%	–
Ex tunc	0.0%	–	0.0%	0.0%	0.1%	–
Sum	0.0%	–	100.0%	0.0%	100.0%	–

By considering only 'non-zero' rulings, the number of relevant cases in all the countries investigated dropped from 6436 to 2506. Putting rejections aside implies that the proportion of the number of rulings per country also changes. Certainly, the proportion of rulings of the Romanian Constitutional Court changed most significantly, dropping from 31.8% (2046) to 5.5% (373) of all rulings in our database, while the relative weight of Hungarian and Polish data increased slightly (Table 9.8).

Statistics show that three-quarters of all 'non-rejection' rulings were substantive unconstitutionality, but one-quarter shows high variance between omission, procedural unconstitutionality, constitutional requirement and CIIA (Table 9.9). We get an even more colourful picture if we take further elements of judicial rulings into account and disaggregate rulings into weak, average and strong forms of rulings (Table 9.10)

By also taking country variances into account, we might argue that some tendencies and peculiarities are even more visible by focusing on 'non-zero' rulings. Table 9.11 shows that only the Hungarian Constitutional Court was keen to play on the whole field and decided in a similar manner only in every third of its rulings (average substantive unconstitutionality). Otherwise, it used other instruments very frequently: the distribution of ruling types is very steady, which means that, considering its 'non-zero' rulings, diversity was one of the most characteristic hallmarks of the HCC. Furthermore, Table 9.11 suggests that the German court's favourite ruling type was, by far, strong substantive unconstitutionality. Three-fifths of its 'non-rejection' rulings were a declaration of severe substantive unconstitutionality; consequently, a certain kind of imbalance was present in the practice of the FCC. Nevertheless, the distribution of the remaining two-fifths of its 'non-zero' rulings shows more steadiness as compared to all other courts (with the exception of Hungary). Perhaps the

Table 9.8 Number of rulings with and without rejections (by courts)

	Nr. of rulings	*%*	*Nr. of rulings without rejections*	*%*
CC	367	5.7	169	6.7
FCC	291	4.5	167	6.7
HCC	1326	20.6	722	28.8
PCT	2144	33.3	937	37.4
RCC	2046	31.8	373	14.9
SCC	262	4.1	138	5.5
Sum	6436	100.0	2506	100.0

Table 9.9 Ruling types without rejections I (full dataset)

Ruling types without rejections	*N*	*%*
OM	137	5.5
PROC	138	5.5
CR	226	9.0
SUBST	1952	77.9
CIIA – RES	53	2.1
Sum	2506	100.0

Table 9.10 Ruling types without rejections II (full dataset)

Ruling types without rejections	*N*	*%*
OM – weak	46	1.8
OM – strong	91	3.6
PROC – weak	44	1.8
PROC – average	44	1.8
PROC – strong	50	2.0
CR	226	9.0
SUBST – weak	754	30.1
SUBST – average	878	35.0
SUBST – strong	320	12.8
CIIA – RES	53	2.1
Sum	2506	100.0

Table 9.11 Ruling types without rejections (by courts)

	CCC	*FCC*	*HCC*	*PCT*	*RCC*	*SCC*
OM – weak	0.6	0.0	6.1	0.0	0.0	0.7
OM – strong	0.6	2.4	11.8	0.0	0.3	0.0
PROC – weak	0.6	3.0	0.7	3.4	0.3	0.0
PROC – average	0.6	0.6	2.1	1.7	1.3	4.3
PROC – strong	2.4	7.8	1.4	0.1	5.4	1.4
CR	5.9	13.2	13.3	4.4	15.0	0.7
SUBST – weak	30.2	9.0	12.6	58.4	13.1	0.7
SUBST – average	53.3	5.4	32.8	30.3	44.5	66.7
SUBST – strong	5.9	58.1	13.6	1.7	19.8	18.1
CIIA – RES	0.0	0.6	5.7	0.0	0.3	7.2
Sum (in %)	100.0	100.0	100.0	100.0	100.0	100.0

Romanian Constitutional Court's practice could be described as highly diverse if we consider only those rulings in which the court found something unconstitutional. Interestingly, the Slovak court was very severe if it found a law unconstitutional: two thirds of all its 'non-zero' rulings were average substantive unconstitutionality, a further one-fifth was strong substantive unconstitutionality and 7% restrictive constitutional interpretation *in abstracto*, which means that the Slovak court was activist in the sense that in 92% of 'non-zero' cases it constrained the legislature very heavily. By contrast, softening its rulings was characteristic for the Polish Constitutional Tribunal (58% substantive unconstitutionality) and to some extent also in the Czech case (30% weak substantive unconstitutionality). It is true, however, that all three courts played from a rather poor playbook and picked up most frequently (in more than four-fifths of the 'non-zero' cases) two ruling types accompanied by other ruling types in 11–17% of cases.

9.4 Frequency of strength values compared

9.4.1 Frequency of strength values

As explained in the Introduction and in the chapter on methodology (Chapter 2), if we are keen to explore the diversity of judicial rulings, the frequency of ruling types might be an appropriate indicator for the variance of judicial rulings. To have an even more refined picture about the practice of CE constitutional courts and to answer the question of to what extent CCs have constrained the room for manoeuvre of the legislatures, we have produced a database which assigned to each ruling a score from zero to 10 with an interval of 0.5 (see Chapter 2, Section 2.6). Nevertheless, we had to face once again some kind of uneven distribution of the data (Figure 9.5).

Rejections with 'zero' scores account for almost half the cases in each country; thus, we might be once again interested in the diversity and distribution of the relative weight of the remaining cases. 'Non-zero' rulings might theoretically vary between scores of 0.5 and 10, which means that they could take on 20 different values. This is certainly a wide scale and data show that not all possible scores became reality in the analyzed cases. Although theoretically all 20 combinations are possible, the middle of the scale is almost entirely empty (Figure 9.6). Approximately 17% of all 'non-zero' rulings of the database fall between scores 1.5 and 2.5, and only a slightly more (19.8%) between scores 0.5 and 3. There is a huge gap with no rulings between scores 3.5 and 5.5 followed by the vast majority of rulings with scores between 6 and 9, with a very dense concentration of rulings with a score of 6.5 or 7.

Certainly, there are once again differences among countries: the distribution of scores is steadier in Hungary and especially so in Germany. In Germany, the highest rate of a score is only 19.8% and several stronger scores peak around 10%, which means that the German court combined elements of rulings very

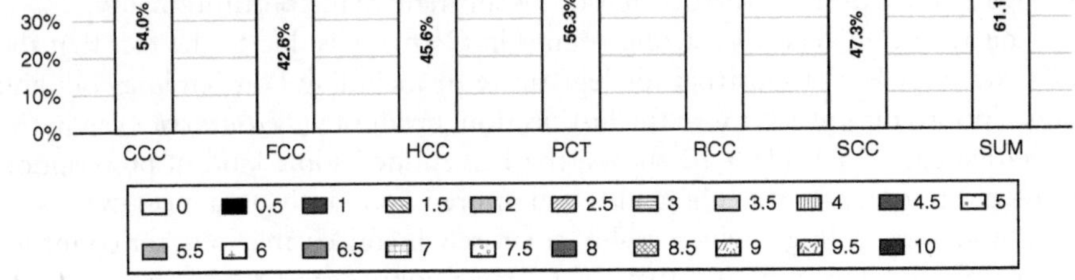

Figure 9.5 Distribution of strength values (by courts)

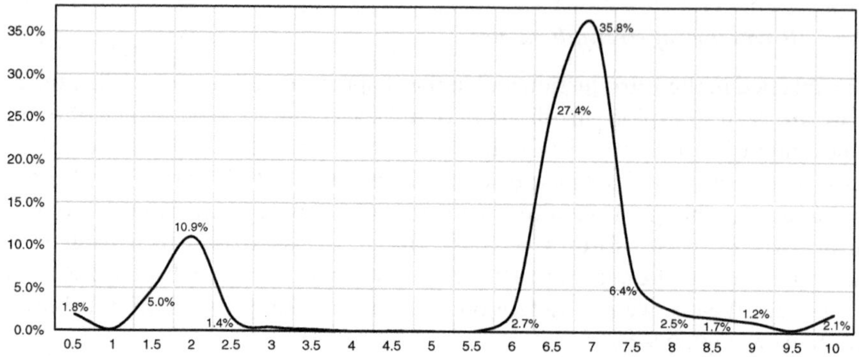

Figure 9.6 Distribution of 'non-zero' strength values (full dataset)

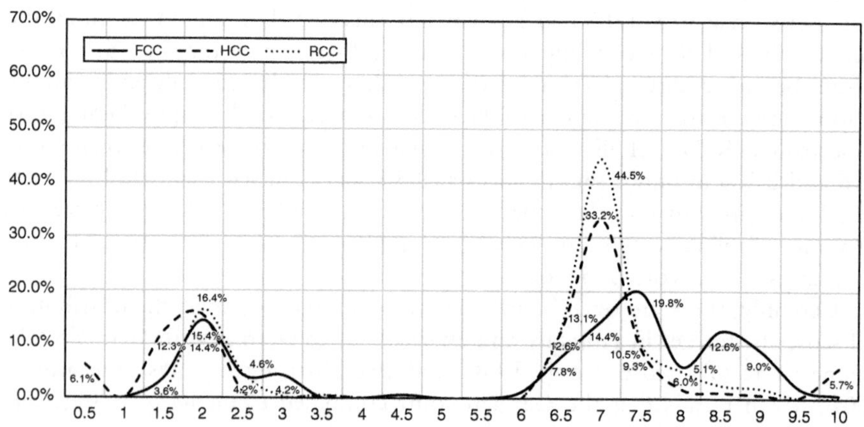

Figure 9.7 Distribution of 'non-zero' strength values (FCC, HCC, RCC compared)

differently (Figure 9.7). In comparison to the ruling types, which showed that the Hungarian Constitutional Court made highly diverse rulings while the German FCC favoured strong substantive unconstitutionality, the scores here indicate that the German court was more sophisticated (and clearly stronger) than the Hungarian if it came to the declaration of substantive unconstitutionality.

This relative diversity of strong rulings in Germany is due to the fact that the FCC was very keen to instruct the legislature by including non-binding/binding prescriptions or directives into the justification, headnote (*Leitsatz*) or even in the operative part. As Table 9.12 shows, the FCC added some kind of prescription (remedy) to every fourth ruling and, even more importantly, to almost every second 'non-zero' ruling – which is almost entirely inconceivable in other countries of the region.[4] This indicates that the German court played the most active role as a positive legislator in the region, which might be perhaps explained by its age and authority. On the other hand, however, the Hungarian Constitutional Court

Table 9.12 Distribution of prescriptions (FCC)

	REF/REJ	*OM*	*PROC*	*CR*	*SUBST*	*CIIA*	*Sum*
No prescription	0.0% (0)	0.0% (0)	68.4% (13)	0.0% (0)	50.4% (61)	0.0% (0)	25.4% (74)
Non-binding prescription	0.0% (0)	25.0% (1)	0.0% (0)	0.0% (0)	9.1% (11)	0.0% (0)	4.1% (12)
Directive	0.0% (0)	0.0% (0)	26.3% (5)	0.0% (0)	18.2% (22)	0.0% (0)	9.3% (27)
Binding prescription	0.0% (0)	75.0% (3)	5.3% (1)	0.0% (0)	22.3% (27)	0.0% (0)	10.7% (31)
Constitutional requirement	0.0% (0)	0.0% (0)	0.0% (0)	100.0% (22)	0.0% (0)	100.0% (1)	7.9% (23)
NA	100.0% (124)	0.0% (0)	0.0% (0)	0.0%	0.0% (0)	0.0% (0)	42.6% (124)
Sum	100.0% (124)	100.0% (4)	100.0% (19)	100.0% (22)	100.0% (121)	100.0% (1)	100.0% (291)

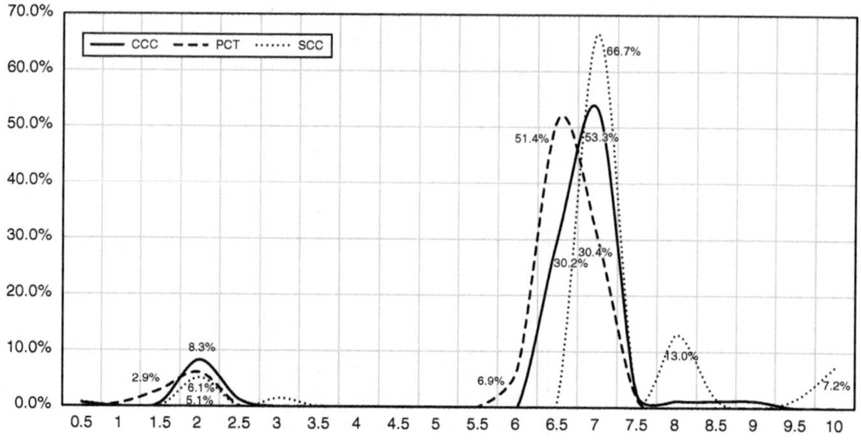

Figure 9.8 Distribution of 'non-zero' strength values (CCC, PCT, SCC compared)

strived to be as soft as it could at the other end of the scale: one-third (33.8%) of its 'non-zero' rulings fall between 0.5 and 2, while the same proportion is clearly lower for all other countries.[5] This is partly due to the several rulings of the HCC declaring legislative omission, which is almost entirely absent from other courts' practices, and shows that the HCC, although becoming activist by declaring unconstitutionality, several times relied on its softest power by declaring legislative omission without prescriptions.

Other countries' performance concerning the diversity of the strength of judicial rulings shows significantly lower variance. In the Czech Republic and in Poland, four-fifths of all 'non-zero' rulings take on a score of either 6.5 or 7, and the same is true for Slovakia, though with the scores 7 or 8 (Figure 9.8). This shows once again that diversity was not the strength of these three courts.

9.4.2 Standard deviation of strength values

Following the argument about why 'non-zero' rulings are worth a separate analysis, one more question emerges, which concerns the question of diversity of judicial rulings. Since diversity might be expressed not only in terms of frequency of ruling types but also in terms of frequency and distribution of the strength values, we might be interested in the standard deviation of the strength of judicial rulings in general and on a yearly basis as well. Standard deviation shows how diverse judicial rulings were. High scores of standard deviation suggest that the court made rulings with highly different values, while low scores show that the court played rather on a narrow field and made rulings with strength scores quite close to each other.

Scores hint at high variance in Hungary and Germany (and to some extent in Romania), while in Slovakia, the Czech Republic and above all in Poland low variance of strength values is dominant (Figure 9.9). If we are keen to disclose the longitudinal changes in standard deviation, we have to turn to the standard

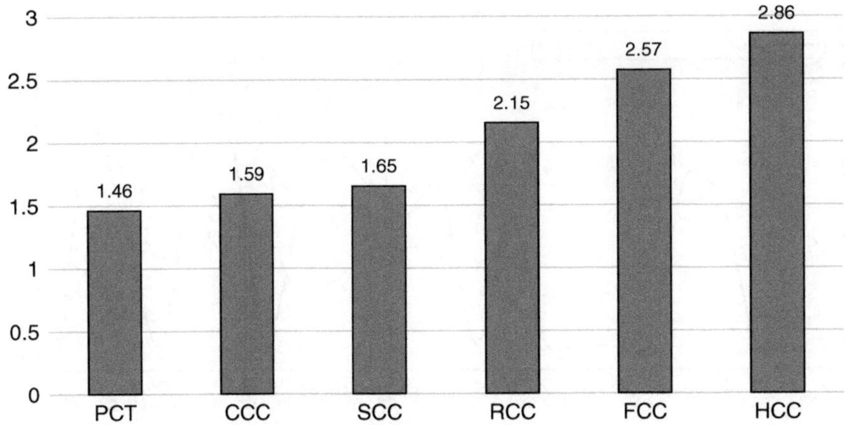

Figure 9.9 Standard deviation of average 'non-zero' strength values in comparison

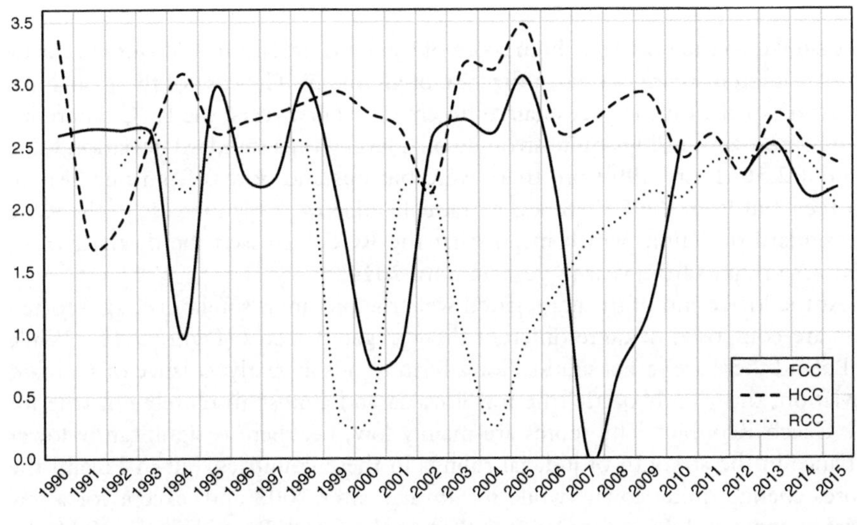

Figure 9.10 Standard deviations of average 'non-zero' strength values (FCC, HCC, RCC compared by years)

deviation data as disaggregated on a yearly basis. Interestingly, both high scores of aggregated yearly standard deviations as well as low scores of aggregated standard deviations show a very different picture if we disaggregate them into a yearly dataset.

While the Hungarian court's performance is a result of rather consistent adjudicational practice, i.e. the standard deviation of strength values was consistently high in all years, the scores of the German FCC show big differences several times from one year to another (Figure 9.10). This means that the FCC in one year made quite diverse rulings, while in another year the strengths of its rulings were

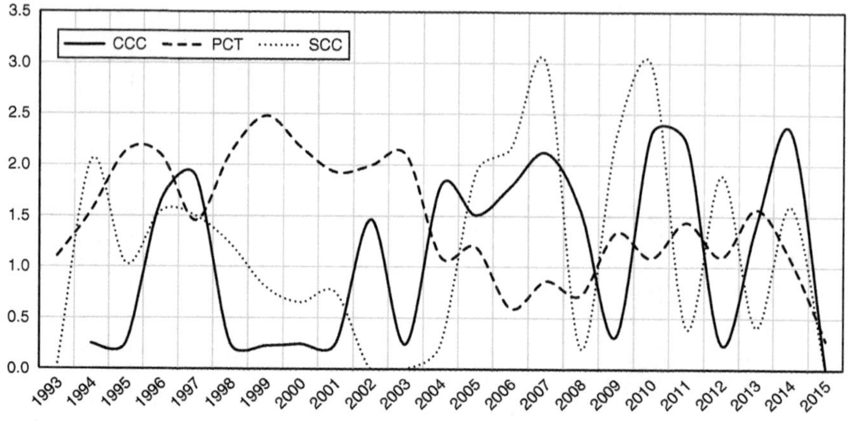

Figure 9.11 Standard deviations of average 'non-zero' strength values (CCC, PCT, SCC compared by years)

very similar to each other. A high score of standard deviation is accounted for by greatly different yearly scores in the case of Germany. The case of the Romanian Constitutional Court is once again different: in its first years, the RCC differentiated its non-zero rulings quite strongly on a level with a standard deviation value around 2.50. From 1999 on, there were big ups and downs from one year to another, but from 2005 there was a gradual and slow yearly increase of the value of standard deviation, which means that the RCC increased the diversity of its non-zero rulings from year to year up until 2014.

At the lower end of the aggregated scale the picture is similar, i.e. aggregated data are composed of quite different disaggregated scores (Figure 9.11). While in Poland there are rather gradual long-term trends in yearly variance of standard deviation, this is only partly true for Slovakia and almost absolutely not true for the Czech Republic. The scores are mainly low, i.e. there is significantly lower variance in the strength of judicial rulings in these countries, but in Poland the scores change quite slowly, while in Slovakia after 2003 and, except for a few years of constant low scores (1998–2001), in the Czech Republic from 1994, the standard deviation oscillates yearly with almost no variance of the strength resulting in an average level around the score 2.0.

9.5 Average strength of judicial rulings in comparison

Frequency of strength values depict in a somewhat more detailed manner what we were discussing in previous sections, i.e. the diversity of judicial rulings. Nevertheless, if we want to answer the research question concerning to what extent have constitutional courts constrained the legislature in six CEE countries, we have to turn to the average strength of rulings as compared in general and on a yearly basis as well. Once again, it might be useful to analyze the dataset separately: first by considering all data, then by focusing only on 'non-zero' rulings.

Having a very general picture of the data, i.e. comparing the average strength of all rulings between 1990 (1993) and 2015, we are faced with some surprising results. It was clearly the Slovak Constitutional Court which constrained the legislature most heavily in the given time period on average, even more strongly than the German FCC with its past of 40 years of constitutional adjudication. Although to date the research has not focused on the operation of the SCC, our comparative data show that the SCC's salient performance is certainly worthy of more intensive analysis. On the other hand, somewhat surprisingly, not only the Slovak and the German constitutional courts but even the Czech Constitutional Court are slightly ahead of their Hungarian counterpart, which was considered earlier to be one of the strongest courts both in the region and worldwide. By looking at the aggregated general data in Figure 9.12 it becomes clear that the general performance of the HCC was certainly not outstanding and did not constrain the Hungarian legislation heavily in the last 25 years.

This means that, although the institutional design provided the HCC with strong 'equipment', which supported the court in building a reputation in Hungary and also internationally, the data of our research project point to a rather careful and modest practice of constitutional adjudication in Hungary. The HCC was able to build its reputation by involving and making decisions very frequently, while at the same time not heavily constraining the legislature. While the Slovak and Hungarian CCs caused a certain astonishment with their general performance, the same certainly does not hold true for the Polish Constitutional Tribunal. As expected, the PCT was rather passive and constrained the legislation less than any other court in the region apart from the Romanian Constitutional Court. As explained in the chapter on the Romanian Constitutional Court (Chapter 7), this low-profile performance of the RCC was mainly due to the somewhat unusual institutional design, which did not provide the plenum of the RCC with a preliminary process of examination and classification of cases. Due to this special institutional arrangement, a vast number of rejections were produced by the RCC, especially between the years 2001 and 2005. The extremely low

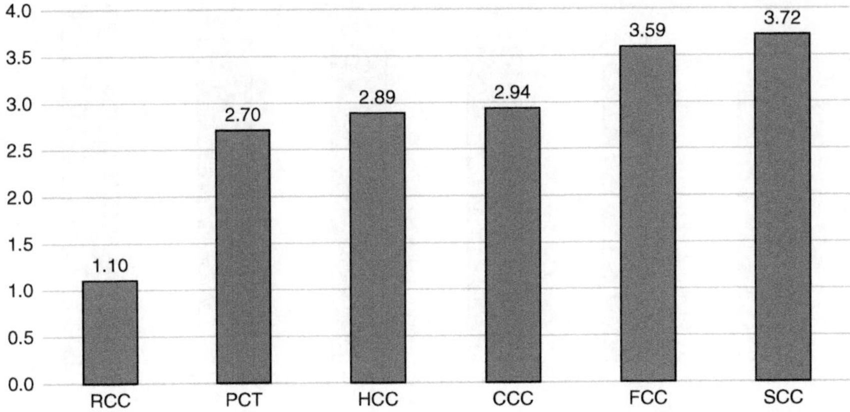

Figure 9.12 Average strength values compared

general score is partly a consequence of this institutional design. This imbalance in the constitutional adjudication of the RCC will be even more apparent if we compare the 'non-zero' rulings of the CEE courts.

When we focus on the question of what happened when the courts ruled some kind of unconstitutionality, three unexpected findings should be highlighted (Figure 9.13). Once again, the Slovak Constitutional Court proved to be highly severe if it came to a declaration of unconstitutionality. The SCC, during its 23 years of functioning, was by far the most rigorous court in the region, followed by the Czech, German and Polish courts, which performed quite similarly if only 'non-zero' rulings are considered. Here comes, however, the second stunner: the Romanian CC's underperformance disappears almost entirely if we compare only 'non-zero' rulings, which means that the RCC, if it ruled some kind of unconstitutionality, was almost as tough as most of its counterparts in CE. However, most unexpected is the very low score of the HCC, which clearly shows what we hinted at above: namely, that the HCC, if it declared unconstitutionality, tried to soften its rulings more frequently than any other court in the region. While the general performance of the courts got closer to each other if we focus on 'non-zero' rulings, the distance between the HCC and other courts is almost as significant as it is between the SCC and the other four courts at the other end of the scale.

Average strength might, however, oscillate yearly, which means that we should turn our attention to the analysis of the longitudinal changes of average strengths. Starting once again with the analysis of the full dataset, by comparing the yearly oscillation of the average strength values we might discern three groups of countries. Courts belonging to the first group, i.e. HCC and PCT, show relatively steady performance (Figure 9.14). The average strength of their rulings ranges between scores 2.0 and 3.0, except for the first year of both courts with scores close to 5.0. This means that both courts started their work by indicating that they might and/or will be important constraints on the legislature.[6] Nevertheless, this energetic and rather courageous entering the battlefield was

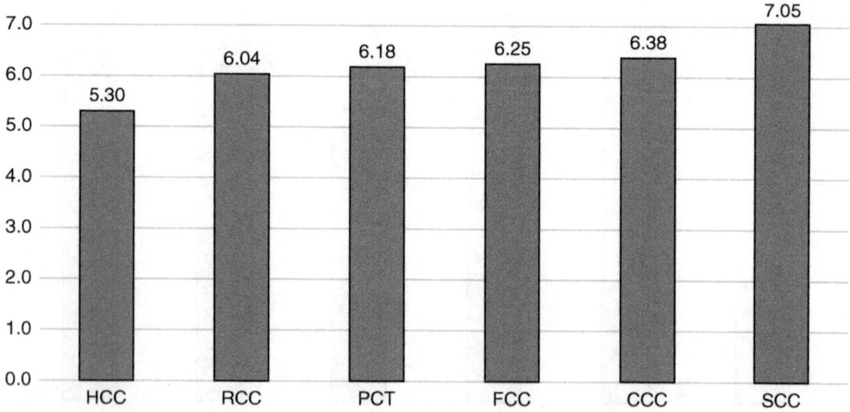

Figure 9.13 Average 'non-zero' strength values compared

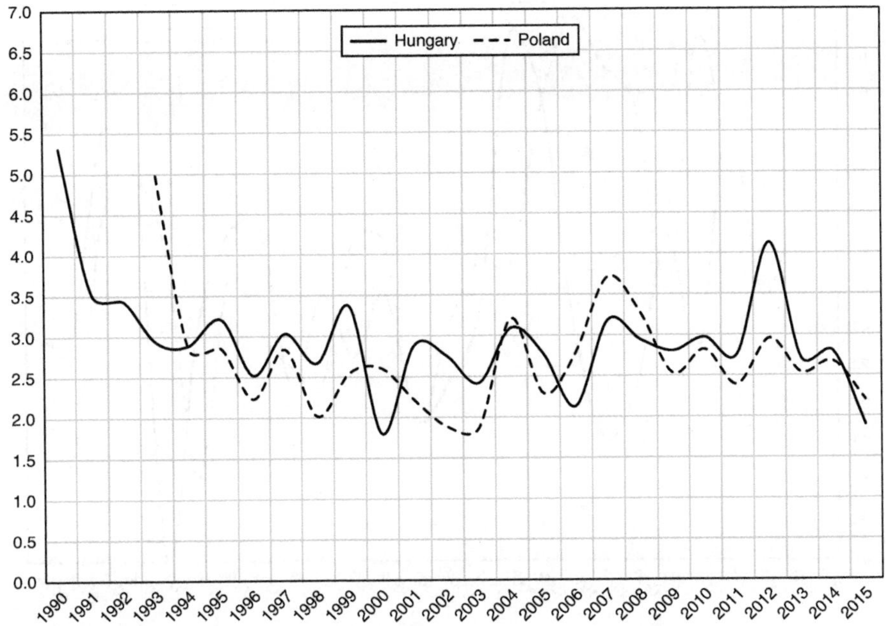

Figure 9.14 Average strength of rulings (HCC, PCT compared by years)

not followed with a similar ambition in the following years. Rather, both courts showed a steady performance (with some special years) with low variances of and low scores in general. To put it briefly, these courts, after having had a relatively strong start, fairly constantly reserved more room for manoeuvre for the legislature. Some years are perhaps more salient, but not as much as the case, for example, in Germany or Slovakia.

By contrast, scores of the German FCC and the Slovak Constitutional Court have oscillated intensively within a couple of years, sometimes even from one year to another (Figure 9.15). This variation shows extreme years with scores 'zero' and scores between 6 and 7. This means that, for example, very strong rulings were declared in Slovakia between 1994 and 1998 (with the exception of 1995) and in Germany in 1999 and 2000, while there was a year in Germany where all relevant cases were rejected (2011). Data suggest that the adjudicational practice of these courts appears more incalculable and unpredictable, while they look like very tough courts. On the other hand, there is a relatively clear trend in the Slovak case, which means that after the Mečiar era the court's stringency dropped significantly from an average of 5.77 (1993–1999) to 3.14 (2000–2015). Big ups and downs from one year to another were, nevertheless, characteristic for the Slovak court's adjudicational practice, as was also the case in Germany. In general, we are certainly not wrong in arguing that an important characteristic of these courts was their highly volatile adjudicational practice, with several very tough years followed by very soft years. This leads to the general conclusion that

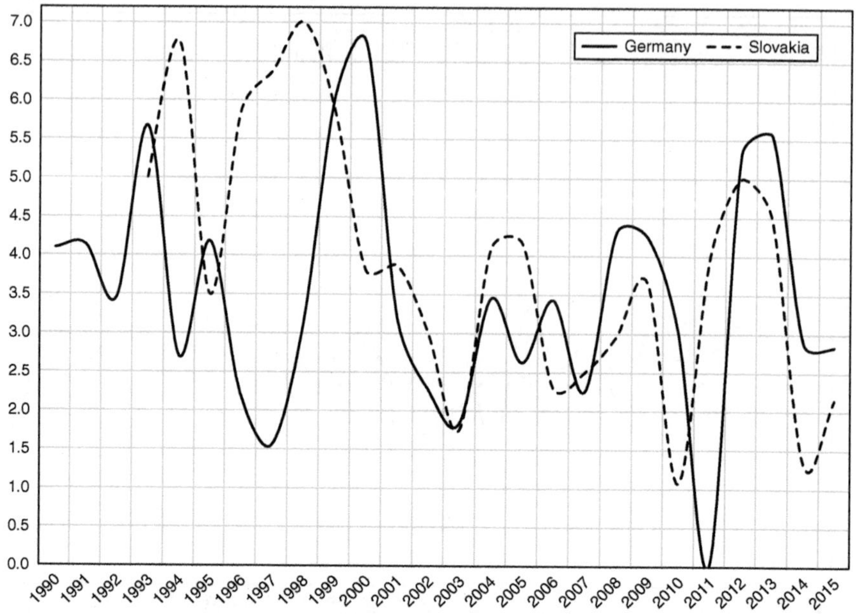

Figure 9.15 Average strength of rulings (FCC, SCC compared by years)

both courts constrained their legislatures severely in several years, while sometimes they allowed the legislature more room to manoeuvre.

The constitutional courts of Romania and the Czech Republic form a cohesive group only from a special perspective. In contrast with the Polish and the Hungarian courts, they certainly did not begin their adjudicational practice with weighty ‘punches’ in their first years, but entered the political field rather smoothly (Figure 9.16).[7] While abrupt changes in average strengths of judicial rulings from one year to another are not characteristic for these courts, certain gradual changes are discernible. Starting with a decent score around 3.0 or 4.0, the yearly average strength of judicial rulings in the Czech Republic began to decrease slightly (but not dramatically) in order to reverse this process in 1998. From that year on there was a gradual but constant increase in average strength until 2004. Between 2005 and 2007, there were three years with a significant decrease, while the pre-2005 level was reached once again in 2009. After that the CCC had a relatively steady performance, although the last year included in our investigation hints at a more impulsive decrease of the score of average strength. In contrast, the scores of the RCC show ups and downs in its first three years, but from 1995 to 2004 a gradual decrease is clearly discernible. However, we have to stress once again that a huge number of rejections between 2001 and 2005 certainly heavily influenced this ‘trough’ in the longitudinal curve of average strength. Values ranged between 1.0 and 2.0 from 2007 to 2013 and scores of average strengths reached the mean values (between 2.0 and 3.0) only in the

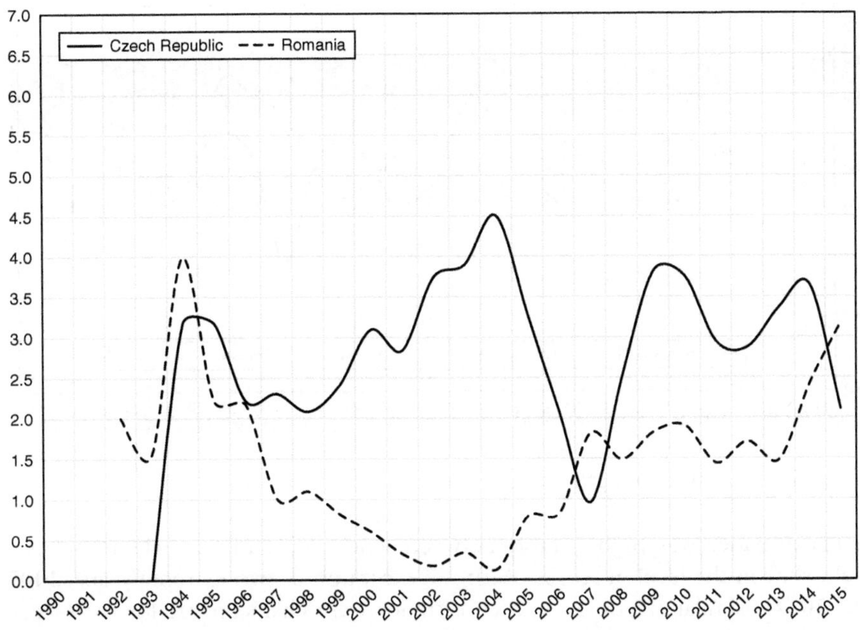

Figure 9.16 Average strength of rulings (CCC, RCC compared by years)

final years, with a massive increase in 2014 and 2015. We might argue that both courts show decreasing or increasing long-term trends without extreme fluctuations from one year to another.

Turning to the longitudinal trends of 'non-zero' rulings, comparison of the complete data and the dataset restricted to the 'non-zero' rulings might be carried out in two ways: either by within-case analysis of individual countries or by cross-country analysis. To begin with, cross-country analysis of 'non-zero' rulings suggests that the SCC was the most severe court in the region from 1990 up to the mid-2000s, although this implied a clear trend of decreasing strength of 'non-zero' rulings. Scores of the German FCC were registered once again on a wide scale, as was the case in the analysis of the complete dataset. Here scores range from 3.67 to 8.5 (Figure 9.17). These hectic changes of 'non-zero' rulings occurred several times from one year to another, which means that the FCC's hectic character was not due to changes in the number of rejections but rather to the variance of non-zero rulings. Longitudinal data also show that the Romanian CC's non-zero rulings matched the average strength of non-zero rulings of CE courts. It peaked with a score of 7.33 in 2003 when the RCC was most severe among CE countries' courts, considering only the 'non-zero' rulings. While from 1993 to 1998 the RCC's 'non-zero' rulings belonged to the lower end of the scale, this changed after 1999 and even more after 2003. Data on the Polish court show some zigzags between scores 5.0 and 6.0 in the early years, but after 2004

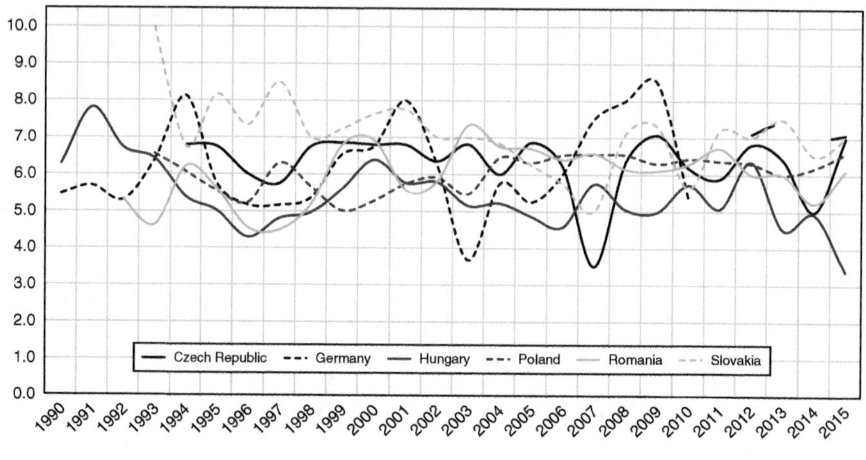

Figure 9.17 Average strength of 'non-zero' rulings in comparison

its performance was highly stable between scores 6.0 and 6.5, which means a slight shift in the level of scores. With the exception of two extreme years (2007 and 2014), similar steadiness and consistency were characteristic for the Czech CC from the beginning. Scores of the CCC line up between 6.0 and 7.0.

We can argue that both courts epitomize the 'average court' considering 'non-zero' rulings. The case of the HCC is interesting: in the first four years of its functioning the HCC showed sturdiness (with average scores ranging from 6.27 to 7.80), followed by a dynamic fall which stopped in 1996 at 4.29. This score is the fourth lowest score of 'non-zero' average strength in our database. After a less dynamic increase, the scores stabilized at a clearly lower level between 5.0 and 6.0, with a declining tendency after 2011.[8] Obviously, the Hungarian court 'competed' most of the time from 1994 on for having the lowest average scores concerning the average strength of 'non-zero' rulings.

All in all, longitudinal analysis of the 'non-zero' rulings reveals that the Slovak Constitutional Court persistently outperformed other courts in the region up to the mid-2000s, while the HCC underperformed them more or less consistently from 1994 on. The German FCC maintained its hectic performance, producing extreme years at both ends of the scale, while the Czech and the Polish courts proved to be the most consistent courts (if we put the two extreme years of the CCC aside). The Romanian court moved up to the other courts' average quite consistently, after being relatively soft in declaring unconstitutionality in its first years.

Nevertheless, it might be of interest to compare longitudinal changes of average strength of the complete dataset and the dataset based only on 'non-zero' rulings country by country. Analyzing the data and graphs from this point of view shows that the difference between the average strength of judicial rulings and the average strength of 'non-zero' rulings varies from country to country.

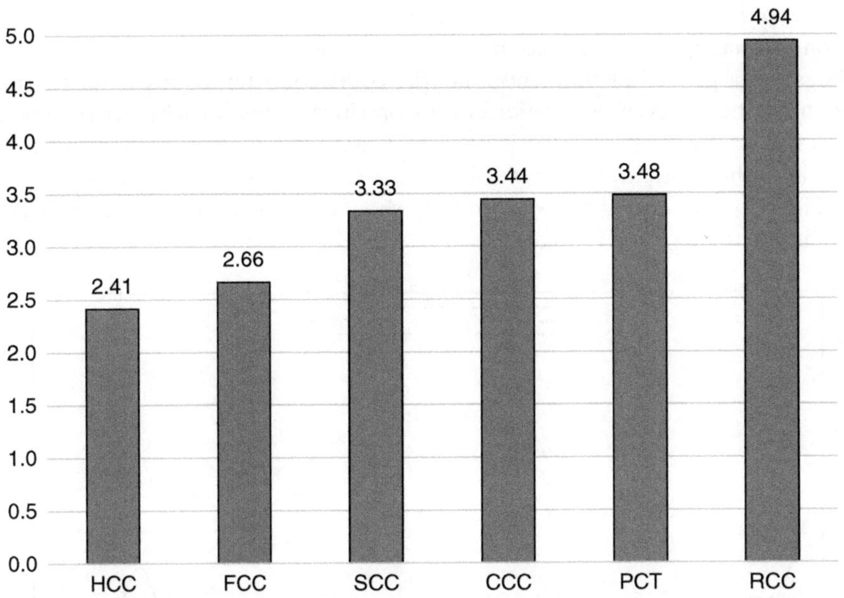

Figure 9.18 Differences of average strengths of rulings with and without 'non-zero' rulings

As the previous analysis explained, the greatest difference between the two indicators was produced by the RCC. This was once again a result of the high number of rejections in the early 2000s. The difference is clearly smaller in the case of Poland, the Czech Republic and Slovakia, and even smaller in Germany and Hungary. This data simply reflects the relative weight of rejections, which heavily influence the strength of rulings (Figure 9.18).

Courts with high differences between the two indicators, i.e. with high scores in Figure 9.18, might not be characterized in general as strong or weak courts; rather, we have to separate their general attitude and their attitude towards what kind of unconstitutionality they declared. They might be very tough when they find some cases unconstitutional, while declaring unconstitutionality is less frequent than in other countries. Is a court which 'punches' rarely but then with high intensity a strong court or a weak court? Is it a sign of weakness or stringency? On the other hand, courts with a relatively low score of difference between the two indicators were quite consistent in all aspects in being either rather permissive or rather severe; thus, their adjudicational practice might be characterized quite easily as strong or weak in general. General attitudes, average strength of rulings and average strength of non-zero rulings could, however, change in the long run or even in a short time period, producing consistent changes of both indicators at the same time; but they can show divergences and convergences as well. Therefore, longitudinal changes should be also investigated from this perspective.

The within-case analysis might reveal whether low scores of average strength are due to the number of rejections or whether the court softened its rulings even beyond declaring several rejections. This proves whether a trend of weakening rulings was a general phenomenon, i.e. the court consistently made weaker rulings and softened even declarations of unconstitutionality, or whether the court looks like an inconsistent actor in the sense that while rejecting several cases it 'punched' the legislature severely if it came to a declaration of unconstitutionality. The two lines on Figures 9.19 to 9.24 show the changes of average strength with and without 'zero' rulings.

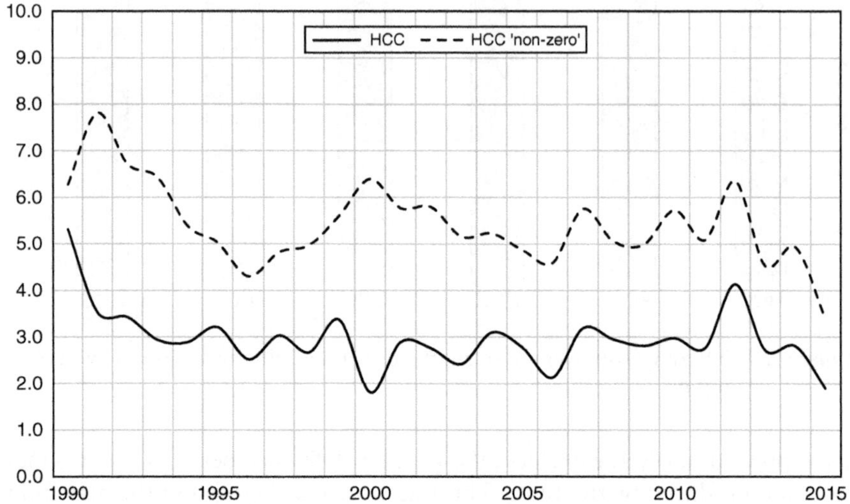

Figure 9.19 Average strength of rulings with and without 'non-zero' rulings (HCC by years)

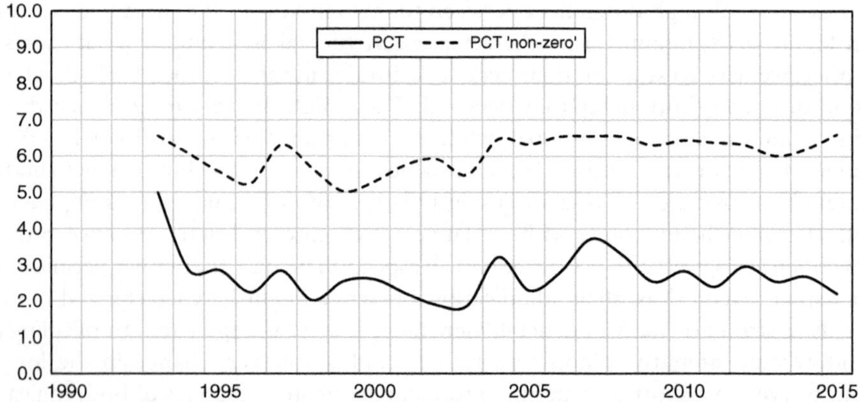

Figure 9.20 Average strength of rulings with and without 'non-zero' rulings (PCT by years)

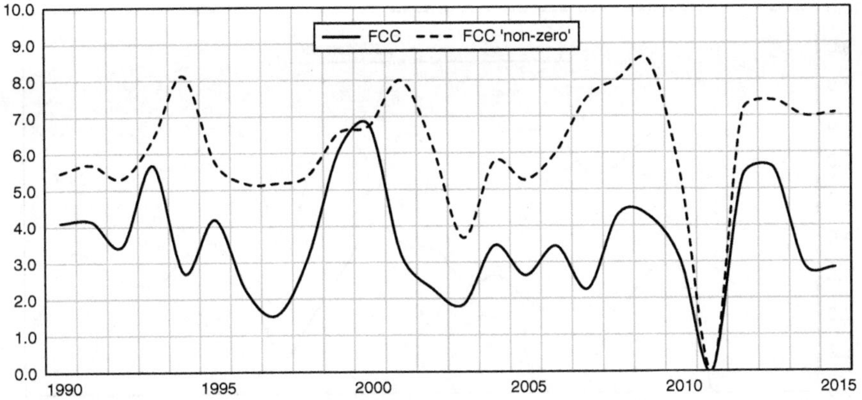

Figure 9.21 Average strength of rulings with and without 'non-zero' rulings (FCC by years)

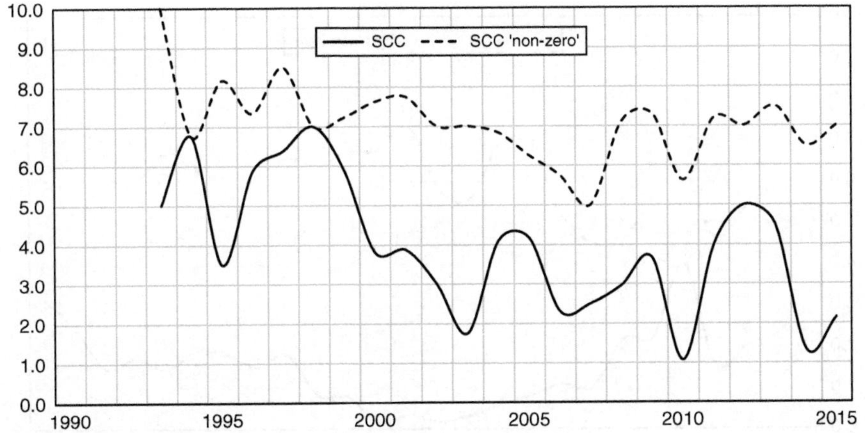

Figure 9.22 Average strength of rulings with and without 'non-zero' rulings (SCC by years)

By reading the figures we might discern three tendencies: first, if the two lines run in parallel it means that softening and strengthening of the rulings depends not on rejections, i.e. the court's behaviour is consistent. If their rulings are weaker in general, they are softer also in declaration of unconstitutionality, and, *vice versa*, if the general strength is increasing it is due to the more severe declarations of unconstitutionality. Second, if the two lines diverge and the difference is getting relatively bigger, it means that while being more permissive in general, i.e. rejecting more cases, they are more severe if it comes to a declaration of unconstitutionality. If the difference is quite big between the scores of general average strength and average strength of 'non-zero' rulings, this shows a divergence

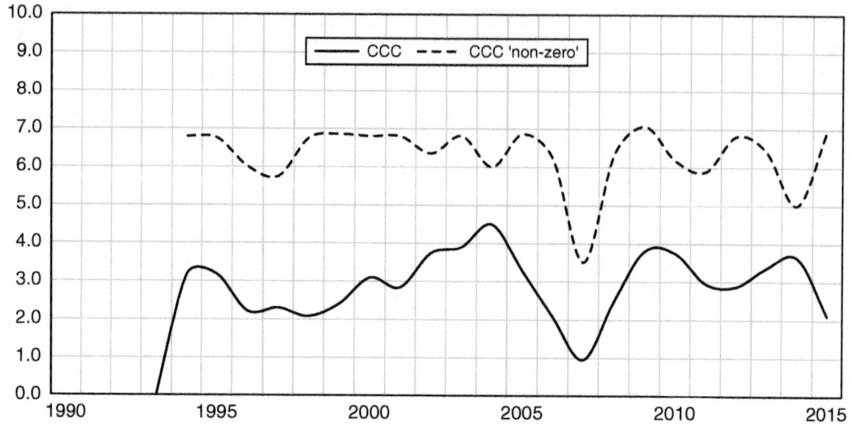

Figure 9.23 Average strength of rulings with and without 'non-zero' rulings (CCC by years)

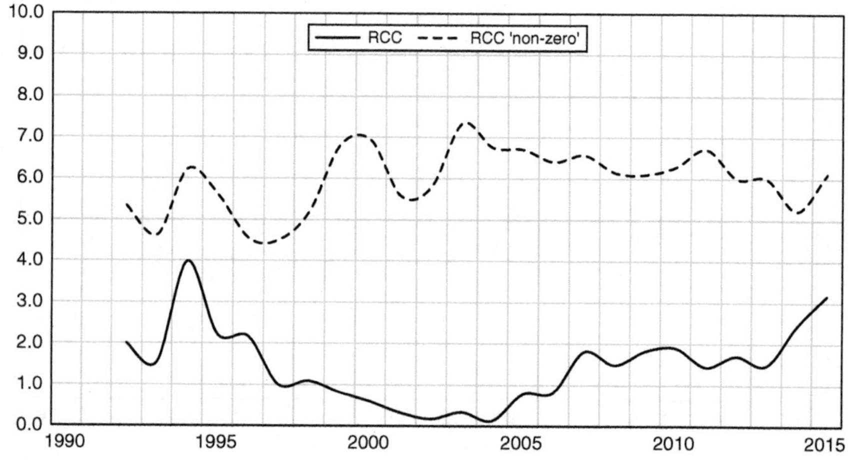

Figure 9.24 Average strength of rulings with and without 'non-zero' rulings (RCC by years)

between the general attitude and the specific cases in which the court declares unconstitutionality of a more severe form. Third, if the two lines converge and the difference is getting smaller, it means that the court's attitude became either generally stronger or generally weaker, depending on whether it simply rejected more cases or simply declared weaker forms of unconstitutionality (at the same level of rejections). Thus, convergence might also lead towards higher or lower levels of strength.

To start with the first tendency, this is characteristic for Hungary and Poland. (Figure 9.19 and Figure 9.20). While the average difference between average strength of all rulings and average strength of non-zero rulings was bigger in Poland, trends in average strength and average strength of non-zero rulings were relatively consistent with each other in both countries. There were some years with diverging scores (such as 1991 and 2000 in Hungary, or 1998 and 2015 in Poland), but the general picture is obvious: the number of rejections did not really influence the general attitude of the court.

If they rejected more cases, they were also softer in their ruling of unconstitutionality, and, *vice versa*, if they rejected fewer cases, they were more severe in their ruling of unconstitutionality. They consistently changed their attitude towards the legislature whether it was about declaring constitutionality or unconstitutionality. This led to a more or less consistent difference between the two indicators (around 2.4 in Hungary and 3.5 in Poland).

Germany and Slovakia form another group of countries (Figure 9.21 and Figure 9.22). As we have stressed in the longitudinal analysis of average strength of all rulings and average strength of non-zero rulings, both countries' curves attest to rather hectic adjudicational practice from both perspectives. The question emerges, however, whether these hectic changes tended coherently in one direction or not. Now, the picture is rather confusing: there are several years with highly diverging trends and the differences between the two indicators fluctuated heavily, ranging from 0.0 (in 2000 and in 2011) to 5.42 (in 1994) in Germany and from 0.0 (in 1994 and 1998) to 5.25 (in 2003) in Slovakia.[9] This means that convergence and divergence of scores were more typical in these countries than consistent difference between the two indicators. To put it in another way, these courts did not soften their rulings of unconstitutionality, even if they found significantly more cases constitutional (rejections). Sometimes they even declared stronger rulings, which led to a high divergence in the two indicators discussed here.[10]

Convergence of the trends is also discernible in both countries, which means that even if they found more cases unconstitutional (fewer rejections) they declared some form of weak unconstitutionality rather than a strong form of it. This discrepancy in trends of the two indicators is a giveaway for being able to make distinctions: while being more or less permissive/severe in declaration of unconstitutionality, as in the previous year, the courts could also counter-steer and declare, contrary to their general attitude towards finding cases constitutional/unconstitutional, more severe/permissive unconstitutionality.

As a third group, the Czech Republic and Romania shared something in common once again from a very special perspective (Figure 9.23 and Figure 9.24). In both countries, gradual and long-term changes in difference between the two indicators are discernible. While in the Czech Republic a slow and gradual convergence is visible from 1998 to 2004, the same is true in Romania from 2004 to 2014. In the case of Romania, it is also interesting that the difference between the two indicators decreased in the last two years (2014–2015) to a level rather characteristic of Hungary. This means two things at the same time: first that rejections were no longer as dominant as in the early 2000s and second that the RCC tended to declare a slightly weaker form of unconstitutionality if they found the case unconstitutional.

It is important to note, however, that in countries with extreme or gradual divergence and convergence, consistent adjudicational practice, as in Hungary or Poland, was not completely absent. There are time periods in which the two curves move together in the same directions in these countries as well.[11]

9.6 Dissenting opinions compared

After having analyzed the diversity and the strength of majority rulings, we now turn to the dissenting opinions. Since we were interested mainly in the operative part of the judicial rulings, we have excluded all concurring opinions from our investigations, because judges publishing a concurring opinion agree with the tenor of the rulings, i.e. they accept the operative part, while they would have argued in a different way. The several ways of reasoning are, however, not in the focal point of our project.

We are aware of the fact that the number of dissenting opinions does not exactly reflect the voting behaviour of judges. There have certainly been several rulings where dissenting judges have not published any dissenting opinions; they have simply voted against the proposal which was accepted by the majority at the end of the process. There might be several reasons why judges do not publish dissenting opinions, although they voted against the proposal. From the perspective of public opinion, these reasons are nevertheless not so important. We assume that if a judge absolutely disagreed with a ruling she or he should have informed the public about the reasons for her/his dissent. Thus, we rely on dissenting opinions, which are not only informative but also instructive for public opinion. By keeping this in mind, we can start with the analysis of dissenting opinions.

Looking at the data on the numbers of dissenting opinions (DOs), it is first obvious that there are countries where publishing DOs is highly infrequent. In Germany, although publishing DOs has been allowed since 1971, the number of DOs is very low: altogether there were 35 DOs published to the rulings relevant from the perspective of the project. On the other hand, in Hungary 885 DOs were published, which is a really high number, though the absolute numbers are perhaps rather deceptive, since they might depend on the number of judges sitting on the benches of the court and the number of relevant rulings we included into our research project. Consequently, we decided to focus on the proportion of rulings with at least one dissenting opinion instead of their absolute numbers. Here, once again, we have to stress that our units of observation are not judicial decisions but rulings. This means that one judicial decision might contain several rulings and several dissenting opinions which oppose different rulings of the same decision.

If we start with the general picture and focus on the average number of rulings with at least one DO published from 1990 to 2015, we might discern three groups of countries (Figure 9.25). As noted above, very few DOs were published in Germany and in Romania, while in Poland and Hungary there were somewhat more. In Hungary DOs appeared in relation to every fourth ruling, which is already a significant proportion. It is, however, not as 'impressive' as

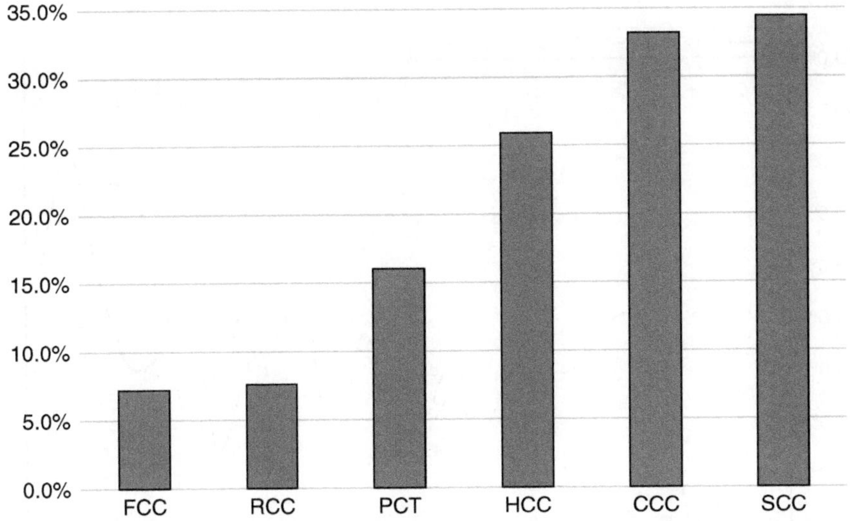

Figure 9.25 Proportion of rulings with at least one dissenting opinion in comparison

the percentage of DOs in the Czech Republic and in Slovakia: in both countries, every third ruling had a dissent. This might be an indicator of a polarized court, as we noted above, but it is not necessarily a political polarization. There might be several reasons why judges dissent. Differences in the political background of the judges might influence and certainly have influenced the publication of several dissenting opinions in the region, but – as this part of the project was a quantitative analysis – we have not attempted to disclose the motivations behind the dissents. Frequent dissents, nevertheless, show that the composition of the court is very heterogeneous, which certainly has advantages as well as disadvantages.

The general picture might be refined if we consider the longitudinal changes in the proportion of rulings with at least one dissenting opinion. If we consider the courts with the highest proportion of rulings with at least one DO, we might discover that the distribution of DOs is rather uneven in the 25 (or 22) years of their functioning (Figure 9.26). For all three courts it is characteristic that the proportion of rulings with at least one DO increased significantly towards the end of the time period under investigation. In Hungary, in the first eight years this proportion ranged between 3% and 16% and in the next 12 years between 19% and 34%, which indicates a gradual increase in the number of dissenting opinions. A radical shift is discernible after 2010: starting at 51%, the proportion of rulings with at least one DO peaked in 2015 with over 70%. With bigger fluctuations, a similar process is observable in Slovakia. While in the first years there was no ruling with a DO at all in Slovakia, in 2013 there was no ruling without one.

Even if we put aside this extreme data of 100% of rulings having at least one DO because of the very low number of rulings, we can ascertain that the Slovak court along with its Hungarian counterpart changed from one of the most

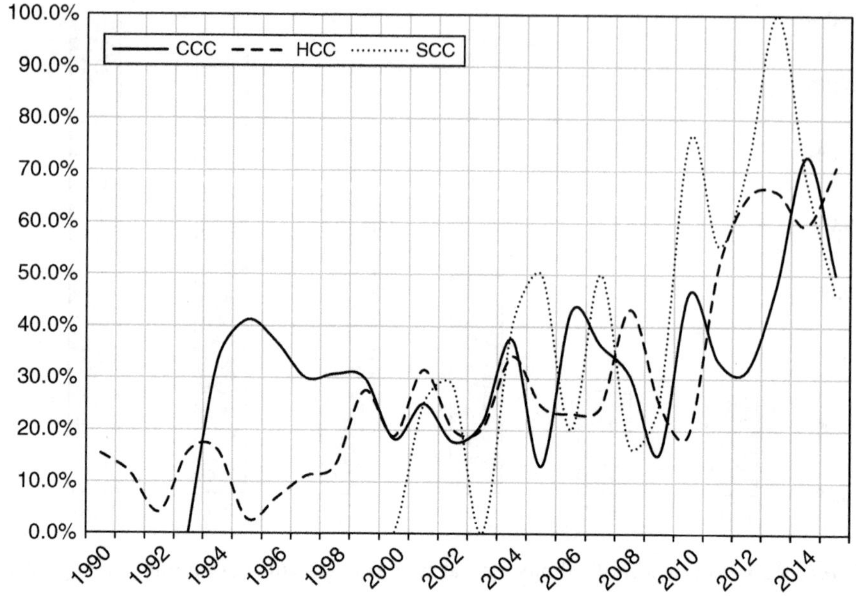

Figure 9.26 Rulings with at least one dissenting opinion (CCC, HCC, SCC compared by years)

cohesive judicial bodies in the region to one of the most polarized ones. The curve depicting the proportion of rulings with at least one DO in the Czech Republic shows a somewhat different pattern. If we disregard the year 1993 because of the extremely low number of rulings, it is more than obvious that the CCC was never a unanimous body, or the judges of the CCC were never reluctant to publish their dissenting opinion. From the very beginning the proportion was clearly above 30%, which is a very impressive number. After some years of decrease a slightly increasing tendency with bigger fluctuations is discernible from 2004 onwards, with a more radical increase from 2012 on. This means that the CCC was more polarized from early on, with a slight intensification of the polarization from the mid-2000s and a radical shift in the final years under scrutiny. All in all, the proportion of rulings with at least one dissenting opinion was very significant: in Slovakia and Hungary, it clearly accounted for more than 50% after 2010 and 2011 respectively, while in the Czech Republic it was always over 20% and several times over 40%.

While producing some extreme years and/or a gradual but less significant increase of rulings with at least one DO, the Romanian and the Polish court seem to have been less divided (Figure 9.27). The RCC published DOs to less than 10% of its rulings up to 2009, while this ratio ranged between 10% and 20% after 2010. Except for the extreme years of 2006 with its 1.8% and 2007 with its 50%, the Polish court's curve moved between 5% and 15% from the beginning up

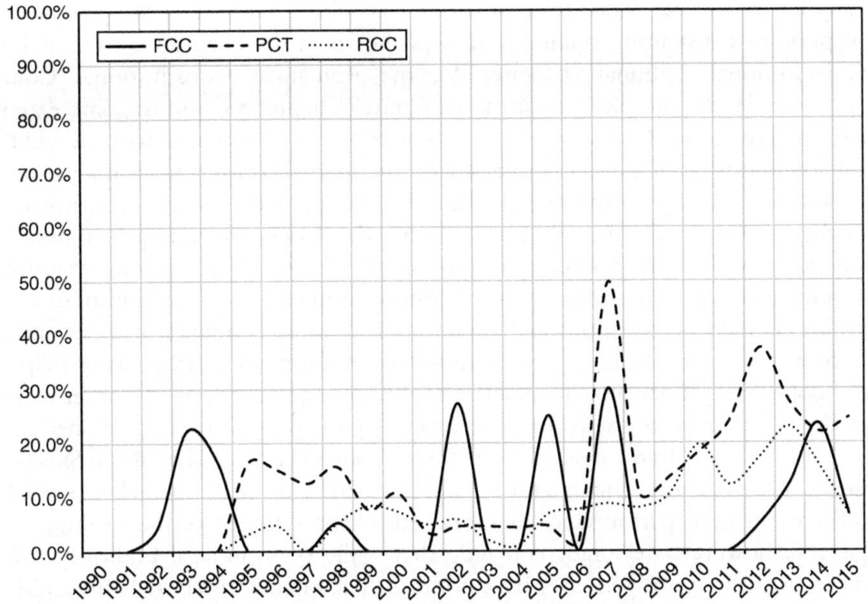

Figure 9.27 Rulings with at least one dissenting opinion (FCC, PCT, RCC compared by years)

to 2009 and then shifted up a level after 2010, with a proportion ranging from 19% to 38%. This means, however, that both courts' scores are clearly below the scores of the Slovak, Czech and Hungarian courts, not to mention the German court with its very low absolute number and proportion of rulings with at least one DO.

9.7 Conclusions

The descriptive statistical analysis of the JUDICON dataset helped us map systematically the multi-faceted realities of constitutional adjudication in six Central European countries. We now might have a general impression on how courts in CEE used their instruments to reconcile political decision-making with constitutional principles. It turned out that some courts (HCC and FCC) were more engaged in selecting a wide range of forms of judicial rulings, while others (RCC, CCC, PCT) were content with more simple forms. While the Polish, Hungarian and, foremost, the Slovak court 'punched' hard right after they were established, even these courts drew back their 'horn' and, sooner (PCT, HCC) or later (SCC), abandoned being a formative power of the political system. Certainly, the German court has always been most inclined to enlighten the legislator as to how unconstitutionality should be remedied, but even the FCC could not be characterized as an extremely activist court.

Nevertheless, in some cases, external political conditions might explain the variation of diversity and strength of judicial rulings, as well as the proportion of published dissenting opinions. As was shown in the chapters on the Polish Constitutional Tribunal (Chapter 6), the Romanian Constitutional Court (Chapter 7), the Slovak Constitutional Court (Chapter 8), and to some extent also the Hungarian Constitutional Court (Chapter 5), external factors and political conditions (sometimes combined with the internal transformation and composition of the court) might have heavily influenced the general performance of these courts in all aspects, i.e. concerning the variety and strength of judicial rulings, as well as the number and proportion of dissenting opinions. Plausible arguments have been presented in the country studies on the mechanism of how politics influenced constitutional adjudication in these countries. If direct influence was not conceivable, open or more covert forms of court-packing helped the politicians influencing the practice of the courts; this led, on the other hand, to the polarization of the courts as indicated by the proportion of published dissenting opinions. In the case of open attacks, courts tried to resist (like in Slovakia in the 1990s or in Hungary and Poland after 2010 or 2015), which was partly reflected in their performance as measured by the strength of their rulings. In general, however, we might conclude that while these judicial bodies became more and more polarized, they have not really constrained too heavily the legislators of their respective countries.

Certainly, in other cases the courts have not been exposed to political influence and intervention as in the countries mentioned above. The Czech Constitutional Court, while preserving its high reputation, has not been under heavy political pressure, and the same holds true for the German Federal Constitutional Court. As explained in the respective country studies, the general performance of these courts does not suggest that the strength or variance of their rulings is connected to special political circumstances. While the election of the judges in both countries is part of high politics, institutional arrangements (in the Czech case) or political culture (in the German case) might prevent politicians from charging courts or judges with political involvement and intentions. The practice of constitutional adjudication in these countries seems to be driven by other factors than politics.

Nevertheless, unduly political involvement of the courts, as presented by some politicians' narratives, is not characteristic for other courts of the region, either. While, to some extent surprisingly, the Slovak Constitutional Court made the strongest rulings in the 1990s, the SCC has never become a third legislator, as explained by Erik Láštic and Max Steuer in their analysis (Chapter 8). Even the Romanian Constitutional Court started as a low-profile institution and became part of the political game only after it got the full competence of annulling legislative acts in 2003 (see Chapter 7). Certainly, political actors discovered and used the courts as a new instrument for their ponderous games, which led to a clear-cut polarization of these courts soon after the political actors realized the stakes of sending their own candidates to the court. This holds true not only for the Slovak and Romanian courts, which experienced political pressure as early as in the 1990s (SCC) or in the late 2000s, but also for their Polish and Hungarian counterparts. Nevertheless, these courts either only pretended to be activist, like the PCT, and very rarely took strong decisions (see data above and the country study in Chapter 6), or they even tried to elaborate soft forms of rulings which might have implicated some form of dialogue on constitutional issues, like in the Hungarian case (see also data above and Chapter 5). Looking back to these strategies from 2018, we must, however, admit that they were not always successful in implementing their original intent.

While this last chapter aimed to present the 'big picture' from a comparative point of view, the studies of the present volume attempted to highlight the possible country-level explanations. Nevertheless, a general explanation of judicial behaviour is a task for the future. As mentioned in Chapter 2 (Section 2.8), the next step in exploring the practice of constitutional adjudication in Central Europe will be to assess the explanative factors of the phenomena we presented in this volume by quantitative methods. Our research community is keen to continue with using the JUDICON project's dataset for unfolding the possible explanative factors of diversity and strength of judicial rulings, and frequency of dissenting opinions and dissenting coalitions.

Notes

1 For example, in Hungary this work is done by the Secretary General of the Hungarian Constitutional Court.
2 It is, however, not completely clear what the reason is and what it means that the ruling/decision ratio is low or high. A high or low ratio might depend on the practice of how courts merge various motions, whether they concentrate only on one issue or aim to resolve more motions in one decision; whether they consider the issue as a complex phenomenon which requires separate rulings or whether they can afford to pick up only one motion since the administrative staff had preselected and refused all other motions. There might be several reasons for this variance of rulings/decision average proportion; thus, we would not draw any conclusions from the difference among countries in this regard.
3 Due to the extremely high number of rejections, which has its origin in the institutional design, data of the Romanian Constitutional Court might distort the general impression to some extent; thus, we always indicate general data without Romania.
4 In Hungary and Slovakia, some kind of prescription was added to only around 9% of the rulings; the same data is 2.5% in the Czech Republic and in Romania, while in Poland there were not any prescriptions at all (!).
5 CCC: 9.5%; FCC: 18%; PCT: 9.5%; RCC: 16.9%, SCC: 5.8%.
6 It should be noted, however, that the relatively high scores around 5.0, which were characteristic for the early years of both courts, do not seem to be highly outstanding in comparison to some scores in Slovakia or Germany. In both countries, the scores of several years significantly surpassed the score 5.0 and ranged between 6.0 and 7.0.
7 The first year of the CCC is more deceptive with its score 'zero', since there was only one relevant decision in that year. It is better to start the analysis of the CCC with year 1994 and its 15 rulings.
8 The HCC also produced the lowest score with an extreme of 3.37 – a low score even for the complete dataset, which also includes the zero rulings.

9 Zero difference means that either there was no rejection at all or all rulings were rejections. In Germany, the zero differences were the result of two different phenomena: first, in 2000, the zero difference was due to the fact that there was no rejection at all in that year, while in 2011 the zero differences came from the fact that all relevant cases were rejected by the FCC.

10 See the diverging curves in Germany in 1994 or 2007, or in Slovakia from 1993 to 2000 in almost every year, even in 2004. Certainly, the divergence and convergence of the indicators were more characteristic for Slovakia.

11 SCC after 2006; CCC 2004–2013; RCC 1993–1996; FCC 2001–2006.

Index

a posteriori review: at the CCC 37, 54; at the FCC 98; at the HCC 99; at the PCT 129; at the RCC 155, 159–63, 165, 168–71, 177–8
a priori review: at the HCC 98–9; at the PCT 129, 136, 139, 143; at the RCC 155, 158–63, 165–6, 168–71, 174–5, 177–8; at the SKK 185
abortion: and the SCC 201–2
acquis communautaire: and the RCC 158
actio popularis: and the HCC 97–9, 215; and the SCC 207n13
activist court *see* judicial activism
Adenauer, Konrad 64, 90n13
appointment of judges: to the CCC 33–6, 43, 49, 52–4; to the RCC 155, 159, 167–8, 176; to the SCC 184–5, 191, 198, 204, 207n6, 208n18; *see also* election of judges
attitude (general): of the CEE courts compared 235, 238–9, of the HCC 120; of the PCT 130, 142; of the RCC 158, 168, 177
attitudinal model of judicial behaviour 26; and the HCC 117, 120; and the PCT 134
austerity: in Hungary 108
authority: of the constitutional courts in general 1; of the CCC 38, 53; of the FCC 2, 64–6, 91n23, 218, 224; of the HCC 108, 114, 120; of the PCT 128, 137, 150–1; of the RCC 155, 157; of the SCC 191, 202

Bagi, István 119
Balsai, István 118
benches (adjudication by): at the FCC *see* Senates of the FCC; at the PCT *see* councils of the PCT
Bihari, Mihály 112–13, 119, 123n24
black box (court as) 78, 133
Bokros, Lajos 108
Bragyova, András 116, 119
Brandt, Willy 64
Brewer-Carías, Allan 9, 187
Bricker, Benjamin 10, 27n1
Bridge (*Most-Híd*) 205

caseload (workload): of the CCC 35, 40; of the FCC 62–3, 66; of the PCT 130–1; of the RCC 161–165; of the SCC 189–90
Ceausescu, Nicolae 157
Čentéš, Jozef 203, 209n24
Christian Democrat Peasant Party (*Partidul Ţărănesc Creştin Democrat*, PNTCD) 173
Christian Democratic Union (*Christlich Demokratische Union*, CDU) 76
Christian Social Union (*Christlich-Soziale Union*, CSU) 76
Čič, Milan 186, 208n22
Civic Democratic Party (*Občanská demokratická strana*, ODS) 41, 47
Civic Platform (*Platforma Obywatelska*, PO) 126, 142, 144–5
Comparative Agendas Project (CAP) 25–6
competences: of the constitutional courts in general 26, 28n11, 32–3, 2014; of the CCC 33–7, 43; of the FCC 61–4, 65, 87; of the HCC 98–9, 110, 122n4; of the PCT 128–30; of the RCC 158–61, 178, 179n4, 244;

of the SCC 185, 187, 207n13; *see also* formal power of constitutional courts
competence collision: *see Organstreitver fahren*
complete annulment: definition 16; as a strong ruling type 18, 21; weighting of completeness 23; and the FCC 69; and the HCC 103, 105; and the PCT 139, 220
composition (personal): of the constitutional courts in general 6, 241, 244; of the CCC 35–6, 40, 43, 45, 47, 49, 50, 53, 56, 58n26, 58n29; of the FCC 62, 77–8; of the HCC 97–9, 107–11, 113, 121; of the PCT 129, 137; of the RCC 159, 174, 178; of the SCC 185–6, 209n24; *see also* structure and organization of the court
constituent power (*pouvoir constituant*) 15, 21, 28n12, 187
constitution-making 15, 28n12; in Romania 157
constitutional amendment: in the Czech Republic 33, 42; in Hungary 99; in Poland 127–8, 151n3; in Romania 158–62; in Slovakia 185, 191, 194, 203, 207n6, 209n28
constitutional complaint: and the CCC 35, 37; and the FCC 62, 68, 86; and the HCC 98–99; and the PCT 129–131, 144, 157; and the RCC 160, 162–3, 165, 171; and the SCC 185, 187, 189, 207n5
constitutional crisis: in Poland 126–7; in Romania 155, 158; *see also* constitutional conflict
constitutional conflict: in Hungary 99; in Poland 134, 136; in Romania 160, 163; in Slovakia 184
constitutional interpretation *in abstracto*: in general 5, 15, 23, 28n12; declared by the CCC 37–8; declared by the FCC 69, 81–2; declared by the HCC 98, 104–5, 108–10, 218–9; declared by the PCT 129; declared by the RCC 171–2; declared by the SCC 185–6, 192–4, 203, 222
constitutional requirement: in general 15–17, 23, 28n10, 217–9, 221; declared by the CCC 38, 45–6, 55; declared by the FCC 82–3, 90n13; declared by the HCC 105–8, 120; declared by the PCT 135, 141–2; declared by the RCC 171, 178; declared by the SCC 192
councils: of the PCT 143–5
court-packing: in general 32, 244; in Hungary 99, 110, 119–20; in Poland 126, 150
Czech and Slovak Federal Constitutional Court (CSFCC) 33–5, 38, 57n6, 58n23, 185
Czech Constitutional Court (CCC) 2, 32–60, 101–2, 145, 185, 213–246
Czechoslovak Constitutional Court 34
Czine, Ágnes 115–16, 118

Dębska, Hanna 132–3
decision by non-decision 191, 198
Democratic Alliance of Hungarians in Romania (*Romániai Magyar Demokrata Szövetség*, RMDSZ) 167
democratic consolidation: in general 8, 100; and the HCC 100; and the PCT 126
democratic transition: in general 32; and the CCC 32, 34, 38–9, 44; and the FCC 70; and the HCC 96–7, 100, 102, 108, 110, 120; and the PCT 127–8, 132–3, 135, 138–9, 142, 150; and the RCC 158
Dienes-Oehm, Egon 116, 118
Direction – Social Democracy (*Smer–sociálna demokracia*, Smer–SD) 188, 191, 204, 208n18
dissenting opinion: compared in CEE 204–3; in general 2, 6, 12; network analysis of 24–5; and the CCC 49–55; and the FCC 63, 78–81, 91n23; and the HCC 100, 103–4, 109, 111, 113–20; and the PCT 137, 143, 146–150; and the RCC 155, 168, 173–8; and the SCC 189–91, 194–8, 200–5
diversity of judicial rulings: in general 1, 3, 12–14, 18–21; of the CCC 44–7; of the FCC 68–71; of the HCC 104–10, 120–1; of the PCT 134–45; of the RCC 169, 172; of the SCC 192–3
Dobrík, Ľubomír 195–6, 208n21
Dzurinda, Mikuláš 186, 188, 192

election of judges: in general 26; of the CCC 33–6, 43, 49, 52–4; of the FCC 62–3, 89n3; of the HCC 97–9, 108–9, 110, 112, 115–16, 120,

122n8; of the PCT 126–30, 134, 137–8, 146, 148, 151; of the RCC 155, 159, 167–8, 176 ; of the SCC 184–5, 191, 198, 204, 207n6, 208n18; *see also* appointment of judges
electoral system: and the CCC 41, 56; and the RCC 171
equality of rights: and the FCC 84; and the RCC 158; and the SCC 200
Erdei, Árpád 119
EU accession 158, 190–1
European Convention on Human Rights: and the CCC 45–6
European Court of Human Rights: and the CCC 43, 46
exception of unconstitutionality: and the RCC 159–60, 162
ex nunc temporal effect: in general 16, 23; and the CCC 37, 54; and the FCC 70, 219; and the HCC 105; and the PCT 139, 220; and the RCC 163
ex tunc temporal effect: in general 16, 23; and the CCC 37; and the FCC 69, 83, 218–9; and the HCC 105; and the PCT 139, 219; and the SCC 199, 209n24

Fenyk, Jaroslav 51–53
Fico, Robert 186, 188, 191–2, 196–8, 203–5
Fidesz (Fidesz-KDNP) 98–9, 110, 112,–13
Filip, Jan 51–2
formal powers: of constitutional courts in general 5–6, 10–11; of the SCC 185; *see also* competences of constitutional courts
Free Democratic Party (FDP) 76
Freedom Union (*Unia Wolności*, UW) 148
fundamental individual rights: and the CCC 41, 46; and the HCC 100, 107; and the RCC 158, 178; and the SCC 184, 186–7

Gajdošíková, Ľudmila 195–6, 202
Garoupa, Nuno 146–7
Gašparovič, Ivan 196, 198
German Federal Constitutional Court (FCC) 2, 61–95, 101–2, 213–4, 218, 221, 224, 227, 229, 231, 233–4, 243
Gionea, Vasile 172–3
grand coalition: in Germany 76; in Romania 175

Harmathy, Attila 119
Havel, Václav 34–5, 42–3, 50
headnote (*Leitsatz*) 2, 17, 24, 224
Herczegh, Géza 123n24
high politics (mega-politics) 34, 41, 45
Holeček, Milos 47–48
Holló, András 106–7, 112, 119
Hönnige, Christoph 9
Hungarian Constitutional Court (HCC) 2, 8, 12, 28n12, 29n14, 33, 38, 49, 50, 68, 96–125, 140, 145, 158, 161, 167, 207n13, 213–4, 218, 221, 224, 226, 229–30, 234, 243–4
Hungarian Socialist Workers' Party (*Magyar Szocialista Munkáspárt*, MSZMP) 97

impeachment 166, 181n24, 185
impossibillismo 151
individual rights 158, 178
institutional design of constitutional courts *see* structure and organisation of courts
institutionalist model of judicial behaviour 134, 136
interpretive ruling 141–2

judicial activism: and the CCC 38, 47, 50, 53; and the FCC 74, 87, 243; and the HCC 100, 105, 108, 226, 245; and the PCT 127, 133, 135–6, 138, 150, 158, 245; and the RCC 178; and the SCC 199, 222
judicial coalition (of dissenter judges): in general 24–5; and the CCC 33–4, 49, 52–4; and the FCC 80; and the HCC 117–20; and the PCT 149–50; and the RCC 176–8; and the SCC 190–2, 195–8, 202, 205
judicial deference: and the HCC 100, 120; and the PCT 138, 150
judicial governance: and the FCC 85
judicial independence: in general 26; and the CCC 41; and the HCC 98; and the RCC 158; and the SCC 202
judicial partisanship: in general 2; and the FCC 80; and the HCC 115, 119–20; and the PCT 127, 129, 132, 134, 137, 143–5, 146–8, 150–1; and the SCC 205; *see also* party preferences of judges
judicial self-restraint: and the FCC 74, 87; and the HCC 102; and the PCT 135, 138

judicial supremacy: and the CCC 32; and the HCC 96–97; and the PCT 122n1, 128–9, 135–7; and the RCC 158, 160, 178; *see also* parliamentary overriding of court decisions
Juhász, Imre 118

Kantorowicz, Jarosław 146–7
Kelsen, Hans 186, 201
Kelsenian model of constitutional adjudication 32, 34, 140, 187
Kessler, Zdeněk 40, 46–8, 53
Kirchhof, Ferdinand 77
Kiska, Andrej 204
Kiss, László 116–17, 119
Klaus, Václav 35, 40–3, 49, 50, 54
Kohl, Helmut 76
Kovács, Péter 119
Kukorelli, István 119

Lábady, Tamás 118
Ľalík, Milan 192, 195–8, 208n23
Law and Justice Party (*Prawo i Sprawiedliwość*, PiS) 126, 142, 144–7, 149–50
legislative omission: in general 14, 21, 27n8; and the CCC 37, 44; and the FCC 69, 82; and the HCC 103–9, 120, 219, 226; and the PCT 140; and the RCC 171; and the SCC 187, 192
legislative self-restraint: and the FCC 102; and the PCT 137
Lenkovics, Barnabás 112, 115
Lévay, Miklós 119
Lewaszkiewicz-Petrykowska, Biruta 134
logic of appropriateness 78, 80

Macejková, Ivetta 186, 194–6, 198, 203, 208n23
Mazák, Ján 186, 194
Mečiar, Vladimír 42, 186, 190, 206n3, 208n18, 209n25
Merkel, Angela 76
Mészáros, Lajos 195–6, 202
Mihai, Lucian 172–3, 182n39
Muraru, Ioan 172–3

National Salvation Front (*Frontul Salvării Naționale*, FSN) 157
ne bis in idem principle 142
negative legislator (court as): *see* positive legislator (courts as)
Németh, János 111–12

Orbán, Viktor 109
Organstreitverfahren: in general 32; and the CCC 35, 55; and the FCC 62, 66, 68, 83; and the PCT 129, and the RCC 160; and the SCC 203
Orosz, Ladislav 195–6, 202

Paczolay, Péter 99, 112–13
parliamentary majority: in general 26; in Germany 82; in Hungary 113; in Poland 126, 138, 143; in Romania 174; in Slovakia 184, 204–5
parliamentary overriding (of court decisions): in Hungary 97; in Poland 135–7; in Romania 155, 158, 160, 169
partisanship: *see* judicial partisanship, party preferences of judges
party preferences of judges: in general 25–6; and the CCC 49, 56; and the HCC 98, 113, 118–20; and the PCT 130, 137, 146–7; and the RCC 167–8, 176; and the SCC 205; *see also* judicial partisanship, political influence
People's Party – Movement for Democratic Slovakia (*Ľudová strana – Hnutie za demokratické Slovensko*, ĽS-HZDS) 186
PiS: *see* Law and Justice Party (*Prawo i Sprawiedliwość*, PiS)
Pokol, Béla 118
polarization: of the CEE courts 2–3, 214, 241, 244; of the CCC 2, 53, 56; of the FCC 79; of the HCC 103–4, 108–9, 112–13, 114–15, 120, 241–2; of the RCC 155, 167, 175; of the SCC 198, 201, 205, 208n16
policy maker (courts as): in general 26; in the Czech Republic 39, 41, 47, 55–6; in Germany 61, 74, 76, 84–5, 87; in Poland 134, 136, 139, 144
Polish Constitutional Tribunal (PCT) 2, 5, 33, 38, 68, 96, 98, 101, 126–154, 158, 161, 214–6, 219, 221, 222, 226, 228–30, 232–4, 242–5
Polish People's Party (*Polskie Stronnictwo Ludowe*, PSL)
political fragmentation: and constitutional courts in general 26; and the CCC 56–7; and the PCT 137, 150; and the RCC 167
political fragmentation: *see* political (in)stability

political influence (on judges): in general 25–6; and the CCC 32–4, 39–42, 49–50, 52–3, 56–7, 242; and the FCC 75–6, 85–7; and the HCC 107–11, 113–15, 118, 120; and the PCT 127, 129, 131–6, 142–6, 148, 150–1; and the RCC 155–6, 166–8, 171–3, 175–6, 177–8; and the SCC 193, 197, 198–205; *see also* party preferences of judges, judicial partisanship
political (in)stability: in the Czech Republic 41, 43; in Romania 167–8, 171–2, 176–8
political polarization: in general 26, 214, 241, 244; in Hungary 108, 115; in Poland 127, 142, 148; in Romania 175; in Slovakia 205
politically salient decisions: in general 25; and the CCC 35, 39, 43, 56; and the FCC 82, 85–7, and the HCC 101–2; and the PCT 143
Politics Can Be Different (*Lehet Más a Politika*, LMP) 122n8
Popa, Nicolae 172–3, 181n28
positive legislator (courts as): in general 2, 9, 15, 17, 23, 28n12; the CCC as a 55; the FCC as a 213, 224; the HCC as a 106–7; the PCT as a 133; the RCC as a 156, 158, 178; the SCC as a 184, 187, 198–9, 205
preliminary examination: and the RCC 162, 229
prescription (remedy): in general 2, 4, 14, 17, 21, 24, 217; and the CCC 38, 45, 54; and the FCC 69, 83, 90n11, 213, 218–9, 224–5; and the HCC 103, 105–6, 226; and the PCT 139; and the RCC 178, and the SCC 202
president: of the constitutional courts in general 6; of the CCC 35–6, 47–9; of the FCC 77; of the HCC 98,–100, 108, 110–14; of the PCT 128, 130, 133, 143–4, 146, 149; of the RCC 157, 159, 172–3; of the SCC 184, 192–5, 198, 202
procedural unconstitutionality: in general 4, 14–15, 23, 217; vs. substantive unconstitutionality 28n9; and the CCC 45–6, 55; and the FCC 69–70, 81–3, 218; and the HCC 103–5, 108, 110; and the PCT 140–1; and the RCC 167, 171–2, 178; and the SCC 193
pro futuro temporal effect: in general 4, 16, 19, 21, 23; and the CCC 37, 55; and the FCC 69, 90n11, 219; and the HCC 120; and the PCT 139, 219–20

qualitative partial annulment: in general 16, 19, 23, 29n13, 29n14; and the FCC 90n11; and the PCT 139, 219–20
quantitative partial annulment: in general 16, 19, 23, 29n13, 29n14; and the FCC 69; and the HCC 105; and the PCT 139, 220

Radičová, Iveta 186, 188, 204, 208n18, 208n23
Rechtsstaat principle: and the CCC 38, 57n6; and the PCT 128, 132, 134, 141, 150; *see also* rule of law
reputation: of the CCC 43, 244; of the FCC 64–6, 218; of the HCC 100, 229
referendum: and the CCC 37; and the SCC 200
retroactive effect *see ex tunc* temporal effect
Romanian Constitutional Court (RCC) 2, 62, 98, 101, 145,150, 155–83, 214,–6, 218, 220, 222, 226, 228–30, 232–5, 239–40, 242–4
roundtable negotiations
rule of law in general 14, 28n9, 32; and the CCC 44, 54, 56; and the FCC 76, 81, 83; and the HCC 100–1; and the PCT 141; and the SCC 199–201, 205; see also *Rechtsstaat* principle
ruling types: in general 5–6, 18–21, 216–22; of the CCC 37, 44–47, 56; of the FCC 69–71, 82–3; of the HCC 104–7, 109–110, 120; of the PCT 134–146; of the RCC 169–72; of the SCC 192–3
Rychetský, Pavel 35, 48–9, 53, 56, 57n12

Safjan, Marek 133, 149
Salamon, László 118
Schmidt, Helmut 64
Schröder, Gerhard 76
self-empowerment: of the FCC 64, 74; of the HCC 108
separation of powers: and CEE courts 8; and the CCC 37; and the

HCC 108; and the RCC 158; and the SCC 195, 199, 202
Šimáčková, Kateřina 52
Šimíček, Vojtěch 51–2
Slota, Ján 186
Slovak Constitutional Court (SCC) 2, 3, 37, 42, 57n9, 68, 101–2, 140, 145–6, 184–212, 214, 229–30, 233, 243–5
Slovak National Party (*Slovenská národná strana*, SNS) 186, 205
Social Democratic Party (*Partidul Social Democrat*, PSD) 167, 181n28
social policy: and the CCC 41; and the PCT133, 136; and the SCC 201; *see also* welfare policies
Solidarity (*Solidarność*) 127–30, 137, 148, 151n4
Solidarity Electoral Action (*Akcja Wyborcza Solidarność*, AWS) 148
Solt, Pál 123n24
Sólyom, László 100, 102–9, 111–14, 118–19
Special Court (Slovakia) 198, 202–3
state budget: and the CCC 41; and the PCT 136, 141
Stępień, Jerzy 146, 149
strategist model of judicial behaviour 26, 214, 245; and the FCC 71; and the HCC 109; and the PCT 127, 132, 136, 142, 147
strength of judicial rulings: definition of the 4; vs. strength of constitutional courts 10–1; measuring the 21–4; of the CCC 39–44; of the FCC 71–6; of individual judges of the FCC 77–9; of the HCC 102–3, 107–10; of individual judges of the HCC 115–17; of the PCT 145–7; of the RCC 165; of individual judges of the RCC 174; of the SCC 191; of individual judges of the SCC 197
Strausz, János 119
structure and organization: of the CCC 33–6; of the FCC 61–3; of the HCC 97–99; of the PCT 127–31; of the RCC 158–61; of the SCC 184–6
Stumpf, István 118
substantive unconstitutionality: in general 15, 23, 216, 218, 221–2; and the CCC 44, 46–7, 55, 222; and the FCC 68–71, 81, 83, 218, 221, 224; and the HCC 105–6, 108, 110, 221; and the PCT 135, 138–42, 146, 219, 222; and the RCC 171–2, 178, 192–3, 218–9, 222
Sulyok, Tamás 118
Sunstein, Cass 9
switchman 201
Szalay, Péter 118
Szívós, Mária 115–16, 118

temporal effect: of judicial rulings in general 10, 16–17, 23; and the CCC 37, 56; andt the FCC 219; and the HCC 103; and the PCT 139, 220; *see also ex tunc* temporal effect, *ex nunc* temporal effect, *pro futuro* temporal effect
term of the judicial office: CCC 33–6; FCC 61–3; HCC 97–99; PCT 127–31; RCC 158–61; SCC 184–6
Tersztyánszky, Ödön 118
Tersztyánszkyné Vasadi, Éva 119
transitional justice 28n9; and the CCC 41, 45, 54, 56
Trócsányi, László 119
trust of the citizens: in courts in general 26; in the CCC 43; in the HCC 100, 229, in the FCC 64–6, 87; in the PCT 137, in the RCC 155, 158; *see also* reputation
Tsebelis, George 9

Uhlíř, David 52
US Supreme Court 62, 133

Vanberg, Georg 137
Varga Zs., András 116, 118
Vida, Ioan 172–3
de Visser, Maartje 10
Vörös, Imre 118
voting record: of the FCC judges 80, 90n21

welfare policies: and the FCC 82–5, 87; *see also* social policy

Zegrean, Augustin 172–3, 182n28
Zeman, Miloš 35, 49–50, 54, 56,
Zemánek, Jiří 52
Zoll, Andrej 130, 136

For Product Safety Concerns and Information please contact our EU representative GPSR@taylorandfrancis.com Taylor & Francis Verlag GmbH, Kaufingerstraße 24, 80331 München, Germany

Batch number: 10725973

Printed by Printforce, the Netherlands